Television News Anchors

FOR JEAN

*If love would die along with death,
this life wouldn't be so hard.*
—Andrew Vachss, novelist, in *Sacrifice*

Television News Anchors

An Anthology of Profiles of the Major Figures and Issues in United States Network Reporting

Edited by
THOMAS FENSCH

New Century Books

Copyright © 2001 Thomas Charles Fensch

All rights reserved. No part of this book may be reproduced or transmitted in any form or by any means, electronic or mechanical, including photocopying, recoding, or by any information storage and retrieval system, without permission in writing from:

New Century Books
P.O. Box 7113
The Woodlands, Tx., 77387-7113

Library of Congress Number:
2001118695

ISBN: Hardcover
0-930751-23-X
ISBN: Paperback
0-930751-24-8

This book was printed in the United States of America.

Table of Contents

Acknowledgments	ix
Timeline: The Development of Network News	xi
Introduction: The Electronic Front Page	1

The Early Years — 9

Edward R. Murrow
"This Is Murrow"
  Time *staff writers* — 10

"TV News Did Not Just Happen — It Had to Invent Itself"
  Desmond Smith — 18

Walter Cronkite
"The Most Intimate Medium"
  Time *staff writers* — 26

Chet Huntley & David Brinkley
"An Accident of Casting"
  William Whitworth — 36

Cronkite Again
"*Playboy* Interview: Walter Cronkite"
  Interviewer: Ron Powers — 70

The Present: Issues — 91

"Network News Is: ☐ Dead ☐ Dying ☒ King of the Mountain"
  William J. Small — 93

v

"The Anchors: Who They Are; What They Do; The
    Tests They Face"
  Alex S. Jones 99

"Anchor Wars"
  Edwin Diamond 111

"Women in Journalism Anchored by Lack of Substantial
    Change"
  Kenneth R. Clark 122

"Off Camera: Newswomen on Bosses, Bias and the Future
    of the Tube"
  Peggy Orenstein 126

"Blurred Lines: TV Network News Is Making Re-Creation
    a Form of Recreation"
  Kevin Goldman 140

"CNN at the Front Line of News"
  Jonas Bernstein 147

The Present: Faces 155

Roone Arledge
"Rooneglow"
  Judy Flander 157

Ed Bradley
"Ed Bradley's Two Muses: Work, Music"
  Mary Corey 166

David Brinkley
"A Touch of Wit: Journalist David Brinkley Has Seen
    It All and Reported It Well"
  Maria C. Johnson 169

Tom Brokaw
"NBC's Air Apparent"
  James Kaplan 174

Catherine Crier
"'The Revolution Will Be Televised': A Year in the
    Life of Catherine Crier"
    Interviewer: Kevin McHargue — 181

Walter Cronkite
"Rolling Stone" Interview
    Interviewer: Jonathan Alter — 186

Sam Donaldson
"ABC's Television Tiger: Sam the Man"
    Jane F. Lane — 197

Douglas Edwards
"CBS' Original News Anchor Signs Off"
    Mark Schwed — 203

Linda Ellerbee
"And So It Has Gone"
    Michele Stanush — 205

Peter Jennings
"The ABC's of Peter Jennings"
    Norman Atkins — 209

Tom Johnson
"Q & A"
    Interviewer: Patricia Villarreal de Macias — 222

Ted Koppel
"Ted Koppel's Edge"
    Marshall Blonsky — 225

Charles Kuralt
"Kuralt Finds Serenity on the Road Less Traveled"
    Jean Marbella — 235

Jim Lehrer
"The Secret Life of Jim Lehrer"
    Hap Erstein — 238

Table of Contents

Robert MacNeil
"MacNeil Says 'NewsHour' an Ideal TV Anchor Job"
   Todd Hegert   243

Roger Mudd
"Association with PBS Is Still Good News for Roger Mudd"
   Michele Greppi   245

Jane Pauley
"In Wake of 'Today,' Jane Pauley Learns America Loves Her"
   Diane Holloway   248

Dan Rather
"Bushwacked!"
   Richard Stengel   250
"I Was Trained to Ask Questions"
   Richard Zoglin   257

Max Robinson
"Tragic Fadeout"
   Marilyn Milloy   263

Diane Sawyer
"Star Power"
   Richard Zoglin   277

Bernard Shaw
"The Anchor Under Fire"
   Jeannie Kasindorf   285

Mary Alice Williams
"News Star Burns Brightly for NBC"
   Susan White   288

Annotated Bibliography   291

Index   297

Acknowledgments

Grateful acknowledgment is made to the following for permission to print or reprint copyrighted material:

"This Is Murrow," *Time,* © 1957. Reprinted by permission.

"TV News Did Not Just Happen—It Had to Invent Itself" by Desmond Smith, *Smithsonian* magazine (June 1989). Reprinted with permission of *Smithsonian* magazine and the author.

"The Most Intimate Medium," *Time,* © 1966. Reprinted by permission.

"Huntley and Brinkley: An Accident of Casting" by William Whitworth. Reprinted by permission of *The New Yorker* magazine, © 1968.

From "The *Playboy* Interview: Walter Cronkite," *Playboy* magazine (June 1973). Reprinted with permission of *Playboy,* © 1973. All rights reserved. Interview conducted by Ron Powers.

"Network News Is: ☐ Dead   ☐ Dying   ☒ King of the Mountain" by William J. Small. Reprinted with permission of *The Washington Journalism Review.*

"The Anchors: Who They Are; What They Do; The Tests They Face" by Alex S. Jones. Reprinted by permission of *The New York Times* Company, © 1986.

"Anchor Wars," by Edwin Diamond from *Rolling Stone* (Oct. 9, 1986). Reprinted by permission of Straight Arrow Publishers, © 1986.

"Women in Journalism Anchored by Lack of Substantial Change" by Kenneth R. Clark. Reprinted with permission of the Knight-Ridder News Service.

"Off Camera: Newswomen on Bosses, Bias and the Future of the Tube" by Peggy Orenstein. Reprinted with permission from *Mother Jones* magazine, © 1989, Foundation for National Progress.

"Blurred Lines: TV Network News Is Making Re-Creation a Form of Recreation" by Kevin Goldman. Reprinted by permission of *The Wall Street Journal,* © Dow Jones & Company, 1989. All rights reserved worldwide.

"CNN at the Front Line of News" by Jonas Bernstein. Reprinted with permission of *The Washington Times.*

"Rooneglow" by Judy Flander. Reprinted with permission of *The Washington Journalism Review.*

"Ed Bradley's Two Muses: Work, Music" by Mary Corey. Reprinted from *The Baltimore Sun,* © 1989.

"A Touch of Wit: Journalist David Brinkley Has Seen It All and Reported

x   Acknowledgments

It Well" by Maria C. Johnson. Reprinted with permission of *The Greensboro* (N.C.) *News and Record.*

"Tom Brokaw: NBC's Air Apparent" by James Kaplan. Reprinted with courtesy from *Vogue,* © 1988 by the Conte Nast Publications.

"Catherine Crier: 'The Revolution Will Be Televised'" by Kevin McHargue. Reprinted with permission of Texas Student Publications (TSP), the University of Texas at Austin.

"Walter Cronkite: The *Rolling Stone* Interview" by Jonathan Alter from *Rolling Stone* (Nov. 5, 1987). Reprinted by permission from Straight Arrow Publishers, © 1987. All rights reserved.

"ABC's Television Tiger: Sam the Man" by Jane F. Lane from *M* magazine (Sept. 1989). Reprinted with permission of Fairchild Publications, © 1989.

"CBS's Original Anchor Signs Off" by Mark Schwed. Reprinted by permission of *The Los Angeles Herald Examiner.*

"Linda Ellerbee: And So It Has Gone" by Michele Stanush. Reprinted with permission of *The Austin* (Tx) *American-Statesman.*

"The ABC's of Peter Jennings" by Norman Atkins from *Rolling Stone* (May 4, 1989). Reprinted by permission of Straight Arrow Publishers, © 1989. All rights reserved.

"Q & A: Tom Johnson Reveals How CNN Took a Gamble on Controversial War Coverage and Pummeled Other Networks Before They Ever Got Off the Ground" by Patricia Villarreal de Macias. Reprinted with courtesy from Images, *The Daily Texan,* © 1991.

"Ted Koppel's Edge" by Marshall Blonsky. Reprinted with permission of Georges Borchardt, Inc. for the author, ©1989 by Marshall Blonsky.

"Kuralt Finds Serenity on the Road Less Traveled" by Jean Marbella. Reprinted from *The Baltimore Sun,* © 1989.

"The Secret Life of Jim Lehrer" by Hap Erstein. Reprinted with permission of *The Washington* (D.C.) *Times.*

"MacNeil Says 'NewsHour' an Ideal TV Anchor Job" by Todd Hegert. Reprinted with permission of *The Colorado Springs Gazette Telegraph* and the author.

"Association with PBS Is Still Good News for Roger Mudd" by Michele Greppi. Reprinted by permission of *The Atlanta Journal and Constitution.*

"In Wake of 'Today,' Jane Pauley Learns America Loves Her" by Diane Holloway. Reprinted with permission of *The Austin* (Tx) *American-Statesman.*

"Bushwacked!" *Time, Inc.* © 1988. Reprinted by permission.

"I Was Trained to Ask Questions." *Time,* © 1988. Reprinted by permission.

"Tragic Fadeout" by Marilyn Milloy. Reprinted with permission of the author.

"Star Power," © 1989. The Time Inc. Magazine Company. Reprinted by permission.

"The Anchor Under Fire" by Jeannie Kasindorf. Reprinted with permission from *New York* magazine, © 1991 News America Publishing Incorporated. All rights reserved.

"News Star Burns Brightly for NBC" by Susan White. Reprinted with permission of the Knight-Ridder News Service.

Timeline: The Development of Network News

1944 NBC newsman Paul Alley puts together the first network newscast. It is treated as a curiosity.
1945 NBC hires a news staff; Ed Murrow has a documentary unit at CBS.
1948 Douglas Edwards begins a 15-minute nightly newscast for CBS – the first of its kind in America. John Cameron Swayze is at NBC.
1949 John Cameron Swayze begins broadcasting on CBS. His show, "The Camel News Caravan" was sponsored by Camel cigarettes. A burning Camel cigarette in an ashtray was regularly shown on camera.
1950 Walter Cronkite joins CBS News, beginning a remarkable three-decade-plus career as a newsman with CBS.
1951 Douglas Edwards begins a 15-minute evening news show for CBS, telecast in black and white. "The Today Show" begins on NBC.
1953 John Daly is anchor at ABC. Characteristics of newscasts at this period: the personality newscaster, with some stills and some black-and-white film. Segmentary format – news, sports, weather, easy to produce and sell. Networks have started to hire their own cameramen.
1954 Edward R. Murrow confronts Senator Joseph McCarthy on television – the subsequent Army-McCarthy hearings are broadcast by ABC as a news event.
1956 Chet Huntley and David Brinkley begin to co-anchor NBC's Nightly News. Their trademark closing: "Good night, Chet," followed by "Good night, David, and good night for NBC News." Videotape recorders become available to local stations.
1959 "CBS Reports" begins – as a response to TV quiz show scandals.
1960 John Cameron Swayze moves to ABC. Characteristics of the newscasts of this period: the magazine format, with more flexibility in content and length of stories and more room for show biz elements in program planning, less advertiser control. "Anchormen, with reporters" also describes this period.
1962 Walter Cronkite begins anchoring for CBS. Transmitting equipment is becoming smaller. John Glenn's space launch is covered live from Florida.

Timeline

1963 President John F. Kennedy's assassination is covered live by all networks. Reporting live from Dallas is Dan Rather. The Cuban missile crisis is covered live by all networks. Ron Cochran is anchor at ABC. CBS and NBC move from 15-minute to 30-minute evening news shows.

1965 Peter Jennings is anchor at ABC. Color news film is developed. Edward R. Murrow dies at 56.

1966 The Vietnam War is broadcast by all networks on the nightly news. It becomes America's first "living room war."

1967 ABC changes its evening news show from 15 minutes to 30 minutes, long after its competition had 30-minute shows.

1968 The news shows enter prime time. "60 Minutes" premiers with Mike Wallace and Harry Reasoner. Anchors: Howard K. Smith and Frank Reynolds at ABC. Walter Cronkite expressed doubts about the Vietnam War on the CBS network; Lyndon Johnson believed if he lost Cronkite, he had also lost mid-America. Johnson subsequently declines to accept a second term "if offered."

1969 Charles Kuralt begins traveling throughout the country in a motor home for "On the Road."

1970 Anchors: at ABC, Howard K. Smith and Harry Reasoner; at NBC, John Chancellor.

1973 The Watergate hearings are broadcast from Washington, D.C.

1976 Barbara Walters becomes the first woman anchor at ABC; she is paired with Harry Reasoner. The chemistry of the two didn't work. ABC then tries a trio of anchors: the first black man, Max Robinson, in Chicago; Frank Reynolds in Washington and Peter Jennings in London. This combination also failed to be cohesive for ABC.

1980 Ted Turner's Cable News Network begins CNN live news 24 hours a day. It initially loses $16 million, but has seven million viewers. "Nightline," with Ted Koppel anchoring, is begun by ABC as a series of reports about the U.S. hostages in Iran; it is an immediate hit.

1981 Dan Rather replaces Walter Cronkite as CBS anchor.

1983 "The MacNeil-Lehrer NewsHour" is expanded from 30 minutes. Most news presented by Robert MacNeil and Jim Lehrer—and others—is analysis.

1990 Douglas Edwards dies in October, at 73.

1991 The war with Iraq is broadcast live by CNN and all three networks. CNN scores a clear victory with its 24-hour coverage. The estimated cost to broadcast from the war in the Persian Gulf: $1–$1.5 million per week each for CNN, ABC, CBS and NBC. (The costs are in personnel and equipment at various locales, plus two million dollars per week in lost revenue from advertisements not shown during the war coverage.) Like the Vietnam War years before, the war with Iraq becomes America's "living room war," except CNN now provides a "24-hour-a-day war."

1991 John Daly, war correspondent and network journalist with CBS and ABC, dies in February, at 77. Daly, who was also director of the Voice of America from 1967 to 1968, was best known for hosting the show "What's My Line" from 1950 to 1967.

Introduction
The Electronic Front Page

The origins and growth of television network journalism and the advent of the television news anchor appear to be uniquely American developments. The evening television news and the evening news anchor—at the local and national level—are now American icons and, as such, are the focus of endless analysis, debate and argument.

The network news and the news anchor at the Big Three networks—ABC, CBS and NBC—were previously summarized in three words: ratings, ethics, costs. At any given time, one network would be in front of the other two.

Added to that is the "tyranny of time." Stories are measured in minutes and seconds; there is never enough time to tell a story completely. Reporters become "talking heads"; audio becomes "sound bites"; one snappy sentence from a presidential speech equals one sentence of rebuttal from the opposition senator. Story length can be measured with a three-minute egg timer, with sand left over for the next story.

Years ago, Walter Cronkite called the evening news "a front-page service." (See "The *Playboy* Interview: Walter Cronkite," June 1973.) He said, "The number of words spoken in a half-hour evening news broadcast—words spoken by interviewees, interviewers, me, everybody—came out to be the same number of words as occupy two-thirds of the front page of the standard newspaper. We are a front-page service. We don't have time to deal with the back pages at all."

While ABC, CBS and NBC still broadcast a nightly "front-page" of the news, there have been a variety of major changes for the three major networks. The first major change has been ownership—when Cronkite spoke to *Playboy* in 1973, all of the three major networks were independent—now all are owned by other firms: ABC by Capital Cities Corp; NBC by General Electric and CBS is owned in part by the Tisch interests. This change in ownership means that cost-cutting and the bottom line on the balance sheets will become more and more important to corporate owners. And that may translate into lower and lower news budgets. Since losing their independence, all three news operations have been involved—although reluctantly—in management efforts to cut the number of employees in the news operations.

Changes which have also occurred relatively recently include: far more coverage, with the use of light-weight mini-cameras and satellite links; the

2   Introduction

institution of regional "feeds"; a general "softening" of newscasts; substantially more reliance on local affiliates to cover the news; the successful advent of "Nightline" and other attempts by the networks to institute more news programs, often in a "magazine" format; the increasing fragility of the star system in broadcast news; and consideration and experimentation by all networks in all-night programming, and cable programming, not only to compete with CNN, but to compete with all other cable and satellite services.

The biggest change, however, was cemented into place during January 1991: the war with Iraq signalled the adulthood of the fourth player—CNN News. Bernard Shaw and his colleagues clearly engineered a coup with their reporting from Baghdad. And suddenly the media world began to wonder: in the future, will the competition be CNN versus the others, now destined to play a media version of catch-up?

The anthology form—in this case, a collection of articles spanning over 30 years—may well be the best form to show the development, causes and concerns in television journalism, as writers come to these interviews, and these stories, with a variety of questions, differing backgrounds and from differing points in time. The end result is a comprehensive collection which no writer, at any one point in time, could duplicate. As an example, three articles about Walter Cronkite are included: a 1966 *Time* cover story, "The Most Intimate Medium"; his 1973 *Playboy* interview and his 1987 *Rolling Stone* interview. As Cronkite had such a remarkable career in television journalism spanning over three decades, these interviews are all included as benchmarks—readers can evaluate Cronkite's responses over a period of years to determine his concerns over the years; ethics of stories during these times, judgments, mistakes (in the *Rolling Stone* interview he admits missing Woodstock as a major news event) and his constant (or changing) perceptions over a substantial period of time.

And what of the others? Included are vignettes or portraits of: Roone Arledge, who engineered ABC's rise to the top of the Big Three; Ed Bradley; Tom Brokaw; Sam Donaldson; Peter Jennings; Ted Koppel; the late Max Robinson; Dan Rather; Bernard Shaw; Diane Sawyer; Mary Alice Williams and others.

The issues are also presented here: the system of the network anchors; and women in television journalism. What do we see in these articles if we look carefully?

The massive travel demands and pressures to meet deadlines, even from the earliest days of television reportage: "He covered the London air raids from the streets and rooftops, made a point of dining under a skylight in a Soho restaurant. Against CBS orders, he went on 25 bombing missions over Germany and broadcast from a British minesweeper in World War II. He has rushed to floods, tornadoes and hurricanes, made three different trips to cover the Korean front—one during his month's vacation—and once had to be hospitalized for exhaustion on his return. Last season, between interviews with Nasser in Cairo, Chou En-lai in Rangoon and Tito on the island of Brioni, he dashed off to cover the Suez invasion." *Time* magazine called this "chasing fire engines on a global scale."—from "This Is Murrow," 1957.

Ethics and objectivity: "Like any other journalist worth his salt, Murrow concedes that, for all the lip service paid to it, there is no such thing as true objectivity in handling the news. The job, as he sees it, is 'to know one's own prejudices and try to do the best you can to be fair.'"—from "This Is Murrow."

Sponsor intrusion into news programs: "NBC's first nightly news telecast was sponsored by Camel cigarettes. It was called the *Camel News Caravan*. As part of the contract, the advertising agency insisted that an ever-lit Camel cigarette must be burning in an ashtray located prominently at John Cameron Swayze's elbow."—from "TV News Did Not Just Happen—It Had to Invent Itself."

The pseudo-event for publicity purposes has always been a bane of the profession: "'I know we're being used,' admits NBC's David Brinkley, as he looks ahead toward November's fast approaching election day. 'I simply decide how to handle the story on the basis of who is using us, and how, and why.'" —from "The Most Intimate Medium," 1966.

Objectivity in the news (again): "'I find an almost excessive lack of bias on television,' says Howard K. Smith. 'We are afraid of a point of view. We stick to the old American belief that there is an objectivity. If a man says the world is round, we run out to find someone to say that it is flat.'"—from "The Most Intimate Medium," 1966.

Writing techniques and style: "'The most elusive thing in our medium,' Huntley's friend Zelman has said, 'is the simple declarative sentence.' Brinkley can write such a sentence. William Monroe, director of news for NBC's Washington bureau, says of Brinkley's work, 'He writes prose of tremendous clarity, prose that is meant for the ear. There is no parallel to him as a writer in this medium.'"—from "An Accident of Casting," 1968.

Freedom of the press vs. governmental restrictions: "Freedom of the press and speech seems to imply that anybody can write or speak out, whether he's literate or not. Erecting standards would also suggest that you're going to legislate against the underground press, and I think that's a mistake. If you're going to accept journalists only if they conform to some establishment norm, you won't have the new blood and free flow of new ideas that are absolutely essential to a vital press. I don't know that Tom Paine could have passed a journalism-review test."—Walter Cronkite in "The *Playboy* Interview: Walter Cronkite," 1973.

The size of the national TV audience: "Each evening network newscast has a far larger audience per appearance than any newspaper or news-magazine. Indeed, no daily newspaper's weekday circulation comes close to the viewership of a weeknight network newscast. The *Wall Street Journal*'s circulation—the largest in the country—is less than two million. *USA Today*'s paid circulation is about 1.33 million, and only three other dailies (the *New York Daily News,* the *Los Angeles Times* and the *New York Times*) have circulations that exceed one million. In contrast, the top-rated network newscast in the last quarter of 1988—Rather's on CBS—reached 9.7 million homes. ABC, slightly behind, was reaching more than 9.5 million homes and NBC was seen in more than nine million. If Rather or Jennings or Brokaw were ever seen by as few people as read the *Wall Street Journal* or even *Time* (circulation 4.3 million), the anchor would be replaced."—from "Network News Is: ☐ Dead ☐ Dying ☒ King of the Mountain," 1989.

Similarities of network anchors: "The anchors are strikingly similar—perhaps too similar if diversity is a virtue. All three are middle-aged Anglo-Saxon male Protestants. Mr. Rather is 54 years old. Mr. Jennings will be 48 tomorrow and Mr. Brokaw is 46. All have close ties to wives and children and live in uptown Manhattan apartments. All are attractive and have the polished look of men who are extra attentive to their appearance. They appear to share basic middle-class values such as sympathy for the average citizen, a taste for hard work and concern about the world their children will inherit. Their journalistic skills would make them a welcome addition to any news organization. Each says he has considerable respect for his rivals. All are fiercely competitive, both as reporters and anchormen."—from "The Anchors: Who They Are; What They Do; The Tests They Face," 1986.

Differences between anchors: "In fact, Dan, Peter and Tom, and their programs, are distinct from one another—as distinct as their on-air personas are from the men playing the anchor's role. What we see *isn't* what we see. It's more intriguing. And the audience, subconsciously, knows this. Viewers have read the implicit iconography of the evening news and aligned themselves in accordance with their understanding of the subtext of each man and program. The proof is all there in the ratings books. Demographics don't lie.

"The iconographic Dan, of course, is country & western, appealing to an older, idealized America of the imagination. Peter is urban, projecting an image with which a more youthful market can identify. Tom positions himself somewhere in between—in the middle—an avatar of suburban values. Together they form a three-way mirror of America that tells us where the country is today—*vide,* the tightened race among the triple demographics of the news. They also tell us where the country is heading tomorrow, as the weight of viewer numbers shifts toward one or another end of the scale."—from "Anchor Wars," 1986.

Missed opportunities: "I wish I had gone to Woodstock, of course. Oh, gosh, I thought of that many times. I really missed a story there. I missed the personal experience by not being there."—Walter Cronkite in the *Rolling Stone* interview, 1987.

How Ted Koppel gains an advantage on an interview subject—while the subject is in an empty studio, with nothing but a television camera facing him or her, and an ear piece in one ear, fielding Koppel's questions: "So there is no eye contact, not even your eye to image-eye, no instantaneous recognition of the interlocutor; rather, a sequential passage of words through your ear. In fact, it places the interviewee in a foreign perceptual world where the guest no longer has the benefit of two dimensions—spatial/instantaneous as well as temporal/sequential. Using language, you still possess the power of analysis, but you cease to react automatically, as the human animal. By removing his person from you, Koppel cunningly deprives you of your animal instinct, of the will you could muster in an eye-to-eye, mano-a-mano exchange."—from "Ted Koppel's Edge."

Ethics for women in television news: "What would you tell a young woman fresh out of college, 22, 23 years old, who wanted a career in television journalism? What would she need to have the right stuff now? Ann Rubenstein (New York City correspondent for the "NBC Nightly News"): "I can tell her some things she ought to do, morally and ethically, once she's in. Hang onto her own code of ethics. Do not depend upon those of her employers. They'll ask her to do things that you shouldn't do. You must really decide for yourself what you're going to do and not do. And what price you are willing to pay for whatever they're offering. Otherwise you're going to find yourself one day standing out in the snow with a microphone and sticking it in the face of a woman who's just had her son killed and asking her how she feels about it. Because somebody told you that's the way to get to the top." — from "Off Camera: Newswomen on Bosses, Bias and the Future of the Tube."

On Diane Sawyer and other television mega-stars: "The crucial question, however, is not whether news stars deserve the money but whether they deserve the stature. Although most are competent reporters, they have reached their positions largely because of qualities that have little to do with journalism: the way they look, the tone of their voices, their on-camera charm. Yet they have influence that betokens great wisdom and judgment. They are the people America listens to, relies on, trusts. The major events of the day are filtered through their eyes and ears. News becomes bigger news simply because they are present — in Paris for a presidential visit or Tiananmen Square for a nation's aborted experiment with democracy. The danger is that as stars become more and more important in the high-stakes world of TV journalism, they are overwhelming the news they purport to report." — from "Diane Sawyer: Star Power."

Earlier perceived racial biases of the networks: "To be sure, all the tyrannies of TV news are constantly fought against and often held at bay. Few, if any, network producers worried about offending Deep South viewers with their civil rights coverage, for example. ABC earned the nickname, 'African Broadcasting Co.'; CBS became the 'Colored Broadcasting Co.'; NBC, the 'Negro Broadcasting Co.'" — from "The Most Intimate Medium," 1966.

Each reader may find even more outstanding and critical issues within these pages; just as each viewer finds different topics and stories important as he or she watches television news shows; so too each reader of this book may find different topics of ethical and personal interest within these pages.

One of the added advantages in an anthology collection — or a book of history — is the larger question posed by early stories: has this problem been solved? Taking an historical perspective through these pages allows the reader to ask: have the networks solved the problems of racial and ethnic balance in stories? Have they solved the "tyranny of time" in newscasts? How do they propose to solve the dilemma of the "cult of personality" of the multi-million-dollar-a-year "News Gods?" How do they solve the problem of the "pseudo-event," staged by a special-interest group simply for television cameras? How do they solve the multifaceted problems of ethics and objectivity? How do they face the problems of freedom of the press vs. government restrictions? How do they face the problems of outside ownership of TV networks? How do they deal with CNN and other cable offerings which are cutting deeper and deeper

6   Introduction

into the over-all ratings of the three major networks? How are they dealing with women in television journalism? How are they including blacks and other minorities in television news? How are they facing the problems of "tabloid television"?

These questions are not only questions which network news executives must face and answer—they are also questions which television news viewers, critics—and interested readers—should also face.

In a collection such as this, it is important to know the background of the writers: who are these contributors, what orientation do they have, what expertise do they bring to their work, what critical vision do they have of television news or the broadcast industry? Are the writers sheltered inside the world of academia? Are they magazine writers who specialize in media coverage? Are they solely television critics for daily newspapers, perhaps far more used to writing reviews of "Dallas" or "Falcon Crest"? Are they ex-broadcast employees with particular axes to grind? Knowing the background of the writers will help the reader keep a mental calculus of the material. This book represents a wide variety of backgrounds and expertise. Briefly, the contributors and their backgrounds are:

Desmond Smith ("TV News Did Not Just Happen...") is a television history critic and now hosts a financial news show on Canadian television.

William J. Small ("Network News Is ... King of the Mountain") has been president of NBC News and United Press International, former vice president of CBS News, is a professor of communication at Fordham University's Graduate School of Business and is the author of *To Kill a Messenger: Television News and the Real World* (1970).

Edwin Diamond ("Anchor Wars") is a media critic and a frequent contributor to *New York* magazine and other publications. He is the author of three books about television, *Good News, Bad News* (1978); *Sign Off: The Last Days of Television* (1982) and *The Tin Kazoo* (1975).

Marshall Blonsky ("Ted Koppel's Edge") teaches communication courses at New York University.

Magazine writers and their magazines include:

William Whitworth (Huntley and Brinkley: "An Accident of Casting"), *The New Yorker* magazine;

Ron Powers (*Playboy* interview—Walter Cronkite, 1973), *Playboy*. Powers later won a Pulitzer prize for his coverage of television, writing for *The Chicago Sun-Times*.

Peggy Orenstein ("Off Camera...") is managing editor for *Mother Jones* magazine.

Judy Flander ("Rooneglow") is a contributing editor to *Washington Journalism Review*.

James Kaplan ("Tom Brokaw...") is a contributor to *Vogue*.

Jonathan Alter (Walter Cronkite interview—1987) is media critic for *Newsweek*.

Jane F. Lane ("Sam Donaldson...") is a contributor to *M* magazine.

Norman Atkins ("The ABC's of Peter Jennings") is a contributor to *Rolling Stone*.

Introduction 7

Richard Stengel ("Bushwacked!") is a staff writer for *Time*.

Richard Zoglin ("I Was Trained to Ask Questions" and "Star Power") is a staff writer for *Time*.

Jeannie Kasindorf ("The Anchor Under Fire") is an editor at *New York* magazine.

Newspaper writers and the publications they work for include:

Alex S. Jones ("The Anchors"), *The New York Times*.

Kenneth R. Clark ("Women in Journalism..."), the Knight-Ridder chain.

Kevin Goldman ("Blurred Lines...") is a staff writer for *The Wall Street Journal*.

Jonas Bernstein ("CNN at the Front Line of News"), *The Washington Times*.

Mary Corey (Ed Bradley...), *The Baltimore Sun*.

Maria C. Johnson (David Brinkley...), *The Greensboro* (N.C.) *News & Record*.

Kevin McHargue (Catherine Crier...), editor of *The Daily Texan*, the University of Texas at Austin.

Mark Schwed (Douglas Edwards...), *The Los Angeles Herald Examiner*.

Michele Stanush (Linda Ellerbee), *The Austin American-Statesman*.

Patricia Villarreal de Macias (Tom Johnson), *The Daily Texan*, the University of Texas, Austin.

Jean Marbella (Charles Kuralt...), *The Baltimore Sun*.

Hap Erstein (Jim Lehrer...), *The Washington* (D.C.) *Times*.

Todd Hegert (Robert MacNeil...), feature editor for *The Colorado Springs Gazette Telegraph*.

Michele Greppi (Roger Mudd...), *The Atlanta Journal*.

Diane Holloway (Jane Pauley...), television critic for *The Austin American-Statesman*.

Marilyn Milloy (Max Robinson...), *Newsday*.

Susan White (Mary Alice Williams...), the Knight-Ridder News Service.

This book pulls these articles together to present a collection of broadcast history, issues, personalities and perspectives not available in any other source or collection.

It is a cliche in journalism — but nonetheless true — that journalism is only a mirror of society. This book attempts to show how television journalism and the anchor system developed and what the current reporters and anchors think of their profession, their problems, their competitors.

For in the mirror of television journalism, the more we know them, the more we know ourselves.

The Early Years

Television network news was fortunate to have Edward R. Murrow during these formative years. Murrow, variously called "the Bishop," "the Professor," or "God" gave television news much of its authority, objectivity and grace. Much of the rest of the television news industry during these years was mired in mediocrity and staffed by ex-newspaper reporters, ex-radio people and others who had little regard for the potential impact of television news. Murrow understood its potential when others chose to accept the mediocre. The quality behind Murrow was very thin. As Desmond Smith observes in his article, television was a medium that had to "invent itself"; the invention was often ungainly and progress toward quality was slow. (And sometimes, looking backward, laughable).

By the early 1960s, television news was stabilized to the extent that anchors such as Walter Cronkite were worried about the objectivity of their craft; media-government confrontations were evident if not inevitable and the quality of equipment and technology was growing (as were funds for equipment and profits for the networks).

The idea of the co-anchor or news team grew from experimentation to an acceptable form for the networks. William Whitworth's lengthy examination of the Huntley-Brinkley team reveals not only their success, but their blossoming as cultural icons. Murrow, Cronkite, Huntley-Brinkley (and a few others) quickly discovered the dark side of media success — they had to accept the role of public figures, which often hindered their reporting.

By the time of publication of Ron Powers' 1973 *Playboy* interview with Walter Cronkite, the media-government rupture was complete. Notice how much of the *Playboy* interview is devoted to Cronkite's analysis of media-government confrontations — and, as an allied issue, television coverage of the Vietnam War — "America's first living-room war," as it has been called.

Race or sex as an issue in the selection of news reporters or anchors is not seen in these stories of the earlier days of television network news. There was also not an abundance of the soft issues which are difficult for television news to cover — social issues which don't have a good/bad dichotomy; slowly changing social mores; economic news which can't be compressed into two-minute "sound bites," etc.

Edward R. Murrow

"This Is Murrow"

> *It is appropriate to begin this book with a* Time *magazine cover article about the man who set the standard for television news and commentary—Edward R. Murrow. Murrow has since been the subject of three exceptional biographies:* Prime Time: The Life of Edward R. Murrow *(Alexander Kendrick, 1969);* Murrow: His Life and Times *(A. M. Sperber, 1986) and* Edward R. Murrow: An American Original *(Joseph E. Persico, 1988). Murrow's career in the early days of network television journalism reveals habits, concerns and ethics which anchors still wrestle with over 30 years later: his frenetic personality; and his then offbeat ideas of coverage: "He wants to put a crew on the caboose of a freight train and let the cameras grind all across the U.S." From this* Time *article can be seen the many changes in television journalism since the Murrow days of the early 1950s.*

Amid the trite and untrue that shed a honky-tonk glare from the nation's TV sets come moments that pierce reality and live up to television's magic gift for thrusting millions of spectators at once into the lap of history in the making. As television moved this week into its second decade, chances were that some of the best of such moments in the new season would come from a dark, high-domed man with a hangdog look, an apocalyptic voice and a cachet as plain as his inevitable cigarette. His name: Edward R. Murrow.

Many have come and many have fallen in TV's growth to immature maturity, but CBS's Ed Murrow, 49, marches on as TV's top journalist. Six years after his *See It Now* pioneered the technique for capturing the sights and sounds, persons and events that shape the news, it is unchallenged by any newer or better technique for exploiting TV's potential or overcoming its shortcomings. The combination of brains, integrity, attractiveness and showmanship that makes him such an effective journalist also establishes Murrow, in his role of star on the trivial but popular *Person to Person,* as one of TV's five top-rated entertainers.

By the Ears. From his pinnacle atop the nation's TV antennas, Murrow commands a huge circulation. The monthly *See It Now,* which starts its new season next week (Sun. 5 P.M., E.S.T.), draws viewers in a Nielsen-estimated 3,850,000 homes; his *Person to Person* (Fri. 10:30 P.M. E.S.T.), now in its fifth year, flickers weekly into more than 8,300,000 homes, and his ten-year-old

---

This article was written by Time *staff writers during a period when* Time *did not give by-lines to staff members.*

radio broadcast, its audience shrunken by TV competition, still enables Murrow to get more than 1,000,000 Americans by the ears every weekday evening at 7:45, E.S.T.

In prestige and awards, he outrates anybody in TV. He has been laureled not only with eight honorary degrees, but four colleges (one of them: his alma mater, Washington State) have offered him their presidencies. In addition, he has been showered with nearly 100 assorted prizes and honors, including so many George Foster Peabody Awards for various feats that the Peabody judges gave him another just for "being himself."

The VIP's VIP. Murrow was the author of TV's most explosive telecast: the March 1954 show that indicted Joe McCarthy out of the Senator's own mouth in film clips. He did not bother to clear the show in advance with CBS, and in turn CBS decided retroactively that it had lent Murrow the network's right to editorialize. The network lists him only as one of its hired hands, but Murrow is something of a power in himself, with his own generously financed domain and the strong personal loyalty of key CBS news staffers. His unique status stems from (1) his close friendship with Board Chairman William S. Paley, with whom he deals directly, (2) his onetime role as a major architect of its news staff and policy, and (3) the hard fact that if CBS ever loses him, it will be NBC's gain. CBS pays him well over $300,000 a year. To a questioner who demanded at a stockholders' meeting why he got more money than Paley or CBS President Frank Stanton, the board chairman himself replied: "His value seems to be higher."

Apart from his rating in television, Murrow is a VIP's VIP. After dinner at the White House on Dec. 7, 1941, Franklin D. Roosevelt confided to him just what losses the Japanese had inflicted at Pearl Harbor that morning. When his broadside against McCarthy provoked the Senator to counterattack, President Eisenhower pointedly described Murrow as his friend. Carl Sandburg calls him a poet. He is a longtime friend-at-the-bar (Scotch, a little water, no ice) of Sir Winston Churchill. Interviewer Murrow is often more celebrated than the celebrities on *Person to Person,* sometimes must work to bridge the gap. When Rocky Graziano appeared, he urged the prizefighter to call him Ed. Replied Graziano on the air: "Oh no, Mr. Murrow, I can't do that."

Wide & Weird. The world of electronic journalism that Murrow bestrides runs a course far wider than the one from the tabloids to the *Times* and weirder than anything in between. It echoes with the weepy singsong of Gabriel Heatter, still broadcasting after 32 years, the now-stilled, intelligent frog croak of Elmer Davis, the cocksureness of Fulton Lewis, Jr., the literate wit of Eric Sevareid, the pear-shaped tones of Lowell Thomas. Gone now from radio is Winchell's clattering telegraph key and breathless bleat; too seldom heard is aging (70) H. V. Kaltenborn's clipped assurance. The news comes by short wave and on tape, the newsmen in snazzy ties and boutonnieres (ABC's popular John Cameron Swayze), and even in pairs (NBC's intelligent and informative duet, earnest Chet Huntley and wry David Brinkley). TV's journalists flit all over, like the technically muscle-flexing *Wide, Wide World,* or work in a simple star chamber, like Interviewer Mike Wallace. On too rare occasions, the newsmakers themselves step before the cameras: Kefauver dueling with a faceless

Frank Costello, John McClellan patiently at work on Teamster Jimmy Hoffa and his voluble forgettery. Daily, the networks pour money, manpower, miles of cable and film into an often losing race to out-distance the spoken word.

What gives Murrow his big edge in prestige and following over his rivals? He does not write so well as his own colleagues Sevareid and Howard K. Smith, or ad-lib with the graceful ease of ABC's John Daly, CBS's Walter Cronkite and Robert Trout, or analyze the news with the pungency of ABC's Quincy Howe. As a reporter, he is not always as knowledgeable as ABC's Edward P. Morgan. Murrow's political superficialities in his pundit's dialogue with Sevareid in CBS's presidential-election coverage last year, sounded as if he had worked too much with the top of his head and not enough with his legs. As a digger and ferret, he was no match for NBC's Martin Agronsky or CBS's Richard Hottelet.

As an interviewer, Murrow's reputation suffers from the insipid conversations he conducts on *Person to Person* (and even some of his *See It Now* interviews show a lack of the flexibility to follow up an opening instead of going on to a prearranged question). *Person to Person* (sponsors: American Oil Co. and Hamm Brewing Co. alternating with *Life*) makes its pitch mainly to viewers who want to rubberneck in celebrities' homes. It deliberately casts Murrow, sitting in a Manhattan studio, as a discrete electronic guest whose job it is to make polite chit-chat, not ask probing questions. Murrow's own discomfort is sometimes visible, but he sold *Person to Person* as a package to CBS this year in a capital-gains deal, thus is undoubtedly committed to go on with it. The show does have what one frequent viewer calls an "idiot fascination," and it is a prime moneymaker for CBS.

One big answer to the question of Murrow's supremacy is that, in TV, Journalist Murrow deliberately by-passes the challenge of the spot news; he lets others try to work out—if ever they can—a way in which TV can cover the day's events as effectively as radio, which not only beats TV on most news but provides more of it. The rest of the answers are more personal: one is what TV hucksters call sex appeal. Murrow is tall (6 ft. 1 in.) and compact (175 lbs.). His saturnine good looks and taut doomsday voice project virile authority. *Person to Person,* which also displays his urbane charm and ready smile, attracts far more women than men viewers, according to Trendex surveys, and in deference to this finding *Person to Person* technicians (so far unknown to Murrow) are now under orders to adjust camera angles and lighting to compensate for the latest recession in his hairline and to make the most of his expressive hands.

Furrows in Murrow. As a performer, Murrow has expert technique. During the blitz, when he served as Britain's Boswell, his "This [pause] is London" carried the thrill of Britain's finest hour across the Atlantic. His timing can make silence more eloquent than words. Between his ominous tone and his spare, understated writing springs a tension suggesting that, as one listener put it, "he knows the worst but will try not to mention it."

Beyond personality and technique, Murrow's persuasiveness is rooted in a prickly social conscience and a sense of mission about keeping people informed. An NBC cynic has versified: "Nobody's brow furrows like Edward R. Murrow's." Murrow's worried look is genuine. "He internalizes world events," says a friend. "They flow right through him like a stream. The fall of Britain would have been as meaningful to him as the loss of a child to one of us." This outsized sense of responsibility fills Murrow's work with conviction and sincerity. Says a colleague: "Above all of us in this business, Ed Murrow is the one who can make serious matters appeal to large audiences."

Alarms & Excursions. Beyond that, as solid a reason as any for Murrow's edge is simply that he is a fine reporter with sight and sound; he has a gift for capturing actuality in its moods and nuances as well as its meaning. Many a veteran of printer's ink has been, in the words of one of them, "faintly scandalized that such good reporting can be done by a man who never worked on a newspaper in his life." Fellow reporters have nicknamed Murrow "the Professor" after his academic past and "the Bishop" for his solemn cadences, but they agree with Walter Lippmann that he is "really first rate."

Murrow's alarms are almost always matched by his excursions to the scene of the news. He covers his stories with an intensity that courts exhaustion and a passion for physical danger that is the despair of his friends and employers. Says his friend and boss, Bill Paley: "You could almost call it a drive to self-destruction. He's never happy unless he's working. When he looks like death, that's when you feel a happy glow."

He covered the London air raids from the streets and rooftops, made a point of dining under a skylight in a Soho restaurant. Against CBS orders, he went on 25 bombing missions over Germany and broadcast from a British minesweeper in World War II. He has rushed to floods, tornadoes and hurricanes, made three different trips to cover the Korean front—one during his month's vacation—and once had to be hospitalized for exhaustion on his return. Last season, between interviews with Nasser in Cairo, Chou En-lai in Rangoon, and Tito on the island of Brioni, he dashed off to cover the Suez invasion.

"The Little Picture." Murrow's zest for chasing fire engines on a global scale sometimes forces him to commute across oceans to keep his weekly date on *Person to Person*. By the time the show's technicians have torn their five tons of equipment out of a visited celebrity's home, Murrow may be on a plane to Washington to lay the groundwork for a new *See It Now* or closeted in a projection room to edit film for one already in work. At the end of a routine day's conferring, writing, filming or reporting, he must also make his nightly radio deadline—"This [pause] is the news." Murrow has little interest in food ("He could eat scrambled eggs three times a day," says an associate), gets four to five hours sleep a night, manages at best two weekends out of three with his wife Janet and his son Charles Casey, 12, at his 280-acre farm at Pawling, N.Y., close by the estates of his occasional golfing friends, Lowell Thomas and Thomas E. Dewey.

For all of Murrow's outpourings of energy, *See It Now* is a complex team operation. Almost as important to the show as Murrow is big (6 ft. 1 in.), bustling Co-Producer Fred W. Friendly, 43, who went to work with him 11 years ago after proposing the idea for their *I Can Hear It Now,* a replay from the recording files of voices and history of 1932-45, brought out by Columbia Records. The record and its sequels led to a radio program, and then to the TV show. Without film training or TV experience, Murrow and Friendly together worked out the *See It Now* technique for getting at the heart of current issues and problems by narrowing their focus on "the little picture" — the human beings intimately involved.

Twenty to One. The technique, which borrows from radio, movie and printed journalism (and owes a huge debt to *The March of Time,* which made the mold for film journalism), is the most realistic reporting yet devised for documentary film. Unlike any documentary before it, *See It Now* sends its cameras after a story without any script, shoots everything with sound, never dubs afterwards, never rehearses an interview, shoots as much as 20 hours of film for one hour of the final product — a ratio greater than any other TV show, newsreel or Hollywood itself. The method is costly in effort and money — $100,000 a show (plus $75,000 for TV time). Though Sponsor Pan American World Airways picks up part of the tab, CBS loses money on the program. Murrow and Friendly may spend as much as a year preparing a single show, e.g., *Automation, Weal or Woe?,* or follow a breaking news story on two hours' notice and come back with the memorable *Clinton and the Law.*

Last week one of *See It Now*'s four full-time field teams (each consists of a reporter-director, cameraman, assistant cameraman and sound man) finished a job in Alaska for a show on Alaskan and Hawaiian statehood and flew to Tokyo to join Marian Anderson on a three-month tour of Southeast Asia. Two teams were finishing film for next week's show, *The Great Billion Dollar Mail Case,* a critical look into the U.S. Post Office. A fourth crew was filming in Europe. In Manhattan headquarters, Friendly pruned incoming footage for perusal by Murrow and began a first draft of next week's narration. Says Friendly, who suffers a severe case of Murrow-worship, a malady rife in the TV world: "My relation to Ed is that of first sergeant. He's the company commander. Everything I edit I edit with Ed's eyes. I write with his fingers." He denies what many pros say — that he gets too little credit: "I get a lot of credit that belongs to Ed."

Eye & Ear. Each show grows first out of hours of talk by Murrow and Friendly. Friendly then briefs the staff, sometimes in a jointly signed memo. After years with *See It Now,* the staff has soaked up the kind of perceptiveness for human and atmospheric detail that Murrow showed in wartime London when he dramatized the blitz with such tellingly simple touches as the sound of unhurried footsteps, caught by his microphone on the sidewalk as Londoners walked calmly to their air raid shelters.

When Murrow and five teams made the eloquent *This Is Korea — Christmas, 1952,* the Murrow-and-Friendly advance memo explained: "We want to portray the face of war and the faces of the men now fighting it ... The best picture we could get would be a single G.I. hacking away at a single foxhole in the ice of a Korea winter..." Murrow brought back the vivid sight and sound of a marine's shovel rasping futilely at the earth. Other memorable *See It Now* moments for eye and ear: a Buchenwald tattoo on the arm of an Israeli jet pilot; a "rehabilitated" Mau Mau warrior singing *Onward, Christian Soldiers;* the ding of a bullet taken out of a G.I.'s spine as it was tossed by the surgeon to a nurse and dropped into a cup in her hand.

In the gap left in news-in-depth reporting when *See It Now* abandoned its weekly schedule of half-hour shows two years ago for monthly hour-long shows, all three networks have tried to use something of its approach. Though such programs as NBC's *Outlook,* CBS's *World News Roundup,* ABC's *Open Hearing* are often well done, they suffer from a lack of *See It Now*'s huge budget, its lavish shooting, its long experience. They also lack Edward R. Murrow.

"Foghorn Voice." Murrow, who lives on Park Avenue and gets his suits from a Savile Row tailor, started out, on April 25, 1908, named Egbert, the son of a tenant farmer, in a log-slab house near Pole Cat Creek in North Carolina's Guilford County, 12 miles south of Greensboro. He was the youngest of Ethel and Roscoe Murrow's three boys. The eldest, Lacy, rose to be an Air Force brigadier general in the 18th Tactical Air Command, and is now a transportation consultant in Washington. The other, Dewey, is a contractor in Spokane. "I had one pair of shoes a year," says Ed Murrow. "I can't remember when I didn't have to work."

When he was five ("a fat little boy with a regular foghorn voice," recalls a cousin), the family moved to Blanchard, Washington, 70 miles north of Seattle, where his father (who died two years ago) became a locomotive engineer in a logging camp. Ethel Murrow, now nearing 80, was a frugal, hard-working Methodist who read her boys a Bible chapter every night until they went off to college. She wanted Egbert to be a preacher; he now regards religion as "more ethics than faith." She recalls him as a lad with a strong sense of duty and determination, who could not wait to grow up to his brothers' level. Typically, when a photographer was once posing the two brothers in their school clothes, little Egbert, not yet old enough for school, grabbed a book and crashed the picture with a mature scowl. He began earning money at 15. At 16, when his boss in the logging camp began calling him Ed, he gladly dropped the Egbert.

Academic Fringe. At Edison High School young Murrow won the school's popularity contest, graduated at the head of his class. In Washington State College, as a speech major, campus politician, actor, debater and R.O.T.C. cadet colonel, he honed his voice, enunciation and speaking technique, made Phi Beta Kappa.

For five years after his graduation, Murrow hustled on the academic fringe, first as a $25-a-week president of the National Student Federation, then as assistant director of the Institute of International Education. The jobs entailed speechmaking on 300 U.S. campuses, European travel, arranging international student exchanges. Firsthand glimpses of the rise of Hitler in Germany appalled Murrow. He joined an emergency committee that helped to bring 288 displaced German scholars to safety. "It was the most satisfying experience I ever had," he says. During the same period, on a train to a student conference in New Orleans, he met a pretty Mount Holyoke graduate named Janet Brewster. They were married in 1934.

A year later CBS hired him as its director of talks and education, and in 1937 sent him to London as "European director," a one-man foreign staff charged with arranging cultural programs. As an assistant on the Continent, Murrow hired from the now-expired Universal Service a newsman named

William L. Shirer. Soon the two switched from "cultural stuff" to report the Austrian *Anschluss,* and then, as Europe hurtled toward war, Murrow began hiring the core of what is still the best news staff of the networks. Among the "Murrow boys," as CBS calls them: Eric Sevareid, Larry LeSueur, Charles Collingwood, Richard Hottelet, David Schoenbrun and Bill Downs.

The war made Murrow one of radio's legends. In New York, CBS staffers formed a Murrow-Ain't-God Club so they could view him with proper detachment. (When Murrow got wind of it, he demanded charter membership.) His vivid picture of Londoners under fire stirred the heart of the U.S. and stands as one of the war's memorable reporting jobs.

Head-On Clash. Back home, Murrow became CBS vice president in charge of news. After a year and a half he decided that he did not like paper work, budgets, and "most of all, I didn't like firing people." Before he went back to broadcasting with a $150,000-a-year sponsored news show, he took a hand in writing what is still the network's policy forbidding its news analysts to inject editorial opinion into their "objective" interpretation. After Bill Paley added him to the CBS board of directors in 1949—a post he held until 1955—Murrow eyed TV even more distrustfully as a platform for a newsman's personal opinion. He asked in a memo: "Is it not possible that . . . an infectious smile, eyes that seem remarkable for the depths of their sincerity, a cultivated air of authority, may attract huge television audiences regardless of the violence that may be done to truth or objectivity?"

Broadcaster Murrow does not practice the objectivity that Policymaker Murrow preached. He could be accused of using the word "objectivity" sloppily. For, like any other journalist worth his salt, Murrow concedes that, for all the lip service paid to it, there is no such thing as true objectivity in handling the news. The job, as he sees it, is "to know one's own prejudices and try to do the best you can to be fair." He admits to open violations of the CBS policy, notably in some sharply partisan *See It Now* shows on civil-liberties issues. The climax was the McCarthy show—and an uproar that produced 50,000 letters, phone calls and wires (four to one for Murrow, by CBS's count). In defense of such violations, Murrow says that "most of the time" he has forthrightly identified them as such on the air.

Yet on his nightly news show, Murrow conveys, by his choice of items and his showman's command of tone of voice, the news as Edward R. Murrow wants it to be understood. Example: on the State Department's obstacles to travel of U.S. newsmen to China, Murrow's reporting has dripped with disapproval. The Murrow aphorism ("A Word for Today") that closes the newscast is often chosen to make an editorial point. Something as simple as a *See It Now* shot of a subject's grimace or surreptitious scratch can carry as much condemnation as a Chicago *Tribune* editorial.

Murrow admits to prejudices shaped by his background; he tends to favor labor, farmers, Britain, underdogs (and, in the opinion of some Republicans, Democrats). He says he owes allegiance to no party. He speaks often of the rule of law and the right of dissent. But the enormous impact of his few overtly controversial broadcasts during the McCarthy era has given him a reputation for the kind of partisanship that he usually succeeds in keeping under control.

"This Is Murrow" 17

Spread Thin. A few who have known him for years think that Murrow has grown vain and pompous—an impression that his style also induces in some of his audience. Vanity is an occupational hazard that a performer has to watch as a woman watches her weight. Living in a swirl of hero worship, Murrow is obliged to recall the Murrow-Ain't-God Club. He smokes too much (three packs of Camels a day), is still gnawed by nerves before every broadcast; even in the air-conditioned studio, doing his radio show, he drips sweat and jiggles his legs tensely. He is a procrastinator and a soft touch. He has little small talk in social conversation. He has an intemperate streak that pushes him beyond sensible limits in poker playing, makes him work 40 hours at a stretch in a projection room or overdo the plowing on his farm. Sometimes in company he drifts off into trancelike gloom. Though he can be an amiable companion to the bottom of the bottle, he has a reserve that keeps his closest friends at arm's legnth. "I've never had any intimate friends," he once confided. "If I were in serious trouble, I would have trouble knowing where to turn."

In his TV career Murrow has become more of a performer and an editor, something less of a reporter and a creator. He is spread thin by three shows. The news roundup on his radio program has always been written by an assistant, but for the last four years ex-Broadcaster Raymond Swing has had a big hand in preparing the interpretive "end piece" that Murrow used to write alone. *Person to Person* was thought up by Co-Producers Jesse Zousmer and John Aaron (formerly associates on the radio news show), and they leave Murrow little more to do than the viewer sees on the screen. The workaday brunt of *See It Now* is borne by Friendly and staff. Murrow's role keeps him from doing much legwork as a good reporter should. He knows it, and his forays to the news fronts are spurred by the strongly felt need to replenish his credentials with the raw facts.

Work & Play. Murrow sometimes talks wistfully of quitting for six months or a year just to "keep silent, listen in on myself." As a man who "never learned how to play," he also would like more time for his hunting (he is a good wing shot), fishing and golf (lefthanded). He has little time now to enjoy his money, is uneasy about the celebrity that has robbed him of his anonymity in streets and restaurants, and he wears the burden of being able to be very proud of the medium in which he works. Murrow thinks that TV at large threatens to become an "opiate" and that the network managements lack "guts." His son Casey is permitted to watch TV only half an hour a day.

But almost in the same breath that he talks of quitting, Murrow may spout plans for big new projects. Forthcoming on *See It Now*: the peaceful uses of atomic energy; the best from an eight-hour Murrow interview with Harry S Truman. Murrow and Friendly have made an exciting pilot film of a new TV show called *Small World,* starring not Murrow but "my colleague" Eric Sevareid, which will present personalities in different parts of the world, joined in conversation through radio circuits and simultaneous movie photography. (But viewers may not see it; so far, CBS has been unable to sell it to a sponsor.) He wants to put a crew on the caboose of a freight train and let the cameras grind all across the United States.

Murrow's success is, by its lopsided domination, a reflection on the state of television journalism as a whole. For all its variety and originality, his achievement also leans hard on formula, and TV's trail is littered with the remains of formulas dead of overexposure. The fact that nothing new or exciting is in view to take Murrow's place is explained in great part by the nature of television. It is primarily an adman's medium conceived in escapism and dedicated to the proposition. Its role in communicating information plays second fiddle to the canned comedies, saddle-soap operas and variety shows. In its daily efforts to cover the news, television has not really made up its mind what it is trying to do. TV men are exhilarated by their technological power to reach at one instant into almost every living room in the United States, yet timid about using it to edify. So far, for all the earnest thought and energy that is devoted to it, electronic journalism has illuminated with bright flashes but few steady beams of light. Perhaps that is the best it is destined to do.

"TV News Did Not Just Happen — It Had to Invent Itself"
by Desmond Smith

Desmond Smith calls the period from 1951 to 1963 "television journalism's adolescent period," and indeed it was. While it has been said that necessity is the mother of invention, necessity has not always been the mother of good invention, as the news anchors' "desk accessory wars" and the heavy equipment of this period show.

As the creator of *60 Minutes,* Don Hewitt is one of the best-known, highest-paid producers in television news. In the summer of 1946, he was a 23-year-old former war correspondent looking for a job. When he swaggered into the offices of the *New York Herald-Tribune,* still wearing his uniform, he learned that the only position available was the same one he had when he worked there before the war — copy boy. Eventually he became a photo editor for Acme Newspictures, where, a year later, a friend phoned him about an opening at the Columbia Broadcasting System (CBS) for someone with picture experience.

Desmond Smith is the senior producer of "Venture," the Canadian Broadcasting Corporation's business program. He has worked for ABC, NBC, and CBS.

Hewitt was puzzled. "Why in the hell would CBS want someone with picture experience?" he asked. "They don't need pictures in radio."

"Not radio," his friend said. "Television."

Hewitt said, "What-a-vision?"

"*Television.*"

"You mean you sit home and look at pictures in a little box?"

"Yeah," his friend said.

Hewitt said, "Nobody's got that. It's Buck Rogers."

"*They've* got it," his friend said.

"The hell they have," Hewitt said.

"The hell they haven't," his friend said. "You want to see it?"

So Hewitt went down to CBS's cavernous studio in Grand Central Terminal, talked to some people—and got hired as an associate director. "I walked in and there were cameras and booms and lights and I felt like Judy Garland in the Emerald City," he recalled during a recent interview. "I couldn't believe the place. And that's how I got into television."

Don Hewitt wasn't the only hard-boiled newsman in the years right after World War II who put television on a par with Dick Tracy's wristwatch. It was something that could happen, indeed probably would happen, but not for a long time. Back then, people got their news from radio, papers and the newsreels shown at movie houses. Radio was big and getting bigger, reaching audiences in the tens of millions. Top news commentators like Raymond Gram Swing, H. V. Kaltenborn and Gabriel Heatter had little regard for television, a medium with almost no audience and few advertisers. "No one in radio wanted to have anything to do with us," recalls Art Lodge, who was a television news writer with the National Broadcasting Company (NBC) in 1950 and became a producer.

The problem, according to Reuven Frank, was that television did not look like a good bet for the future. Frank was president of NBC News from 1968 to 1973, and again from 1982 to 1984. He was hired as a television news writer in 1950 after visiting the network's screening rooms at 106th Street and Park Avenue in the old Pathé Building. Like Hewitt, Frank, then 29, had no radio or television experience; he had been working as a night city editor at the *Newark Evening News*. "I asked this guy how come he hired me," he remembers. "'Well,' he said, 'Nobody in radio who is worth anything thinks it's gonna last.'"

Under the circumstances, that wasn't surprising. Television news had barely begun to invent itself. Walter Cronkite, a gutsy war correspondent and former Moscow bureau chief for United Press, entered the broadcasting booth in 1950 as the first reporter assigned exclusively to television in CBS's Washington bureau. In those days, television news was still a hybrid of newsreels and radio-style reporting. Videotape, mini-cams and three-way satellite hookups had not yet been developed. There was no such thing as computer graphics or instant replay. No one had ever used the word "anchorman" (let alone "anchorwoman"). Ted Koppel was ten, Diane Sawyer was five, Connie Chung was four. There were only about ten million homes with television sets in the entire country, compared with more than 90 million today.

By 1970, things had changed. Most Americans were getting most of their news from the tube and the three networks, CBS, NBC and ABC (the American Broadcasting Companies), were getting better and better at providing it. The anchormen and reporters talking to people in their kitchens and living rooms had become so familiar it sometimes seemed as if they were members of the family. Cronkite, the eager young newscaster of the 1950s, was maturing into the trusted father figure of the '70s, and would become the silver-haired Uncle Walter of the '80s, loved by millions, voted in polls the "most trusted man in America."

This is the same Walter Cronkite, mind you, who in 1954 played straight man to a puppet. It happened after he was appointed host of CBS' new morning show. Since one of the stars of NBC's hugely successful *Today* show with Dave Garroway was a chimpanzee, the creative minds at CBS decided to pair Cronkite with several puppets, including one named Charlemagne the Lion. It didn't work, and eventually Cronkite was replaced by Jack Paar. Cronkite received a number of letters from viewers who were not happy to see him go. Among them was one that said, "Jack Paar won't be as good in the morning as you. I know—I'm his mother."

That sort of silliness was fairly typical of the often wacky era in which network news came of age. It began in 1951, when it became possible to operate a network coast-to-coast, using a combination of coaxial cable and microwave relays. It ended in the early '60s, when the evening news programs were expanded to 30 minutes, ushering in a new period of growth and technological sophistication. During the golden years between those two benchmarks, the pioneers of network news learned how to do their jobs.

By the end of 1948, the year Don Hewitt joined CBS News, the CBS television "network" consisted of fewer than 30 stations. Hookups were such that programs originating in New York couldn't even get as far as Chicago. When CBS's first evening news program, *Douglas Edwards with the News,* started up, its audience was barely measurable. In time, however, it would become the most-watched weeknight news program on television, with some 38 million viewers—a greater "circulation" by far than any newspaper or magazine in the world.

There was never any question in William S. Paley's mind that television was the wave of the future. The son of a wealthy cigar maker, Paley took over the fledgling CBS radio network in 1928. In the 1930s, he began hiring people for radio who he felt would be good in the new medium. Now nearing 90, Paley is still chairman of CBS and recently, surrounded by Picassos and Dubuffets in his magnificent office on the thirty-fifth floor of corporate headquarters in Manhattan, he talked about the way it was. "I saw the war coming, so I phoned Ed Murrow, who was in Europe lining up speakers for our talk programs. I told him to hire some good people." Murrow hired some of the best reporters in the world, including William L. Shirer, Howard K. Smith (who later became an anchorman at ABC), Robert Trout, Eric Sevareid and Charles Collingwood.

As Paley had anticipated, a number of the journalists Murrow signed up eventually formed the nucleus of the CBS television news team. They already knew how to go out and "get" a story, and then present a concise analysis of what they had learned. After a little training and some on-the-job experience, they began to get familiar with the video dimension.

Until the early 1950s, when they began hiring their own cameramen, the networks relied on the newsreel companies to provide their filmed material. The newsreels usually sent a script along with the film, which writers at the networks would redo. Phil Scheffler, the senior producer of *60 Minutes,* worked with Douglas Edwards. "One afternoon we opened a can of film," he recalls, "and the caption said, 'Hordes of Chinese prisoners captured on the west coast of Korea.' I remember saying to producer Don Hewitt, 'This footage looks awfully familiar,' and Don agreed. We looked back in our files. Sure enough, a month earlier the newsreel people had sent us the same footage, only that stuff was captioned, 'Hordes of Chinese prisoners captured on the east coast of Korea.'"

The earliest newscasts were pretty crude. No invisible boom mikes, no offscreen Teleprompters, no glitzy sets, no hookups to live action in faraway places. The newscaster simply read the news directly from the written page into a big microphone located smack-dab in the middle of a plain desk. Then some smart young director decided to hang a clock in the background, just so the audience would know it was all happening live before their eyes. Then an even smarter young director on a rival network added a second clock with the time on the West Coast (even though no one on the West Coast could watch New York television before 1951). Pretty soon it degenerated into a game of "Can you top this?"

If Douglas Edwards at CBS had three clocks and a calendar, then NBC's John Cameron Swayze, a dapper man who usually wore a red carnation in his buttonhole, had to have a map. So maps proliferated. Not to be outdone, Edwards' producer added a world globe, a black telephone (evidently in case Edwards had a sudden urge to call the President), In and Out baskets, and an executive pen set. "It was fatuous and meaningless," says Sandy Socolow, now the executive producer of *World Monitor with John Hart.* "I'm not sure anyone cared except the ten or twelve people in each network's newsroom. For them, it was fun."

Socolow was a writer with a "news of the day" type program on the old Du Mont network, which went out of business in the mid-'50s. The program was sponsored by Bond, which was (and for that matter still is) a large-volume men's clothier in Manhattan. The newscaster for that program was a hard-driving professional named Mike Wallace. "Every evening Mike would show up for the 15-minute broadcast, get out of his street clothes and into a Bond suit," Socolow recalls. "After delivering the news, he would stand up and the camera would follow him as he moved from behind the desk to another area. Here Mike would go into an impassioned spiel about Bond suits, pointing out special features about the one he had on and usually concluding with an offer to sell you a suit just like it — with not one but *two* pairs of trousers."

That kind of commercialism was pretty much par for the course in television's early days; it was a holdover from radio. Many radio programs, including the news, were bought by the sponsors and controlled by their advertising agencies. NBC's first regular nightly news telecast was sponsored by Camel cigarettes. It was called the *Camel News Caravan*. As part of the contract, the advertising agency insisted that an ever-lit Camel cigarette must be burning in an ashtray located prominently at John Cameron Swayze's elbow. "The ad people were insatiable," according to Reuven Frank, who was one of the *Caravan* writers. "They wanted 'Camel' to show up in every picture." But they did not want cigars to show up at all. There was, Frank says, a "gentleman's agreement" to avoid shots of people with cigars. The single exception permitted was Winston Churchill.

Sponsor influence extended even to the coverage of special events. The matchup between Senator Robert Taft and Gen. Dwight Eisenhower at the 1952 Republican Convention made gripping television, and so did the emergence of Senator Adlai Stevenson at the Democrats' get-together. But an attractive TV hostess named Betty Furness stole the spotlight at both shows. Furness was the spokesperson for Westinghouse Electric Corporation, which sponsored all television coverage by CBS at both conventions that year. Day after day, she talked about the finer points of refrigerators and ranges while the cameras cut back and forth between the floor fights and the spnsor's kitchen set. By the time the conventions were over, it seemed to many viewers that Furness had filled more airtime than the nominees — and, in fact, she had.

After the 1948 conventions, which were the first to be commercially telecast, network news and politics became entwined like ivy on the college wall. Most nightly newscasts carried a lot of Washington news. One reason was its availability. News from Europe had to be shipped by plane. News from the Soviet Union, Eastern Europe, China and most of Africa wasn't available at all. But from 1948 on, all three networks had a coaxial cable joining Washington and New York. Congress always had a story or two in the works and politicians were usually willing to talk.

Dwight Eisenhower was not comfortable with television; his predecessor, Harry Truman, was. Truman became the first "television President." Homey, outspoken and accessible, he was made for the medium but the medium often had a hard time keeping up with him. CBS cameraman Herb Schwartz was covering Truman on one of his visits to New York.

Getting a Leg Up on Harry. "Every morning when he came out of his hotel for his daily walk," Schwartz says, "we'd be waiting with our cameras rolling, and he'd just walk off briskly down the street. CBS had just developed a portable sound-on-film camera and we decided to test it out on Truman." The camera was battery operated, so Schwartz and his colleagues made up a tray, like the kind cigarette girls used to hang around their neck, and put the battery and other apparatus on top of it. When Truman stepped outside, they were ready. "He kept walking and talking for several minutes," Schwartz says, "which was about as long as we could manage to keep walking backwards in front of him. We ran most of it on the news that night."

In New York, Ed Murrow and his longtime radio associate, producer Fred Friendly, added a new dimension to the relationship between Washington and the networks with an extraordinary documentary program that debuted on Sunday, November 18, 1951. Viewers who tuned in that night saw Murrow swivel in his chair, squint directly into the camera and say, "Good evening. This is an old team trying to learn a new trade." He was 43. Friendly was 36.

The program was called *See It Now* and it set a new standard of hard-hitting journalism for television news. Once *See It Now* got rolling, many Washington politicians and bureaucrats who previously had been only too willing to sound off in front of the cameras began ducking out the back door. The program's impact was tremendous because it was so bold. It took on such topics as the plight of America's neglected migrant workers, the discharge of Airman Milo Raduvolich as an alleged security risk and an argument over the right of free speech in Indianapolis. There was nothing else like it on television — certainly not the regular newscasts, locked as they were into 15-minute digests of the day's happenings.

See It Now became audacious in its presentation, too. It originated from a television control room, not just a set, establishing a realistic format that is still standard in TV news today. It became noted for its thorough reporting and incisive editing. It also broke new ground by taking advantage of television's ability to move around. Its film cameras went everywhere. In one astonishing piece of legerdemain, the viewer at home saw Murrow look up at two TV screens, one with a picture of New York Harbor, the other with the Golden Gate Bridge in San Francisco, "Three thousand miles," wrote one critic, "compressed to the vanishing point.... This was television."

The program's most enduring legacy, however, was its willingness to tackle tough issues. And the best example was its unflinching look at Joseph McCarthy on March 9, 1954. The ultraconservative Senator from Wisconsin was then at the height of his anticommunist crusade. For years, he had bullied and outmaneuvered journalists and politicians alike. Murrow and Friendly showed McCarthy in action, then analyzed his charges and tactics. "This is no time for men who oppose his methods to keep silent," Murrow editorialized at the end. "We can deny our heritage and our history but we cannot escape responsibility for the result." Viewer reaction was overwhelmingly favorable.

In the late 1950s, the rivalry between NBC and CBS intensified with the arrival of Robert E. Kintner as president of NBC. A onetime Washington columnist turned broadcasting executive, Kintner had previously worked for ABC. He was a hard-driving, ferociously competitive man who conducted rounds of dictation with as many as three secretaries at once. He was determined to make sure NBC was never beaten on a news story. He had three television sets in his office, one for each network, and whenever he saw something that displeased him he promptly fired off a memo to his news chief, William McAndrew. His record: 35 memos in two days.

Getting an Exclusive with Fidel. During that period, news producers were putting more and more emphasis on getting their reporters and their cameramen into the field. In 1957, much to NBC's chagrin, CBS managed to get a team into the Sierra Maestra of Cuba for ten days of interviewing and filming with Fidel Castro. Then a 31-year-old revolutionary lawyer, Castro predicted that he and his followers would soon overthrow the regime of President Fulgencio Batista. Earlier, Batista had claimed that his 50,000-man army had wiped out the rebels, but an American newspaperman challenged that assertion. CBS decided to take on the dangerous task of finding Castro and getting an exclusive interview on the air.

Veteran cameraman Wendell Hoffman went to Havana with reporter Robert Taber for a prearranged rendezvous with Castro in a secret mountain camp. Since any such contact was strictly forbidden by the Batista government, Hoffman had to find a way to conceal his 250 pounds of equipment from troops in the field and at military roadblocks. The problem was solved for him by Castro's emissaries, who devised a way to hide the gear in the side panels of the automobile the party would be using. When Hoffman learned they would also be trekking through mountainous terrain, he gave away his 90-pound tripod. It took Hoffman and Taber two days to cross Cuba, and several more days of climbing. "It was tough," says Hoffman, who now lives in Manhattan, Kansas. "I got blisters as big as silver dollars from fording rivers and then walking in wet boots."

The newsmen spent ten days with Castro and his men, filming every day. Then, after struggling back down the mountains and driving 150 miles through roadblocks, Hoffman caught a plane to New York. The stories made from the film—on the evening news and in a documentary special—created a sensation. There was no doubt, after the CBS pictures, that Castro was alive and well. Not quite two years later, he entered Havana in triumph—a victory he had foretold in halting English before Wendell Hoffman's camera.

A postscript. After being congratulated on his coup by John Daly, then the president of CBS News, Hoffman dropped in on the camera department. "Where's the camera?" the supervisor asked. Hoffman, all six feet two inches of him, glared down at the man. "The camera weighed 50 pounds," he explained. "I had to carry it up the danged mountain but I was danged if I was going to carry it back. If CBS wants that chunk of metal so much, why don't *you* go back to Cuba and get it?"

By the late '50s, the CBS and NBC networks had grown to about 200 stations apiece (ABC was far behind), which meant that almost any place in the United States where news was happening, a crew could cover it and send it back to New York from a local affiliate. A little more than a decade later, the sky would no longer be the limit for television. The orbiting of American communication satellites would put the delivery of news into outer space.

The competition kept heating up. After NBC introduced *The Huntley-Brinkley Report* in 1956, based on the novel idea of using two anchors instead of just one, Douglas Edwards' longtime lead in the ratings began to evaporate. David Brinkley, a witty young Southerner with curly brown hair and a mischievous grin, had been a writer at the network's Washington station. Chet Huntley, a somber, solid citizen from Montana, had been working as a newsman in Los Angeles. Together they became the most famous duo in the history of television news. Their sign-off—"Good night, Chet" ... "Good night, David, and good night for NBC News"—was Reuven Frank's brainchild and pretty soon people were saying it all over the country.

Huntley was cast in the Murrow mold. Sometimes Brinkley refused to take the news all that seriously. Once, following a debate in which the Republicans wanted to change the name of Boulder Dam to Hoover Dam, Brinkley suggested that everything would be all right if the former President "would change his name to Herbert Boulder."

One Era Ends, Another Begins. By 1963, television journalism's adolescent period was just about over. The business was going to get larger, more powerful and even more competitive. ABC made its big move into news in 1963 when it hired Elmer W. Lower, a onetime *Life* magazine writer and CBS News Washington bureau chief, as president of its news division. And 1963 was also the year when the evening news got longer. Confronted with the huge ratings success of the Huntley-Brinkley team, CBS had replaced Douglas Edwards with Walter Cronkite, who had presided over the coverage of three national conventions and all of the U.S. space shots. Next, it announced that it was taking the evening news from 15 to 30 minutes. NBC quickly followed suit. ABC went to the half-hour format in 1967.

On Cronkite's first half-hour broadcast, President John F. Kennedy appeared for a "conversation" with the newscaster. Eight-one days after that, Kennedy's assassination in Dallas wrenched television news into a new era. Cronkite the anchorman became Cronkite the family man, reliving the events of that terrible week with a grieving nation. A decade earlier, television news had possessed no such power, no such editorial abilities, no such technical resources.

Today, the networks are in trouble. Declining audiences, soaring costs, and competition from cable, pay and satellite TV have ushered in yet another era — this time one of austerity that puts new pressures on news operations. It's hard to predict how Americans of the next century will learn about what's going on, but one thing seems fairly certain: reporting the news won't be as much fun as it was in the beginning.

There was, for example, the time when a plane crashed in New York's East River and Don Hewitt, then an evening-news producer, chartered a tugboat to visit the wreck site with a CBS camera crew. A crew from NBC arrived about the same time in a rowboat with an outboard motor. "They came put-putting along with a camera and a dish aimed at the Empire State Building," Hewitt recalls. "I told the captain of the tug to maneuver between them and the Empire State Building so they couldn't transmit past our boat."

In the process of maneuvering, the tug bumped into the rowboat. When Hewitt got back to the office, he found out that Frank Stanton, the president of CBS, had received an irate complaint from the people at NBC, who alleged that Hewitt had tried to sink them in the East River. "I'll never forget what I said then," Hewitt recollects. "I said, 'Crybabies!'"

Walter Cronkite

"The Most Intimate Medium"

Walter Cronkite's tenure as anchor has no equal. Cronkite joined CBS in 1950 from the wire service world of United Press; he became anchor in 1962, serving in that capacity until 1981, when he was replaced by Dan Rather. In this 1966 article, Cronkite worries about the "tyranny of time (limitations)" in television journalism, the "front page" treatment television journalism is giving to the news and the then-lack of professional training for television journalists.

By his own definition, the man behind the big U-shaped desk is a managing editor. All day, with wire-service teleprinters clacking behind him, he and his associates have kept a close watch on the spasmodic flow of the world's news. They have assigned stories, selected pictures, edited and rewritten copy. They have argued the relative news value of a battle-action file from Vietnam and bloody films of students rioting in Djakarta; they have checked on the latest peace rumor out of Washington, the day's speeches at the United Nations. Now, deadline is approaching, and the big problem is whether that World Series game out in Chavez Ravine will end in time for them to carry the score.

So far, the frenetic activity would be familiar to any newsman on any big-city daily. But deadline brings a difference. No presses roll. Show business moves into the newsroom, and lights dim beyond the rim of the desk. The day's debris is shoved off into the shadows. As technicians man their equipment, a makeup expert goes to work on the managing editor. At the last moment he runs a comb through his blond hair, shrugs a neatly pressed jacket over his wrinkled shirtsleeves, and shoots his French cuffs. It is 6:30 p.m. Cameras zero in, and CBS's Walter Cronkite, Jr., begins his half-hour evening report. Now, by his own definition, his role has changed. On the color TV tube he becomes part editor and part ham.

Out of this unlikely combination, Cronkite has constructed an on-screen personality that makes him the single most convincing and authoritative figure in TV news—no mean rank in a medium where competition is uncompromising, where the three nationwide networks scrutinize one another's shows and crib from one another's operations in a desperate drive for the top of the ratings. As a better-informed public has demanded more and more information about current events, TV news programs have changed from loss leaders and have begun to start paying their way. And as the networks have made the

Like the 1957 Time *article on Edward R. Murrow, this article was published in* Time *during a period when* Time *did not give by-lines to staff writers.*

most of them, news shows like Cronkite's have become one of the most important and influential molders of public opinion in the United States. Some 58 percent of the U.S. public gets most of their news from television, reported an Elmo Roper poll last year.

How to Be Used. For better or worse, television has become an established part of the democratic process—a fact of life in the United States that is not lost on any politician. Senator Robert Kennedy candidly admits that he would rather appear for 30 seconds on an evening news program than be written up in every newspaper in the world. "President Johnson," says White House Press Secretary Bill Moyers bluntly, "feels that television offers him the most direct, straightforward and personal way to communicate with the people. It is not someone else's attitude or interpretation of what the President said. It's the purest form of communication, and I think the most desirable."

Today the well-heeled political candidate spends all he can to buy television time. When money runs low, he uses his ingenuity to organize "news events"—a post-office dedication, say, or an appearance with an illustrious visitor—anything that will lure the ubiquitous television camera. "I know we're used," admits NBC's David Brinkley, as he looks ahead toward November's fast-approaching election day. "I simply decide how to handle the story on the basis of who is using us, and how, and why."

However the story is handled, its impact is predictable. Together, the Cronkite and Huntley-Brinkley reports are watched by an estimated aggregate of 30 million people, and it is claimed that 70 percent of that audience is made up of adults. One particularly popular news special, such as Pope Paul's visit to the United States last year, can easily focus the attention of 150 million viewers. Even at the dullest point of the Fulbright hearings on Vietnam, several million people were tuned in.

"Newspapers try to transmit facts," says Voice of America Director and onetime NBC Correspondent John Chancellor, "but television is the transmission of experience in its rawest form." Putting the pageantry of a Kennedy or a Churchill funeral into countless living rooms, is an achievement that the most moving newspaper description cannot duplicate; the sight of a young Dominican being shot in the back by a U.S. paratrooper can jolt the home viewer far more than any account of the same tragedy in print.

No Back Pages. "Television," says ABC's Howard K. Smith by way of explanation, "is not just a picture medium. It is pictures, plus words, plus personality." When the words and the personality belong to a Walter Cronkite, they generate what CBS Vice President Gordon Manning calls "believability." Talking to the camera as if it were an attentive stranger, Cronkite projects an air of friendly formality, of slightly distant courtliness. His millions of viewers at the other end of the tube respond with consistent warmth.

No matter how ordinary the event, no matter how stirring the picture, the news that Cronkite and his colleagues bring into the American home always carries a kind of subliminal authority. The effect can be traced, says Cronkite, to the almost embarrassing intimacy of the camera. Even more important, he says, everything the viewer sees and hears comes to him on what amounts to an electronic front page. What the managing editor chooses for him, he cannot

28 The Early Years

Walter Cronkite during the Vietnam war years (photo courtesy Walter Cronkite).

avoid. He cannot skip from headline to headline and browse among stories. They are all read aloud, right to the end. "There are no back pages in our kind of journalism," says Cronkite. Everything is up front where it cannot be overlooked.

Amplifying Prejudices. As a result of its extraordinary impact, television news has become a powerful force encouraging social ferment. Early in the civil rights revolution, Negro activitists made it perfectly clear that wittingly or unwittingly, the television cameraman was their ally. Marches were staged and demonstrations timed to get full coverage. By reporting the whole movement, television added to its momentum. The sight of Bull Connor's dogs attacking Birmingham Negroes served as a catalyst for the conscience of most of the nation.

To be sure, as TV news cameras moved north with the civil rights riots, their films had another effect. Ironically, television, which had given such a boost to the civil rights movement, began to obstruct it and contribute mightily to the white backlash. "Take the case of some recent footage on the Atlanta riots," says M.I.T. Political Scientist Harold Isaacs. "What you saw was a black blur of a face, two shining eyes, flashing teeth — shouting 'Black power!' That stirs up all too basic reactions in people." Says V.O.A.'s Chancellor: "It's a mistake to think that TV alone makes up people's minds on broad questions. What it does is amplify their prejudices."

It can also gather its audience into a cohesive whole with a sureness that is unmatched in any other area of communications. By its coverage of the assassination of President Kennedy and the murder of Lee Harvey Oswald, TV news demonstrated its tireless capability and versatility. For millions upon millions, the President's funeral became a heart-moving personal experience. "Television held the country together over the transition period in a unique way and helped preserve the whole democratic process," says one-time FCC Chairman Newton Minow, who exempts TV news from his charge that the medium is a "vast wasteland."

Space from All Angles. Aware that they now have on their hands a commodity of indefinable power and, inevitably, incalculable value, the networks are putting more time, money and ingenuity than ever into their news programs. Both CBS and NBC now allot about one-quarter of their programming to news and public affairs, ABC somewhat less. The Cronkite and Huntley-Brinkley reports, which used to run for only 15 minutes, were increased to a half-hour in 1963; and ABC's *Peter Jennings with the News* will go to a half-hour this January. Together, the three networks will spend $148 million on news this year—their budgets have been boosted 200 percent from five years before.

For the coverage of astronautics alone, the networks will shell out a combined $20 million this year to handle all angles of the story—from anxious wives awaiting the return of the astronauts to the various manufacturers who have contributed to the space capsule. With 30- to 40-man staffs in Vietnam, CBS and NBC spent over $500,000 apiece on war coverage last year. With the help of the Early Bird communications satellite, television managed live coverage of the Gemini 6 splashdown.

Out of Context. The range is virtually unlimited, the impact almost awesome, the promise increasingly impressive. Yet there is general agreement that TV news still falls short of its potential. "It is hard for television newscasting to serve the more mature purposes of journalism," says Harold Fleming, director of the Potomac Institute. "It is hard for TV to give perspective, to put things in context."

Cronkite, for one, agrees. TV, he feels, is shortchanging the vital, reportorial aspect of journalism. "The networks," he says, "including my own, do a first-rate job of disseminating the news, but all of them have third-rate news-gathering organizations. We are still basically dependent on the wire services. We have barely dipped our toe into investigative reporting."

For one thing, even though the networks are steadily building up their reportorial staffs, they still have too few men in the field. In Washington, a correspondent may cover Capitol Hill one day, the Labor Department the next; on the following day a story may take him out of town. He has little time to develop expertise in any one area.

Once a story is assigned, the reporter goes to work and a kind of "tyranny of time" sets in. Interviews are filmed, the films are given to leather-jacketed couriers who hop on motorcycles and rush to the studio while the reporter chases down the next subject for camera and sound crews. By the time the reporter himself gets back to the studio he sometimes finds that the producer has put his story together in a surprising manner. After being told that he will be given ten seconds in which to mouth an introduction to a 20-second slice of film, with perhaps 15 seconds of narrative later on, the reporter is likely to explode: "Yeah, but when do I get to tell what else happened?"

Cold-Eyed Calculation. Holding equal sway with the tyranny of time is the tyranny of pictures. To the television reporter, his producer is a man who dotes on "fender-bender crashes, fires, demonstrations, fights." The more striking the pictures, the greater the chance that they will get on the air. "This is the boy-oh-boy, look-at-the-people-riot syndrome," says one CBS correspondent. A correspondent's response to the syndrome is understandable. Getting on the air is the name of the game — especially if the reporter himself is visible on film while supplying comment; under the TV fee system, he earns at least $50 extra every time he appears on camera.

Then there is the matter of money. The expense of flying film from Vietnam, for example, developing it on the West Coast and then leasing a line for $3,000 an hour to transmit the pictures to New York for inclusion in a program is likely to have an overbearing effect on news judgment. Even if the pictures do not live up to the raves cabled in by the man in the field (who probably had not seen them and was depending on his photographer's word), they may price their way onto the program.

It is that same sort of cold-eyed calculation that keeps the network news programs where they are on the television schedule — always on the unhappy edge of "prime time," which runs generally from 7:30 P.M. to 11 P.M. Nobody in the management end of the business wants them on prime time because their low Nielsen ratings (generally around 14) would presumably keep people from dialing in any high-rating entertainment show (Nielsen rating: 21) that followed. And no local stations want a network news program at 11 P.M. — which is where Cronkite would like to be — because they can make twice the money at that time with local spot ads on their own local news show. So Cronkite goes on at 7 P.M. in the New York area, just when the average commuter has arrived home to concentrate on his first martini. In Chicago, he is broadcast at 5:30, in San Francisco at 6:30 and in Los Angeles at 7:00. A large share of his potential audience is inevitably lost.

Old Objectivity. Of almost equal importance is the tyranny of advertisers. Though the newsmen, with good reason, proclaim their freedom, the sponsor's influence is still apparent. Commercials, the newsmen occasionally boast, are restricted to a small percentage of a news program's time, far less than the percentage of space given over to ads in successful newspapers. But it is also true that those commercials appear right in the middle of the electronic front page. Few newspapers give their advertisers such considerate treatment.

And network executives are notoriously timid about antagonizing anyone — particularly the people who pay their bills. Which means that there is a pervading reluctance to take sides on any issue. "I find an almost excessive lack of bias on television," says Howard K. Smith. "We are afraid of a point of view. We stick to the old American belief that there is an objectivity. If a man says the world is round, we run out to find someone to say it is flat." Network executives are also quick to delete any portion of a news program that might offend any powerful segment of the audience. Top management, said the late Edward R. Murrow, "with a few notable exceptions has been trained in advertising, research, sales or show business. But by the nature of the corporate structure, they also make the final and crucial decisions having to do with news and public affairs. Frequently they have neither the time nor the competence to do this."

Little has changed since Murrow's speech almost a decade ago. Summing up for all those now who make their livings "dealing with producers, directors, business executives, salespeople, sponsors, agents, set designers, accountants and all others in the new, huge superstructure of human beings hovering over the frail product," CBS's Eric Sevareid was hard put to describe the rigors of putting on a news program. "The ultimate sensation," he finally decided, "is the feeling of being bitten to death by ducks."

Raw & Lively. To be sure, all the tyrannies of TV news are constantly fought against and often held at bay. Few, if any, network producers worried about offending Deep South viewers with their civil rights coverage, for example. ABC earned the nickname, "African Broadcasting Co."; CBS became the "Colored Broadcasting Co."; NBC, the "Negro Broadcasting Co."

Of all the shows on all the networks, it is Cronkite's that most consistently triumphs over the built-in drawbacks of TV newscasting. His reporters have learned to respect his news judgment; his producers have learned that he will back that judgment with a fierce pride. Despite the cost, he will not hesitate to remake the tape of his show when new film or a new story cries out for space — even after the original broadcast has already gone on the air in some parts of the country. He is determined to keep up with what he and other TV commentators like to call the "raw news," the "hard news" of day-to-day events — which is to say, the late-breaking stories that have always made up some of the liveliest stuff of journalism.

For all the lure of news in the raw though, it was wariness born of long experience as reporters that caused Cronkite and his executive producer Ernest Leiser to hesitate and worry for hours over whether to run the now-famous film sequence showing U.S. Marines in August 1965 burning a Vietnamese village. Were the pictures fair to the U.S.? To the Marines? Or was their message somewhat out of balance? In the end, it was decided that the pictures were simply too good to pass up. So, along with a narration by CBS Correspondent Morley Safer, Cronkite's audience saw a filmed report that represented most of what is best and most of what is distressing in TV's coverage of the war.

Message of Urgency. The very sight of Safer, gaunt and haggard, out there in the midst of battle, brought the war to the screen with undeniable immediacy. It testified to the reporter's scorn for danger as he tracked down his story. No Marine rifleman was more exposed to enemy fire than Safer and his crew as they lugged their bulky equipment to the outskirts of the hamlet called Cam Ne. The very sound of Safer's voice, excited yet sure, carried a message of urgency. "This is what the war in Vietnam is all about," he intoned, as the camera panned over crying women and old men. In his careful solemnity there was an echo of CBS hero Edward R. Murrow reporting World War II on radio: "This is London."

It was clear what Safer meant. To him, the war in Vietnam was all about husky, well-equipped Marines burning down an entire village, leveling 150 homes "in retaliation for a burst of gunfire." If there were Viet Cong around, Safer said, "they were long gone." And the Marines, he intimated, were wreaking a kind of harsh vengeance as the day's operation burned homes, "wounded three women, killed one baby, wounded one Marine and netted four prisoners — four old men who could not answer questions put to them in English. Four old men who had no idea what an ID card was."

Perhaps the emotional phrases were only to be expected in an emotional situation. And the fact is that even if Safer had gone out of his way to try to explain or excuse the Marines at Cam Ne, his words would have had little effect. To try to put pictures of one village burning into proper context, to balance that one incident against all the other activity that makes up the war in Vietnam, would be all but impossible. On TV news, pictures make their own front-page context; it takes a skillful script indeed to give them an added dimension, to remind the viewer that they are only part of the story. All too often the reporter in the field only adds a little wordy color or asks an inane question: "Seen action like this before, Marine?"

Bang! Bang! Bang! NBC's Chet Huntley, for one, is worried that too many TV reporters in Vietnam concentrate far too much on Safer-like shots, the kind of flaming action that ensures an appearance on the air at home. The military thinks that too many correspondents are out there for their "own personal aggrandizement," Huntley told a *Variety* reporter recently. ABC's Howard K. Smith took the same tack when he returned from a recent visit to Vietnam. During the Buddhist demonstrations, he said, "television gave the impression that the whole country was rioting, instead of 2,000 out of 17 million." Television, he complained, "still gives the impression that it is an American war out there. You never see a Vietnamese action." His colleagues, he said, were completely ignoring all the work on pacification. They look for what will get on the air, "and that's bang, bang, bang. We're missing all the nation-building."

Others among the regular Saigon TV corps agree. "Let's be truthful," said one of them in *TV Guide* as he offered a straightforward explanation for all the battle footage he and his competitors are sending home. "Here in Vietnam you can get your face on the network three or four times a week. It's risky, but it's money in the bank. We're all war profiteers."

The accusation is harsh. Vietnam is television's first war; the medium's mistakes are due as much to overall inexperience as they are to individual overinvolvement. The networks are learning fast; the quality of their coverage is improving steadily. It had better. By next year, if the Vietnam conflict continues, a new communications satellite high over the Pacific may make live coverage available. Then TV's first war will become the war brought home to the American living room even as it is fought.

News Sense. Apart from its troubles with the "raw" news of immediate events, television has demonstrated that it is perfectly possible to unite film with text in a news program that is both balanced and provocative. Taking one of the most abstruse and complex of current topics — the Common Market —

John Chancellor made it understandable as well as entertaining in a special that few critics thought would come off. By examining some of the blatant misuses of federal highway funds, Brinkley showed what a cutting edge investigative TV work can have. Many people have ridden the fabled Orient Express, but NBC's Edwin Newman was the first to take a television camera along and he exposed the ride for the grueling, unglamorous trip it is. "Why do we have to wait for the Fulbright committee to examine our China policy?" asks Edward P. Morgan. "Television should have gotten the idea well beforehand."

To meet such criticism, says Cronkite, the television industry will have to train its own journalists. It will have to build a corps of correspondents with well-developed news sense and a disciplined news judgment. Until that happens, however, TV will continue to raid the other media — as it did in the case of Walter Cronkite, who has worked for both radio and television and brought to them a pervasive background of news experience.

Born in St. Joseph, Missouri, brought up in Kansas City, Cronkite found reporting far more exciting than his studies and dropped out of the University of Texas in his junior year. For a short while he found his niche as a radio sportscaster, and he achieved a measure of local renown with his talent for the then-popular practice of replaying football games with nothing but wire-service copy, a sound-effects man and his own fertile imagination to give the listener the effect of an on-the-spot description. He improvised elaborate descriptions of players and cheerleaders, even pretended to recognize friends in the stands. Once when the wire service broke down, he kept a game going for 20 minutes on imagination alone. "I marched them up and down the field — with frequent and protracted time outs. When the wire finally came back, I discovered that Notre Dame had scored. I had them on their own 20-yard line. I had to get them all the way back downfield to score in a hurry."

Success with Chalk. The sportscaster soon grew restless in radio; it involved too much show business to suit him. Besides, he had met a girl named Mary Elizabeth Maxwell, and he had the distinct impression that she would not marry him until he became a bona fide reporter. Cronkite joined United Press in Kansas City, Missouri, and Betsy married him. They have three children: Nancy Elizabeth, 18, Mary Kathleen, 16, Walter Leland III, 9.

In 1942, Cronkite became a U.P. war correspondent. He covered the North African landings, then the air war out of London. Put in charge of U.P.'s operations in the Low Countries after the invasion, he often arrived in towns ahead of liberating Canadian troops. "I got a lot of garlands and heard a lot of welcoming speeches. The Canadians were not amused."

At war's end, Cronkite went to Moscow for two grim years as U.P. bureau chief. Back in the United States, he was offered a job as a KMBC radio correspondent in Washington. The pay was good, but Cronkite was dubious. "News is a newspaper's business," he bluntly told KMBC, "and it isn't radio's business." He finally accepted, though, at double his United Press salary, which, after ten years, was still only $125 a week. When the Korean war broke out, he was hired by CBS and made an impromptu TV debut giving a lecture on the war, complete with chalk and blackboard. He was such a hit that against his better judgment he was soon shifted to television news. "It was a time," he says, "when no self-respecting newsman wanted anything to do with this new electronic beast."

Cronkite was not long in getting the beast under control. In 1952, CBS News Director Sig Mickelson picked him up to anchor the network's coverage of the national political conventions, and he did such a workmanlike job that he found himself in the top rank of newscasters. Suddenly he was a star. He bgan to have his own news shows—*Twentieth Century* and *Eyewitness to History*.

Drowned in Din. Despite Cronkite's unqualified success as a newsman, the network persuaded him to try to be an entertainer as well. Reluctantly, he agreed to host a CBS morning program to compete with Dave Garroway's *Today Show,* and he found himself a hostage to show business. A gag writer was hired to write his lines, and he lost control of the program. "I was reasonably charming," he insists to this day, "but the whole thing didn't work out."

One morning when he arrived for work, he learned from a TV gossip column that he had been replaced by Jack Paar. "In the course of the day, I discovered that the Hollywood version of the networks is quite correct. I called CBS executives all day long and couldn't reach a single one. The order was out to all secretaries that no one wanted to talk to me." It was small consolation to open his mail and read one brief letter: "Jack Paar won't be as good as you. I know—I'm his mother."

After this debacle, along came Huntley-Brinkley with their breezier approach to the political conventions of 1956. "I was the old hand," says Cronkite, "but they received the critical attention." To make matters worse, by the 1964 conventions, the network competition was out of hand. Lugging their equipment with them, television reporters swarmed over the convention floor. Quiet and restrained, Walter Cronkite tended to get lost in the crush. CBS executives became so panicked by the Huntley-Brinkley ratings that they rigged Cronkite with a new headset—one earphone tuned to the podium, the other to the control room. Their anchorman could not make much sense out of anything. "It was as bad a job as I have ever done," he remembers. Completely agreeing, CBS replaced him at the Democratic Convention with the team of Roger Mudd and Bob Trout. The replacement got even worse ratings than Cronkite.

Demoted though he was, Cronkite bounced back. The audience for his evening news program, which he had taken over in 1962, continued to grow. "Sometimes Cronkite goes too far and tries to tell everything like the New York Times," says Fred Friendly, who, as CBS news president used to be Cronkite's boss. "But he is a success because he cares so deeply for the news." As Cronkite puts it: "I like working with the commodity, in the way a farmer likes to work with the black soil of Iowa."

Although he now earns $200,000 a year—a combination of fees and a base salary of about $25,000—Cronkite is still easygoing and gregarious. Thanks to his philosophy, "If it's for sale, buy it," he owns a 35-foot ketch that he sails with his family in the waters around Long Island. In the 1950s he took up sports-car racing, even drove a Lancia in the Sebring 12-hour race. Once, while tearing through the Great Smoky Mountains, he went off on a turn and plunged

100 feet into a stream. He was well belted in, and he emerged unhurt, but these days Betsy frowns on the sports-car bit.

In a business where ulcers are an occupational disease, Correspondent Cronkite seems to have only one persistent worry: that he may be shrinking. "When I was a young man," he says, "I could happily say I had achieved the American ideal of being six feet. Now I have to stretch hard to make it." Retorts his wife: "Nonsense, Walter has always been just a hair under six feet."

No Snow Job. Whatever his height, Cronkite has earned top billing in a star system that rivals any in show business. Alongside him are Huntley and Brinkley; ranking just below are such newscasters and commentators as CBS's Sevareid and Harry Reasoner, NBC's Frank McGee, ABC's Howard K. Smith. Wherever they go, the stars are instantly recognized. When they cover a story, their presence makes a story in itself. Their casual power to shape the news is immense. Ralph Renick, news director of Miami's Station WTVJ, says he will never forget the expression on Cronkite's face after his program ran a film of Negro children being beaten by whites in Grenada, Mississippi. "He positively recoiled," says Renick. "That hurt look was the most powerful kind of editorializing. It was as effective as Huntley and Brinkley getting their opinions across by sly side comments and making mouths."

The stars themselves have mixed feelings about playing the role of what Brinkley calls the "all-wise, all-knowing journalistic superman." Brinkley is bothered because "it's just impossible to know everything that is happening all the time, to really know what you're talking about." Cronkite has further complaints. Among the 1,000 or so letters he receives each week are some disconcerting notes from women who claim to have discovered a secret message in his broadcast beamed to them alone and are eager to arrange a tryst. But no such beefs from the stars will make the system go away. "People tend to believe certain individuals in times of crisis," says Sevareid. "They get a feeling with a broadcaster. They know if he is trying to do a snow job."

In the battle of the stars for ratings, Huntley-Brinkley and Cronkite seesaw back and forth as public tastes vary between a preference for the wry quip and the more stolid Cronkite style. Though he thinks a Brinkley bon mot is well worth waiting for, *New York Times* TV Critic Jack Gould admires Cronkite's "uncanny ability to fight fatigue." As a critic in the Providence *Journal* put it: "Viewers rarely recall or relish a Cronkite statement. They believe it instead."

No Bulk. They believe it despite all the lingering aspects of show business. Resentful as TV newsmen are of the very word "show," the smell of greasepaint still clings to their programs. Last week CBS announced that its newsmen would be making one-shot appearances on entertainment shows to publicize their election-night broadcasts. Thus Cronkite, among others, will soon make his debut on *I've Got a Secret* and *Captain Kangaroo*.

By now they will take it in stride. Television news knows its power. It has come a long way since the days when pencil journalists demonstrated their contempt for their upstart rival by carrying clackers to news events to foul up sound tapes and by unplugging the cables of the TV equipment.

The networks, Cronkite is happy to say, have shown considerable restraint and responsibility in not stooping to a tabloid treatment of the news, the crime and sex coverage that he is sure could quadruple their audience. They are moving, he believes, not in the direction of sensationalism but toward greater professionalism. The widespread use of communications satellites, he says, will cut down the high costs of landline charges; and with the savings, he hopes, the networks will build up their news-gathering services. Further miniaturization of equipment will make TV teams less obtrusive when they go out on a story. One man equipped with a pocket or lapel camera will be able to replace five. "He won't attract attention," says Cronkite. "He won't make news by just being there. A source will talk more easily when the lights and the big eye are not on him."

However much television news improves, though, Cronkite is convinced that it can never replace printed news. Though he feels that a half-hour news program is the equivalent of the front page of a very good newspaper, he realizes that all those other pages are still missing. "We do such a slick job," he says, "that we have deluded the public into thinking that they get all they need to know from us. And the people, if they are to exercise their franchise intelligently, need a flow of bulk information. We can't give it to them."

Chet Huntley and David Brinkley
"An Accident of Casting"
by William Whitworth

The accidental pairing of a westerner from Montana—Chet Huntley—with a North Carolinian—David Brinkley—led NBC to a phenomenal anchor team with as much popularity and staying power as Walter Cronkite. William Whitworth's 1968 profile is surely the longest and most comprehensive article published about Huntley and Brinkley.

Straining for words adequate to describe the stature of giants, the trade magazine *Editor & Publisher* once declared that Chet Huntley and David Brinkley were the biggest team in broadcasting history since Amos 'n' Andy. The comparison was more pertinent than Huntley and Brinkley would perhaps

When this article was published, William Whitworth was a staff writer for The New Yorker *magazine.*

care to concede. For they long ago ceased to be mere newsmen and became personalities, taking their place in American popular culture beside such immortal duos as Blanchard and Davis, Abbott and Costello, Roy Rogers and Trigger, and Fibber McGee and Molly. Their sheer famousness, impressive enough by show-business standards, is downright unreal by the standards of journalism, electronic or otherwise. According to surveys by Home Testing Institute/TvQ, Inc., Huntley and Brinkley are recognizable to more adult Americans than are such superstars as Cary Grant, James Stewart, the Beatles, and even John Wayne. If either of them ventures outdoors almost anywhere in North America, he is likely to be surrounded by fans, one of whom will quip "Good night, Chet," or "Good night, David" — lines that are always socko with the onlookers.

The stars are not gratified by this aspect of their celebrity, since it makes covering a story out in the field difficult for them. It was during the 1960 Democratic Presidential primary in West Virginia that Brinkley discovered his fame had begun to interfere with his work. Then he had to give up trying to cover Hubert Humphrey after it became apparent that West Virginians would rather meet a TV star than a Presidential candidate. Friends recall that Brinkley returned to Washington irritated, dejected, and a little embarrassed. Since then, he and Huntley have both sounded off periodically about the evils of show-business ballyhoo in journalism. If anyone mentions these outbursts to the first producer of "The Huntley-Brinkley Report," a cynic named Reuven Frank, who is now president of NBC News, Frank shrugs and says, "They take the money." Precisely how much they take is not ascertainable by an outsider, but the figure is handsome enough that when NBC executives discuss it they will give or take a hundred thousand dollars or so. An NBC vice-president who was asked recently about a newspaper report that Huntley and Brinkley were each paid four hundred thousand dollars a year stared thoughtfully into space and then replied, "Four? Oh, I don't know. It's probably more like three." Four or three, it must be a record for journalists, though it isn't exorbitant at all for the stars of a show whose gross annual income — around 29 million dollars — is said by some network people to be larger than that of any other NBC program except "Saturday Night at the Movies."

It is one thing to achieve success in television and another to maintain it. Huntley and Brinkley have maintained theirs as have no other television journalists and few other television performers of any sort. It seems strange to think so, but this year's college freshmen can only dimly remember a time when there wasn't a "Huntley-Brinkley Report" on the air. Now in their twelfth year together, Huntley and Brinkley have a survival record that puts them in a class with such stars as Ed Sullivan, James Arness, Johnny Carson, and Lassie. Huntley and Brinkley have done more than become rich and famous, however. In a period when television began to rival the newspapers as a news medium, they and the staff behind them were contributing to the development of the nightly television news program as a form. When Huntley and Brinkley became a team, in 1956, pioneers such as Fred Friendly and the late Edward R. Murrow, then both with CBS, had brought the television documentary to a high level of development, but the nightly television news program was still in its infancy. The show that Huntley and Brinkley replaced, for instance—the "Camel News Caravan," featuring John Cameron Swayze and his carnation—was little more than a newsreel. With innocent pride in scooping the movie theaters by a few days, the "Caravan" offered silent-film reports on beauty contests, horse races, and fashion shows, as well as the day's catastrophes and political headlines. "The Huntley-Brinkley Report" and its competitors at CBS, interacting with each other over the years, have evolved a nightly format that, for all its shortcomings, is much sounder journalistically and far more advanced technically. And Brinkley, meanwhile, has altered to a considerable extent the tone of American news broadcasting. Until he rose to stardom, the dominant style was a grave one, formed in the crisis years before and during the Second World War and best exemplified by Murrow's work. Brinkley brought to the industry an understated wit, an irreverence that seemed to be based on a coherent viewpoint rather than on a pose (such as the professional-brat stance now popular in print), and, perhaps most important, an ability to write a simple declarative English sentence. Today, intentionally or not, television announcers throughout the land imitate his delivery, and even Walter Cronkite, of CBS, has admitted that he avoids watching "The Huntley-Brinkley Report" for fear of slipping into unconscious mimicry of the Brinkley cadence.

The quality that is mentioned without fail when Huntley's friends try to describe him is niceness. A typical comment goes, "Chet is warm, he's friendly, he's unaffected, he's—well, he's just so damned *nice*." What these friends are talking about can be seen by anyone who spends even a short time around Huntley. He has a way of putting people at ease and making friends instantly. He is cheerful and gregarious, and he can take a joke at his own expense. He never seems to be merely polite but always to be genuinely interested in what other people have to say. After five minutes of his company, women decide that he is kind and reliable, and men want to put an arm over his shoulder and buy him a drink. The power of Huntley's niceness was demonstrated one evening last year at a party, when he was introduced to a man who had never before seen him in person but had conceived a terrible hatred of him. The man was a television announcer, and the party at which he met Huntley took place during the American Federation of Television and Radio Artists strike against the three television networks—a strike that Huntley failed to support, thus enraging many AFTRA members, and especially the announcer. When Huntley walked away after chatting with him for a few minutes, the announcer turned to the man next to him and said grudgingly, "Well, damn it, you're right. He really *is* a nice guy—the dirty son of a bitch."

On camera, Huntley is somber, distant, and, in Brinkley's words, "relentlessly serious." People who know him well say that his serious manner is no act, that he really worries about all the horrible news he has to spring on the American public night after night. Somehow, though, women viewers are able to see right past this almost chilly public image and detect Huntley's essential niceness. Many a man has had the experience of watching Huntley deliver a news item in his sternest manner and then hearing his wife or mother or grandmother say, with a smile, "That *sweet* Chet!" Women apparently receive

ABC journalist David Brinkley (photo courtesy Capital Cities/ABC, Inc).

a signal from the home screen that men don't, and quite a few of them are moved by it to write in and tell Chet what an absolute honey he is. Some of them write so often that Huntley's secretary can spot their work without reading it or even opening the envelopes, which she labels by author—"Inez," "Hazel," "Myra," or "Dorothy," to name a few of the regulars. "Hi, Sweetie," the breezy Myra began one of her notes not long ago. "I suppose I'll celebrate my 60th birthday before you seem able to shift into an easy chair, & give me a boost, & a rest & a little money, for breakage. I am not in too good a shape, for the long wear and tear of the last 9 yrs.... Honey—Remember—When I phone, set that Damn Date, so I can relax. I am worn out, with you going & me watching H-B (& now taped). Send $100 by wire, & I prefer the Pa RR station. I can get there, & feel better. The ride is pleasant, & I get upset on the bus.... We put up a pretty rose trellis yesterday. Fan shaped & the buds are just ready to burst, thorny as the dickens..."

A recent letter from Inez was filled with family and neighborhood news. "Don't be surprised if you hear of this house burning," Inez warned. "Kids have been lighting fires in the basement again. Mrs. Jackson will deny it—she pays no attention to it. Alene and Dale know it is true. They play with fire around outside too. It has been awfully dry (had a shower last evening). The kids stay up and play at night—unless Alene is here. Mrs. Jackson can't do anything with them—and they're getting past Alene. She took the kids to Jackson today. Alene was very drunk last nite—but got dinner. I expect to go to the dentist in the morning. At least one tooth will be pulled I'm sure.... Mrs. Jackson fussing about bills as usual—grocery bill $150 she said. These kids eat more than I do. Her Veteran check for them is still $100—33⅓ each. Her dependent children Social Security check for three is $62.50. Dale gives her $100.00. She gets about $62.00 or so for Social Security and a small R.R. pension check. I imagine $20.00 or so. Dale calls her moneybags. He thinks she gets plenty, handles it poorly...."

After "nice," the word that Huntley's friends apply to him most often is "naïve." This sounds like criticism at first, naïveté being one of the least desirable qualities in a journalist, but the friends don't mean it that way. They think of Huntley as authoritative in his work but fear that he is unduly tenderhearted and free of skepticism in his private life. "He's a terribly regular fellow," his wife says of him. "The word 'naïve' keeps coming to mind, though that's probably not really what I mean. He's very trusting. He assumes that people are honest, and if they disappoint him he's just overcome. With him, you're right until proved guilty." Irving Wall, a lawyer and close friend of Huntley's, once described him as "one of the most unsophisticated people I've ever known," but it was clear that this was simply part of Wall's affectionate notion of Huntley as "a log-cabinish man" of "plainsman strength." Another acquaintance of Huntley's said of him recently, "I don't know how to put my finger on it, but there is something naïve about Chet. He lets people take advantage of him. It's as though he never quite made the move from Los Angeles—or from his home town in Montana—to New York. He gets excited about things that other people are already tired of, and he has some odd opinions. Like, his idea of the greatest writer in the world is James Michener."

"I find Huntley extremely difficult to understand," Robert Northshield, the executive producer of "The Huntley-Brinkley Report," has said. "You know, a great part of the time he looks like a 12-year-old kid—kind of wide-eyed and sentimental, and trying to be tough. And other times he's a very worldly-wise fellow. He's extremely impulsive and gets carried away with his own expectations and hopes. You remember during the AFTRA strike he had this great idea to get out of AFTRA and form his own union, just for real news people. Well, I don't think anybody ever worked harder than he did on that. For a couple of days. And then I don't know what ever happened to it. For all I know, he worked very hard on it for a couple of months, but it kind of whimpered out and died."

When Brinkley was asked a few months ago what he thought of these evaluations of his partner, he said, "'Naïve' may not quite be the word. I think it's sort of cattle-country, farmerish, not lack of sophistication but just refusal to accept what passes for sophistication in this part of the country." Brinkley felt stubbornness to be a more important aspect of Huntley's personality than the alleged naïveté. "Huntley is given to taking positions that he believes in and that are perhaps unpopular, and refusing to budge, come hell or high water, and I kind of admire that," Brinkley said. "A terribly minor example of this is that he insists on pronouncing the capital of Hungary 'Buda-*pesht*.' This is correct in a sense, but actually not. The word has long since been Anglicized. As 'Rome' has. We don't call it 'Roma.' We don't call the capital of France 'Paree.' So 'Budapest' is a thoroughly accepted pronunciation, but Huntley refuses to say it! Just absolutely refuses! And everybody has said, 'Chet, now come on! It's "Budapest"!' And William R. McAndrew [the late president of NBC News] — I think McAndrew *ordered* him to say 'Budapest.' And he just refused!" The memory of this willfulness delighted Brinkley. He chuckled quietly, and his mouth twisted into the little smile that he can never suppress on camera when he does stories about Senator Everett Dirksen.

"What does Chet say when people argue with him about this?" Brinkley was asked.

"Well, I think what he says is that his way is correct and the hell with you," Brinkley said, a chuckle swelling into joyous laughter.

It's doubtful whether being thought of as a farmerish, unsophisticated, cattle-country man would leave any other resident of New York as equable as it leaves Huntley. He is a Westerner who is proud of it and who looks the part. Now 56 years old, he is still ruggedly handsome. He stands six feet two inches tall and weighs just under 200 pounds. His face is tanned and creased, like that of a man who is accustomed to being outdoors and squinting into the sun, as Huntley is. There is probably nothing else that interests him quite as much as farming — as a hobby, as a business, as a national political problem. His face brightens noticeably if the subject comes up in conversation. "To see growing things is probably the most satisfying piece of business in the world," Huntley has said. "It doesn't matter whether it's a rosebush or a purebred bull. It's so different from writing or broadcasting. A field of alfalfa is tangible." Huntley's work at NBC keeps him indoors and in the East much of the time, far from fields of alfalfa and other tangibles, but he does what he can to compensate. His office — a little one on the fifth floor of the RCA Building, in Rockefeller Center — is decorated in the least Eastern fashion possible, with such rustic touches as an old rolltop desk, an 1870-model Winchester, and a brass spittoon. For six years, he owned a 300-acre cattle ranch at Stockton, New Jersey, to which he could retreat each weekend, but he sold the place last August after suffering a $90,000 loss on its operation. He had a sizeable interest in a cattle-feeding lot in Iowa and in a cattle ranch in Montana until recently. These gave him more financial than spiritual pleasure, however, since he seldom saw them, and not long ago he sold his interest in the ranch and most of his interest in the lot.

Huntley was born in Cardwell, Montana. He spent the first 13 years of his life on a 960-acre cattle and sheep ranch at Saco, Montana, that was operated, with little success, by his grandfather, his great-uncle, and his father, Percy Huntley, who was a railroad telegrapher as well as a rancher. Huntley attended Montana State College in Bozeman; the Cornish School of Arts, in Seattle; and then the University of Washington, in Seattle, from which he graduated in 1934. His first goal was a medical career of some sort, but the family's financial troubles during those Depression years made the required schooling impossible. The idea of doing something in radio suggested itself when he discovered, as a college orator, the intense pleasure of speaking in public while others listen with approval. He got hooked for good on communicating during his last year of college, when he worked at a little 100-watt radio station in Seattle—KPCB (now the 50,000-watt KIRO). "I did everything from sweeping out the joint to spinning records, writing advertising copy, dreaming up new programs, and running the transmitter when the engineer was out for coffee," Huntley recalled recently. He gave up record-spinning long ago, but he has been in radio and television ever since the first job, and this early start makes him one of the senior men among the big network names in broadcast journalism today. He is also one of the very few men of any seniority in the business who have no newspaper experience to speak of. From KPCB, Huntley went on to radio stations in Spokane and Portland, and then, in 1937, to the NBC affiliate in Los Angeles. There, to supplement his salary, which was fairly tiny, he took a second job, at $15 a week, as announcer for the nightly dance-band broadcasts from Earl Carroll's restaurant. Huntley wasn't proud of having to moonlight, but he liked music and he enjoyed listening to the grandiose schemes of the band's young piano player, Stan Kenton. Huntley joined the CBS affiliate in Los Angeles in 1939, at a time when Murrow was building the European reporting staff that was to help make CBS preeminent in news until well into the fifties. During the forties, Huntley got into the Pacific Theatre on two or three brief assignments, and he went to Europe in 1949 for several weeks, but he spent most of his time in Los Angeles, where he covered such continuing stories as the industrial development of California and the relocation of Japanese Americans. At CBS in the late forties, and at the ABC Los Angeles affiliate from 1951 to 1955, Huntley made a name for himself as a commentator on the news as well as a broadcaster of it, and as a liberal. The late forties and early fifties, of course, were bad times for liberals in radio and television; anti-Communist vigilante groups became powerful in the broadcasting industry on both coasts even before the rise of Senator Joseph R. McCarthy. Huntley, who said nice things about the United Nations and criticized McCarthy, did not escape the notice of the vigilantes. But he survived, and in 1954 he had the satisfaction of winning a slander suit against a woman vigilante who had harassed him. Unlike such radio commentators as Raymond Gram Swing, whose career was badly damaged, Huntley came out of that era in good shape professionally. When NBC hired him in 1955 and brought him East, he was known to be described by some people as NBC's answer to Murrow.

In the years since then, Huntley apparently has been both more and less than the answer to Murrow. He has been a bigger success commercially than he or NBC could have dreamed in 1955, but although he is held in great esteem throughout the industry and has won every available award for television commentators, his peers do not seem ready to rank him with Murrow or with other past greats, such as Elmer Davis. There is a wide range of opinion about his journalistic abilities. At one extreme, there is the unidentified NBC employee who was quoted in the *World Journal Tribune,* during the AFTRA strike, as saying, "Many of the guys think Huntley's position is ridiculous. He talks about newsmen. He's not a newsman. He's a reader. I've never seen him on the street." This view is unfair. While it is true that the mechanics of the nightly television show are such that Huntley does not write all or even most of what he says on the air, he can point to a number of television specials for which he has done most of the reporting and writing, and to his radio commentaries, all of which he writes. At the other extreme are the people in the business who say that the issue, as it was stated in the *World Journal Tribune,* is irrelevant. "Huntley is in television, not the newspaper business," one of these people has said. "He is simply a competent journalist. He doesn't pretend to be a pundit or an investigative reporter. He's intelligent, he does his homework, he has a magnificent voice, he can communicate in the medium as few others can — he's totally professional." Somewhere between these extremes, there is the opinion of Sam Zelman, a CBS News executive producer who has known Huntley since his days at CBS and ABC in Los Angeles. "Chet lifted himself by his bootstraps," Zelman said several months ago. "He was a country boy, utterly without sophistication, when he came to Los Angeles. He read the *New York Times,* the Manchester *Guardian,* and the *Economist,* and he sort of rewrote them. It's less than fair to say he rewrote them, but basically that was it. He did a synopsis of what he had read. This sounds like a put-down in one way, but it's also another way of saying he was more conscientious — more serious — than most of the others in the business then. Most guys were just tearing wire copy. Chet was studious. Still, I wouldn't say he has a news background. He's covered things, but the discipline is different on a newspaper. You don't even have to be able to spell on radio and television. I guess you *can* get a news background in broadcast journalism, but, believe me, that's the hard way."

Huntley has made quite a bit of money at NBC, and he is thought to have held on to a large part of it. He is not known as a big spender. He still has about $15,000 invested in the Iowa cattle-feeding lot. He also has an interest in three radio stations on Long Island — WRIV, in Riverhead, and WALK and WALK-FM, in Patchogue — which he estimates is worth a quarter of a million dollars. At one time, he had almost half a million in his unsuccessful ranching venture in New Jersey. One of his most valuable investments is the three-story house he owns, in Manhattan, on Sixty-ninth Street between First and Second avenues. The house is occupied only by Huntley and his wife, Tippy. (Huntley and his first wife, Ingrid Rolin, were divorced in 1959. They had two daughters — Sharon, 27, now Mrs. Dan Arensmeier, who lives in Rochester, New York, and Leanne, 24, now Mrs. Eskandar Khajavi, who lives in San Francisco. In 1959, Huntley married Tipton Stringer, who was then the weather girl at WRC-TV, the NBC station in Washington, D.C.) Now that Huntley has given up his New Jersey ranch, he spends a good deal of time in his house, cooking, reading, sorting out his thoughts about the state of the world, and dodging phone calls. "At home, Chet will not dial the phone, and if it rings he won't answer it," his wife says. "He's learned to hate it. Interruptions drive him crazy." This is not to say that Huntley is antisocial. He doesn't frequent night clubs and restaurants, but he enjoys an evening of conversation or bridge with such friends as Irving Wall, his lawyer; S. Hazard Gillespie, another lawyer; and Dr. Kenneth Riland, Governor Rockefeller's physician. These friends report that Huntley is a delightful host, that he prepares a terrific bowl of chili, and that his supply of niceness is inexhaustible. "He can sit through an evening of perfectly miserable cards and be as cheerful as can be," Gillespie says.

Except on special assignments, such as national political conventions, during which they share equally in the reporting and ad-libbing, Huntley and Brinkley have very dissimilar jobs. Brinkley's gives him a chance to write and report, but Huntley's seldom does, for a number of reasons. Huntley's beat, in a sense, is the whole world minus Washington. The best stories on his portion of the program tend to be photographable—wars, natural disasters, riots, and the like—and so are covered by camera crews and correspondents, whose reports need little from Huntley beyond a few words of introduction. As for the non-visual stories—the ones that Huntley simply reads on the air, with perhaps a map or a drawing in the background—these are based, for the most part, on wire-service reports, which must be verified, condensed, and rewritten to meet the program's style and time requirements. The contribution that Huntley can make here is also limited, because the stories are so diverse in subject matter and origin that he—or anyone else not at the scene of the event—is unlikely to know much more about them than what appears on the wires; besides, there are too many of them each day for one man to handle. Occasionally, there will be an item of particular interest to Huntley, perhaps concerning foreign affairs or race relations, and then he can express himself by writing what amounts to a little editorial. Once in a while, he will take a few days off to go out and cover something.

In Washington and the federal government, Brinkley has a beat that, though it is complex, is certainly tidier than Huntley's, since it is not scattered all over the world. The most important stories in Washington are likely to be abstract rather than photographable, and therefore to lend themselves to treatment by Brinkley instead of by a camera crew. Brinkley doesn't get out of the office to cover stories much more often than Huntley does, but, unlike Huntley, he is in a position to know or find out more about a story than what appears in the wire reports. Since he has close friends at all levels of government, from the Cabinet down, it is not unusual for him to find himself writing about someone he has dined with or played poker with the previous evening. And whether or not he is well acquainted with the principals in a story, he can call them or visit them. Consequently, Brinkley is able to put his stamp on most of the material he handles, and to write every word he says on the air.

"An Accident of Casting"   45

There are people in the business — mostly at NBC, of course — who say that Brinkley's writing is the best ever done in television journalism. This isn't a wild claim, considering the quality of much of the competition. "The most elusive thing in our medium," Huntley's friend Zelman has said, "is the simple declarative sentence." Brinkley can write such a sentence. William Monroe, director of news for NBC's Washington bureau, says of Brinkley's work, "He writes prose of tremendous clarity, prose that is meant for the ear. There is no parallel to him as a writer in this medium." Another Brinkley admirer is Robert Doyle, who was formerly an NBC producer and director and is now chief of the television division of the National Geographic Society. "David has done a lot to change television coverage, with his ability to give the facts of a story so simply and coherently," Doyle says. "He can convert a mass of information into a simple account without talking down. He and television are perfectly matched." Brinkley achieves this simplicity and economy by using plain, almost homely English instead of the bureaucratic prose that reporters sometimes slip into in Washington, and by maintaining an extreme skepticism about the importance of each story he deals with. After covering Washington for 25 years, he seems convinced that there hasn't been a really new idea in town since the thirties. "David has a kind of ruthless attitude toward what is news and what is not," says John Chancellor, a contributing editor on the Huntley-Brinkley show. "I think we've been refreshingly free of a lot of Washington-insider stuff as a result. Boy, I come in here in the afternoon saying, 'This is absolutely the most important thing in the world,' and it's not, of course, and the next day you know it. But David isn't excitable like that." Much of the daily flow of news leaves Brinkley not only unexcited but bored. "I think the press — meaning all of us — devotes too much time and space to so-called official news," Brinkley said recently. "I'm not trying to pass myself off as any kind of example to be followed, but I hear a lot of younger guys, on radio and television, reporting on some bill in Congress because it moved from a subcommittee to a committee. Well, a bill in Congress, before it gets through — Let's see, there's introduction, subcommittee hearing, committee vote, vote on the floor. That makes six steps in the House and six in the Senate, plus signature — 13 steps, each of which can be a piece of news, if you want. But you see it in the papers every day, you hear it on the air a lot, because it's easy to get. It's police-court, blotter-type news, about which nobody really cares."

The public knows Brinkley best not for his stern news judgment or his ability to write simple declarative sentences but for his wryness. Even people who can't remember whether his name is Huntley or Brinkley know when they see him on the screen that he's the funny one down in Washington. One form in which this wryness appears is the one-line gag. To take a famous instance, during the argument over whether or not the name of Boulder Dam should be changed to Hoover Dam, Brinkley suggested on the air that it would simplify everything if Hoover would change *his* name to Herbert Boulder. The real substance of Brinkley's wit, however, lies not in memorable gag lines but in his delivery and in the cumulative effect of a steady, daily stream of dry remarks. The laughs sometimes come at unlikely moments, as one did in a story that Brinkley wrote and delivered last August: "the most unseemly burlesque of a funeral anyone ever saw occurred today in Culpeper, Virginia, about 70 miles from Washington. The Army gave permission for George Lincoln Rockwell, the murdered Nazi, to be buried in a national cemetery in Culpeper, Virginia, about 70 miles from Washington. The Army gave permission for George Lincoln Rockwell, the murdered Nazi, to be buried in a national cemetery in Culpeper, because under the law he was entitled to it. But the Army said no Nazi emblems, swastikas, or ceremonies would be allowed inside the cemetery, and that the funeral must be conducted with reasonable dignity. At the appointed hour — 11 A.M. — a hearse arrived with Rockwell's body, and along with it a band of followers wearing Nazi-type uniforms and swastikas. They were told unless they took off the swastikas they couldn't come in. They refused. Then, here's how it went. [The film rolled, showing Rockwell's followers scuffling with the soldiers.] Four hours later, the Army refused to give in ... the Army cancelled their permission to bury Rockwell ... the cemetery closed for the day ... the crowd was dispersed ... and the Army left a guard on the cemetery to keep them from trying to sneak the body in at night. [The film showed a hearse pulling away, with the defiant Nazis.] The hearse left, and the Nazis with it. So, tonight, as they say, the funeral arrangements are not yet complete." The last line — one frequently used in routine newspaper obituaries — combined elements of surprise, apt quotation, and ironic understatement, and conveyed Brinkley's distaste for Rockwell, for Nazis, and for the stir at the cemetery. And, in an almost horrible way, it was extremely funny on the air.

Some of Brinkley's most spirited writing is never seen or heard by most of the public, since it goes into his answers to letters from disgruntled viewers. Brinkley tries not to fret over the mail, in order to conserve his time, but occasionally an especially critical letter will irritate him beyond silent endurance. When that happens, the author receives a harsh rebuke. "In response to your note, no, I was not much interested in the piece you wrote in the UAW paper," one such reply said, "I found it thin, shallow, and in general too sophomoric to be taken seriously...." Another began, "My advice to you is to calm down. And if you wish to offer lectures to those reporting the news, you ought to listen more carefully to what they say.... Nowhere did I say or suggest this included all members of the Senate, Republican or otherwise, and therefore your various excited accusations are based on false premises and so are false themselves." A man in the District of Columbia who informed Brinkley that he had "forfeited" his credentials as a newsman by editorializing on the air received this reply, which sums up so much of what Brinkley feels about viewers' criticisms:

> Dear Dr. P_____:
> Thank you for your note. But I believe you have let your emotions run out of control. I caution you against this unwise and possibly dangerous surrender and urge on you the virtues of cool and dispassionate analysis.
> You say you heard "editorialization and speculation." Had the statements you heard been oriented toward your own personal point of view, I daresay you would not have found them to be editorial or speculative at all, but rather would have found them to be fair and responsible renderings of the facts. In about thirty years of reading mail from

readers and listeners, I have learned that a "biased opinion" simply is anything the writer does not like to hear.

The truth is that there were no opinions expressed at all, biased or otherwise. We merely tried to assess, without any value judgments by us, the political aspects of the war and the race problem in this country. I think you will agree this is a fair subject for analysis at this time.

It is understandable that you might have found some of what we said not to your liking, but I must say I was distressed to find that toward the bottom of the page, warmed by your anger, you have lapsed into arrant academic snobbery, inquiring into my credentials to perform as a "pundit," and saying if you want opinions you will seek them from an "expert." Just what discipline produces expertise in President Johnson's current political troubles? To suggest, as you do, that only political scientists are qualified to discuss this is merely silly. But if you really care, I will try to have a transcript of my academic credentials forwarded to you for your private and unhurried perusal. I believe you will find them impressive and perhaps reassuring.

Thank you again for your note, and my best wishes to you.
Sincerely,
David Brinkley

When Senator Dirksen suggested not long ago that the marigold be selected as the national flower, Brinkley objected on the grounds that the marigold wasn't pretty and that it smelled bad. A man named Gaston Ley, of Carmel, California, wrote in to say that, the way things were going these days, the marigold's characteristics made a good choice. Ley also noted that someone on the program had reported that a man in California had been executed "for the first time in four years." "It would have been interesting," Ley wrote, "to know how far back this man's previous execution (or executions) had taken place, and, maybe, when a subsequent execution was likely to occur." Brinkley replied:

There is something in what you say, but I still don't like the marigold. A flower ought to be a relief from ugliness and sordidness, not a confirmation of it.

As for California executing a man for the first time in four years, I daresay if that ever does happen, it will happen in California. You are all far ahead of the rest of us in the unreal, the unbelievable and the unacceptable. I think — or fear — that California (not Carmel) is what all of the U.S. will be in time, and some time thereafter, all the world.

Then, and only then, should we adopt the marigold.

Naturally, not everyone at the other networks is ready to declare Brinkley the best writer in the business, or is enthusiastic about the kind of job he does in Washington. When Sig Mickelson was president of CBS News, he criticized Brinkley for "disc-jockey journalism," and Richard Salant, Mickelson's successor, once asked in a speech, "Are we satisfied when the viewer turns off the program at its end only with a recollection of some quip of the news broadcaster?" In fairness both to Brinkley and to the CBS executives, it should be noted that these criticisms were made in the early days of the Huntley-Brinkley success, when the CBS News staff apparently was in a state of perpetual pique over its loss of prestige and the humiliations it was suffering in the ratings war. A more recent criticism of Brinkley came from a respected and knowledgeable man at CBS News who said, "I feel that by injecting so much style over there they very frequently don't tell the story. I think David undoubtedly writes well, and perhaps best of anybody in the business. But I really feel that the news is fairly well distorted many times by David's taking a single angle and getting his little twist on it. I don't think that's good reporting." When a complaint is made about Brinkley in Washington, it is usually that he doesn't work hard enough — by attending press conferences and government briefings, for instance. Brinkley's answer is that he works extremely hard, from ten in the morning, when he may be calling on a senator or an Administration official, until late at night, when he often is attending a party and, in his opinion, working more than he is partying. He thinks that there is more information to be had from his social and professional contacts than at press conferences, which government officials are likely to use as a forum rather than as an occasion for submitting to hard questioning. And, though government officials are amazingly accessible to reporters, Brinkley's contacts must be considered exceptionally good. In recent years, his social circle has included people as diverse as Jack Valenti, Robert Kennedy, Edward Kennedy, John W. Gardner, Robert McNamara, and Eugene McCarthy.

In general, Brinkley's standing in Washington is high. Howard K. Smith, the ABC commentator, has praised his writing, and Roger Mudd, a CBS Washington correspondent, has said, "Brinkley, of all the TV guys here, probably has the best sense of the city — best understands its moods and mentality. He knows Washington and he knows the people." Until James Reston, now executive editor of the *Times,* moved to New York recently, he and Brinkley were considered the top men in the city's press corps as party catches or as celebrities. "If the Prime Minister of Britain came to town and the British Ambassador wanted to pick a dozen people for him to level with, Brinkley and Reston very likely would be included in the group," a White House aide said not long ago. While both men are influential men, Brinkley's influence is of a different sort from Reston's, because of the differences between their media. Politicians apparently regard newspaper columnists as purveyors of ideas, who have considerable influence in Washington itself, and television commentators as editors and packagers, who have great national impact because of their ability to convey a mood to the general public. "People in the government would clear almost anyone off their schedule for Brinkley," Russell Baker, the *Times* columnist, remarked recently, "yet they aren't as interested in what Brinkley says as they are in what Lippmann says, for instance." And a Presidential assistant observed several months ago, "A story on television doesn't create the flap in the government that a story in print does. Politicians pay more attention to it when it's in black and white. But I think the nightly news shows may set the tone of the news more than the papers do. The treatment of news on television probably determines whether most people end up the day thinking that everything is all right or thinking that the nation is going to hell."

In Washington, Brinkley and other television commentators are at a competitive disadvantage with newspapers, because they go on the air in the early evening, when many government officials are still in their offices. These people will say that they have the highest regard for Brinkley but that they just can't get home in time to see the show. No such alibi is offered by President Johnson, who has nine television sets in the White House and is said to watch all three network news programs frequently, despite the fact that the Cronkite show and the Huntley-Brinkley show go on the air in Washington at the same hour. Some people feel, in fact, that "watch" is too weak a verb to describe the President's fierce scrutiny of television news coverage, especially of an event such as a Presidential address. Almost before his own image has faded from the screen on these occasions, it is said, the President has dashed into his office, seized his little electronic control box, pressed a button that causes sliding doors to part and reveal three of his television sets, and tuned in all three networks. There he remains, alert for instant replays or for comments on his performance, until the correspondents sign off. Correspondents who have dared to make such comments say that the next day, or as soon as he can get his hands on them, the President gives them critiques of their work that are startling in their frankness. At NBC and around the White House, it's thought that Brinkley has been a little out of favor with the President in recent months, possibly because of Brinkley's doubts about the war in Vietnam and some pointed remarks he has made about the influence of the military establishment in American life. He is no longer invited, as he once was, to see the President at Camp David on a weekend or at small, informal gatherings at the White House.

While Brinkley's political views may occasionally be unwelcome at the White House, they are frequently misunderstood elsewhere. In the South and the Midwest, judging from his mail, viewers often take him for what he has called "a bloody-shirt Northern Liberal Radical." Among his friends in Washington, where many people are accustomed to neat categories and accept the present-day definitions of "liberal" and "conservative," he is thought to be unclassifiable and unpredictable. In the pages of *TV Guide,* he has been described as slightly right of center. All three estimates are wrong. Brinkley is an old-fashioned, lower-case liberal, skeptical of doctrinaire programs and distrustful of concentrations of power, whether on the right or on the left. His scorn has fallen with equal force on the radical right, the radical left, conservatives, liberals, Democrats, Republicans, big business, big labor, the government, and the military. "I would call myself liberal but not very," he says. "That sounds like an evasion, but I don't like categories. I don't like, for example, the A.D.A. doctrinaire view of everything that comes along. They look at a problem, decide what the liberal position is, seize it, and then relentlessly defend it. I think that's utterly God-damned nonsense. I'm much more pragmatic than that. I have some views that liberals would find distasteful. It isn't that I'm scared or shy to be this or that, but before I would offer any answer on any political problem, I'd want to know what the question was." John Chancellor says that Brinkley is angered by anything he considers unjust, and that he cannot abide fools. Rogues are apparently another matter. On the air, for instance, Brinkley can seldom hide his pleasure in presenting items about Adam

Clayton Powell. "I just find people like that amusing," Brinkley explained recently. "There is so much hypocrisy and phony piety in Washington that it is refreshing to find an Adam Clayton Powell, who lives the way he wants to and makes no pretense about it. I love the story about the congressman who visited Powell in his House office and was offered his choice of Scotch, bourbon, or champagne on ice. When his colleague commented on such opulence, Powell told him, 'This is what comes of serving Jesus.'" Huntley perhaps finds less amusement in the news, but his political reactions to it coincide pretty closely with Brinkley's. "I like to think I'm what you would call a classic liberal," Huntley has said. "By liberalism, I mean an open-mindedness, a feeling that ideas are not dangerous and let's consider them all. As for the A.D.A. kind of liberalism, I've always thought the A.D.A. was founded on a false premise—that Roosevelt's New Deal ought to be continued. Two or three years before the A.D.A.'s founding, Roosevelt himself said the New Deal had ended. That period is gone, and we're into something new. So I think the A.D.A. is much too orthodox today. You can anticipate what its policy is going to be on almost any issue."

When Brinkley's fans see him in person for the first time, they often are surprised by his size. Like Huntley, he is well over six feet tall. Next, they are likely to be struck by the fact that the famous Brinkley cadence is not just a professional, on-the-air manner; he really talks that way all the time. Then there is a disappointment: after years of saying funny things on television, Brinkley turns out not to be a comic or the life of the party. People who make this discovery often go away saying that Brinkley is "withdrawn" or is a "strange man," as though he were a hermit or a mystic. He has been described in print so many times as a "loner" that even a few of his friends now offer this designation to strangers as a psychological insight. However, Brinkley appears to be simply a quiet, reserved, introspective man who is not fond of small talk but is sociable enough. If he is sometimes aloof in public, it is perhaps because being treated as a celebrity makes him uncomfortable.

In any case, Brinkley probably is much less of a loner now than he was during his childhood, in Wilmington, North Carolina, where he was born in 1920. He remembers himself as a lonely boy. His father—like Huntley's, a railroad man—died when Brinkley was eight years old. He had two brothers and two sisters, but they were all grown and at work while he was still in elementary school, so they afforded him slight companionship. In his solitude, Brinkley acquired what he now calls a "sort of disease"—the book-reading habit. By the time he was ten, habit had become addiction, and he was visiting the public library six or seven times a week. In high school, Brinkley excelled at English, took E. B. White as his literary hero, and began to think of himself vaguely as a writer. That notion led him to take a part-time job at the Wilmington *Star-News,* where he quickly established himself as a reporter and as a composer of simple declarative sentences. Brinkley stayed on at the paper after graduation from high school, in 1938, since the family couldn't afford to send him to college. In 1940, for reasons that he can't remember, he signed up for a year in the Army, and served it as a supply sergeant in the infantry rifle company at Fort Jackson, South Carolina. Brinkley spent the next two and a half years with United Press (now United Press International) in Atlanta, Montgomery, Nashville, and Charlotte. He attended college classes in his spare time during this period at the University of North Carolina and at Vanderbilt, but he never received a degree. It was while he was with U.P. that Brinkley found his real vocation. One of his assignments in the Atlanta bureau was writing for the radio wire—taking stories from the regular newspaper wire and rewriting them in what U.P. imagined was a suitable style for radio (the more clichés the better, he was advised). After he had done that for several months, Brinkley decided he had a special talent for writing for the ear, as opposed to writing for the eye. Still, he had no particular desire to work exclusively in radio and none at all to be *on* radio. He did want more money, however, and so, late in 1943, he went to Washington and applied for a job at CBS. CBS turned him down, but NBC hired him. For the next several years, Brinkley wrote news scripts for announcers to read on the air, covered Washington as a reporter, and appeared on television, which was then still a gadget. He rose steadily in the bureau, and by 1950 he was doing regular Washington spots on the "Camel News Caravan." Though he was winning admirers among his colleagues and among the younger producers, Brinkley remained relatively obscure right up to the time he was teamed with Huntley for NBC's television coverage of the 1956 political conventions. "Brinkley was a nobody then," Reuven Frank recalled recently. "He had a better assignment than some, in that he was doing the inserts on the Swayze program, but other than that, he was no different from a dozen other guys working out of the Washington office. And he could hardly get on radio. Television was not quite established then. The big show was the radio show—Morgan Beatty's. And they didn't like Brinkley much—he was a smart-aleck."

Brinkley seems almost embarrassed by the amount of money he has made since those days. He says that he is overpaid, but he consoles himself with the thought that he and Huntley don't earn as much as they would if they were a pair of TV cowboys instead of a pair of newscasters. Brinkley is not the capitalist that Huntley is. He has no investments and he owns nothing, he says, except 60 acres of land in the mountains of Virginia and a two-story Georgian home in Chevy Chase. Brinkley lives modestly, by show-business standards, and his home is relatively quiet, even though it involves a wife, three sons, a swimming pool, a big, noisy collie, and a considerable amount of mandatory party-giving. Brinkley's wife is the former Ann Fischer, a pretty, petite brunette who once was a U.P. reporter, and his sons are Alan, 19, a student at Princeton; Joel, 16; and John, 13. Brinkley doesn't care much for such convivial suburban diversions as drinking, swimming, and tennis; he prefers the solitary pleasures of carpentry, at which he is expert, and reading. His favorite pastime, though, may well be his work. "That's the one thing in the world he's really comfortable with," says Mrs. Brinkley.

To anyone accustomed to the poverty-stricken atmosphere of a newspaper office, there is something dazzling about the financial side of a network-television news operation. A TV news producer dispatches platoons of men and charters planes more casually than a city editor approves an expense account for a $1.98 lunch and a cab ride. "One thing about the networks is that they've really got the dough," says Douglas Kiker, a contributing editor on the Huntley-Brinkley show. "There's none of this penny-ante stuff. They base their decisions about what to cover on news values." Kiker is acutely aware of such matters, having served as White House correspondent for the New York *Herald Tribune* during that paper's threadbare dying days. Only ten years ago, NBC's annual news budget was ten million dollars. Last year, it was about 52 million, excluding sports coverage, and the CBS budget was no doubt similar. The annual budget for "The Huntley-Brinkley Report" alone is more than six million dollars. It may be unfair to compare network news expenditures with those of the newspapers and wire services, since the operations of the three are so different, but, just for the record, here are the approximate annual editorial budgets for three of the nation's most important papers: the Los Angeles *Times,* eight and a half million dollars; the New York *Daily News,* ten and three-quarters million; and the New York *Times,* $20 million. (The *Herald Trib*'s was running to almost six million at the paper's death.) The Associated Press budget is $56 million, and the budget of United Press International is close to $49 million. While the networks' news expenditures have increased greatly, so have their news revenues. In 1962, when "The Huntley-Brinkley Report" was still a 15-minute show, there were two and a half commercial minutes available per broadcast, at an average price of $18,000 a minute. Today, on the 30-minute show, there are five commercial minutes available per broadcast, at an average price of $29 million — it is now said to be the second-largest among all NBC programs. (The first-place show, "Saturday Night at the Movies," has rates ranging from 45,000 to 57,000 per commercial minute, and its annual gross is 36 million.) What the Huntley-Brinkley show's annual *net* income may be, the outsider can only guess. NBC executives will not discuss the profits of individual shows, on the reasonable theory that loose talk might encourage sponsors to think they're overcharged and stars to think they're underpaid. But an NBC man who is in a position to know says the rule of thumb in estimating net income is that the net equals the gross minus 50 percent (15 percent for ad-agency commissions and 35 percent for compensation to local stations for carrying the network show) and minus production costs. If this formula is correct, it would indicate an annual profit of about eight million dollars for "The Huntley-Brinkley Report." NBC executives, however, regard such calculations as academic, because, they say, the network news operation as a whole does not break even.

Profit or not, a network news show is a big undertaking financially. It is also a big one, physically, involving more personnel and equipment than the viewer might guess from what he sees on the screen. In fact, most of the people involved in such shows, including the principals, have no clear idea how much manpower it takes to get the news on the air each night, and some of them would apparently rather not think about it. Several months ago, while reminiscing about the good old radio days, Huntley said, "Back then, you wrote it, you edited it, and you went down in front of the microphone and put it on the air. There was no pre-recording. And maybe, if you were fortunate, a couple of times a month you could have the experience of walking away from it saying, 'Well, that was about as close to a good job as I possibly shall ever come.' That doesn't happen often in television, because there are too many things that can go wrong, and they usually do. For one thing, there are too many people involved. I don't know exactly how many, but it's real group journalism, and sometimes you feel that your contribution to the total was minute. And there are some nights you *hope* it was." Roger Mudd expressed the same thought recently when he said, "Man, the machinery is really there—it's like the French civil service."

A breakdown of that machinery, including everyone from writers to motorcycle couriers, was made for one Huntley-Brinkley broadcast last fall by Walter Kravetz, an NBC News associate producer and director. His estimate was as follows:

Basic New York and Washington staff (Producers, directors, news editors, writers, production assistants, secretaries)	35
Basic engineering crew in New York (Live studio, film studio, tape room, stagehands, electricians, makeup artist, stage manager)	29
Basic engineering crew in Washington (Same as above)	17
News-film department (Camera crews, film editors, lab crew, messengers)	47
Graphic artists and visual personnel	16
Master-control-network engineers, New York, Chicago, Los Angeles	18
Staff in Los Angeles, for live switch to Los Angeles (Talent, producers, directors, film crews, engineers)	21
American Telephone & Telegraph people used to route show on network	130
Live talent (Huntley, Brinkley, Chancellor, etc.)	7
Total	320

The total could easily have been higher. If there had been a three- or four-minute report by satellite from, say, Tokyo via Lani Bird II, it would have meant the involvement of a hundred more men or so: employees of AT&T or one of the other carriers (IT&T or RCA), in New York; of the Communications Satellite Corporation, at the satellite ground station in Brewster Flat, Washington; of the Kokusai Denshin Denwa Company, Ltd., which handles Japan's overseas communications, at the ground station in Ibaraki, Japan; and of Nippon Hoso Kyokai, a Japanese television network, in Tokyo.

This is not to say that the Huntley-Brinkley staff consists of three or four hundred people. The correspondents in the film, the film crews, and many of the technicians and engineers are not on the Huntley-Brinkley staff proper but work for NBC News or for the network, and make contributions to the nightly broadcast only when they are called upon. The day-to-day work of the show— the writing, the copy editing, the film editing, and much of the reporting—is done by 50 or 60 people in New York and Washington. Among the members of this basic staff are, in New York, Huntley, the executive producer, the producer, three news editors, three writers, a field producer, two directors, a supervising film editor, 12 film editors, and a production assistant; and, in Washington, Brinkley, an associate producer, three writers, a director, four film editors, and a production assistant. Robert Northshield, the executive producer, believes in overlap and flexibility—in the words of one of his employees—so it is sometimes difficult to define the duties that go with a particular job on the Huntley-Brinkley staff. In general, producers and news editors make editorial decisions, writers write, film editors edit film, directors run the control room, and field producers go out into the field to scout potential stories and to help camera crews and correspondents put their reports together. But in New York a producer or a news editor sometimes writes, and a writer may find himself serving as a correspondent or a field producer. And in Washington the writers are really field producers and reporters instead of writers, because Brinkley likes to do all the writing.

Whatever his job, almost everyone connected with the program must be concerned at times with film—shooting it, processing it, editing it, watching it and evaluating it, or writing copy to complement it. The members of the Huntley-Brinkley staff regard tasks of this sort as both a pleasure and a headache. "If God had wanted to create the most awkward possible way of covering news," says William Hill, an NBC producer, "he would immediately have chosen film." The awkwardness seems to be experienced most keenly by the writers and the correspondents, nearly all of whom are former newspaper reporters. In covering a story, the newspaper reporter needs no physical equipment except a pencil and a notebook; he can travel fast and light. The television correspondent must travel with—at the very least—a cameraman, a sound man, an electrician, and more than 60 pounds of equipment, including cameras, recorders, high-intensity lights, microphones, exposure meters, and cables. He has to worry not only about the substance of a story but also about the logistics of getting it: How can they get from here to there? Can they rent cars, or should they charter a plane? Where will they sleep? More important, he must greatly alter the reporting methods that he learned in the newspaper business. The newspaper reporter's basic technique is the interview—asking people for information and opinions. The television correspondent has to gather the same facts in the same way, but he can't stop when he feels that he understands the story. He must then produce a little movie about it, and his bosses usually prefer a movie that consists of something more than interviews. In 1963, Reuven Frank, in a memo that was first known around NBC as "The Koran" and is now called simply "The Memo," set down his ideas about how to cover news on television. "The Memo" had this to say about interviews:

> An interview can too often be a crutch. Getting a picture of an event as it happens takes effort and luck, sometimes a lot of both. Neither is needed to back some hapless eyewitness, or even participant, against a wall and let him tell what happened. It is too easy to consider this an adequate substitute.

"An Accident of Casting"

Most people are dull. That is, they communicate ineptly. If they are dull, their description of interesting events will be dull. Sometimes they are interesting, but for the wrong reasons. They suffer from speech defects, tic, or strabismus, and what may make them interesting is precisely what interferes with their contribution to information. Those who communicate eptly—politicians, actors, and the like—tend to be self-serving....

Some interviews are devices for putting a reporter's notes on the air. This is hardly fair to a sponsor paying $2,000 a minute [prices have gone up], even if it does not all go to the reporter. Every beginning journalist is trained to talk to as many people as he can at the scene of a fire or a murder and note what they say—usually in thick copy pencil on newsprint cut into copy paper or on the backs of envelopes. He would have been bemused if when he returned to the city room instead of having him write his story—from his notes—his city editor would have sent his smudged copy paper or envelope to photo-engraving. Most spot interviews of eyewitnesses are in this category....

It takes a professional journalist to know what sentence in a speech or in his own interview should be pulled to the top, set in large type, quoted in the headline and the bannerline. In our business, we cannot pull that sentence out and up. The audience must pick its own sentences and set its own front page around it and do it before we have passed that story and gone on to the next. Television interviews have value, but it is not the same value printed interviews have.

The best illustration I can think of is this: we have evolved so far in television that the Sunday afternoon interviews of the famous and frightening are much more useful to the Washington bureaus of the wire services and the *New York Times* than they are to the television audience. They still make news, if what appears on the front pages is the criterion for news. But unless he is waiting for a lead sentence to be spoken, even a professional is likely as he listens to miss the one big news story of the program. Certainly the audience is not sure what it heard until it reads the Monday morning newspapers.

After Frank had dealt with interviews, he described some of the kinds of things he would prefer to see in the correspondents' miniature movies, as in this paragraph from a section of the memo called "News as Film":

Sound can establish the environment of your event. So can picture. Very few events we trouble to cover are not enhanced by including a feeling of where they took place. This is not the tired newsreel cliché called the establishing shot—a wide picture usually of the exterior of a building inside which what interests us is taking place. But the inside walls, the spectators, the minor actors, pictures of the scene from high up, from far away. In a Congressional hearing, we should see the table of legislators, the crowd in its seat, even the cameras banked together. Recently a Chicago alderman was murdered in his office. We had good pictures of the corpse under a blanket on the floor, the desk at which he was working when he was shot, the chair in which he was sitting. Another network had a walking shot through the door of his office as it opened, past the phalanx of policemen, the lights of the film man—our lights, presumably—the scurrying, the tension. It looked like a crime in Chicago.

56   The Early Years

The former newspaperman in television must also learn a new style of writing. "It's much more difficult than most people think," says Kiker, who has nine years of newspaper experience and has been with the Huntley-Brinkley show since last August. "I never knew what these people did. I thought they had it easier. But it's two different worlds. You have to remember that television is pictures. If the Mayor says X is going to happen, and someone else says X *and* Y are going to happen, then in a newspaper story you can hedge and qualify. You can say that 'It is said that' or 'On the other hand,' and so on. You can prove a point by putting all these blocks together. But on TV you don't have room for all that. You have to just haul off and say it. It takes very tight writing. You have to write dialogue for yourself — a news story in dialogue form. And it's not vertical writing, it's horizontal writing — writing to time instead of space." Wallace Westfeldt, associate producer, in Washington, of the Huntley-Brinkley show, describes television writing as "the art of not writing, of shutting up and letting the film tell it." Fred Friendly, Murrow's old associate and a former president of CBS News, recently said of reporting and writing for television, "A television reporter can look at the Green Bay–Detroit game and see the same thing you see, but *tell* you something you *can't* see. That's where Brinkley is great. When he looks at an event or a film, he doesn't just see captions."

Neither Huntley nor Brinkley runs "The Huntley-Brinkley Report." Huntley spends his time writing and then taping his two daily radio commentaries, and reading as much as possible in an effort to maintain some degree of expertise in world affairs. He has no interest in coping with the hundreds of details involved in assembling a nightly broadcast. He can influence the shape of a particular show, however; if he suggests a story as a lead item or a closing item, or complains that the coverage of some continuing story has been out of balance, he is certainly listened to. Brinkley has plenty of leverage, too, and chooses to apply it to a much greater extent. For all practical purposes, he is the producer of the Washington segment of the program. The boss of the entire show is Robert Northshield, the executive producer. Northshield, a big, jovial man in his mid-forties, succeeded Reuven Frank in June, 1965, and Frank later went on to become vice-president of NBC News. (Frank became president in June of this year, shortly after the death of William McAndrew.) Northshield previously had been the general manager of NBC News, and before that he had been producer of public-affairs programs at ABC, producer of "Adventure" and "Seven Lively Arts" at CBS, and a reporter at the Chicago *Sun-Times.* His television work had received considerable critical acclaim, including a Peabody Award and awards at the Venice and Edinburgh film festivals.

Northshield's method of running the show is firm yet casual, and in his staff's offices, which occupy a small suite in the RCA Building, the atmosphere is lighthearted. There is a lot of banter in editorial conferences, which sometimes resemble a chat at the water cooler among office pals. Staff members lounge around reading the *Times,* and stroll in and out of the office at will. Everyone, from secretary to star, is on a first-name basis. Anyone visiting the office before noon might think that he had wandered into some obscure NBC division whose duties were vague and not very urgent. But the look of things is deceptive. Assignments have been made the day before, by Northshield or by the show's producer, Lester Crystal. Correspondents are at work in other cities and other countries, and are in touch with Northshield and Crystal off and on all day, by phone. On other floors, film is being processed, and reports from correspondents are being videotaped. The writer missing from his cubicle is less likely to be on a coffee break than to be upstairs watching a filmed or taped report, for which he will have to write copy if there is no accompanying narration or if the narration is unsatisfactory. Northshield, a news editor, and the supervision film editor may be screening film in other rooms. Something similar, on a smaller scale, is going on in Washington, under the direction of Brinkley and Westfeldt.

By noon, Northshield has seen some film, discussed story ideas with his producer and with the Washington staff, spoken to a correspondent or two, and read as much wire-service copy as possible. These chores will occupy him throughout the day, right up to air time. By 3 P.M., Northshield says, he is beginning to tense up. "I'm worrying about what we have and don't have. The first question is: Have we covered everything? Second: Do we have enough? Third: What's the lead, and do we have a closer?" Unless he is delayed by an important late-breaking story, Northshield will begin trying to make a rundown—a list of the stories that will be used on the program, with an estimate of the time to be allotted to each—between 3:30 and 4:00. Perhaps six or eight of these stories will be filmed or taped reports, varying in length, usually, from one and a half to three and a half minutes. The 20 or so other stories will be briefer, nonvisual ones, to be condensed from wire reports by Huntley, Brinkley, and the staff writers. Shortly before five, Crystal holds a story conference with the writers and gives them their assignments. Each man's is likely to be brief—anywhere from 30 seconds to three minutes of copy, which, at Huntley's speaking pace of three words a second, means from 90 to 540 words. But the writers often find it hard to complete their work by air time, at 6:30. Gilbert Millstein, a news editor who came to the show in 1965 with 25 years of experience at the *Times,* the *News, Time,* and the *Saturday Evening Post,* says that boiling several stories down to 540 words for television is as difficult as turning out a two-column piece—about 1,500 words—for the *Times.*

Because of this and other production hazards, the calm that has prevailed in the Huntley-Brinkley offices most of the day often gives way at 5:00 to an excitement bordering on frenzy. Like the excitement occasionally found in a newspaper office or backstage at a theater, it is heightened by the approach of a deadline and by the necessity of performing well under pressure and in public. An important difference is that in television there is no such thing as stopping the presses or delaying the curtain. The show must go on at 30 minutes and no seconds after 6:00, and must go off at 58 minutes and 34 seconds after 6:00. Yet it is not unusual, when there are late stories, for one of the writers to be still working furiously 15 minutes after the broadcast has begun. Neither is it unusual for Northshield and his production assistant, who times each story as it is delivered on the air, to discover in the middle of the broadcast that they are running several seconds behind and don't know exactly how they will get off the air on schedule. In anticipation of such a difficulty, a minute or two in each rundown is reserved for what is called "pad" — brief, less important stories that can be dropped at a signal from Northshield. A few more seconds can be gained by cutting short the credits and the theme music. At the end of a broadcast, the mood in the control room is usually one not of reflection or self-criticism but of simple relief.

The show is seen live, at 6:30 P.M. Eastern time, in many parts of the East, the South, and the Midwest, and is taped for rebroadcast at other hours in other areas of the country. New York gets both the Huntley-Brinkley show and "The CBS Evening News with Walter Cronkite" on tape, at seven. This delay allows the staff of each of the two shows to watch its own product live, on monitors, and then to tune in the competition immediately afterward. Each staff tends to rate the shows as fairly even, but to give a slight edge to its own show. CBS people, including Cronkite and Mudd, seem to feel that the Cronkite show offers more hard news and that it is a little sounder journalistically. "There is a general feeling that Cronkite covers more news and that Huntley-Brinkley has a tendency to 'edit long,'" Mudd said recently. "On a speech or a press conference, we might run a minute and they might go two and a half. Sometimes this is very effective. Nobody has decided what an evening show really should do — cover a lot of things fast or a few things well. Still, there is a cursory feeling about the Huntley-Brinkley show, a feeling that after you watch it you don't know quite as much about as many things. They're more likely to go for the long, soft feature. For instance, they gave about eight minutes to the last voyage of the *Queen Mary* and made only one point over and over — that the world doesn't have time for that kind of luxury anymore." Cronkite sees another difference in the shows. "Brinkley in particular and Huntley occasionally will participate in what might be called an instant analysis or a comment on the news in a sort of parenthetical manner," he says. "I'm not suggesting which is the more viable approach, but that's something we scrupulously avoid."

The members of the Huntley-Brinkley staff all have a high regard for the quality of CBS reporting, but they don't think much of the writing on the Cronkite show. In their discussions of the subject, a recurrent phrase is "U.P.I.-style writing." Justly or not, for many journalists, "U.P.I.-style writing" is a synonym for journalese — for clichés, melodrama, overstatement, oversimplification, and corny brightness. "We always felt that as writers they couldn't carry our shoes," Patrick Trese, a former Huntley-Brinkley writer who now covers politics for NBC News, said several months ago. "They had a U.P.I. approach, while we were worrying about little details like sequence of tenses. We'd say 'Communist China' and they'd say 'Red China' — little things like that." Gilbert Millstein says, "I think there is a sophistication and a simplicity in our writing that they don't have on the Cronkite show. They can be embarrassing. We wince at that last line of Cronkite's — 'And that's the way it is.' And they have a fake folksiness. Sometimes their transition from one story to another will be something like 'By the way.'" And William Hill says, "It's very often a standoff in substance and picture. But they seem a little more sensational to me at times. What they choose to lead with, for instance. It kind of boils down to adjectives — making things seem black and white, worse or better than they are. A lot of their stuff must be read in the same light as U.P.I. That is, take the adjectives out and see what it really means."

An evaluation from outside the business was offered in 1963 by *Newsweek*, which characterized the Cronkite show as "sort of a visual *New York Times* with a twist — 'all the news that fits we show,'" and described the Huntley-Brinkley show as the equivalent of "a good afternoon newspaper." Brinkley considered the comparison silly. "I think, to the extent it has any relevance at all, it would be the other way around," he said recently. "Those terms are very loose and fuzzy. I think our approach to the news would be more like that of the *New York Times* than Cronkite's is. I suspect — I couldn't be positive, because I don't see his show enough, but I suspect we cover more of the important dull news than Cronkite does. I doubt, for example, that he's done as much as we have with the conflict between the President and Wilbur Mills about the tax and economic argument."

Until two or three years ago, a majority of the public and of the critics seemed to agree with the Huntley-Brinkley staff that its show was the better one. Now, they may not. During the past year, the CBS show has taken the lead in the ratings, and it is becoming more and more common to hear newspapermen and politicians say that they find Cronkite "more solid." This apparent shift was reflected in a *Time* cover story on Cronkite in October of 1966. "Of all the shows on all the networks," *Time* said, "it is Cronkite's that most consistently triumphs over the built-in drawbacks of TV newscasting." It would be difficult to prove *Time*'s assertion or one to the contrary. Anyone who can manage to see the shows back to back every night for a month or so is likely to feel that there is little to choose between them when they are judged on news content rather than on style or personality. Very often, of course, they are not judged on content; style and personality have been important factors in the competition between NBC and CBS over the years. For a time in the late fifties and the early sixties, "The Huntley-Brinkley Report" was clearly superior to its CBS counterpart as a news medium, but its strength with the public and the critics may have been based as much on fashion as on quality. For instance, *Newsweek* complained in 1961 that CBS reporting was occasionally "saddled with an air of doom and gloom, a hang-over from the Ed Murrow era," and similar observations were appearing in other magazines and newspapers. Thus, Murrow was being discarded as casually as an out-of-date hemline, and his approach to television news was suddenly just a quaint mannerism from the past — "that doom-and-gloom stuff." The new model was Brinkley, whose light touch was especially welcome after the general grayness of the Eisenhower years. If Brinkley and NBC benefitted from that contrast, perhaps Cronkite is now benefitting from one of another sort. Today — when the atmosphere is psychedelic rather than gray, and the effort to offer the public new excitements in the media is so strenuous that a soft drink or a new shade of lipstick is likely to be represented as something "naughty" or "outrageous" or "hip" — perhaps some viewers find reassurance in the mustache, the pipe, and the avuncular manner of Walter Cronkite.

NBC's initial pairing of Huntley and Brinkley—for its television coverage of the 1956 political conventions—seems to have been more an act of desperation than a logical decision. Reuven Frank now thinks of it as "a show-business accident—an accident of casting." At the time, CBS had the dominant network news operation, in prestige, ratings, and personnel. In the weeks of planning before the conventions, NBC's problem was not so much choosing an anchor man from a list of potential ones as thinking up any names worth putting on the list. Frank remembers that the early candidates included a man ready for retirement and a man who was young and attractive "but merely a stumblebum." Frank and several of the other younger producers and executives wanted either Huntley or Brinkley, each of whom was still relatively unknown, and they could not decide which they preferred. "And then," Frank has recalled, "one of the great compromisers said, 'Why don't we put the two of them together?,' meaning the old guy and the stumblebum. And we—and this was principally me, the producer of Huntley's 'Outlook' show; Bill McAndrew, who was director of news; and Joe Meyers, who was manager of news, and is dead now—we said, 'Let's put *those* two together,' meaning Huntley and Brinkley. It was like the light bulb going on over someone's head in the comics. The light bulb went on almost simultaneously for the three of us." Since the decision turned out later to have been such an important one for NBC, there are other versions of how it was made, featuring other participants, but Frank's will serve as well as any. Though CBS received the highest ratings for its coverage of the conventions, Huntley and Brinkley had some critical success, and considerably enhanced their reputations. This led to their assignment to the nightly show, which was 15 minutes long, as replacements for Swayze. Frank thought that using two men was a terrible idea for the show, but he agreed to become its producer.

Several months ago, Frank, a prematurely gray man in his late forties, who is both soft-spoken and emphatic, received a visitor at his office in the RCA Building and reminisced about the show's first months. "It was quite an opening show," Frank said. "It may have been the worst news show in history. We went on with no dry run at all. We had a little time in the studio on a Saturday, and on Monday, October 29th, we went. The Hungarian revolution was fresh—maybe a week old. The Israelis jumped off against the Suez Canal on the twenty-ninth. We had *no* facilities, and we were brand-new—we had gotten rid of the entire Swayze production crowd. You know, we were all experienced in the business, but the neuromuscular patterns of a daily program, for those of us who had done one, were something in the past. I'd been on the Swayze show for years, but that was a year and a half or two years before. It requires a certain attack. Your juices have to flow just a certain way or else you're not going to make it. And we were a very small staff, and very poor. Besides which, a resident genius had taken over the designing of the set—he's no longer here— and had instructed our set designer that what he wanted was a set for a *ballet* about the news. The genius had no journalistic background, and, boy, the set really looked it. Don Hewitt, over at CBS, used to call it the Martian Ballroom. The thing was supposed to give the effect of having pillars, and it was a big semicircle—a studio big enough for a production of 'Hamlet.' On one side of it was a monitor, where we had Brinkley. On the other side, all across the face of the studio, was a projection screen for maps and still pictures. And in the back were these things that looked like scimitars growing out, so that at a certain angle it did look like pillars, where you were going to get a lady in diaphanous robes floating around in a classical ballet. But whatever shot you took of Huntley, one of these Goddamned things would grow out of his head. And we went crazy. During a piece of film, Huntley had to go running back and forth across this stage, because someone here had committed money to the development of an inflatable globe ten or 12 feet high, with physical features correct to the logarithmic scale. They had put a lot of money in it, so somebody said, 'Use that.' So there was this *thing* in the center of the set, and they wanted Huntley to point to it. And I said, 'Well, he can't run this way and that, we just don't have enough time in a 15-minute show.' It was a marvelous globe, except that it had no relevance to this kind of program. Finally, we took a lot of photographs of it and did our maps on the photographs, and that was great.

"Our budget then was murder. I guess it was a fifth or a sixth of what they have now. And I had to amortize this huge set and I don't know how many tens of thousands of dollars on this globe, plus the fact that this studio was not ours, but ours for four hours a day. So I had to have stagehands come in and inflate the globe and then deflate it and truck it down to our warehouse on Eighteenth Street and truck it back. I had stagehands and teamsters, but I had no money for news coverage. Well, around January they said, 'You've got to cut your budget—you're spending too much money.' And I said, 'Fine, I'll tell you how I'm going to do it.' Now, in those days, news people reported to entertainment people. So I couldn't just say, 'Look, if I can get rid of this *junk,* I can save almost ten thousand dollars a week.' I had to give it to them in their terms. I said, 'I've worked out a new concept for the program.' And they said, 'Yeah? What's that?' I said, 'I call it the closet-to-closet concept.' And all these guys, with very solemn looks, they said, 'Well, would you explain that?' And I said, 'Well, it seems to me that for news presentation, material is more important than setting. A newsman can do a news show in a closet.' And they nodded and said, 'Well, all right." And I said, 'Well, I want a closet in New York and a closet in Washington.' And I got them. I had an announcer's booth eight and a half feet wide and 22 feet long, with a glass window fronting the hall. And I went to Hjalmar Hermanson, that wonderful designer, and I said, 'I want this thing to look like it extends from Sixth Avenue to maybe Third.' So he gave me a Mercator-projection map with forced perspective. Then we got little clocks for the wall, and painted a door no more than a couple of feet high. It was the damnedest forced perspective, and it cost nothing. And I got another set for Brinkley, with nothing on it, just Brinkley. Without damaging the corpus of my program, I saved about eight grand a week.

"But at the beginning of the program was a dog. It just died. The stuff was awful, and nobody knew us, and we had to fight our way. But that kind of keeps you going. Sponsors stayed away in droves. We were on in those days at 7:45 P.M., which is network time. Douglas Edwards, at CBS, had run away from Swayze, after years where it was reversed—where Swayze was actually the highest-rated program in television, I think. We were running a seven

Nielsen, which is, you know, miserable. And then we went down to a four. And Huntley and Brinkley and I often talked about the fact that we were trying to do a program the way we wanted to do a program, because we couldn't understand all those audience-measurement things. I was prepared to be called in to the front office on a Friday night and thanked for my noble and vigorous effort, because I don't think we were doing a job for them. You know, here was their No. 1 news show, and, no matter how badly you do it, your principal news program must pay the core costs of your news operation. And we weren't getting any income. We weren't bringing it in. Personally, if I'd been an advertiser I don't think I would have bought the show. The guys were not used to each other. The format was new. People used to make fun of the closing—the 'Good Night, Chet.' Including Huntley and Brinkley, who kept begging me to stop using it. I'm the guy who wrote that. Supposing you had been the man who first said 'So's your old man,' or 'Your mother wears Army shoes,' or something else that got into the language—'Good night, Chet.' 'Good night, David.' 'And good night for NBC News.' And when the guys complained, I said, 'Look, you must end a program.' And Brinkley said, 'Not this way, it makes us sound like fags. It's corny.' I told them if they could think of a shorter one, all right, and they never did.

"The summer of 1957, the program was sustaining for 13 weeks. You couldn't give it away. And why Kintner [Robert Kintner, former president of NBC] and Bob Sarnoff didn't do just that, I don't know. There was one entire quarter when we didn't have a commercial minute on the program. Then, all of a sudden, it started to take off—I believe in the spring of 1958. It was coincident with, and not unrelated to, Texaco's buying the show out. There had been improvement in the show, and there had been improvement in the ratings, too, I believe."

Things got better for the show and its stars in 1958, but in 1960 and thereafter they got wonderful. At the 1960 conventions, Huntley and Brinkley won all the critical attention and defeated their CBS opposition, Cronkite and Murrow, by a humiliating margin in the ratings. "It wasn't only the political old guard that perished in Los Angeles," Jack Gould wrote in his TV column in the *Times*. "The pontificating commentators of television also succumbed in the early hours of yesterday; they couldn't withstand the fresh breeze of David Brinkley's wit." Gould went on to rub it in, in another piece: "The National Broadcasting Company's team of Chet Huntley and David Brinkley swept away the stuffy, old-fashioned concept of ponderous reportage on the home screen. They talked as recognizable humans, sprinkled their observations with delightful wit, and were easily the TV hit of the week." CBS News did not fully recover from its convention defeat for nearly seven years. Maintaining their momentum after the conventions, Huntley and Brinkley took a commanding lead in the ratings with their nightly show in 1961 and 1962. Simultaneously, they took an equally commanding lead in the publicity battle, winning award after award, and becoming the subject of frequent magazine and newspaper articles. In 1962, CBS fought back by removing Douglas Edwards from "The CBS Evening News" and replacing him with Walter Cronkite. Under Cronkite, the show improved and increased in popularity, and for a time in the summer of 1963 it drew even with "The Huntley-Brinkley Report." But 1964 brought another convention debacle for CBS. Cronkite fell so far behind Huntley and Brinkley in the convention ratings that CBS replaced him as anchor man with Roger Mudd and Bob Trout, and they fared even worse. Huntley and Brinkley held on to their edge in the ratings most of the time through the next three years—until late in 1967, when Cronkite seemed finally to have caught up with them for good.

If ratings and polls have any degree of accuracy at all, then both shows have now attained an audience of spectacular size and an influence that is probably beyond calculation. Early this year, it was estimated that during any given minute of a broadcast 19,240,000 people were watching the Huntley-Brinkley show, and that the total audience per broadcast was 21,550,000. The equivalent figures for the Cronkite show were 19,680,000 and 21,930,000. And as the audience for each show has grown, so, apparently, has each show's authority with the public. A long-range Roper poll (which had been challenged by other researchers but still may be evidence of a trend) indicates that television is now the nation's primary news source, and—more surprising—that the public places greater faith in what it sees on television than what it reads in newspapers. One of the questions asked in the Roper poll was "If you got conflicting or different reports of the same news story from radio, television, the magazines, and the newspapers, which of the four versions would you be most inclined to believe—the one on radio or television or magazines or newspapers?" In 1959, 29 percent of those polled chose television as the most believable, and 32 percent chose newspapers. In 1967, the figures were 41 percent for television and 24 percent for newspapers.

Despite all this public acceptance, Huntley-Brinkley staff members and other television news people sometimes feel unloved and misunderstood. This is because so many harsh and, in their opinion, unfair things are said about them by television critics, mass-media critics, newspapermen, and academics. Although the TV people admit that television news has many shortcomings, they feel that some of the standard criticisms of it are not judgments at all but simply assertions—unproved and unexamined notions that gain authority through repetition. Several assertions of the sort they have in mind were included in the 1966 *Time* cover story on Cronkite. For instance, there was the old assumption that television news is a branch of show business and is under the thumb of the advertisers. "Of almost equal importance [with other "tyrannies" besetting television news] is the tyranny of advertisers," *Time* said. "Though the newsmen, with good reason, proclaim their freedom, the sponsor's influence is still apparent. Commercials, the newsmen occasionally boast, are restricted to a small percentage of a news program's time, far less than the percentage of space given over to ads in successful newspapers. But it is also true that those commercials appear right in the middle of the electronic front page. Few newspapers give their advertisers such considerate treatment." Instead of showing just how "the sponsor's influence is still apparent," *Time* offered a metaphor—"commercials appear right in the middle of the electronic front page." But since, as Cronkite told *Time,* "There are no back pages in our kind of journalism," it is difficult to imagine where the commercials would appear except on the "electronic front page." If the advertisers do exert any influence on the nightly shows, it is so subtle that the correspondents and writers themselves are unaware of it. "I think our medium—television—is the freest and most nearly independent news medium on earth," Brinkley said recently. "There are a few newspapers that would fall into the same category, but not very many. The *Times* is one. It is hard to name more than a handful of others, and none of them is circulated truly nationally. NBC—the management of the network—has no editorial position on anything. No one at NBC, since the day I came to work here, has ever once limited, suggested, or implied that I should take this or that line on anything." Herbert J. Gans, a sociologist with the Center for Urban Education, in New York, who is making a long-range study of the mass media, remarked recently, "Despite the old stereotype that media employees report the news as their owners and advertisers see fit, this is not true of national television and magazines, however true it may be of the local press. People who work in the media I have studied so far are surprisingly free from outside interference on the part of nonprofessionals and business executives, and can decide on their own what to cover and how to cover it."

A related criticism is that television news shows, since they are under the influence of advertisers, are naturally timid. *Time* said, "And network executives are notoriously timid about antagonizing anyone—particularly the people who pay their bills. Which means that there is a pervading reluctance to take sides on any issue. 'I find an almost excessive lack of bias on television,' says Howard K. Smith. 'We are afraid of a point of view. We stick to the old American belief that there is an objectivity. If a man says the world is round, we run out to find someone to say it is flat.'" In an article in *Nieman Reports,* in December, 1963, Karl E. Meyer, a foreign correspondent for the *Washington Post,* wrote that television discourages contentiousness, and "favors the bland vendors of Fact—the Huntleys and the Cronkites who convey a personal opinion only through inscrutable movements of the eyebrow or a slight modulation of a mellifluous voice." Such observations are offered frequently, despite the evidence to the contrary that is displayed regularly on the network news programs. Huntley and Brinkley both deliver outright editorials when they are upset or irritated by something, and their correspondents in the field often go far beyond the newspaper and wire-service notion of objectivity. For some time now, it has been almost impossible to watch the Cronkite show or the Huntley-Brinkley show without seeing a reporter standing in an outdoor setting somewhere and delivering a little homily on race relations or making historical, political, and tactical judgments about the war in Vietnam. To take only one instance, Kiker was not bashful about including his personal judgments in his reporting from Vietnam last February. Much of what he said on the air could have appeared in a newspaper only as part of an editorial or a news analysis by a columnist. In one report he said, "South Vietnam's cities will never be the same because of these guerrilla attacks, and neither will the war. These attacks represent a major turning point—a point equal in historical importance to the beginning of the bombing of the North, or the large-scale introduction of U.S. troops. . . . At press briefings, the U.S. Mission is *trying* to give the impression that all this is just a temporary setback of no major consequence. Until these attacks come, American officials here were bragging about the great progress being made in the war—bragging so much that new charges of a lack of credibility are bound to result.... Despite official claims of great progress, Vietnam's rural-pacification program was making little progress even before the attacks. Now its very existence is threatened.... It's inevitable that the South Vietnamese Army will be clustered more closely in these cities, because the government simply cannot afford to take more chances with its key urban strongholds. This would mean that a diminished American force would be fighting the Vietcong alone for control of the countryside. And that's *not* the way this war is going to be won."

Perhaps the most serious criticism of television news is that—hampered by its need for pictures, for brevity, and for appeal to a national, mass audience—it is superficial. Television newsmen agree that their coverage often is superficial, compared with that of the *Times,* but they are tired of being compared with the *Times.* "The whole approach of this sort of criticism is wrong," a network correspondent said recently. "We aren't supplying an inferior sort of newspaper coverage—we're supplying *television* coverage. The newspaperman considers pictures an annoying necessity for us, but we consider them simply part of the medium, and the source of much of its impact. Being condescending toward us for our reliance on pictures is like knocking a newspaper article for not being a book, or a movie for not being a novel. Our coverage just gives another aspect of the news. It's only part of the news, but sometimes it's an important part." Reuven Frank had something similar in mind when he wrote, in his 1963 memo, "The highest power of television journalism is not in the transmission of information but in the transmission of experience.... There are events which exist in the American mind and recollection primarily because they were reported on regular television news programs. We have found a dimension of information which is not contained in words alone. The rebellion in Hungary; Little Rock; the Berlin Wall; Suez; the 1960 Democratic primaries; Khrushchev's visit; de Gaulle; the hurricane at Lake Charles, Louisiana.... Each member of the audience has his own list. Television brings to reporting the transmission of experience, and here it is matchless. But not all of the major stories of the past dozen years were created by television. The Supreme Court nine-to-nothing decision in Brown vs. Board of Education worked a major permanent change in American society, but television could not report the decision itself as well as newspapers could. The failure of any Communist country to feed itself may be the climactic fact of this century. It is primarily a story for magazines and books."

As surely as television news programs must have pictures, they must have a large, national audience, in order to attract sponsors and survive. This means limiting the selection of stories to those which the producers consider of national or international importance, or of general interest. Again, however, television news people apparently regard playing to this audience as a unique characteristic of the medium, rather than as a troublesome chore or a mandate for superficiality. Considering the parochialism of so many local papers, they feel that they are performing an important educational service by reaching millions of people with a serious, though cursory, report of the news. Few of them have any desire to put on a broadcast version of the *Times* or *Foreign Affairs* and thus to reach only a small audience that is already served by other media. And, though none of them think television alone is an adequate source of news, some of them believe that the disparity between their coverage and that of the newspapers is not quite as great as the heft of a *Times* might make it appear. Brinkley, for one, is inclined to think that there is often less going on than meets the eye, and that the "real story" about what's up often is that nothing is up. "There are many days," Brinkley said recently, "when there is so little real news that we have a hard time finding anything to lead the program with that is not embarrassing to use as a lead. Well, on those same days the *Times,* which is the closest thing we have to a national newspaper, will come out with 60 pages. And it *looks* like a paper fat with news. But when you get down to it, it's not. A fourth or a third or sometimes half of the front page might be local news, which we wouldn't use. Inside, it's full of ads, more local news, trade news of one kind or another, business news, industrial news, analyses of the Broadway season so far, and stuff like that — stuff that we wouldn't use if we had it and had the time for it." Brinkley would reject such stories not because he thinks his audience has a narrower range of interests than the *Times*' audience (though it surely has) but because of a basic difference between broadcasting and print. The broadcasting media exist in time, and the print media exist in space. In this sense, it is television that is the linear, one-thing-at-a-time medium and the newspaper is the mosaic, to borrow the terms of Marshall McLuhan, the Canadian media oracle. In other words, the television viewer must either watch the news program or not watch it; the newspaper reader can skim or ignore stories and skip around in the paper, choosing what interests him. The Huntley-Brinkley staff members assume that using a *Times* approach on television would mean a daily show two or three hours long. They assume further that it would be unwatchable, because the viewer would have to watch all or most of it in order to see the part that really interested him. How many people would read the *Times* if it were available only at a certain hour of the day, and if they had to read every word of it, on a long, slowly unwinding roll of paper?

However defensive the network news people may be about their critics, they are not satisfied with the job they are now doing on the nightly shows. They admit that a lot of details are ignored in a show based, as the present ones are, on the assumption that a four-minute report on the air is a long one. Most of them also admit that television news is still weak in first-hand, investigative reporting, and that its reliance on the *Times* and the wire services is enormous. As a possible remedy, both NBC and CBS have studied the idea of a nightly one-hour show — a compromise between the present half-hour show and the hypothetical, unwatchable three-hour one. So far, there seems to be more enthusiasm for a one-hour show at CBS than at NBC. But neither network can expand its show without the cooperation of the affiliated stations, which are reluctant to give up another half hour of local time and the advertising revenue that goes with it. For if local television is often bush-league journalistically, it is strictly big-time financially. The NBC affiliate in one fairly large Southern city, for example, receives $453 per broadcast from the network for carrying the Huntley-Brinkley show; but its own local news show, when all the commercial time is sold, has a gross revenue of $8,500 per broadcast, or $2,210,000 a year. NBC executives say that, for now, the expansion idea has been rejected.

Brinkley and Reuven Frank are skeptical about the value of a longer show anyway. They wonder if an hour show would produce reporting of greater depth or simply more of what is already being offered. It was a desire for more depth, within the limitations of the 30-minute program, that led NBC last August to make the greatest change in the Huntley-Brinkley show since late in 1963, when the Huntley-Brinkley and Cronkite shows were both expanded from 15 minutes to 30. On August 21st, after several months of discussion and two weeks of rehearsal, NBC added to the Huntley-Brinkley show four so-called contributing editors, to cover stories and to engage in ad-lib conversations about the news with each other and with Huntley and Brinkley. The contributing editors included three experienced NBC correspondents — Chancellor, Sander Vanocur, and Jack Perkins — and Kiker, then a newcomer to the medium. The new approach, suggested by Brinkley, was modelled on NBC's highly successful convention coverage, which always featured Huntley and Brinkley, as anchor men, talking informally with each other and with reporters who were roaming among the delegates. Brinkley's idea was that using this approach nightly could make "The Huntley-Brinkley Report" more informative. He thought that some unrehearsed questioning from him and from Huntley might shake the contributing editors out of the slick, conventional patterns of reporting and, in a sense, startle them into telling everything they knew about a story. Before each broadcast, the participants were to be told which stories were up for ad-lib discussion — or "crosstalk," as it was called — but careful planning was to be avoided, in order to insure informality.

The morning after its premier, the revised show received a cautiously favorable welcome from Jack Gould in the *Times*. Gould approved of the attempt to provide more background material at the expense of film footage, and commended NBC for its "venturesome initiative." During the next couple of weeks, the Huntley-Brinkley staff people were like children with a new toy. They used the crosstalk at every opportunity, and delighted in the smooth way in which Brinkley and the others handled the tricky business of live, ad-lib news analysis. As it happened, the experiment was being watched with some pleasure at CBS, too. One CBS producer who was asked what he thought of the change replied, with a happy smile, "I love it, it's awful." It was not really awful, but neither was it a complete success. Although the correspondents were performing well, aside from getting off a few inevitable non sequiturs, they were seldom saying anything in their ad libs that was especially interesting or that could not have been included in their regular reports. Mail on the change was fairly heavy. The viewers who approved of it were rapturous, and those who didn't were outraged. A furious resident of Summit, New Jersey, wrote not only to NBC but also to a sponsor, the American Home Products Corporation, vowing that until the new approach was scrapped he would not combat his sinus congestion with Dristan or shave his face with Aero Shave. The pro and con factions were about evenly represented in the mail, and NBC executives considered this a bad sign. They reasoned that the happy viewers would simply keep watching, the unhappy viewers would switch to Cronkite, and the Cronkite viewers who might like the new Huntley-Brinkley show would never know about it—responses that added up to a loss of viewers. Then there was an even worse sign. For the previous couple of years, Cronkite had moved ahead in the ratings during the summer months but had dropped behind again in the fall. NBC's perhaps smug theory was that during the summer "their people"—the young and well-to-do—were too busy with tennis and surfing and yachting to watch television, and that the absence of these swingers gave Cronkite, with his oldsters and shut-ins, the advantage. But in 1967 Cronkite was still ahead in late September and early October. This development was so jarring that it almost excited Paul G. Klein, the vice-president in charge of audience measurement in NBC's research department, who is known for a degree of detachment about television that is unusual among the medium's executives. ("TV is based on the principle of least obnoxious," Klein has said. "You don't sit down to watch a *show,* you sit down to watch TV. Then it's just a matter of 'What's on?' You're turning on TV to eat up your life.") When the Huntley-Brinkley show fell two points behind Cronkite in the Nielsen ratings, a naïve acquaintance of Klein's asked him if that was bad. "Is that *bad*?" Klein repeated. He paused, as though trying to summon up words to describe a concept beyond the comprehension of a layman. "It's *terrible!*" he finally said, in a low, mournful tone. Friends of Northshield's say that a few minutes before 6 P.M. on October 5th, Julian Goodman, the president of NBC, called Northshield into his office and told him that the ratings were down, which Northshield already knew, of course. The conversation was casual, but Goodman's choice of that hour—shortly before air time, when Northshield was extremely busy—seemed to underscore the gravity of the situation. That night, Brinkley, Chancellor, and Vanocur flew in from Washington for a long discussion of crosstalk with Northshield, Huntley, and Kiker. Northshield is said to have told them that a crisis might be approaching.

As far as an outsider can tell, the crisis never came. There were no firings or reorganizations. The crosstalk ceased to be a nightly feature, but it is still used for reporting important stories. Huntley and Brinkley have remained behind in the ratings; their audience has decreased slightly, but Cronkite's has increased considerably. Crosstalk and ratings aside, the new approach may have helped the show. The reporting has probably been strengthened by the addition of the four contributing editors, who, unlike the other NBC correspondents, work exclusively for "The Huntley-Brinkley Report," and are not on call for such shows as "Today" and "The Frank McGee Report." Some network people regard the inclusion of Kiker among the four as an especially good omen for the future of television reporting. His swift rise at NBC is said to show that a reporter can succeed in television journalism on a journalistic basis, without the usual star qualities. Kiker's accent is Southern, and though he is nice-looking, he is not glamorous. "I'm not handsome," Kiker said recently. "I've got big ears. I've thought about putting some dark stuff in them to make them look smaller. But then I wouldn't be that reporter at NBC with big ears—I'd be that dirty-eared reporter at NBC." Northshield, in particular, is pleased that Kiker seems to have been accepted by the NBC brass. "I've known about this guy ever since he was at the *Trib*," Northshield said not long ago. "I remember when he made a camera test, looking for a job. I was impressed that anyone would *give* him a camera test. He had everything else, and yet when you look at him... If there was anybody at NBC who was willing to spend the money to tape him, even knowing what he looked like — why, hell, then obviously I had it licked."

The addition of the four regulars to the show has been welcomed enthusiastically by Huntley and Brinkley, who are now able to get out and cover stories more often; both stars had been complaining for some time about their confinement in the studio. The network, for its part, sees a possible long-term advantage in the constant public exposure of the new men. Huntley and Brinkley obviously must retire someday, and when they do, one or more of the contributing editors should have attained star status and should be ready to replace the superstars. Huntley and Brinkley both think of retirement — or at least quitting the nightly show — in a vague, wistful way these days. Both say that they are not tired of the news business but that the routine of the regular show is wearing.

"The work is endlessly interesting, but it is confining," Brinkley says. "Every night, rain or shine, sick or well, news or no news, you have to be in the studio at six-thirty-oh-oh-oh-oh. Broadcasting is the only thing done by human beings that is always punctual. The *only* thing. Everything else is late sometimes or early sometimes. So this absolutely unyielding routine does get to be a little difficult." He says that sometimes during the next year or two he may begin to fade out of the show — taking off one night a week, then two, and so on, until he is completely out. Then he would like to do some writing and produce a television show occasionally, he says.

Huntley has thought about returning to Montana and entering politics. "I would have to make up my mind by 1972," he said several months ago. "I'll be 60 by then. I wouldn't want to use a Senate or House seat as a form of relaxation, and I don't know how much this trade is taking out of me. Sometimes I feel it's taking my very blood. Of course, the people of Montana would be justified in saying, 'What goes here? What makes this guy think he can come back and claim elective office?' But if I had a fighting chance, and if I didn't have to hurt anybody, and use elbows and claws, I might try it." Huntley says he can imagine himself running in either of the major political parties. Some of Huntley's friends are against his running for office, on the ground that he is too tenderhearted for politics, but Brinkley thinks it might not be a bad idea. "As a politician, Huntley would, I suspect, continue to do things that he believed in and thought were right — things that vast numbers of people disliked — and would persist in doing them in spite of all entreaties to the contrary," Brinkley said recently, with a broad grin. "So on that score I think he would be a pretty good politician. We could use a few guys like that. He might serve only one term, but it would be a good time while he was there."

Cronkite Again

"Playboy *Interview: Walter Cronkite*"

Interviewer: Ron Powers

When this interview was conducted for Playboy magazine, Walter Cronkite had been anchor at CBS for over 10 years. Notice how different this is from the 1966 Time article; issues are now more complex. Instead of the "tyranny of time," the lack of professionalism and the "front page" aspects of television journalism, the 1973 issues are press-administration confrontations and other issues much more subtle and less easily solved.

When Playboy reprinted this article in its anthology The Playboy Interview, *published by Playboy Press, 1981, editor G. Barry Golson added the following two paragraphs of Introduction:* "Since 1971, the Nixon administration had been orchestrating an attack on what it saw as the liberal bias of the press, with the alliterative vice-president, Spiro Agnew, leading the charge. That 'the most trusted man in America,' CBS's Walter Cronkite, should speak out on the issue meant it was important. That he should do so in Playboy meant he wanted his message to reach an audience larger than the number of viewers who tuned in to the CBS 'Evening News.' (The CBS news program has an audience of about 14 million; Playboy's total readership is about 22 million.) But what was unusual was how forcefully—even passionately—Cronkite spoke about newsmen's rights. Abandoning his avuncular neutrality, he lashed out at the Nixon spokesmen and defended the independence of the media. The interview remains a rare look at 'Uncle Walter' off-camera, and on a podium.

"The interview was conducted by Chicago Sun-Times *TV critic Ron Powers, who later won a Pulitzer prize for television coverage. Queried by Northwestern's Medill School of Journalism in 1977, Cronkite said that his interview in* Playboy *was 'one of the best ever done with me.'"*

If God had set out to create a prototypical middle American, He could have done little better than limn the image of the sad-eyed 56-year-old man—at his CBS anchor desk in New York—whose military-drum-roll voice, sending modulator needles flickering toward the bass registers, has become part of our collective consciousness. But while Cronkite is regarded by the public as a

Ron Powers has won a Pulitzer prize for his commentary about television.

fatherly, sympathetic figure, he has a rather more volatile reputation among his colleagues in the broadcast industry, where he's known as a tough, jealous and outspoken guardian of newsmen's rights.

To get a summing up of Cronkite's own feelings about his 40 years in journalism and about the current contretemps between the Government and the press, Playboy assigned TV critic Ron Powers to interview Cronkite in New York. His report:

"Walter Cronkite is a Walter Mitty in reverse: He is a famous man who has fantasies of being ordinary. His office—a pristine cubbyhole just off the 'Evening News' set at CBS' big broadcast barn on West 57th Street in New York—proves it. There are the obligatory 'serious books' about Presidents and nations, the plastic-lined wastebasket, the three TV sets and the 'Facts on File.' But there is also a large, sentimental oil painting of a sailing boat (boating is Cronkite's favorite recreation), a box of chocolates and a cardboard-cutout statue of Apollo spacemen, a grade-schooler's gift that Cronkite keeps as a souvenir.

"He never loosened his necktie as we talked, but he propped his feet up on his desk and alternately clasped his hands behind his head and fiddled with his stretch socks. His eyes, so penetrating on the screen, seem pale and sensitive in person. He has the old-time journalist's knack of forming his thoughts into cogent, parsable sentences as he speaks, and he displayed a gift for the lyric phrase when talking of his reveries at the helm of his boat or of memories of childhood days in Texas.

"I frequently sensed a mild, resigned puzzlement that the life of a superstar had come to him. He was unfailingly courteous with me, but on the topic that was obviously foremost in his mind—current Government ploys to muffle newsmen in the pursuit of their work—he was neither mild nor resigned. He was visibly steamed, in fact, when we discussed the subject, which I broached in my first question."

Playboy: You are perhaps the most outspoken of all newsmen in defending broadcasters' rights against Government intimidation. In fact, you have used the word conspiracy in describing the Nixon Administration's efforts to discredit the press. How would you characterize this conspiracy?

Cronkite: Let me say, first of all, that after I used the word conspiracy the first and only time, in a speech to the International Radio and Television Society in New York a couple of years ago, I began to regret the use of the word—only because I found that there were still people who equated conspiracy with some of the witch-hunts of the past. The word has nearly lost its true meaning. Having said that, I still feel that this is basically what has taken place: a well-directed campaign against the press, agreed upon in secret by members of the Administration. I can't see how it's possible to have such an orchestrated, coordinated campaign without some prior plan and agreement—which really comes out to be a conspiracy.

Playboy: Can you trace it to one person in the Administration?

Cronkite: I certainly think that the President has to be held accountable, since he's the boss.

Playboy: Do you attribute Nixon's hostility toward the press to his personal bitterness about the way the press has treated him?

Cronkite: I think that may be true, although it's very hard to ascribe motivation to anybody. Circumstantially, the evidence would point to that. Certainly, he's had his bouts with the press before; his disappointments have been shown in public. There is the case of the 1962 gubernatorial concession statement in California. There is his failure just in recent months, at a very critical time in history, to appear more frequently before the press and the public to explain the workings of the Administration. I think all these things point to that general attitude toward the press.

I don't know what happened inside the Administration. I don't know at what point its members decided that it would be wise to attempt to bring down the press's credibility in an attempt to raise their own. But I think that's what has happened. It's sort of like that U tube we used to see in physics class that shows the countereffects of pressure: When you put pressure on one side and the level goes down, the level of the water on the other side has to rise. Extending that theory, if you could lower the credibility of the press, you could raise the credibility of the politicians. That must be the underlying theory in their attack.

Playboy: Nearly all politicians have felt the need to control the press to some degree. Is this Administration simply more sophisticated than its predecessors in the techniques of applying pressure effectively?

Cronkite: I don't know that they're any more sophisticated, but they're the first ones who have deliberately set out to *use* those techniques.

Playboy: What has been the chronology of this attack? Was Vice-President Agnew's 1969 Des Moines speech—in which he attacked the "tiny, enclosed fraternity of privileged men"—the start of it all?

Cronkite: I think that was the open declaration in the battle. Before that, it was simply felt that this Administration's antagonism had been about like the antagonism shown by previous Administrations, Democratic as well as Republican—particularly Democratic—toward the press. An adversary relationship, we all agree, is a good thing. But the Agnew attack suddenly became a matter of Administration policy and, more than that, a threat to use Governmental weapons against the press. Then, following Agnew's speech, there was a tightening in attitudes on the part of press-relations people in the Government. It was a subtle thing.

The Administration feels network news must exercise a greater degree of "professional responsibility." I'd have a hard time defining professional responsibility myself. But my hackles rise when I hear it suggested that we're *not* responsible. We in broadcast news have ethics we defend and maintain as strongly as a doctor or a lawyer does; in fact, a lot *more* strongly than some doctors and lawyers I know.

Playboy: Doctors and lawyers have rather well-defined codes of professional standards, but journalists don't. Do you think they should?

Cronkite: I don't really see that they need to be imposed, and I see some dangers in it. Freedom of press and speech seems to imply that anybody can write or speak out, whether he's literate or not. Erecting standards would also suggest that you're going to legislate against the underground press, and I think that would be a mistake. If you're going to accept journalists only if they conform to some establishment norm, you won't have the new blood and free flow of new ideas that are absolutely essential to a vital press. I don't know that Tom Paine could have passed a journalism-review test.

Playboy: One standard that Government already confers on broadcasters is the so-called fairness doctrine, which requires that both sides of controversial issues be presented. You have said you favor its elimination because it imposes artificial and arbitrary standards of balance and objectivity.

Cronkite: Yes. I think the only way to free radio and television news broadcasting from the constant danger of Government censorship is to free it from any form of Government control. The only way to do that is to limit the licensing practice to a technical matter of assignment of channels.

Playboy: Insofar as television is bearing the brunt of this attack, do you feel that CBS is the primary target — that the Administration is still vindictive about *The Selling of the Pentagon* and your own news reports last summer on the Watergate affair and the Soviet wheat deal?

Cronkite: I like to think that we've been in the forefront of the reporting and therefore in the forefront when the flak starts to fly. That doesn't alarm me. I'm not alarmed for CBS. I'm alarmed for the entire country.

Playboy: News analysis on all the networks has dropped off since the Administration's attacks began. There are fewer "instant analyses" of Presidential addresses, for example.

Cronkite: I'm not sure I agree with you. I think that we at CBS bend over backward to be sure that we get an analysis on after every major address. Even when commercial considerations might have dictated going immediately from the address to the next program, we've cut into the top of that program in order to get a few licks in.

Playboy: But are these licks as tough as they used to be?

Cronkite: I don't know. I guess I have to be candid and say that it seems to me that on occasion our guys have pulled their punches. But I've talked with them about it — not officially, because that's not part of my function — and I get the impression that they don't feel they have. But they do feel threatened. This question of "instant analysis," though, is one of the major phonies of the whole anti-network, anti-press campaign. As any newspaperman knows, it's rare that the press doesn't have a major Presidential speech several hours in advance. The newspapers must get it set in type, the editorial writers must have a shot at it for the next day's paper. So there's nothing instant about analysis. The network analysts have longer than the print press to study a speech, in fact, because they don't deliver their analysis until after it's given.

Playboy: Do you think that the public's apparent declining interest in documentaries has anything to do with the Administration's success in discrediting the press? Were you surprised, for example, at the low level of outrage following the Watergate exposé?

Cronkite: I certainly was, very much so. I tie it to the fact that the people say, well, it's just another campaign-year press attack against Nixon.

The Early Years

Playboy: Do you think the public really cares about freedom of the press anymore? Or even about its own freedom of speech or assembly?

Cronkite: I think people care in the abstract. But they don't understand the specifics. We did a poll on the Bill of Rights at CBS a couple of years ago. We asked people such specific questions as, "As long as there appears to be no danger of violence, do you think any group, no matter how extreme, should be allowed to organize protests against the Government?" Something like 76 percent of the people said no, they don't have that right. But the same people *support* the constitutional guarantee of freedom of assembly. So they believe in the abstract but not in the specific. And this is our problem.

Playboy: Implicit in the Administration's attempts to force the networks to "balance" the news is a conviction that most newscasters are biased against conservatism. Is there some truth in the view that television newsmen tend to be left of center?

Cronkite: Well, certainly liberal, and possibly left of center as well. I would have to accept that.

Playboy: What's the distinction between those two terms?

Cronkite: I think the distinction is both clear and important. I think that being a liberal, in the true sense, is being nondoctrinaire, nondogmatic, noncommitted to a cause—but examining each case on its merits. Being left of center is another thing; it's a political position. I think most newspapermen by definition have to be liberal; if they're not liberal, by my definition of it, then they can hardly be good newspapermen. If they're preordained dogmatists for a cause, then they can't be very good journalists; that is, if they carry it into their journalism.

As far as the leftist thing is concerned, that I think is something that comes from the nature of a journalist's work. Most newsmen have spent some time covering the seamier side of human endeavor; they cover police stations and courts and the infighting in politics. And I think they come to feel very little allegiance to the established order. I think they're inclined to side with humanity rather than with authority and institutions. And this sort of pushes them to the left. But I don't think there are many who are *far* left. I think a little left of center probably is correct.

Playboy: Some critics believe that this left-of-center tendency produces a kind of conventional wisdom for liberals—a point of view that's common to most newsmen. During last summer's convention coverage, for example, George McGovern was repeatedly characterized as a likable but conniving bumbler and President Nixon as an unlovable but efficient manager running a closed shop. According to Richard Dougherty, Senator McGovern's press secretary during the 1972 campaign, the press never rests until it has found a convenient tag. Then, unconsciously, it edits its coverage to fit this preconception. Is this a legitimate charge?

Cronkite: God, it worries me more than almost any other single factor. It's a habit that I justify to myself because of the time element. You quickly label a man as a leftist or a conservative or something, because every time you mention him, it's almost impossible to explain precisely where he stands on various issues. But labeling disturbs me at every level of our society. We all have a tendency to do it.

Playboy: Doesn't the fact that the same labels tend to be applied to the same people by all the networks—as well as by the print media—imply that there's a bit too much editorial camp-following in the news business?

Cronkite: Don't forget that in political campaigns those who cover a candidate are all living and working together in the greatest intimacy. I mean, there's a lot of cross-fertilization, and these reporters become kind of a touchstone for the rest of the press. That's inevitable, I suppose. But the idea that there's some elitist liberal Eastern establishment policy line is absolutely mad.

Playboy: To the extent that there is at least a tendency to group-think, what do you think the effect of it is?

Cronkite: To the extent that there *is* an effect, I think it's to be deplored. But I don't know that there's anything you can do about it. We're perhaps all conditioned by similar backgrounds, similar experiences. And you'll find, I think, that if we do, indeed, react in a knee-jerk fashion to news stimuli, so do people in every other business.

Playboy: Isn't that the essence of Vice-President Agnew's charge—that newsmen are conditioned by similar backgrounds and experiences?

Cronkite: Again, he's thinking of the elitist Eastern establishment as our common background and experience. I'm thinking about covering the police station in Louisiana in Howard K. Smith's case or North Carolina in David Brinkley's case. That's the kind of experience I'm talking about—experience of America, experience with the people, experience with the burgeoning and overburdening bureaucracy, experience with those who have a tough shake in life. That's the experience I'm talking about.

Playboy: How do you feel about advocacy journalism—the kind of reporting that puts the sort of experience you mention in the service of a newsman's own personal convictions? Is it possible that there isn't enough of this—rather than too much, as Agnew claims—in the media?

Cronkite: I think that in seeking truth you have to get both sides of a story. In fact, I don't merely think, I *insist* that we present both sides of a story. It's perfectly all right to have first-person journalism; I'm all for muckraking journalism; I'm all for the sidebar, the eyewitness story, the impression piece. But the basic function of the press has to be the presentation of all the facts on which the story is based. There are no pros and cons as far as the press is concerned. There shouldn't be. There are only the facts. Advocacy is all right in special columns. But how the hell are you going to give people the basis on which to advocate something if you don't present the facts to them? If you go only for advocacy journalism, you're really assuming unto yourself a privilege that was never intended anywhere in the definition of a free press.

Playboy: In reporting an official statement that a newsman knows to be patently untrue, do you think that in the interest of presenting both sides of a story, he should feel an obligation to report also that it's a lie?

Cronkite: I think you're probably obligated to report it—but you're also obligated to check the records first.

Playboy: Can you think of a story in which a man who's been quoted has been shown by independent checking to be untruthful?

Cronkite: Yes, that happens quite frequently. For example, there's a Pentagon announcement about the purchase of a new weapons system that's going to cost so much, and we point out that development costs have already run a lot more than that. This is a routine part of reporting.

Playboy: The job of corroborating the facts in a story can be complicated by a newsman's closeness with his source. Jack Anderson and others say that most newsmen in Washington are so dependent on high-level sources, so impressed with being able to associate with the mighty, that they become their unwitting allies. Is this a fair appraisal of the Washington press corps?

Cronkite: I think it's a serious problem, and not just for the Washington press corps. It's a serious problem for the county-court reporter, the police reporter in Sioux City or anywhere else. How close do you get to your sources? It's a hard decision. In order to protect your objectivity, you can turn your back on them socially; but by so doing, you can also cut yourself off from inside information.

Playboy: Anderson insists that sources tell him things because they're afraid not to.

Cronkite: Well, I think that's right. But I don't approve of everything Anderson does and everything he prints. He often has inadequate evidence. I think he takes the minor episodes and blows them into what appear to be major scandals. On the other hand, he's the one guy who's doing a consistent job of investigative journalism, at least on a daily basis in Washington. And I do agree with him that there are many reporters in Washington who deliberately seek social favors, to the considerable detriment of their reporting. But there are also a lot of lazy reporters who aren't high enough on the social scale, the impact scale, to get the big invitations. They simply find it's a lot easier to take the handouts and rewrite them than it is to do a day's work.

Playboy: Another problem in Washington news coverage seems to handicap broadcast reporters more than the print press. The networks don't seem willing to spend the money for specialist reporters, and their general newsmen are shunted from story to story, never staying on one for a long time. Doesn't that handicap you?

Cronkite: Yes, there's no question about it. It's part of our basic problem in network news, something the public should be made aware of. The problem is lack of personnel. The reporters we have in the field are the best in the business, I think; most of them are graduates of newspapers and news services, and they are superb. But we don't have enough of them, and we're never going to — simply because we don't have the outlet for them. I mean, we may have room on the *Evening News* for maybe three or four reports oncamera and a total of 10, 12 or 15 other items that are going to run 15 to 20 seconds each. It's pretty hard in those circumstances to economically justify maintaining a staff equivalent to that of the AP or UPI.

In television, we can introduce the public to the people who make the news. We can introduce them to the places where the news is made. And we can give them a bulletin service. In those three particulars, we can beat any other news medium. But for the in-depth reporting that's required for an individual to have a reasonably complete knowledge of his world on any given day — of the city and county and state — we can't touch it.

Playboy: There is a famous story that the CBS news director once pasted up your transcript of the *Evening News* onto a dummy of *The New York Times,* and it covered less than the eight columns of the front page.

Cronkite: Yes. The number of words spoken in a half-hour evening-news broadcast — words spoken by interviewees, interviewers, me, everybody — came out to be the same number of words as occupy two thirds of the front page of the standard newspaper. We are a front-page service. We don't have time to deal with the back pages at all.

Playboy: In recent years, the television press has been criticized not merely for the superficiality with which it reports the news but for actually creating or transforming news events — riots, for example. Do you think that's a valid criticism?

Cronkite: There's a very serious problem with that. Demonstrations have always been staged for the purpose of attracting attention. There's no purpose for a demonstration except to get public attention and — it's hoped — sympathy. Certainly, the demonstrators are going to be where the cameras are. Certainly, they're going to let us know in advance that the demonstration will take place. Certainly, they're hoping for live coverage. Certainly, if you have live coverage, it's going to be a more lively demonstration than if you don't have live coverage. But I don't think that we're responsible for the events. We unquestionably have an influence on them; but so does a newspaper reporter's or a still photographer's presence.

Playboy: But TV camera crews are very conspicuous, whereas a newspaperman can be lost in the crowd.

Cronkite: Lights are the biggest problem. And I guess for that reason the Chicago convention may have been the end of lighted demonstration coverage, because lights attract demonstrators like moths to a flame.

Playboy: Television has been assailed at least as much for its coverage of the Vietnam war as for that of demonstrations against it here at home. Do you think we found out from television — soon enough, at least — what was really going on in Vietnam? In the early war years, network news executives seemed to subscribe to the conventional assumption that American generals and politicians were simply doing what had to be done to preserve freedom, and the war was covered accordingly. It wasn't until long afterward — 1968 and later — that TV newsmen such as yourself began to express doubts about the justness of America's involvement in Indochina. Wasn't this lag in critical reporting one of broadcast news's great failures?

Cronkite: I'm not sure I can give an entirely satisfactory answer. The coverage changed. Yes. It changed. It went through several periods. Let's go back to when American troops were first committed over there in sizable, easily identified units, as opposed to two or three American advisors working with the Vietnamese troops. Up to '65, as our involvement deepened, we were increasing our coverage. We were doing stories on advisors out in the field, and the dangers to them, and the occasional death. But it wasn't a daily flow of combat film. For one thing, we weren't interested in endangering our correspondents to do that kind of thing. But in '65, when we began committing total U.S. units, it was another story. Here were American boys fighting in a war. The news story became these boys at war. If you're going to do that honestly, you're going to have to go up where the blood is flowing. That's where the story is; the story's not back in the base camp. We were taking the war into the homes of America—and that's where it belonged. In a war situation, every American ought to suffer as much as the guy on the front lines. We ought to see this. We ought to be *forced* to see it.

Playboy: But Vietnam wasn't just a visual story. It was a complex story of ideas, of political assumptions, of men's attitudes. To convey an understanding of the war on this level necessitated sophisticated reporting. How high was the journalistic quality of the TV newsmen who went over there in the early years? How about those guys who hung around the press headquarters in Saigon for the so called "five-o'clock follies"—those no-comment news conferences? How long did it take them to realize they had to stop taking handouts and find out what was really going on?

Cronkite: I don't think there was any lag at all. As a matter of fact, I was surprised—and a little annoyed—at reporters during my '65 visit over there. I had gone over believing in what we were doing; I came back concerned because I saw a build-up of forces far greater than our leaders ever told us we were likely to commit. That's when my disillusionment began. But at first, when I arrived, as I say, I was annoyed at the skepticism of the reporters at the press conferences in Saigon. They were accepting nothing at the five o'clock follies. More than seeking information, they were indulging in what I considered self-centered bearbaiting, pleasing their own egos, showing how much they knew. And I was a little offended. I thought they shouldn't betray their extreme youthfulness. Maybe, I thought, they were a little wet behind the ears. I wondered why they didn't just do their jobs, ask the questions and then go on and get the story.

Playboy: Didn't the military have a strong hand over there in directing the flow of news, deciding where a man could go with his camera?

Cronkite: Yes, they did, but they always do in a war situation. And I think that the press ended up getting the truth anyway—and telling it.

Playboy: Well, it wasn't a reporter who uncovered My Lai but a disgruntled soldier, Ronald Ridenhour, who tried for months to peddle his story to the press before *The New York Times* accepted it. There was great resistance on the part of the press to accept his version.

Cronkite: That could very well be, because this sort of story comes to us quite frequently. There are a lot of things that, if we had the manpower and the time and so forth, we could investigate: the letters that come to us about conditions at mental institutions, or in prisons, or the welfare situation, that undoubtedly are true. But as for My Lai, had it come to us first, I don't know precisely how we would have handled it, but I can see where we would have had considerable difficulty in handling it. Here was one soldier's charge; we couldn't have just gone on the air with it. We would have had to go out and spend a tremendous amount of effort to check the thing out. A really overwhelming amount of effort. And we just haven't got the resources to do it.

I think that the attitude of a managing editor, faced with that tip, might very well have been, "God, that sort of thing goes on in all wars. It's probably not as bad as this soldier says it was. As a matter of fact, we've already reported several like that — obviously not as bad as that, but charges that civilians had been shot, and so forth." And just dismissed this story for that reason. My Lai, fortunately, *was* finally uncovered, to the very great credit of Seymour Hersh.

Playboy: You were quoted as saying that if Daniel Ellsberg had brought the Pentagon papers to CBS, you wouldn't have run that story either.

Cronkite: I didn't say that. Somebody else said it, I think. But I'm not sure that it's quite true. I think if he had brought them here, we would have gone to a newspaper and said, "Let's work together on this. Let us summarize them and you present the full text." But the Pentagon papers are a tough one. I don't know that if I were the editor of a newspaper, I would assign a reporter to try to get hold of the secret reports of the Pentagon. In fact, I'm pretty confident I wouldn't.

Playboy: Why not?

Cronkite: Because I think that going in from the outside to get hold of secret papers is legally indefensible. I don't think the press has a right to steal papers.

Playboy: Isn't it just as legally indefensible to print papers stolen by someone else?

Cronkite: No. Once they've come out of the secret files and are in circulation in any way whatsoever, I'd say then that the public is entitled to know whatever anybody else knows. But I don't think an individual is entitled to know what is inside secret files while they're still secret. Please understand, however, that I'm for complete declassification of secret papers. Overclassification is one of the areas in which the Federal Government is terribly culpable. But I think we have to get at it through legal means.

I don't believe we have any right to violate the law. I'm a real old-fashioned guy in that sense: I believe in law and order. I don't like the fact that the phrase has become a code word for bigotry and suppression of civil rights and a lot of other things. I don't believe in that for one damned everloving minute. But if you take the words for what they really mean, I think law and order are the foundation of our society. And I just don't believe that anybody should take it unto himself to violate the law, no matter what good he thinks can be achieved, because you can extend that right up to lynching. Now, what Ellsberg did is for his conscience to work on. I admire tremendously his courage and bravery and his fortitude in doing what he did. But I would never assign a man to do that for CBS.

Playboy: So a public good came from something you oppose in principle.

Cronkite: It's not yet clear that Ellsberg violated the law. The trial is still on as we talk today. Ellsberg, after all, was the *author* of much of this material. He was a participant in it, you know.

Playboy: Whether or not Ellsberg is guilty of a crime, is there never an instance, in your opinion, in which breaking the law could be justifiable? What about civil disobedience as practiced by Martin Luther King?

Cronkite: Clearly, there may come a time when civil disobedience and protest against what is considered an unjust law might be considered proper. I'm inclined to believe, though, that if I had to stand on absolutes, I'd prefer to stand on the absolute of law and order, even in such a case as that. I think there are means in our society to correct injustice, and I don't think that civil disobedience or sticks and stones provide the way to do it.

I'm glad that things have worked out to speed integration in this country — certainly, for 100 years we damn well did far too little — didn't do anything, in fact. I'm glad we've finally gotten off our behinds and gotten going here in the last couple of decades. We have probably been spurred to some degree by the demonstrations that the great Martin Luther King directed. So you've got to say, well, it works on occasion. But I still think the better way would be to do it within the law.

Playboy: The opinions you've just expressed are stronger than any you've ever delivered on the air about this issue — which seems to reflect your views about the importance of remaining an objective reporter. Yet you departed from that policy when you returned from a visit to Vietnam in 1968 and advocated an early negotiated peace in a series of editorials at the end of your nightly newscast. Are you glad you did it?

Cronkite: Glad? I'm not sure. In a lot of people's minds, it put me on a side, categorized me in part of the political spectrum. And I think that's unfortunate. It's a question in my mind now, looking back, weighing the long-term disadvantages with the short-term benefits. When I went over there, I didn't know what I was going to report back, actually. I didn't go over to do a hatchet job. I didn't go over to be anti-Vietnam, to be against American policy. I was leaning that way; I had been very disturbed ever since the '65 build-up. I was particularly disturbed over the lack of candor of the Administration with the American public, about the constant misleading statements as to the prospect of victory — the light-at-the-end-of-the-tunnel stuff. I thought — and I still think — that was the most heinous part of the whole Vietnam adventure. I had also been disturbed about the vast overkill, about what we were doing to the people of Vietnam.

But even then, I was still living with my old feeling of sympathy for the original commitment, in line with Kennedy's promise that "we shall support any friend to assure the success of liberty." Nobody was kidding himself about the nature of the South Vietnamese regime, but we thought we were trying to create conditions that would promote the growth of democracy, give them a right to self-determination. So I went out in '68 still basically believing in our policy but increasingly disenchanted with what we had actually been doing over there ever since '65. Then, after the *Tet* offensive, Johnson and Westmoreland and McNamara were saying we had won a great victory — you know, "Now we've got them; this was their last great effort." And it was clearly untrue. That was what broke my back. That's why I felt I finally had to speak out and advocate a negotiated peace.

Playboy: What do you think was the effect of your editorials?

Cronkite: I think the effect was finally to solidify doubts in a lot of people's minds — to swing some people over to the side of opposition to our continued policy in Vietnam. I must be careful not to be immodest here, but I happen to think it may have had an effect on the Administration itself.

Playboy: On President Johnson?

Cronkite: Yes, although he denied that to me personally. Not just about my reporting but about everybody else's. In fact, in our last conversation, ten days before his death, he went over that ground again, as he did in almost every conversation. It weighed on him very much, apparently. He talked about the *Tet* offensive and he said a lot of people were sure it was *Tet* that really turned him off, and he said it wasn't so and that it wasn't my reports that did it, either.

Playboy: Did Johnson ever confide in you about his feelings on the war? In the course of those last interviews you had with him, did he say anything that contradicted his public statements in office?

Cronkite: No, never. It was one of the disappointments of the interviews we did. I thought, when he was out of office, that he would let his hair down and say, "Well, there were some points where I think we went wrong; there were some things I did that I wish, looking back on it, I hadn't done." But that never happened, either in personal conversation or in the interviews. And I think that's because he didn't entertain any such thoughts. Our private talks were reasonably personal. I'm sure he thought that they were confidential, and therefore there would have been no reason not to say it if he felt it. He was a loquacious man in person, and I believe these feelings would have flowed if he had felt them.

Playboy: Another about-face for you in '68 occurred at the Democratic Convention in Chicago. It seemed almost a coming-out for you in a lot of human ways. It was as though you had gotten fed up with being above the battle. You saw Dan Rather get punched out on the convention floor and you made a reference to thugs. And then you said you felt bad about having said that.

Cronkite: Yes, I did.

Playboy: Do you still?

Cronkite: Yes. I know that outburst kind of makes me more human in the eyes of the public and therefore, perhaps, improves the impression that people may have of me — that I'm not just an automaton sitting there gushing the news each night. But I think that each network ought to have someone who really *is* above the battle. CBS has 24 minutes of news time every evening. I know I could do 22 minutes of news just as objectively as I'm trying to do it now, and then I could put on another hat and for two minutes I could give a scathing editorial opinion, analysis, commentary, whatever you want to call it. It would be right out of the guts and depths of my soul each day, and it probably would be a pretty good piece, I'd like to think. What was revealed about me in those two minutes wouldn't affect the objectivity with which I conducted myself for the 22 other minutes of that program. But I can't for one minute expect anybody else — except, perhaps, another journalist — to believe that.

Playboy: Some critics have discerned traces of editorializing in other facets of your coverage. During the space flights, for example, you were affectionately referred to as "the other astronaut," and your enthusiasm was obvious.

Cronkite: Well, I can see why they would come to that conclusion. I don't fault them for coming to it. I was a space booster; I believed in that program. But I don't think that affected my criticizing the program, which I did on many occasions. I thought they should have gone with an extra Mercury flight, for instance. There were a lot of things in Mercury and Gemini and Apollo — in the matter of equipment and delays and some of the usual hardware problems — that I didn't think were handled right. And I talked about that during the space shots. I didn't ever pull those punches. But that in no way dimmed my excitement over man in space. I think it was the most exciting adventure of our time and probably of centuries; probably since the original explorations of the New World. I have no apologies to make for that.

Now, of course, it's fashionable to criticize all the money that was spent — "We should have used it here on earth" and all that sort of thing — but I still don't think that's right. If you could guarantee that the 24 billion dollars would have been spent on our cities instead of on space, then I would be inclined to agree that the money was perhaps not apportioned in the right fashion. But you know it *wouldn't* have gone to the cities. I think history is finally going to have to make some decisions on this matter. I think that those who are being critical are going to have to eat some words before the whole thing is over, because I think we're going to find that space is terribly valuable to us.

Playboy: On news events such as these, you're not only a correspondent but part of management as well. In fact, your title is managing editor of CBS News. How much editorial responsibility do you have?

Cronkite: It's about like being managing editor of a newspaper. When I assumed that title, some of my friends in the press were critical — not in their columns but they suggested it was some kind of show-business gimmick, a title that had been lifted from the ancient and honorable print media. But when I pointed out what I did, I think I pretty well convinced them it was a sensible title. I participate in making assignments, in the decisions about what will be covered, future programing plans — what we're going to go after and, ultimately, what goes into the program. And I edit the copy. Every word that's said goes through my hands and is usually touched by my hands in some way. I edit almost every piece, rewrite many of them and originally write some of them.

Playboy: If you were to quit tomorrow —

Cronkite: That's a great idea.

Playboy: Would the public get a substantially different picture of the news from CBS?

Cronkite: Not really. I'm not sure, though, that some of the things I eventually hope to accomplish around here would be quite as easily and quickly done by somebody else, because I think I've established a certain degree of credibility with the public and with my employers as to my honesty and integrity. There's a mutual trust there. On that particular score, I may have a value beyond that of the daily broadcaster.

Playboy: Actually, you're not only a network newsman but a TV star. Does that status affect the way you're able to cover a story?

Cronkite: It's a major handicap. There's an advantage to it, quite obviously, in that I can reach people more easily than a less-well-known newsman could. This works around the world, I find. I get in to see heads of state, usually through their American representatives, ambassadors or what not, just because they've seen television coverage. But, on the other hand, just like the camera that appears at the scene of a riot, when I appear I change the nature of the situation. I can't go to a bar and take in an average conversation, because it changes when I'm there: They're talking to the press.

And the same thing is true even when I meet important people. Yesterday a journalist who was doing an interview with a very important person in Washington told me he thought that his interview subject was arrogant and domineering. Well, I haven't seen either of these characteristics in this man, and I said so. My friend said, "Well, he probably *isn't* that way with you. With you, he probably feels he's dealing with an equal, or has some fear of your power, and therefore is much more courteous, much more willing to exchange ideas." And I suppose that's true. But I think if I have enough time, I can break down most barriers. I think if I went back to that hypothetical bar for two or three days in a row, I'd find that I was accepted as a fairly regular fellow and the façade would wither away.

Playboy: How do you feel about the personal side of being a television star? Do you like to be recognized, sign autographs and all that?

Cronkite: Well, the autograph thing is flattering, that's exactly the word for it. But it's exceedingly tiring. It'd be nicer if you could turn it on once every few months, as sort of an ego builder, and then turn it off again. It's not fun to be the center of attention all the time. You know that people's eyes are on you. My wife and I like to dance, and we don't do it very often, but just the other night we were at a big occasion, an opening in New York, and we were Joel Grey's guests. In the early stage of the evening, at the Waldorf, we were dancing; but we suddenly realized, heck, everybody's kind of watching us dance. And that's not fun. I'm not an exhibitionist — at least not quite in that sense. I'd like to be a song-and-dance man; that's my secret ambition, but —

Playboy: Wait a minute. You've always wanted to be a song and dance man?

Cronkite: I've always thought one of the great things in life would be to entertain people with songs and dances and funny sayings. But it's just a fantasy. Another Walter Mitty dream.

Playboy: Has your wife enjoyed the celebrity life?

Cronkite: I think so, to about the same extent I have. That is, I can't deny it's nice getting a good table in a crowded restaurant without a reservation — a few emoluments of that kind. But I think both of us would have liked a more quiet life.

Playboy: How do you escape? What do you do for privacy and enjoyment?

Cronkite: Well, I enjoy totally escapist reading. I duck into historical sea stories. I enjoy the C. S. Forester kind of stuff — and there are 10,000 imitators of Horatio Hornblower who kind of keep me going. It's about a simpler period, a romantic period — strong men doing daring deeds, and a rather simplified moral code — and that makes it rather easy to take. I really enjoy solitude and introspection. That's why I like sailing. I like sitting in the cockpit of my boat at dusk and on into the night, gazing at the stars, thinking of the enormity, the universality of it all. I can get lost in reveries in that regard, both in looking foward to a dreamworld and in looking back to the pleasant times of my own life.

Playboy: Tell us about that dreamworld.

Cronkite: Oh, my dreamworld personally is just to take off on that boat of mine and not have to worry anymore about the affairs of mankind, and about reporting them, and taking the slings and arrows from all sides as we do today, since we can't seem to satisfy anybody. After ten years of it here in this particular spot, it gets tiresome. I'd like to be loved, like everybody else.

Playboy: Do you feel the slings and arrows personally?

Cronkite: Yes, I do. Most of them aren't directed at me personally, but they disturb me deeply anyway. And the criticism comes from both sides. The conservative press picks up the Administration line and hammers that back at us; and the liberal press snaps at us all the time about the things you've been bringing up, quite justifiably: about space, about civil rights, about our coverage of the war. So my dreams are to not have to fight the battles anymore.

My dreams for the world are the same. I get fearful about what the world is coming to. You know, most people are good; there aren't very many really evil people. But there are an awful lot of selfish ones. And this selfishness permeates society. It keeps us from the beauty of where we could go, the road we could travel. Instead of being always on these detours and bumbling along side roads that take us nowhere, we could be on a smooth highway to such a great world if we could just put these self-interests aside for the greatest good of the greatest number. It applies to the industrialist who puts out a product into which he builds obsolescence, and to the guy up in Harlem who throws his garbage out the third-floor window. It's everybody's fault. I just find it hard to understand how man could come so far, how he can be so damn smart and at the same time be so damn stupid.

Playboy: You're not alone in being discouraged with contemporary society; some writers are beginning to call the age we live in "postconstitutional America." They view with particular alarm such trends as the tendency toward unregulated, unlimited surveillance. What's your opinion?

Cronkite: I can't decry it enough. I just don't see how we can live that way. It's not America, and it's not what we believe this country stands for. It's so terrible that I'm convinced there's going to be a great revulsion to it. I think we've come as close as we can to living in a kind of chaotic police state — and I say chaotic because it doesn't have any central headquarters; everybody's doing it. We're living in a state where no one can trust his telephone conversations, nor even his personal conversations in a room, in a bar or anywhere else.

Playboy: Have you ever suspected that your phone was tapped?

Cronkite: Oh, yes. My home phone and the one here at my office. I think anybody in the public eye — even in private business — who believes that his conversations are sacred today is living in a fool's paradise.

Playboy: Would it be fair to describe your position on most issues as middle of the road?

Cronkite: I think it would. I just don't understand hard-shell, doctrinaire, knee-jerk positions. I don't understand people not seeing both sides, not seeing the justice of other people's causes. I have a very difficult time penetrating what motivates such people. I'm speaking now of the particularly militant left as well as the particularly militant right. But I'm also speaking of people in that great center, whom I sometimes despair of when they accept so glibly the condemnation of other factions within our society—whether it's welfare people or the rich.

There are many people in this silent America who are bitter against the rich. We forget that. You know, from my Midwestern background, I know the Archie Bunkers of Kansas City; they're really basically my own family. I know exactly how they felt about all other walks of society, the lower classes as well as the upper. Unless you were a 32nd-degree Mason living on Benton Boulevard in Kansas, City, Missouri, and a white Protestant, there was something a little wrong with you.

Playboy: With that kind of background, where did you get your sense of fairness?

Cronkite: From my parents. My father was a liberal when he was a young man. Though he's basically kind of set in his ways, as older people are inclined to be, he was terribly upset over the treatment of blacks when we moved to Texas. He went down to teach at the University of Texas Dental School in Houston, and also to practice. And the very first crack out of the box, the first social occasion we went to, we were sitting on the porch of this rich sponsor down there, in a fancy section of town—such a fancy section it didn't have alleys—and we ordered ice cream. In those days, nobody had a freezer, so you ordered it from the drugstore. A young black delivery boy brought it over.

There wasn't any alley, as I say, and he parked his motorcycle out in front of the place and walked up the front walk, across the lawn. And this fellow sat, with rage obviously building in him, and watched him come up the walk. When this young man set his foot on the first step of the porch, this fellow leaped out of his chair and dashed across the porch and smacked him right in the middle of the face. He said, "That'll teach you niggers to walk up to a white man's front door." And my father got up and said, "We're leaving." We almost went back to Kansas City. Growing up in the South, one's attitudes are affected quite seriously by such early experiences.

Playboy: Do any other such experiences come to mind?

Cronkite: Well, there was another one that also involved ice cream. This time *I* was the drugstore delivery boy; I did bicycle deliveries and we had a couple of blacks who used motorcycles for more distant orders. They were both great guys. One of them was a particularly close friend of mine—as close as you could be in the environment of Houston at that time. We weren't about to go out together anywhere, but we were good friends at the drugstore and sat out back and pitched pennies and shot crap and a few things like that.

As I say, he was a nice guy, came from a nice family. His mother was a washerwoman, his father was a yardman, but they had great dignity. He had three or four brothers and sisters. Anyway, one night, as he parked his motorcycle and was walking between two houses to deliver some ice cream to the back door, he was *shot* by one of the occupants—the one who hadn't ordered the ice cream. He was listed as a Peeping Tom and the murder was considered justified. Incredible. I mean, this guy was no more a Peeping Tom than I was— maybe less so. Of course, if he'd gone to the front of the house, the guy who ordered the ice cream might have shot him. I almost never got over that case.

Playboy: When did you decide to become a journalist?

Cronkite: About the time I started junior high school, I became the happy victim of childhood Walter Mittyism, and it's never really gone away. *The American Boy* magazine ran a series of short stories on careers. They were fictionalized versions of what people did in life. And there were only two that really fascinated me at that point. One was mining engineering and the other was journalism. Anyway, I started working on the high school paper in Houston and I found that was what I wanted to do. In fact, that's really *all* I wanted to do. I didn't want to go to school anymore. But I did. I worked my way through the University of Texas in Austin as a newspaper reporter and did a little radio. Did a lot of other things, too, such as working in a bookie joint for a while.

Playboy: What was your job there?

Cronkite: Announcer.

Playboy: In a bookie joint?

Cronkite: On the public-address system. When they hired me, they said, "You sit back here in this room, and as the stuff comes over, you read it out over the P.A. system." Well, I'd never been in a bookie joint before, so I gave them the real Graham MacNamee approach on this, describing the running of the race. A mean character ran the place, a guy named Fox, and he looked like one. He came dashing into the room and said, "What the hell you think you're doing? We don't want entertainment, we just want the facts!"

Playboy: Your first critic.

Cronkite: Yeah!

Playboy: When you got out of school, according to your bio, you joined United Press and later covered World War II for them, and among the dispatches you filed was one from the belly of a Flying Fortress during a bombing raid over northern Germany. Under those circumstances, was it good copy?

Cronkite: Well, it had a dramatic lead. Homer Bigart, who was then a correspondent for the *New York Herald Tribune,* and I were at the same base. We were heading for the bomber command headquarters, outside London, to be debriefed after a long day's raid over Germany. We were both tired and I said, "Homer, I think I've got my lead: 'I've just returned from an assignment to hell. A hell at 17,000 feet, a hell of bursting flak and screaming fighter planes.'" I just recited it. I don't know if you knew Homer Bigart, but he stuttered very badly in those days—and he turned to me and put his hand on my arm and said, "Y-y-y-y-y-you wouldn't."

Playboy: Did the experience teach you anything about war?

Cronkite: I didn't need to be taught anything about war. I had already learned about it. But I still didn't understand—and don't understand today—

how men can go to war. It's irrational, it's unbelievable. How can people who call themselves civilized ever take up arms against each other? I don't even understand how civilized people can carry guns.

Playboy: Were you under fire as a correspondent?

Cronkite: Lots. People take a look at my record, you know, and it sounds great. I'm embarrassed when I'm introduced for speeches and somebody takes a CBS handout and reads that part of it, because it makes me sound like some sort of hero: the battle of the North Atlantic, the landing in Africa, the beachhead on D day, dropping with the 101st Airborne, the Battle of the Bulge. Personally, I feel I was an overweening coward in the war. Gee, I was scared to death all the time. I did everything possible to avoid getting into combat. Except the ultimate thing of not doing it. I did it. But the truth is that I did everything only once. It didn't take any great courage to do it once. If you go back and do it a second time — knowing how bad it is — that's courage.

Playboy: After the war, you stayed on in Europe with United Press, finally returning to this country in 1948. Two years later, you joined CBS News in Washington, as a correspondent. Since CBS is a large, competitive organization, how did you manage to rise to your present position there?

Cronkite: I was just plain old lucky to be in the right place at the right time. But I think that to take advantage of luck, you've got to have some ability to do the job. As far as the ability to work oncamera is concerned, that part of it was an absolute accident. I never trained for it; I'm just lucky to have it. Whatever it is, it seems to work. I was also ambitious as a young man and pushed myself along, not to become president of United Press but because I wanted to be where the story was. So I pushed to get where I could go. And I guess the whole thing just built up into a store of experience, and with experience came a certain amount of knowledge.

Playboy: In the years since you've been reporting the news at CBS, we've seen America's belief in its own rightness and invincibility crumble, its moral sense lost, or at least mislaid. Has it been shattering to you — as a man who believes in the system — to see all this happen?

Cronkite: No, not shattering. I'm still sitting here and doing my work; I'm not in a mental institution — although maybe some think I should be. But it *has* eaten at me. Sometimes I think about early retirement, simply to get out of the daily flow of this miserable world we seem to live in. But shattering? I have to say no. I think at times, though, that maybe I'm not as sensitive as I ought to be, that I ought to have gone nuts by now, covering all of this and seeing it firsthand. I sometimes wonder if maybe I'm not really a very deep thinker or a deeply emotional individual.

Playboy: Are you serious about early retirement?

Cronkite: Oh, I don't suppose it'll happen, at least not in the foreseeable future. I've just negotiated a rather lengthy extension of my contract.

Playboy: So you wouldn't have accepted that Democratic Vice-Presidential offer we heard about, had it been made by George McGovern.

Cronkite: No, I don't think so. Well, I don't know. I don't know what I would do with a political opportunity if it actually came down the pike.

Playboy: Would you really have considered it?

Cronkite: Well, if it were seriously tendered—and this is all so hypothetical, because it never was, you know, let's be perfectly honest about it. As I reconstructed it, the McGovern people were sitting around in a meeting and somebody simply said, "Look, I just saw a poll that said Walter Cronkite was the most trusted man in America, what about him?" And I think that's just about as far as it went. Nobody said that there were loud guffaws, but it would have gotten back to me directly if they had gotten any more serious than that. If they *had* gone any further with it, though, they would have uncovered the fact that I'm not a registered Democrat. I'm not a registered anything. I'm a total independent.

Playboy: Do you have any other skeletons in your closet?

Cronkite: Well, I'm just not going to talk about them!

Playboy: Have you ever seen yourself as a statesman?

Cronkite: Well, I must admit I've seen myself as a Senator. I see it in a very romantic way, jousting for justice and that sort of thing, on the floor of the Senate. But I don't know how effective I'd be in the political infighting. And I think we forget how hard public servants work. When you see them in action in Washington, you appreciate that they work awfully hard, long and tough hours. It must also be the most frustrating job in the world, spinning wheels as they do so much of the time. I really wouldn't want to undertake all of that. Far less would I ever want to be President. Even if I were temperamentally suited for the job, which I'm not, I wouldn't regard myself as qualified—except perhaps by good intentions.

Playboy: Do you think Nixon is qualified for the job—temperamentally or professionally?

Cronkite: Well, whether or not I agree with some of the things he's done as President, there's no question that he's had plenty of experience to qualify him for the job. As for his temperament, I think it's regrettable, particularly for a man in his position. I guess I just don't understand a man like Nixon—the completely private man. To stand off and almost hold your hands up and say, "Don't come any closer"—that bothers me in anybody, whether it's President Nixon or my next-door neighbor. It must be terribly sad and lonely to be so aloof, to be unable to throw one's arms around one's fellow man and hug him to you. I think President Nixon would like not to be that way; I think he'd like to be an outgoing, lovable man. But he knows he's not; it's not in his make-up. Somewhere in his genes, he just didn't come out that way. I think it bothers him, and I think it may affect a lot of his thinking.

You understand that I'm doing this analysis from about as remote a position as one can have. As you well know, I'm not exactly one of the inner circle. As a matter of fact, I'm cut off from the White House today, presumably because of my outspokenness about the war and about Administration attacks on freedom of the press. I regret this very much. I'm very sad, at this stage in my professional life—where, rightfully or wrongly, I have acquired a large audience and some prestige—that people in high places aren't inclined to invite me into their groups.

On occasions when I've been with President Nixon—and they've been fairly rare, countable on the fingers of one hand—I've had a tremendous feeling of wanting to reach out to him. I wanted to kind of help him. I wanted to say, "Look, let's let our hair down and talk about these problems." I have no doubt that this man wants to do what's right. But, as I said, I think what he's trying to do in several cases is absolutely dead wrong. I think that the attack on the press is so antithetical to everything that this country stands for that I just can't understand it.

I would love to be able to shut up about all of this. I don't want to stand out here as a spokesman for the free press against the President of the United States and against his Administration. That's not a comfortable thing to have to do. The attacks haven't come from our side, though. We're like the troops in the trench during a cease-fire that's being violated by the other side. You know, if we could just lay down our arms and say, "Come on, the Constitution says we have free speech and a free press, and broadcasting ought to be a part of it; now let's just admit that and acknowledge that this is the way this country has always run, and let's run it that way." Gosh, that would be great.

I just don't understand why the Administration took this position in the first place. The press wasn't that anti-Nixon in '68 or '69. I think most of the liberals in this country would say the press was cozying up to him, if anything. And yet, whammo, this whole explosive attack on the press. It all gets back a little bit, I think, to the President's personality, to his remoteness. He has never been able to sit down with newsmen, put his feet up, get out the bourbon bottle and say, "Come on, gang, let's have a drink; you guys sure laid it into me today." That's the sort of thing that goes on all over Capitol Hill every afternoon. And I think that because President Nixon can't do that, his aloofness grew into coolness, into misunderstanding of the press, and then into antagonism toward the press and eventually into a campaign against it.

Playboy: Why does so much of the public seem to acquiesce in this campaign? Is it something about the times we live in?

Cronkite: I think you put your finger on it right there. It's a revolutionary time and people are never comfortable in a period of revolution. I think they try to regain some sense of security through the use or threat of force. But force isn't the mainstay of our democratic system. Dialog-debate is, and that's regarded with suspicion and indifference by most people at this particular moment in history. I suppose it's only human, when you're backed into a corner in debate, to get mad, to lash out with your fist or to leave the room as a last resort. I think that's what's happening today. Demands for law and order are translated into suppression. As I said before, I believe in law and order, not as a code word but as a keystone—along with freedom and justice—of the democratic process. We've got to stand for law and order. But when the effect of maintaining order is to chip away at the Bill of Rights, to suppress dissent and debate, then I think we're in very serious trouble.

I think these charges by the Administration fall on receptive ears in much of our country, among so many classes of people, because they feel so afraid, so unable to understand, let alone cope with, the tumultuous times we live in, so helpless to hang on to the values they were taught to believe in, so threatened by the revolutionary changes they see going on around them, that they're looking for scapegoats—and the press is a handy one. It's tragic that they can't see the press as the bulwark of their own freedom. I suppose the only reason I keep going, the only reason I haven't been shattered by all this, as I said earlier, is that basically I have hope that it's all going to turn around. In time, I think there'll be a new tolerance, and with it will come a strong resistance to all of these pressures against our liberty.

Playboy: Where will this resistance come from?

Cronkite: I think it'll come from the people. You know, we're shown amazing resilience all these years of the American experience. We go through these dark periods, but eventually we come back into the shining light of day. And I think we'll come back again.

The Present: Issues

The three major network news teams are here to stay although they now have a severe threat — financial cutbacks from the three "outside" corporations which now own them: Capital Cities which owns ABC; General Electric which owns NBC and Tisch interests which now control CBS. Given that, constraints on budgets, foreign correspondents, news crews, bureaus, equipment and development will likely continue at all three networks.

Secondly, the threats from CNN and its 24-hour news operation will continue, and when breaking news occurs, CNN is sometimes in a better position to broadcast continuing stories than are the three major network news operations. If a story occurs in the morning, and CNN has it all day, it's "old news" by the time Brokaw, Jennings and Rather get to it in the evening. Even George Bush has said that in the White House, he gets the news "like everyone else — on CNN."

The final threat is the increasing percentage of American households which are connected to cable. If a household has a 55- (or more) station cable system, chances may be less that the television is turned to one of the three major networks for the evening news.

In the early 1990s, there are striking similarities among all three major anchors. They are older white men, have the same interests, are intensely competitive, and generally have the same outlook on life and how to present the news. And while they have their individual differing images — Dan Rather, the Texas maverick; Peter Jennings, the suave urbane international journalist and Tom Brokaw, the mid-American spokesman, many others, including minority spokespeople and media critics, are increasingly discussing and critiquing the similarity.

Women, blacks and minorities still rank lower economically in broadcast journalism; and while women have risen into selected "second-team" positions, none have yet reached the pinnacle in broadcast news. Blacks and Hispanics remain still further behind women in broadcast journalism, although strong possibilities exist for advancement by blacks and Hispanic journalists in markets where there is a large black or Hispanic population.

News manipulation is still a problem. The *Wall Street Journal* article "Blurred Lines..." examines how CBS's manipulation of facts and situations caused a mini-scandal in broadcast news. The sort of manipulation which is discussed in that article has since been disavowed by the networks, but the temptation to re-create such stories in the future still exists.

Technologically, television has arrived. The availability of satellite "uplinks," of "fly-away" satellite dishes, which can be disassembled, shipped and re-assembled make the world of the 1990s a very small global village. Budgetary problems, sexism, and racial injustices in hiring and staffing remain, as do the grayer problems of news sensitivity and presentation.

"Network News Is:
☐ Dead
☐ Dying
☒ King of the Mountain"

by William J. Small

> *Do "compressed budgets, fallen ratings, the muscle of local stations" and "the appeal of sleaze journalism" add up to the death of network news? William J. Small says no. The death of network news, he implies, is not likely to happen.*

Are the pallbearers gathering to bury network news?

"There is no longer a financial place in the networks for their news organizations," says Robert Wussler, executive corporate vice president of Turner Broadcasting. "It's just a matter of time."

"I'm rather suspicious that network news may be going out of fashion," Rupert Murdoch has said.

Former CBS News President Richard Salant gives a lecture titled, "Network News: Its Future, If Any."

Ernest Leiser, a former executive of CBS News, has written "That's the Way It Was When Network News Died," a fantasy that dates January 10, 1993, as the day network news signs off forever.

Those in the major networks' news divisions often see the present as the worst of times. All three networks changed ownership in the 1980s (General Electric bought NBC, Laurence Tisch of Loews Corporation purchased CBS and Capital Cities bought ABC). Thus only ABC is currently run by people with a broadcast/media background; the others, as Salant has pointed out, come from "jet engines, light bulbs, tobacco and insurance."

New ownership meant a new look at news division budgets. The major networks' news departments, each of whose budgets remained less than $20 million a year in the 1960s and less than $100 million a year through much of the 1970s, were splurging at the rate of $300 million a year each by the middle of this decade. Cutting budgets was overdue—but it hurt, nevertheless.

ABC News' downsizing of staff and expenses was subtle enough to avoid provoking the headlines that attended the later slashes by CBS and NBC. CBS

William J. Small, former president of NBC News and UPI and former vice president of CBS News, is the Felix Larkin professor of communications at Fordham University's Graduate School of Business.

ABC newsman Forrest Sawyer (photo courtesy Capital Cities/ABC, Inc.).

News eliminated one-third of its work force in a 14-month period. NBC News lopped off 300 jobs in two years. Today the network people who survived often appear unhappy and jittery, constantly telling former colleagues, "You don't know how lucky you were to get out when you did."

Network news employees have also become defensive about their product, accepting Walter Cronkite's devaluation of prime-time news as "a headline service." Their loss of confidence manifests itself in arguments over the proper balance for their programs of hard and soft news, investigative reports and analytical segments. In the general malaise of the past five years, all three networks replaced the executive producers of their evening news programs.

The major networks' monopoly on national and world news is a shattered memory. Not only is CNN providing a solid 24-hour news service, but local stations have access every day to dozens of stories from around the world via satellite services, syndicated feeds and regional exchanges. "The sky is full of stuff," says the news director of a network-owned station. "We just take it down from the satellites. We could do a network newscast any time we wanted."

Frank Magid, the ubiquitous local-news consultant, says stations are privately discussing the possibility of dropping Rather, Jennings and Brokaw in favor of their local anchors. If that happens, Magid says, it could trigger a stampede. But the audience hemorrhage weakening the networks is also affecting affiliates, which are cutting their own news budgets.

The conspicuously flourishing branch of broadcast "journalism" is tabloid TV, Geraldo Rivera's domain. In the past, network news departments disdained that variety of news as beneath their professional and ethical standards.

ABC correspondent Jeff Greenfield, speaking to the Radio-Television News Directors Association last December, urged his audience to reject these "video barbarians." Rivera fired back in the *New York Times,* calling Greenfield "macho-phobic" and suggesting that Rivera's high ratings show his audience "is not a lunatic fringe.... It is America and it is watching."

The network news departments, contemptuous as they may be of the "barbarians," cannot be unaware of their parent companies' hunger for ratings. NBC aired Rivera's high-scoring two-hour program on Satanism. And, according to *Business Week,* some former NBC executives claim that General Electric Chief Executive John F. Welch, Jr., and NBC President Robert C. Wright have discussed one way to increase the audience for NBC specials: bring in Rivera and Morton Downey, Jr., as hosts.

It's no wonder that during the same week last October both *Time* and *Newsweek* claimed the networks were tottering at the brink. They are, said *Time,* "sick and fighting for survival." *Newsweek* cited prophecies that network news will be a "mere memory" by the year 2000.

But even all of this taken together — the compressed budgets, the fallen ratings, the muscle of local stations, the appeal of sleaze journalism — does not add up to the imminent death, or even the critical illness, of network news. "Decline and fall" is a catchy phrase. But "decline and recovery" is far more likely in this case. Network news may not be as powerful in the 1990s as it was in the past. The evidence is nevertheless compelling that ABC News, CBS News and NBC News will remain the three most potent American news organizations well into the next century.

The video barbarians have not gained a foothold in network news. All three networks are blessed with exceptional groups of talented journalists. As Salant said early last year, "On its best days, the evening news is brilliant; on its good days, which are more common than its bad days, it is surprisingly informative."

The quality is personified by the anchors, Peter Jennings, Dan Rather and Tom Brokaw, all serious and seasoned journalists. Gone is the tendency of past decades toward one-network dominance based on the Huntley-Brinkley team or on national idol Walter Cronkite. The scene today is one of hot, healthy worldwide competition among three closely matched teams of reporters, producers and anchors.

The parent organizations, the networks themselves, are not dying either. Granted, their combined share of prime-time audience has fallen from 90-plus percent to about 70 percent and continues to drop. But the rate of decline is slowing, and even if it levels off at 63 percent (as CBS projects) or lower, it will still be the largest mass audience known to man, delivered at the lowest cost-per-thousand.

Moreover, each network evening newscast has a far larger audience per appearance than any newspaper or news-magazine. Indeed, no daily newspaper's weekday circulation comes close to the viewership of a weeknight network newscast. The *Wall Street Journal's* circulation—the largest in the country—is less than two million. *USA Today's* paid circulation is about 1.33 million, and only three other dailies (the New York *Daily News,* the *Los Angeles Times* and the *New York Times*) have circulations that exceed one million. In contrast, the top-rated network newscast in the last quarter of 1988—Rather's on CBS—reached nearly 9.7 million homes. ABC, slightly behind, was reaching more than 9.5 million homes, and NBC was seen in more than nine million. If Rather or Jennings or Brokaw were ever seen by as few people as read the *Wall Street Journal* or even *Time* (circulation: 4.3 million), the anchorman would be replaced.

A great deal of attention is paid to the importance of cable, but even though it reaches more than 55 percent of American homes, it is not a genuinely national service. Much of the United States continues to rely on traditional delivery of television. Bitter fights are under way in areas where cable has taken exclusive rights of sports events—something that especially offends households with no cable service. Further, cable networks, even the most popular ones, are not carried on all cable systems. As for competing with network newscasts, CNN's average prime-time audience in the last quarter of 1988 was slightly more than 500,000 homes. PBS's "MacNeil-Lehrer NewsHour" reaches more than three times that number of homes. No daily report, in any medium, matches the size of network television audiences.

While the network news organizations struggle with the new reality of lowered and lowering budgets, there are still good economic arguments for continuing their productions: They remain cheaper than products bought from Hollywood and are wholly owned. Late in 1988, for example, CBS bought four years of baseball rights for $1.1 billion. This price plus production expenses for 12 regular season games, the playoffs and the World Series will end up costing CBS as much or more than running its news division for the next four years. And the news division—with or without budget cuts—will produce many more hours of programming than baseball.

Among the products produced by the three major news divisions are prime-time magazines. CBS currently has three such hours (more than it ever regularly scheduled in the past). ABC has one and plans to introduce at least one more. And though NBC has been unable to come up with a competitive

"20/20" anchor Hugh Downs (photo courtesy Capital Cities/ABC, Inc.).

and lasting prime-time news-magazine despite many attempts over the last 10 years, it is still trying.

The pot of gold at the end of the news-magazine rainbow is a moneymaker with large audiences, such as ABC's "20/20" or CBS's "60 Minutes." The latter is a miracle in terms of audience size, longevity and profitability. The most expensive of all magazines to produce, "60 Minutes" still permits its producer, Don Hewitt, to publicly claim, "I have a show that makes $70 million a year for the network."

Hewitt loves to stir up controversy. At one point he advocated replacing the current network news with pay-per-view, at 50 cents a day, which he thinks would produce up to $900 million a year and leave half of that behind as profit. He has also recommended that networks leave actual newscasts to their affiliates and become television wire services.

It might be more difficult than Hewitt thinks to get five million homes to cough up $182.50 a year to provide that $900 million, even if they could receive newscasts, "Nightline," "Frontline," "60 Minutes" and documentaries, as Hewitt suggests. Furthermore, affiliates are unlikely to provide enough income for his other suggestion: a network-produced electronic AP. That could cost some $200 million a year. As previously noted, plenty of that material is already around—free or cheap—for local stations to pick off the satellites. Consider Hewitt's alternatives and one must conclude that network news, as we know it, will be around for a long time, no matter the economic pinch.

One reason for maintaining the current setup is prestige. Some of the networks' new presiding officers may not feel—as the Stantons, Paleys, Kintners and others did in an earlier era—that news is, as CBS executives often put it, the "crown jewel" of the networks. They do, however, recognize the prestige that comes with a great news organization.

Affiliates share their networks' pride in having an important, national news service. The major news anchors have always been the symbols of their networks (only Johnny Carson's identification with NBC approaches that kind of synonymy). The news figures embody the most important public service the networks provide.

In a little-publicized 1986 study by NBC ("The News Mission Study: Viewer Attitudes and Beliefs About Network and Local Newscasts"), an overwhelming percentage of television viewers said they would turn to networks over local newscasts for major news events, for the most knowledgeable and experienced newscasters and for the most in-depth news. In percentages running to the eighties, they also thought the networks were the proper place to turn for national and world news.

NBC research anticipates neither a change in this nor in the public's desire for separate network and local news to continue. Indeed, one top NBC researcher says that local newsrooms, feeling the budgetary squeeze that networks are going through, are cutting back from long-form, two-hour-or-so newscasts. He adds that the unfulfilled dream of network news executives, a one-hour network newscast, might be realized in the early 1990s because affiliates are demanding more network news service to ease the burden of their growing costs. Such speculation may go against the common wisdom, yet rising local costs are evoking new thoughts about old and even dead ideas.

Even the affiliates of Rupert Murdoch's Fox Television network now express interest in a national newscast, according to published reports. Originally, Murdoch planned none.

There is also the question of Washington. Networks worry, as all corporate giants do, about the impact the federal government has on their business. But despite criticism from the White House and members of Congress, Washington does recognize the influence and importance of network news. When a network argues with Washington for things it wants to happen and, more often, against things it doesn't want to happen, it wraps itself in its public service image. No contribution to the good of the republic is more visible than news coverage. To abandon national news would be to discover quickly its significance to the federal establishment. Anyone who has "worked" Washington knows how true that is.

There is even a new international constituency. Network newscasts and CNN now appear in many places overseas, notably in upscale hotel rooms. The "Today" show is seen at midnight in Australia. Morning broadcasts in France, Italy and Japan carry Dan Rather. While it hasn't yet added much to the bottom line, U.S. network news already reaches an international elite of businesspeople, officials, journalists and other opinion makers. This international recognition and demand adds to the prestige and power of the American commercial networks.

ABC Chairman Thomas Murphy has said, "If we're not in the news business, we might as well be a Hollywood studio." ABC *is* in the news business: It ended 1988 with healthy news ratings and four hourlong documentaries on "Burning Questions" that the nation faces.

Despite the problems of surviving the worst of times with no clear vision of the best of times approaching, it is far too early to write off the news organizations of ABC, CBS or NBC. The sky may be "full of stuff" but, among the news organizations contributing to that traffic, the commercial networks will almost certainly be the heavyweights for the next decade and quite possibly much longer.

"The Anchors: Who They Are; What They Do; The Tests They Face"
by Alex S. Jones

"The networks demand that an anchor be the network's premier showman, top editor and star, symbol of news excellence and the network's single most important living logo." — Alex S. Jones

Alex S. Jones is a reporter for The New York Times, *specializing in coverage of the press.*

Each weeknight, 38 million Americans watch one of the network evening news programs—22 minutes of news and eight minutes of commericals. In this brief envelope of time three men—Dan Rather, Tom Brokaw and Peter Jennings—present the world to a vast audience in a communication so intimate that it leads strangers to greet them automatically as Dan, Tom and Peter. In their role as anchors of the network evening news, the three have become not only celebrities equal to any in Hollywood, but also the nation's best-known journalists, who have come to symbolize continuity and order in the face of sometimes shattering news events. Like town criers, the anchors offer proof each night that "the world's still here and there's going to be another day," said Richard S. Salant, president of CBS News for 16 years, until 1979. While the world the anchors present is often graphically violent, the anchors themselves are reasoned and calm, and the three shows usually lighten the report with something upbeat or heartwarming. "They want it to be a reassuring view of the world," said Les Brown, editor in chief of *Channels* magazine, which covers the electronic media.

But as they go about their job of crafting the nightly news, they are doing so in a television world that is in unprecedented tumult. This summer's extremely close viewership ratings for "CBS Evening News with Dan Rather," "NBC Nightly News with Tom Brokaw" and "ABC's World News Tonight with Peter Jennings"—the ratings are so close that the differences are statistically negligible—have transformed the normally spirited competition among the shows into something fiercer. "It's trench warfare," said Van Gordon Sauter, president of CBS News. "There's everything out there but mustard gas."

The anchors and their programs are caught up in an environment of change that goes far beyond their struggle with each other for ratings. Interviews with the anchors, corporate and news executives, journalists, academics, television research specialists and financial analysts specializing in television paint a picture of the three anchors and their shows in a ferment of transition. New corporate ownership, new competition from cable and independent television as well as the networks' own affiliates and new technologies are exerting enormous pressures, including economic ones such as those that resulted in the dismissal ten days ago of 70 CBS employees. In this supercharged atmosphere, the anchor is the key weapon in the war for journalistic respect and ratings supremacy.

While the anchor's job has always included a bit of showmanship, the role today encompasses conflicts that previous anchors were largely spared. The networks demand that an anchor be the networks' premier journalist and principal showman, top editor and star, symbol of news excellence and the network's single most important living logo. Despite his overwhelming ratings, Bill Cosby is not NBC, Tom Brokaw is NBC.

But who, in a corporate sense, are NBC, CBS and ABC? After decades of consistent ownership and management, all three networks have experienced upheavals in the last year that have raised new questions about how the networks will be operated in the years to come. NBC and its parent, RCA, were officially acquired in June by General Electric; ABC this year became part of Capital Cities, a communications conglomerate; and, in an effort to ward off

Peter Jennings, anchor and senior editor of "World News Tonight with Peter Jennings" (photo courtesy Capital Cities/ABC, Inc.).

unwelcome takeover attempts such as that by Ted Turner, CBS has allied itself with Laurence Tisch, chairman of the Loews Corporation, who now owns 19.7 percent of the company's stock.

Historically, the networks' news coverage has been driven by a desire for prestige as well as concern for profit. But the cost-consciousness among the corporations that now own the networks has prompted cuts to news staffs and, some say, threatens quality. Among news organizations at all three networks there is anxiety about the ultimate impact of the recent takeovers, or the fear of takeovers, and apprehension that the new corporate leadership may eventually include the independence of the news.

Change wrought by technology—particularly readily available satellite transmission—is another of the principal pressures the anchors and their programs face. Local stations now have the ability to cover national and international news, and this has placed them in competition for the first time with the network news shows. There is also new pressure from competing organizations such as Ted Turner's Cable News Network and potential competition from the fourth commercial broadcast network Rupert Murdoch is attempting to assemble. As a result, all three networks are struggling to redefine their shows to make them somehow unique.

Though ratings pressure has always been present, the close competition among the news shows has created what Dan Rather describes as a "ratings madness" that some fear could eventually make news judgment second to ratings success. With outside competition growing, the average viewership of the three network shows combined dropped nearly 18 percent from 1979 to 1984, according to the A.C. Nielsen Company. A rebound in 1985 brought the decline to about 13 percent, but this June's ratings were lower than last year's. Consequently, the agenda-setting role of the nightly news is being questioned and its impact is being challenged by studies that argue that, contrary to what the television industry has long claimed, television is not the main source of most Americans' news. In fact, new research suggests that television news adds little if anything to the body of information people draw from many sources.

Amid all these pressures, the evolution of the nightly news is taking place on two fronts—journalistic and commercial—so thoroughly intertwined that those involved have difficulty separating one from the other. Though all news organizations, including newspapers, must wrestle with maintaining an independent journalistic voice within the context of a business, nowhere are news reporting and news marketing merged as thoroughly as they are in television.

"People in television news are in a tear," said David W. Burke, executive vice president of ABC News. "Good, sound, professional journalism is on one side of the tear. On the other is the method by which we package and deliver material. Some people consider this show business. I don't."

The conflict between journalism and entertainment has never been greater than now for hegemony of the dinner-hour news, the flagship newscast where both millions of dollars in advertising revenue and the networks' pride as news organizations are at stake.

Peter Jennings and William E. Lord, executive producer of ABC's "World News Tonight," along with others, were planning future segments for the broadcast in Mr. Jennings' office in the ABC News headquarters on West 66th Street, near Central Park. "Give away the piece," Mr. Jennings said, meaning that a videotaped news feature that had languished on the shelf for several weeks would be offered to another ABC show, "Good Morning America," or be used on a weekend news program, but would not be aired on "World News Tonight."

Mr. Jennings and Mr. Lord spend most of every day following the news and discussing what should be on "World News Tonight," where a segment should come in the broadcast, how long it should be, and what points it should make. A long segment is over two minutes. An extraordinarily long segment

"The Anchors..." 103

approaches four minutes. Each minute represents about 100 spoken words, which means that the total number of words on a newscast would fill a bit more than half of a typical newspaper page.

Later in the day, the conversation turned to what should be dropped, as "World News Tonight" cannot be expanded to accommodate a heavy news day. If they disagree, Mr. Lord has the final say, but Mr. Jennings' views carry a great deal of weight and, in network television news, an executive producer who does not generally see things the same way as the anchorman is likely to find himself with a new job.

At the Rockefeller Center offices of NBC News and at the CBS News headquarters on West 57th Street, Tom Brokaw and Dan Rather are engaged in the same kind of exchange with their executive producers and staffs. At all three organizations, the competition is never far from anyone's mind.

In their anchors, the three networks have sought a combination of journalistic expertise and mass appeal. Each anchor takes a leading role in crafting his program. Mr. Rather and Mr. Brokaw are managing editors of their broadcasts. Mr. Jennings is senior editor of his, and all three take their titles extremely seriously. Both Mr. Rather and Mr. Brokaw seem to have a veto power over their broadcasts that goes beyond Mr. Jennings's control, but the difference is a subtle one and all three wield enormous power.

The anchors are strikingly similar — perhaps too similar if diversity is a virtue. All three are middle-aged Anglo-Saxon male Protestants. Mr. Rather is 54 years old, Mr. Jennings will be 48 tomorrow and Mr. Brokaw is 46. All have close ties to wives and children and live in uptown Manhattan apartments. All are attractive and have the polished look of men who are extra attentive to their appearance. They appear to share basic middle-class values such as sympathy for the average citizen, a taste for hard work and concern about the world their children will inherit. Their journalistic skills would make them a welcome addition to any news organization. Each says he has considerable respect for his rivals. All are fiercely competitive, both as reporters and as anchormen.

They bristle at the notion that their job is, as Mr. Brokaw says, "to put on makeup and read out loud." But the comparison to show-business celebrities is inevitable. All three have been at the center of advertising and promotional campaigns attempting to boost the image and popularity of the dinner-hour news by promoting the anchors as, in essence, stars of the shows. This promotional effort did not include posing together for a photograph for this article; Mr. Rather declined, though Mr. Brokaw and Mr. Jennings were willing.

All three command star salaries. None of the networks will disclose figures, but officials who asked not to be identified said that Mr. Rather earns about $2.5 million a year; Mr. Brokaw, about $1.8 million; and Mr. Jennings, about $900,000. The greater salaries for Mr. Rather and Mr. Brokaw reflect inner-network bidding wars for their services in the early 1980s.

Despite their similarities, they are also quite different men with different styles in many respects, and though some elements of their personalities are reflected in their broadcasts, some others are carefully kept out.

Peter Jennings is a self-described "weeper," whose eyes can well up as he describes the memorial service for the astronauts killed months earlier in the shuttle explosion. He makes an enormous effort not to cry on the air. He is the only smoker of the three, and sometimes takes a drag on a cigarette while off-camera. Mr. Jennings is a Canadian who says he plans to become an American citizen when eligible in two years. Canada occasionally comes through when he says certain words, such as house, which in his mouth rhymes with loose.

Admirers of Mr. Jennings frequently say that he seems urbane and sophisticated, the most thoughtful of the anchors, although those who do not like his style say it is a bit facile and glib. "World News Tonight" is considered at its best with fast-breaking foreign stories, such as the TWA hostage crisis, when Mr. Jennings's experience as a foreign correspondent seems to give him an edge.

Mr. Jennings seems both pleased and somewhat awed by his ratings success—for decades, ABC's nightly news lagged behind the other networks'—since he became sole anchor three years ago. "When they hired me for this job, I don't think they had any idea whether I would succeed," he says. "I tend to feel the weight of social consciousness a good deal more than three years ago. When you've done the Challenger broadcast and seen what power this electronic beast has, it affects you. Hopefully, it makes you more modest." He says that his attitude toward reporting has been colored by his limited education—he finished the tenth grade in Canada—and his years as a reporter in the Middle East, where he concluded that most issues were inevitably many-sided. He also says his father, who was a journalist, pounded away at fairness. He says that these influences make him cautious about assuming a strong point of view in his newscast, though he doesn't shrink from injecting his perspective when he feels he has special knowledge, such as with subjects like the Middle East and South Africa, where he also worked as a reporter for ABC.

Mr. Jennings describes himself as an internationalist who views the world as a global village. This orientation is reflected in "World News Tonight," which devotes more time than its competitors to international news—67 percent of its average broadcast, according to a recent study of the content of the shows by Leslie K. Davis of the University of Massachusetts and James Smith of the State University of New York at New Paltz. Though all three broadcasts devote over half of their time to international news, CBS gives it the least attention. Mr. Rather's show reflects his greater preoccupation with regional issues, and Mr. Brokaw steers a course between the two.

In each case, the content also reflects the audience of the shows. Mr. Jennings tends to be more popular in large cities while Mr. Rather has strength in small towns, and Mr. Brokaw's audience touches both. The ratings race is so tight that during the second week in July, all three shows were tied, each drawing a 22 percent share of the television audience for the time period, according to the A.C. Nielsen Company. The rest of the audience was claimed by the "MacNeil/Lehrer NewsHour" on the Public Broadcasting Service or, in most cases, syndicated reruns of entertainment shows such as "M*A*S*H."

Rather is a Texan who came up through the ranks at CBS and worked for many years as a top correspondent in Vietnam and at the White House and as an investigative reporter for "60 Minutes." He offers a sense of passion in his broadcasts, and his admirers often say his program is the most sincere and human. His detractors say Mr. Rather's passion is overdone, the emotion sometimes seeming calculated. According to the people he works with, his charged delivery is an accurate reflection of the man, and he is encouraged to be as passionate as feels natural. Mr. Rather is a student of oratory, and says that the television evangelist Jimmy Swaggart, who frequently attacks the three anchors, may be the most effective speaker in the country. Tom Bettag, who recently became executive producer of "CBS Evening News," says that the show seemed to be drifting earlier this year and was somewhat unfocused, in large part because too much time was spent anxiously watching what the other anchors were doing as they cut into Mr. Rather's ratings lead. The broadcast, he says, now has a sharper focus on significant news, is shifting away from frothier subjects, and is giving full rein to Mr. Rather's intensity, which Mr. Bettag says looked somewhat strained earlier this year. News executives at CBS note that Mr. Rather has been found to be the most trusted anchorman in various surveys.

When Mr. Rather contemplates the meaning of his job, he talks with a zealot's fervor about stewardship of a CBS news tradition. Prominently displayed outside the door of Mr. Rather's office is a picture of Edward R. Murrow, the pioneer CBS journalist. He is also fascinated by the intimate bond that anchors form—sometimes to the point of delusion—with their audience. He tells how, when he was an anchorman in Houston years ago, an elderly woman who watched him regularly asked him about a new picture she had just acquired through a Sears, Roebuck catalogue. "She asked did I like it better over the mantle in the dining room, or did I like it better where it was in the living room," Mr. Rather recalls.

One day this summer, as he paced the cramped space that serves as both the newsroom and studio for the "CBS Evening News," Mr. Rather was clearly the dominant presence. It is a tense period for Mr. Rather, who has seen his commanding ratings lead dwindle, and there is palpable anxiety among the staff that the slippage could get worse. Wearing both suspenders and a vest, Mr. Rather seemed to reflect the girded-for-battle atmosphere that permeates the newsroom.

"If I err, I probably err with too much zeal," Mr. Rather said. "I don't have anything else to prove to myself. I don't need money. I have more money than I need. But I really care about this place. Right or wrong, I think CBS News is important to U.S. journalism. Insofar as I'm able to influence its staying that way, I want to do so. In my own mind, this place was a lighthouse of standards of what could be. I think it's tougher to do that now."

Mr. Brokaw's credits as a reporter include coverage for NBC of the civil-rights movement and the White House, but his many years as host of the "Today" show have forced him to contend with the impression that his journalism background is not as rigorous as that of Mr. Rather and Mr. Jennings. He takes pains to make his delivery calm and unemotional, with occasional wry, sardonic humor. Mr. Brokaw's fans find his presentation authoritative, smooth and intelligent, while to his critics his resolute steadiness and deadpan delivery tend to make the broadcast flat. Mr. Brokaw says he is uncomfortable when asked to discuss the meaning of what he does. "I don't get up in the morning and bury my head in my hands," he says, adding: "My instincts are as a reporter. I have a story to tell." In part, the reticence seems to come from an aversion to the flurry of self-promotion that has streamed from NBC in recent months and has centered on Mr. Brokaw. A South Dakotan whose office is spotted with relics and books on the West, Mr. Brokaw comes from a world often suspicious of celebrity. He is quick to lash out at television critics who, he says, make too much of the show-biz side of his job. "I get a little weary of this," he says. "The personality part of television is inescapable. There's one critic who talks about my button nose."

According to William O. Wheatley, Jr., his executive producer, Mr. Brokaw's carefully modulated on-air delivery stems in part from his experience with an interview that appeared in *Mother Jones,* a leftwing magazine, in 1983, in which he described his personal politics, which — like the other anchors' — are basically centrist, but seem somewhat more liberal. Mr. Brokaw has said that the interview was a mistake and that he takes care to keep his personal opinions out of the broadcast. But, as with the other anchors, his views sometimes become apparent. For instance, he does little to hide his distaste for the near-adoration many Americans display for English royalty, which he considers to be contrary to America's democratic traditions.

At times, Mr. Brokaw and Mr. Wheatley disagree on some aspect of the show. "We close the door and work it out," Mr. Brokaw says. "I'm not given to hysterics, but I have very strong feelings. When we honestly don't see eye to eye, we work it out among ourselves. Sometimes I prevail, sometimes Bill prevails. But it is not by sheer muscle that I prevail. Nor does he prevail because of my lack of interest. Anchormen have lots of weight, and you have to be sure you don't throw it around."

The pace becomes frenetic in the cramped NBC newsroom as air-time nears. On one relatively calm news day, ten minutes before the show began, Mr. Brokaw was pounding out revised copy on his electric typewriter in the midst of a debate about whether a short item about a Supreme Court decision should be rewritten to make it clearer. It wasn't, and this was later judged a mistake. At 6:22 P.M., Mr. Brokaw pushed back his chair, put on his jacket, which covered a big turquoise belt buckle he favors, and left the newsroom for the studio from which the show is televised.

Though the public perception of the network newscasts is that the anchors are giving their personal synthesis of the day's events, how much they actually write of what they say can vary greatly from day to day, depending on their interest in various news events and whether they are diverted by addressing conventions of affiliates and other such duties. Mr. Brokaw almost always writes at least the first part of each night's broadcast, and Mr. Jennings writes much of what he says. While Mr. Rather also writes part of his broadcast, he says he does not feel it is particularly important to write the copy himself. All three work with a team of writers who prepare a script that not only conveys information but also is tailored to the style and taste of the anchor. At the very least, the anchors review the script before they go on the air, adding shadings and altering emphasis here and there. In the final moments before the shows

NBC news anchor Tom Brokaw (photo courtesy NBC).

begin, the altered scripts are reviewed by a copy editor to make sure the construction and grammar are proper, then passed to the executive producer for a final look. After a little makeup is applied, the anchors go on the air at 6:30 P.M. and, if there are glitches or late-breaking news, all or part of the show is done a second time at 7 P.M. Usually, however, viewers who see the news at 7 P.M. are mainly watching a videotape of the 6:30 broadcast.

Since the evening network news shows were born in the early 1950s, viewers have watched them change from a 15-minute broadcast focused almost entirely on recapping that day's events to a much more technically sophisticated 30-minute show whose focus is more difficult to define. While the most important of the day's events are still covered, those assembling today's broadcasts say they are seeking a combination of breaking news, background news, coverage of trends, commentary, interviews and light features, all taking maximum advantage of satellite technology and electronic gadgetry to provide the freshest material so that the programs will be entertaining as well as informative.

Despite a popular impression that the shows are very much alike, the Smith-Davis survey found that only about a quarter of the news items they presented were covered by all three programs. About 15 percent of each network's news content was not covered by the others at all.

In the face of new competitive pressure from local stations for national and state coverage, the network shows are increasingly turning to longer, in-depth coverage of fewer news events, and interviews with prominent people. A station in Nebraska now has the ability to cover news in Borneo, transmit it to a satellite using equipment that fits into half a dozen suitcases, and get the signal instantaneously on its own satellite receiver. Goaded by pressure from affiliates who want to include major national and international news in their local broadcasts each afternoon, the networks routinely transmit via satellite portions of the networks' own videotape gathered ostensibly for the network news show—though the networks reserve the best material for themselves. Timothy J. Russert, a vice president of NBC News, says that about 70 percent of those viewing the network evenings news have already watched a local news show which has made the networks acutely aware that many of their viewers have already been exposed to many of the subjects the network news will cover.

Though there is no clear solution to what many network executives call "the redundancy problem," many say that the nightly news of the future will likely be more of a one-man show, with the anchors presenting most of the broadcast while the on-air role for field correspondents will be greatly diminished. In an extremely imitative business, the success of ABC's late-night "Nightline" has been watched with great interest. Ted Koppel, the anchor, dominates the show, which examines one or more timely issues in depth. But there is concern that adapting that format to the nightly news would cause morale to plummet among correspondents, who covet air time, and thus damage the quality of a news organization.

The anchors and other news executives generally agree that the expansion of the network evening news to a one-hour show is extremely unlikely because the local affiliates have been unwilling to give up control of such valuable advertising time. This spring, there were reports that Lawrence K. Grossman, president of NBC News, was interested in creating a so-called "news wheel" in which local stations and network stations would share a longer broadcast, with a period of network news followed by a period of local news. According to many network and local news executives, the idea found little support among the affiliates.

Pressures created by cutbacks of news personnel and intense cost-consciousness have been felt at all three networks, but NBC and ABC seem to have coped with the cuts better than CBS. At CBS, which dropped 120 news positions last year, 70 more employees were dismissed July 17, including the correspondent George Herman, who had been with the organization 42 years, and Don Webster, the CBS Middle East bureau chief, who had been with the network for 25 years. The impact on morale has been devastating, and although the "CBS Evening News" was not affected by the latest cutbacks, Mr. Rather had said before the dismissals were officially announced, "It's hard for me to figure a way our coverage isn't going to suffer some."

Compounding this economic pressure is a concern among many in the news divisions that the new corporate owners will not preserve the traditional hands-off attitude. Top network and corporate executives say they have no intention of impinging on the independence of the news. But the anxiety remains.

And there is a parallel anxiety that the corporate parents will come to view the network nightly news as an advertising vehicle that should put ratings ahead of anything else. Mr. Jennings argues that the ratings battle has sharpened all three news shows, and many news executives say the best strategy for earning higher ratings is a more serious, deeper news show rather than a more frivolous one. But there is wide agreement that if a more sensational news show were successfully launched, it would likely push network news in the same direction. The prime candidate for launching such a show is believed to be Mr. Murdoch's Fox Broadcasting Company, a fourth network of independent stations, and a spokesman at Fox did not rule out such a show in years to come.

The debate about the role of the nightly network news is clouded further by disagreement among news executives — even within the same network — about whether the format is still the agenda-setting vehicle it was when it had a near-monopoly on television coverage of national and international news and when there was not so much competition from other news outlets, such as cable channels, early morning and late night network news and newsbreaks throughout the day, as well as national newspapers and magazines.

According to the recently published *The Main Source: Learning from Television News,* by Mark R. Levy and John P. Robinson, both professors at the University of Maryland, people generally have a basic knowledge of current events that is drawn from a variety of sources, including television, newspapers, magazines, radio and other people, and this level of knowledge is present whether or not people watch television news. It is considerably enhanced, however, by reading newspapers or news magazines, which carry much more information. According to the book, much of which is based on research sponsored by the John and Mary Markle Foundation, viewers of the nightly news comprehend the main points of only about a third of what they see. Though broadcast executives express skepticism about the book's findings, many agree that clarity and context are sometimes lost as the news is compressed to meet time demands, and that concerns about this are coloring the way the nightly news is evolving.

From the public's perspective, the basic question raised by this environment of transition and pressure is whether the nightly news is becoming better or worse.

The anchors — indeed, virtually everyone in television news — insist that the shows are better than ever, and even their most severe critics acknowledge that in some ways they are right. Technological advances, especially worldwide satellite links, have extended the reach and timeliness of the nightly news dramatically. Other electronic innovations, in graphics and special effects, now make the programs more likely to cover abstract subjects such as economics. The shows are more likely to devote more time to fewer subjects, adding depth to the coverage. And the competence of the anchors and their news organizations are not seriously questioned.

110   The Present: Issues

But there have been losses as well. Intense competition and technological innovation have meant that the shows sometimes lose the ability to ponder. Burton Benjamin, who was executive producer of "CBS Evening News with Walter Cronkite" and who says he is an admirer of the present broadcasts, notes that *his* broadcast ended four nights a week with a commentary by Eric Sevareid. Though the current shows all have commentators, ABC and CBS devote much less time to them. The shows almost inevitably end with a crowd-pleasing segment. The use of lengthier segments has meant that breadth of coverage has been sacrificed.

Ongoing criticism from the older generation of television broadcasters and others charges that the nightly news shows have de-emphasized substantive news in favor of "softer" items that are mainly crowd-pleasing and designed to raise ratings. For instance, ABC recently installed "person of the week," a long segment at the end of each Friday's broadcast. Roone Arledge, president of ABC News, says it was created in large part to attract younger viewers, who frequently skip the Friday news in favor of other weekend pursuits. The people profiled have ranged from Speaker of the House Thomas P. (Tip) O'Neill to the pianist Vladimir Horowitz. While Mr. Arledge defends the creation as newsworthy, others have labeled it something else. "You're talking *People* magazine more than you're talking news," sniffs Thomas H. Wyman, chairman and chief executive officer of CBS. Mr. Arledge responds that CBS and ABC do the same sort of thing or worse.

Questions of journalistic judgment have also been raised as a result of the overwhelming competitive climate. For instance, during the race to cover the TWA hostage crisis in Lebanon, Dan Rather's pointed on-air questioning of Nabih Berri, the Moslem leader ostensibly trying to negotiate the release of the hostages, prompted criticism that he had crossed the line dividing journalism from personal diplomacy. This spring, NBC aired an interview with Abul Abbas, the fugitive Palestinian terrorist charged with masterminding the highjacking of the Italian cruise ship *Achille Lauro*. NBC agreed not to say where the interview originated, which drew stinging criticism from government officials and some other news organizations. Both NBC News and CBS News defended what they did as legitimate news coverage.

ABC News drew fire from the other networks and news organizations by limiting access to the ceremony relighting the Statue of Liberty on July 3. ABC had paid $10 million for broadcast rights to the weekend's activities and justified limiting access by arguing that most of the events were entertainment rather than news. But the network installed Peter Jennings to anchor coverage of the entire weekend, blurring his role as a newsman. Mr. Jennings said that he "felt a slight bit of anxiety" about his role.

Despite such incidents, even the most severe critics of the network nightly news shows say that the shows remain within their original framework as serious journalistic outlets. But there remains a concern that the combination of pressures could eventually alter the nightly news into something much less substantial, if more popular and profitable.

"I sometimes fear that I may be the last of my kind of anchorman at CBS," Mr. Rather says. His nightmare, he says, is that the corporations owning the networks will find it easier to deal with more docile anchors than the current crop, with their long journalistic backgrounds and "emotional commitment to the responsibility of the broadcast."

But Mr. Rather adds that he remains an optimist. "If we're about half-smart and a lot lucky, we can keep our standards. I'm not sure we can do so, but I like our chances."

"Anchor Wars"
by Edwin Diamond

How similar are Rather, Jennings and Brokaw as anchors — as journalists? How different are they? And what do these similarities and differences teach us about who they are — and who we are as viewers and as a culture?

"I know a lot of people think I've got the CBS eye tattooed on my ass," Dan Rather says, conceding his public image as a tough, hard-charging tele-journalist. Yet during the day, as he prepares for *The CBS Evening News*, Rather frequently slips out the back door of the CBS Broadcast Center to the playground of the New York City Housing project on West Fifty-sixth Street, taking the air, contemplating life, as immobile as one of the park winos. The real Dan Rather, he says, "simply loves the news."

A few clicks of the dial away from Rather, *ABC's World News Tonight* presents the modish, immaculately groomed Peter Jennings, the very image of the diplomatic correspondent with his English-cut suits and mid-Atlantic diction. Off camera, however, Jennings is tieless, hustling on the phone for stories, dragging on one of the scores of cigarettes he smokes daily, his voice revved up to talk-radio speed. He says he sometimes gets so emotional about stories that he once considered quitting TV "to work for the refugees." His wife, Kati Marton (the third Mrs. Jennings), says the austere man on the screen isn't the man she sees at home.

On *NBC Nightly News*, Tom Brokaw looks like just another pretty face on local TV in, say, San Jose or Phoenix. Around the NBC news room at 30 Rockefeller Plaza, however, a co-worker has rechristened Brokaw "Duncan the Wonder Horse" — in tribute to his prodigious work habits. In his office, Brokaw keeps hand-exercise grips to fight down his tensions; privately, Brokaw is the one with the tattoo, the confrontational style. "I am formed," Brokaw

---

Edwin Diamond is a media critic. He is a frequent contributor to New York *magazine and other publications and is the author of the books:* Good News, Bad News *(M.I.T. Press, 1978),* Sign Off: The Last Days of Television *(M.I.T. Press, 1982) and* The Tin Kazoo *(M.I.T. Press, 1975).*

112 The Present: Issues

says, in what might be considered a reference to one or possibly both of his rivals. "I don't reinvent myself every night."

Who says the camera doesn't lie?

The common perception is that what we see is what we get, that we know *our* anchormen, with their instantly recognizable faces, that we can call them by their first names: Dan, Peter and Tom. Each week night they come into nearly 40 million American households to deliver the news, familiar guests at our hearth: three white, prosperous, middle-aged males—Rather is 55, Jennings, 48, Brokaw, 46—each highly qualified for his work. Even their programs are outwardly similar. After time for commercials is subtracted, each has 22 minutes of stories and the same general rotation of the news—actually, "the olds." Invariably, it's Washington (White House and Congress), War Zones (South Africa and the Middle East), American Heartland (tornadoes, drought, farm foreclosures, 30-car pileups on California highways) and Human or Animal Interest (the boy who fell through the ice, the baby born to the brain-dead mom, Bambi's mother and lost whales).

These rhetorical models have apparently grown so much alike that the viewing public itself gives them almost identical attention. The biggest news about the evening news right now is that the holy writ of the Nielsen ratings shows Rather, Jennings and Brokaw each commanding an audience of about 15 million people, give or take a million or two. Looking at Dan, Peter and Tom and their three evening broadcasts, it's possible to conclude, after Gertrude Stein, that the news is the news is the news.

It's possible, but it would be wrong. In fact, Dan, Peter and Tom, and their programs, are distinct from one another—as distinct as their on-air personas are from the men playing the anchor's role. What we get *isn't* what we see. It's more intriguing. And the audience, subconsciously, knows this. Viewers have read the implicit iconography of the evening news and aligned themselves in accordance with their understanding of the subtext of each man and program. The proof is all there in the ratings books. Demographics never lie.

The iconographic Dan, of course, is country and western, appealing to an older, idealized America of the imagination. Peter is urban, projecting an image with which a more youthful market can identify. Tom positions himself somewhere in between, in the middle—an avatar of suburban values. Together they form a three-way mirror of America that tells us where the country is today—*vide,* the tightened race among the triple demographics of the news. They also tell us where the country is heading tomorrow, as the weight of viewer numbers shifts toward one or another end of the scale.

"I am the keeper of the flame of Ed Murrow, Walter Cronkite and Douglas Edwards."—**Dan Rather.** Television news people pay lip service to Edward R. Murrow as their Founding Father. He's honored for his wartime radio broadcasts ("This ... Is ... London") and his gritty CBS special reports and documentaries. They don't make 'em anymore like the program that took on Senator Joe McCarthy or "Harvest of Shame," the documentary that alerted comfortable viewers to the plight of migrant workers. In fact, they don't make

'em at all; *60 Minutes, 20/20* and the other TV magazine shows normally offer more infotainment than exposé or social consciousness. The network evening news is where the action is now, both for advertising dollars and journalistic prestige. Curiously, Murrow never was a TV news anchor and served only briefly, and poorly, as part of the CBS anchor team during the conventions of the fifties and early sixties. There has been only one proto-anchor, and his name is Walter Cronkite. The word *anchorman,* in fact, was first applied to Cronkite at the 1952 conventions to connote the strongest performer, the man you'd want running the final leg of a relay race.

TV news is divided into two historic periods—the years B.C., Before Cronkite, and the modern era. From the late sixties until he stepped aside in 1981—after a sharp shove—Cronkite presided over the top-rated program. He was, first of all, a consensus figure: he came not only out of a simpler America but also out of the middle of the middle—born in 1916 in St. Joseph, Missouri, the son of a dentist. Neither North nor South, East nor West, rich nor poor. His journalistic training was in the objective mode of the wire services; Murrow hired him from United Press during the war.

Cronkite wasn't always Cronkite. He stumbled badly in the ratings at the 1960 and '64 conventions; the early and mid-sixties belonged instead to NBC's Chet Huntley and David Brinkley. Huntley was a rugged native of the Big Sky country who rode in from a California station and bore a certain physical resemblance to Murrow; Brinkley was from Back East, a Washington reporter who cast a cold eye on politics. The Huntley-Brinkley bicoastal ticket won over the news audience, with Cronkite in the middle distance behind them. ABC, for all practical purposes, was nowhere, a weak, insubstantial news organization with a minuscule constituency: the Almost Broadcasting Company. In 1965, desperate to compete and willing to try anything, ABC put forward a reporter named Peter Jennings as its evening-news anchor. Though Jennings was 26 at the time, he had already worked as an anchor in his native Canada. But the ABC audience, the ABC staff, the ABC affiliates, and the critics, all judged Jennings too young and too pretty for the job; after only two years he was back in the ranks of correspondents.

Cronkite versus Huntley-Brinkley was stage center, ABC the sideshow. Huntley-Brinkley, while not exactly a novelty act, did well enough as long as the news could be lightened up. But by the end of the 1960s, a couple of million people had dialed out NBC and switched to CBS, an unprecedented mass-media movement. The times demanded gravity. A lot of sixties viewers were older folks. News watching, like voting in elections, has traditionally been a middle-aged activity, and CBS's prime-time entertainment schedule appealed to older rural and small-town audiences. This was the era of *The Beverly Hillbillies, Green Acres* and *Hee Haw.* But Cronkite himself also pulled in viewers, for this was also the time of Vietnam abroad and political assassination and racial insurrection at home. Hippies, yippies, strung-out grunts, black rock & rollers, longhairs, women's liberationists—all seemed to be shouting from the screen. Cronkite's modulated, "objective" demeanor calmed the fears of the mainly older, white, male, propertied viewing classes. When the Kennedys and King were shot, when the body bags came home, when the Chicago police

114   The Present: Issues

rioted and when the astronauts got stuck in orbit, it was Cronkite who anchored the nation's emotions in a way Huntley-Brinkley could never quite do. He had authority; in the phrase of Richard Wald, now vice-president of ABC News, Cronkite assumed the form of a paraclete, "a messenger of God." When Cronkite returned from a visit to Vietnam in 1968 and expressed doubt about Lyndon Johnson's war, LBJ concluded that having lost Cronkite, he had lost the country and decided not to run for reelection.

The Cronkite consensus began to come apart as the mass audience became younger and less middle-class and white. The street children and urban rioters of the 1960s joined the settled, TV-watching population of the 1970s. Fred Silverman, the man with the golden gut — his own sensibilities supposedly wired to contemporary pop-cult tastes — was in charge at ABC. His string of highly successful comedy shows and macho action entertainment — *Laverne & Shirley, Happy Days, Starsky and Hutch* — brought younger viewers and especially women to ABC. The popularity of the ABC shows boosted ABC News: at the beginning of the 1970s, less than two-thirds of the 168 ABC-affiliated stations "cleared" the ABC evening news — took the network feed and put it on their air. By the beginning of the 1980s, virtually all of the 200 or so affiliates were clearing it, putting the program on as many "newsstands" as its CBS and NBC counterparts.

By this time, too, the ABC product on the stands had begun to show off a more contemporary look and zippier, computer-generated graphics. Roone Arledge had taken over ABC News. At ABC Sports in the sixties and early seventies, Arledge had helped create the modern TV sports era with instant replays, slo-mo and isolated cameras and honey shots (three-second shots of good-looking women in the stands). He was Captain Success, and he applied the new techniques to ABC News. Bankrolled by Silverman's dollars, Arledge spent money on the news as if it were . . . a sport. The sports division had paid out hundreds of millions for the rights to pro football and the Olympics. What was a million more here or there for on-air news talent?

In the Nixon years, Dan Rather and Tom Brokaw were White House reporters for their networks, each earning no more than $125,000 a year. By 1979, they were both working in New York, Rather for *60 Minutes,* Brokaw for *Today,* each earning perhaps $300,000, when Arledge offered Rather $2 million a year (plus a role in everything at ABC News from anchoring the evening news to hiring and firing staff). Cronkite was earning half that. When Arledge couldn't bag Rather, the sportsman went after Brokaw, who also turned him down. To keep Rather's and Brokaw's loyalty, CBS and NBC had to play — and pay — in Arledge's league. Rather got a pledge that Cronkite would be hoisted as the CBS anchor — and a ten-year contract that guaranteed him nearly $2.5 million. Earlier this year, insiders say, his contract was sweetened again. Rather is now the $3 million-a-year man. Brokaw's Arledge-proof salary is around $1.8 million annually.

"I've learned to live with the money, the celebrity, the criticism. They come with the territory."— Dan Rather. For almost five years, Rather and his *CBS Evening News* have been number one, the program the others have tried to

overtake. He's the front page of CBS News and, like Jennings and Brokaw, is worth every penny of his salary. If his presence can contribute to a shift of just one rating point in the Nielsen numbers, from, say, a 10 to an 11, it can mean as much as $15 million in what CBS can charge advertisers.

Rather doesn't make the first nights, the power meals, the New York scene. He claims to be happiest lunching on a tuna-fish sandwich at the news desk in the Broadcast Center with the evening-news staff, working on the story lineup. His daily prayer is, he says, "God, give me one more day at my work."

Some of this is the kind of "log cabinning" that politicians do: self-serving stories showcasing their modest beginnings, diligent work habits and simple desires. Rather today is a sophisticated journalist who seems to be consciously gearing down his high-intensity persona. A good performer, he's careful not to appear too fast for the room he's working. Yet "the book" on Rather, to borrow a Ratherism, does begin in hardscrabble East Texas. He remembers that Depression-era kids like himself aspired, at most, to be high-school football coaches or airline pilots (in fact, Rather's younger brother is a high-school principal, and his sister is a high-school teacher).

Rather's critics accuse him of constantly redefining himself, pulling on or peeling off sweaters at a tremor in the ratings, changing the color of his hair from black to gray to black again (a charge Rather denies). "Who is that guy inside the suit *anyway*?" asks a CBS colleague. "The one running around here saying, 'I'm Dan Rather.'" Rather says he knows who he is: "I am a reporter who cares about people." In his autobiography, *The Camera Never Blinks,* he describes his father, Irwin "Rags" Rather, as an oil-pipeline worker—a ditch digger—and his mother as a waitress. As a young man, Rather got down into the trenches himself—humbling up still more his humble past.

One of the longstanding indictments of network news—thunder from the left and the right—is that the decision makers are an elite, cut off from "the people," hooked to their closed-circuit communications and their regular morning diets of the *New York Times, Washington Post* and *Wall Street Journal* (more input from people just like them). The state-of-the-art facility deep inside the CBS Broadcast Center where Rather and his producers determine the nightly play of stories is held up as symbolic of their isolation, as are the similar rooms at ABC and NBC across Manhattan. The conference rooms look out on news desks and internal monitors, not the "real world."

But Rather claims to have a different perspective. "If you've come from where I've come from," he says, "standing in a ditch, shovel in hand, working with your back, that's a never-to-be-forgotten experience. No matter how high you rise, you can never get *away* from those formative years. . . ." Then leaning forward, he smiles. "You're thinking to yourself, 'There goes the bullshit part. . . .'" You are, in fact, wondering if Rather is fusing his life with Rags's, but then he adds, "As Henry Kissinger once said, 'And it has the added advantage of being true.'"

There it is: populism with an intellectual face. Not to put too fine a point on it, that's as good a summary as there is of what *The CBS Evening News with Dan Rather* is all about. The CBS broadcast is the People's Republic of Rather. Rather didn't create this state of mind by himself. He had the help of Van

Gordon Sauter, the president of CBS News. When the occasion demands, Sauter can put up his own log cabins. He's also from Small Town, U.S.A. — Middletown, Ohio, no less. His father was a fireman, his mother a saleslady. He went to Ohio University, studied journalism at the University of Missouri, worked on papers in Detroit and Chicago. Sauter knows the territory and when to talk from the heartland. While Arledge is running with the beautiful weekend people in the Hamptons, Sauter says, "I'm fishing in the woods of Connecticut."

When Rather took over the *Evening News* in 1981, and the ratings sagged a bit, it was Sauter who figured out the problem. "Dan was doing the *CBS Evening News — with Walter Cronkite*," he says. CBS's coverage was still Cronkite's straight-ahead wire-service report — headlines, a lot of them from congressional hearings, told with pictures. Rather and Sauter began taking the *Evening News* out of Washington and into the country. They wanted stories for television, built around people and their emotions.

Part of this change was generational, the slaying of the father Cronkite and the older executives who had worked with him and shared his print background. Cronkite wasn't in a hurry to leave, and the memory of the changes still rankles (asked for his opinion of today's CBS news program in a recent *Washington Post* interview, Cronkite expressed admiration for *Entertainment Tonight*). The Rather-Sauter regime promoted producers whose sole experience was in television, who liked video and worked to achieve visual epiphanies or, in Sauter's phrase, "moments." But this change also involved the Reagan eighties gestalt: antigovernment and antipolitics; Miller Time instead of hearings time; This Broadcast's for You evocations of ordinary people's lives; and the community of feelings rather than the parade of authority (including the old authority figure of the anchor).

This doesn't mean the Rather news is an upbeat, Reaganite "shining city on a hill" vision, or the fluff of airhead local news. A few weeks ago, when *The CBS Evening News* reported that USX was shutting down mills and that LTV was going into Chapter 11, Rather quickly moved from the institutional report of Big Steel in trouble to the little people's story of how the closings are affecting one disabled worker, depriving him of medical benefits. "Someone loses his or her job," Rather says, "and I want to show what's being said and felt."

More than 60 years ago, the philosopher George Herbert Mead looked at the newspapers of his day and suggested that there were two models of journalism: informational news based on fact (e.g., Cronkite) and story news intended to create an aesthetic experience and help people relate events to their own lives — the Rather show. "The olds" as much as "the news."

"I can always go back to being a reporter. I'm not too big for it." — Peter Jennings. It's the 3:45 news meeting, and Peter Jennings is going through the *World News Tonight* lineup with seven producers and news editors, six men and one woman; their average age appears to be 35, much like that of a significant percentage of the audience for *World News Tonight*. Bill Lord, the executive producer of *WNT*, is on vacation, and Jennings, who has been the sole anchor for the program since September 1983, is clearly running the meeting.

But even when Lord is there, Jennings (like Rather and Brokaw) still has the anchor's ultimate, though rarely if ever used, power to say, *I don't want to do that piece.*

Jennings and Lord both agree that the toughest workdays are those when there's too much news and those when there's not enough. This day, July 28th, 1986, is shaping up as one of the former; pieces will have to be held, given away (to *Good Morning, America,* for example) or simply killed. Jennings is wired. The producers offer up stories, and he swings hard at them. NASA will be making available a tape transcript of the Challenger crew's last moments—weeks, someone says, after agency officials said no such tape existed. Another producer smells cover-up or, at the least, foul-up. Jennings worries, "Is it too ghoulish? I don't want to be ghoulish." Next: The LTV steel plant in East Chicago is shutting down, but no one can quite place the town. Jennings remembers. It's in Indiana, the old home town of the late Frank Reynolds—before Jennings, ABC's great anchor hope of the post-Cronkite era.

Jennings wants to know, "How sick is Ella Fitzgerald? Do we have a piece ready?" The singer is resting comfortably in the hospital, but it was her heart; an obit should be put together and banked. One producer pitches a yarn about a tiger supposedly loose in the wilds of Pennsylvania. "I can see the picture now," says Jennings. "A bunch of highway patrolmen, guns drawn, peering down the road." No sale. From Washington, the bureau is offering congressional hearings on crack. Jennings makes a prediction: "Not a day will go by for the rest of the year without some politician wanting to get on the air with his statement about a 'crackdown on crack....'" No dissent.

The rest of the meeting goes back and forth on what to do about two features, each qualifying as light show-enders. TV news likes to send the audience off to prime time, and to the advertisers' messages, with a pleasant emotional buzz—the news permitting, naturally. Jennings has to choose between the opening round of the Karpov-Kasparov chess match in London and the story of Mi Dori, the 14-year-old violin prodigy whose remarkable concert with Leonard Bernstein at Tanglewood made the front page of *The New York Times* that morning. The concert was two nights earlier, and no network crews were present. Still worse, the producers are groping to remember the name of the town near Tanglewood. But CBS and NBC read the *Times,* too. Hold the chess piece.

The meeting over, Jennings places a call to Bernstein, rolls copy paper into his Olympia manual, picks up the phone ("Hello! Maestro! How very nice of you to talk to me...") and proceeds to play catch-up on the story, just one more street reporter getting a fill from a news source. Later Jennings puts in some work on his regular Friday-night feature, "Person of the Week," a personality-centered piece intended to engage younger viewers who normally dial out the news on the weekend. "Person" tends to be upbeat, a tribute to national leaders (through the first 17 weeks of the series, only one genuine bad guy made the roster—Jackie Presser of the Teamsters).

That night Jennings leads with the NASA tape, as do Rather and Brokaw. There's a straightfoward piece from Washington on plans for a Reagan-Gorbachev summit, mostly stenographic reporting of official positions. The steel story is also aired, as is a Special Assignment segment on crack by reporter John Quinones. The visual style of this package comes right out of *Miami Vice,* with editing certain to have its greatest impact on what the market researchers call the urban-core audience. There are quick-cut shots of SWAT teams tearing into "crack houses," knocking down doors that are open *anyway;* lots of black and brown people shoved up against the wall or wrestled to the ground; police officials mouthing lines about addict "wildcats" loose in the streets; preposterous statements about New York City having "more crack stops than bus stops." No one challenges the official story. One sequence shows viewers the equipment needed to get in on all the excitement — a Maxwell House coffee can, tin-foil lid, cigarette lighter, crack and you. The whole meringue is topped with a closer shot, in tight, of an eight-year-old, the next crack user, we are to conclude . . . certainly, if he follows the ABCs of it all.

Crack hype infects all three networks, and overall that night's program was not typical. Various content analyses show that *WNT* usually does more foreign news than its rivals. (Predictably, CBS does the fewest foreign pieces, and NBC's international-story content falls in the middle.) The Jennings news reflects the Jennings strengths, and also his basic character, as distinct from his image. Jennings's vaguely Oxonian urbanity is acquired. Though no ditch digger (his father was an executive of the CBC, the Canadian Broadcasting Company), Jennings is a high-school dropout.

Jennings's real school has been the road. After his brief run on the evening news in the mid-1960s, Jennings worked abroad for ABC on and off for the next 15 years. He helped open the ABC office in Beirut — the first American TV news bureau in the Arab world. He interviewed Arafat, covered Khomeini's return to Iran and Sadat's assassination. "Jennings owned the Arab story," according to his friend Av Westin, the veteran ABC News executive. Some American-Jewish groups used to claim that the Arab cause owned Jennings. But the charge is heard less and less now and was ill-founded in the first place.

ABC's rivals hold that Jennings is "too intellectual." Surely, no one would mistake *WNT* for the CBC News, much less *Le Monde.* But Jennings is sensitive to any accusations that the program is not sufficiently "American." His Canadian citizenship doesn't seem to bother his viewers — out of the 900 letters he got after ABC's Liberty Weekend coverage, he says that almost all complimented him and that only three complained about a non-American anchoring the broadcasts. Nevertheless, Jennings works hard cultivating the American beat, just as hard as he works at his Mr. Cool image: "Precisely because I was out of the U.S. for so long, I didn't take anything for a given after I came back." It was Jennings who first suggested a regular American Portrait for *WNT*; Arledge took this basically leaden idea and turned it into the glitzy "Person of the Week."

The early Jennings played James Darren to Sandra Dee: when ABC made him an anchor the first time, it was looking to attract, he acknowledges, a "Gidget-type audience." Abroad, Jennings filled out. After the failed marriages and the glamorous life of a correspondent prowling the world, he now follows a more settled routine with his wife and their two small children in a yup-scale Manhattan apartment. He has circles under his eyes and a developing bald spot at the top of his head (not visible on camera). As Av Westin says, "The sharper edges of the 'Brit' image have been eroded.... He's one of us folks now." The Americanization of Peter has proceeded so well that respondents to a January 1986 Gallup Poll ranked Jennings, among all news people, second only to the gone-but-not-forgotten Cronkite in that most important of all anchor qualities—"believability."

"I've been doing this all my life. This is me."—Tom Brokaw. One critic ticks off Tom Brokaw by referring to his "button nose." Others have judged Brokaw and the *NBC Nightly News* to be "bland," "neutral," "objective." When I suggested to Brokaw that after watching several weeks of all three news programs, a group of us had placed him in the middle between the emotional, populist Rather and the suave, establishment Jennings, Brokaw hardly paused before he said, "I'll take it."

A certain degree of white-collar caution has always characterized Brokaw's organization. The great Huntley-Brinkley team, praised so much for its instant chemistry, was an accident of the laboratory, the byproduct of negotiations between two rival executive forces each pushing its own man. Twenty years later Brokaw himself moved up to the anchor job as a kind of compromise between, on the one side, traditionalist factions loyal to the esteemed veteran John Chancellor and, on the other, more opportunistic, showbiz-minded executives willing to try something completely different to catch CBS—namely, the flash-and-dash communicator Tom Snyder. With the warring factions, Brokaw remembers, came "revolving-door leadership." In the ten years he has been in New York, first with *Today* and now with the *Nightly News,* Brokaw has worked for five different NBC News presidents.

Currently, stability reigns at NBC News, much of it brought by the competent, quiet leadership of news-division president Lawrence K. Grossman. On the whole, NBC is the nice, warm, "tasteful" network. Its biggest prime-time hit is about a family, Bill Cosby's made-for-TV brood. On NBC's morning success, the *Today* show, Jane Pauley is on (real-life) maternity leave. Last December Tom Brokaw was the host of the NBC Christmas special that ended with him and Nancy Reagan, NBC's Leading Man and the nation's First Lady, singing Christmas carols on camera.

Like Rather, Tom Brokaw came out of the heartland—the terrain, though, of the contemporary split-level, not the log cabin. He grew up in South Dakota, where his father was a construction foreman for the U.S. Army Corps of Engineers—the kind of job that would have made him Rags Rather's supervisor. Brokaw was very much the boy next door who marries his high-school sweetheart. Her name was Meredith Auld, and she was the kind of girl who wins the Miss South Dakota title in the Miss America competition.

In the late sixties and early seventies, when he was working for KNBC in Los Angeles, the Brokaws ran with the well-to-do Southern California crowd; he still serves on the board of the Norton Simon museum of art in Pasadena. He also ran on his own, apart from any pack. He took up running, he remembers, long before it became a craze, slogging through the L.A. streets in high tops, a lone runner in a town on wheels. Arriving in New York, neither Brokaw broke stride. He became a friend of Thornton Bradshaw, chairman of RCA, the parent company of NBC. She started Penny Whistle, now a chain of four children's toy stores in Manhattan and the Hamptons, where one birthday balloon sells for $1.50 — without the air ("That's her business," he says amiably, "not mine").

Brokaw competed with Rather once before, and lost, when both were covering the Nixon White House in the Final Days of Watergate — a time of some of Rather's most memorable work. In the current round of competition, Brokaw has the momentum. His program has gained about two million viewers in the last two years, while Rather has lost at least 400,000, giving them both about 15 million nightly watchers. It's necessary to say "almost" and "about," because TV ratings, unlike the circulation figures for newspapers and magazines, are notoriously slippery. Ratings books come with asterisks like measles. There are other services besides Nielsen — Arbitron, for example — as well as the networks' own research, and the numbers often differ.

Then, too, ratings are affected by everything but the phases of the moon (and some have wondered about *their* influence). There's the *Wheel of Fortune* factor: some local stations displaying Vanna White in late-afternoon syndication pull large audiences away from the network news on other channels. There's also the role of so-called lead-in shows; for example, the ABC news programs in Chicago and Philadelphia, two of the top six TV markets, have very strong circulations, helping build audiences for *World News Tonight*. Finally, there's NBC's successful *Today* in the morning and the Cosby megahit in prime time; both may keep certain kinds of viewers tuned to NBC, in line with the TV law of inertia — a dial set at rest remains at rest unless acted upon by an outside intelligence. Superfinally, ratings can be just a matter of how the ball bounces, literally. West Coast baseball match-ups have preempted network news shows in the last several months and decisively changed the ratings numbers. As Brokaw says, "There is no fixed formula for ratings success. I've been down, and I've been up...." The one reasonably sure factor is the trend line. Brokaw is up.

Why? Check the correct answer and step up and claim a network-news presidency, paying in the low seven figures. Brokaw takes the moderate, sensible view that ratings success comes from a combination of elements — all of the above, but also the *substance* of the newscasts. For example, Robert Bazell on NBC has done the best reporting on AIDS, while Allen Pizzey on CBS has dominated the South African coverage.

And then there's the anchor. The personality of the leading man is perhaps the only factor the evening-news producers can control. The White House and other officials determine when news is made; the affiliates and station owners are in charge of lead-ins and lead-outs; geography and neighboring buildings can affect the clarity of the picture. But the anchor allows for enterprise. As Brokaw says, "People watch people. They'll watch me as long as I deliver the kind of news they want and need."

Brokaw's kind of news is centrist. *NBC Nightly News*, for example, has been doing the farm-crisis story along with the others. But in search of its own angle, NBC went to the county seat of Cedar County, Nebraska, to see how the shoemaker and other small businesses serving the farmers were being affected. The people who look to NBC for news, according to Brokaw, "live in Walla Walla and El Paso, and they don't get *The New York Times* or *The Washington Post* or *The Wall Street Journal*." If Rather's heart has gone back to Texas and the deep country and Jennings's has moved toward the urban centers, Brokaw talks to the main streets of small cities and commuter towns, where the country's political and consumer power increasingly resides. Of course, TV news is a mass activity engaging large demographic groups all across a broad population. But just as clearly, each of the three anchors speaks to special constituencies. Right now Brokaw's growing audience compels our attention.

Three years ago, Brokaw gave an interview to *Mother Jones,* the left-radical magazine published monthly in San Francisco. Brokaw had just been named the sole anchor of the *Nightly News,* amid some sniping that he was just another pretty boy. "I wanted to demonstrate that I had been around politically," he recalls. Brokaw waded into the interview with some sharp comments about Reagan, whose values, he said, were "pretty simplistic." Further, journalists were letting Reagan get away with "the crock that he was out of work in the '30s" and therefore knew what being poor was like. "He's always been a guy who had a paycheck coming in . . . an extremely rich man who has lived this isolated life . . . in this artificial world, with Nancy out in Pacific Palisades...."

The interview got picked up all over the country. If Brokaw's audience cared, it didn't show; his ratings continued to go up. So did Reagan's. A lot of people see nothing wrong with privilege. They *aim* to live in the Palisades. Reagan's vote-getting vision of the "shining city on the hill" was always upscale, not so much Norman Rockwell's America as Justin Dart's and Betsy Bloomingdale's. The suburbs love them all.

"My best work is still ahead of me. I believe that." — Dan Rather. The network news is done in high-technology style and, most of the time, with journalistic substance. In the past few years, however, the same technology that makes it possible for the seven o'clock news to bring in satellite stories from all over the world also permits strong local stations and new cable networks to gather the same stories — and put them on the air thirty minutes or an hour before the network news comes on. More and more of the audience may decide not to wait for Dan or Peter or Tom. Increasing numbers may turn to Ted Turner's Cable News Network — the news around the clock, the news on demand, the news set to the viewer's schedule rather than the networks'. Rather, Jennings and Brokaw, and their bosses, have all begun to speculate on the next major change in network news, which comes, perversely enough, at a time when the news has arguably achieved its highest quality.

One new format under discussion involves bringing newsmakers on camera and offering interviews or confrontational exchanges. Rather, Jennings and Brokaw over the past year have all begun to do a little of this within the structure of their present programs. But, as they and their viewers well know, the place where this emerging form gets its most prominent exercise is on ABC's *Nightline* with Ted Koppel and, in a more leisurely work-up, on PBS's *MacNeil/Lehrer NewsHour*. The present three-way split in the news audience among Rather, Jennings and Brokaw serves them well, still keeps them in power. But as the local and cable alternatives present themselves, the anchors' constituencies may further weaken. A new consensus personality may arise, not necessarily an authority figure like Cronkite or a demographic mirror like the current three but something much more, well, televisionlike. That is, a personality who thrives on live, unscripted, give-and-take controversy. As interviewers and creators of confrontation, Rather, Jennings and Brokaw are simply not as good as Ted Koppel.

All three of the anchors, unlike one another in so many ways, agree on one thing: They see themselves as newsmen, reporters who can go out and get a story. By the 1990s, they might be back on the streets again.

"Women in Journalism Anchored by Lack of Substantial Change"
by Kenneth R. Clark

Although women in broadcast journalism have gained in prestige and salaries, they still have a long way to travel to match their male counterparts. Here Kenneth R. Clark examines their current status.

First it was Diane Sawyer, hired away from her high-profile post as the only female correspondent ever assigned to CBS's *60 Minutes* for a shot, potentially at an even higher profile at ABC. There she will be paired with Sam Donaldson in what network wags have dubbed "Cheers II: The Sam and Diane Show."

Then it was Connie Chung, leaving NBC after two months of intense negotiations and the chance to develop the new news magazine, *Yesterday, Today and Tomorrow,* to CBS, where she will be sole anchor of *West 57th Street*. Mary Alice Williams, one of Cable News Network's brightest stars, jumped to NBC and the job Chung rejected.

Kenneth R. Clark is a staff writer for Knight-Ridder.

Wealth, fame, power, success. As the cigarette ad says: "You've come a long way, baby." Yet Sawyer, Chung and Williams are celebrity journalists — superstars in or on the threshold of a millionaire-anchor club heretofore dominated by males. For women in television's rank and file, another epigram, written nearly 150 years ago by French author-journalist Alphonse Karr, is more applicable: "The more things change, the more they remain the same."

Things have changed for women in television news since 1983, when Kansas City anchor Christine Craft — fired for being, in her words, "too old, too unattractive and not deferential enough to men" — filed her landmark discrimination suit. But too much, perhaps, has remained the same, making network women restive, if not actually in open revolt.

"'Happy' would not describe all of us right now," said Ann Rubenstein, an NBC correspondent based in New York.

"When my gentlemen friends start complaining about diminishing roles for white males, I find it hard to commiserate," said Beverly Lumpkin, who covers the Justice Department in Washington as an "off-air" reporter for ABC.

"I have noticed that Peter Jennings tends to say, 'Tim Wooten covers Capitol Hill for ABC,'" said Sheilah Kast, who handles the House of Representatives, while Wooten takes care of the Senate. "I haven't heard him say that about me. I want to do a good job of reporting what I'm assigned to report, as opposed to fighting over this little piece of glory or that little piece of glory, but it is the sort of thing that tends, over time, to weigh you down."

Only at CBS, where women outnumber men in the Washington bureau, is there an upbeat note.

"At my network, we're standing pretty high," said CBS Justice Department correspondent Rita Braver, pegged in a recent study at Southern Illinois University as the most rapidly rising female star in the business. "We have three women who are correspondents (Braver, Susan Spencer and Leslie Stahl). Our senior producer is a woman, our bureau chief is a woman, and we have two women in senior slots for the *Evening News.*

"We only have three men in the Washington bureau who are in senior management positions at this point. That may be the next story: How are men doing in television news?"

With such status, it is little wonder that Braver sees no "tokenism" or discrimination at CBS.

"There's not a feeling at all here that anybody is ever going to say, 'That's an awful big job for a little girl,' which is something I once heard, way back when," Braver said. "It's not an old boys' network here anymore. There are a few old girls now."

But what will happen to the "old girls" when their hair gets as gray as Dan Rather's, and when their faces begin to bear the lines that traditionally make men "distinguished"?

Kast, who is active on ABC's Women's Advisory Board, charged with carrying any complaints to news president Roone Arledge, said, "We don't know how the networks are going to react to 50-year-old women," she said. "There is a wave of us around 40 that they seem to be coping with, though we have seen women get on less frequently, then be switched to something else as they

Diane Sawyer, co-anchor with Sam Donaldson, of "Primetime Live" on ABC (photo courtesy Capital Cities/ABC, Inc.).

age. I want to see a woman with gray in her temples who noticeably could be, if not a grandmother, at least the mother of teen-agers."

At NBC, where the frustration level among women probably runs highest, News President Michael Gartner recently called for formation of two "task forces," one on women and one on members of minority groups. Network spokesman Curt Block said no conclusions were expected for perhaps two years.

"Right now, 40 percent of NBC News professionals and management are women," he said. "We're trying to bring that up to 50 percent."

Andrea Mitchell, the network's highest-ranking Washington correspondent,

ABC journalist Carole Simpson (photo courtesy Capital Cities/ABC, Inc.).

who recently switched from White House to the State Department, said such action is overdue.

"Women are taking increasingly prominent roles in some of the anchor responsibilities, but there are still far too few women involved in prominent beat assignments, and far too few being retained regularly on the premier newscasts," she said. "I think a lot of women at the network level have been frustrated by their lack of access to major beats. It's true of all the networks."

Mitchell, however, made it clear that she is frustration-free on her new beat.

"I'm delighted with my current assignment," she said. "I've been given a wonderful opportunity to carve out the beat for NBC in a way that's not been done in the past."

NBC's Rubenstein did not place all the blame for low-level female roles at the network's doorstep.

"The company clearly is in transition," she said. "Women in broadcast journalism took some big hits in the Reagan years, and I wouldn't presume for a second that it's just women in broadcast journalism. (The Reagan era) was very pro-business, with business calling the shots. They did things like disband affirmative action, and that sent messages."

"Off Camera: Newswomen on Bosses, Bias and the Future of the Tube"

by Peggy Orenstein

What do women in television journalism think of their industry, their workplace and its ethics, their roles and their future? Mother Jones magazine gathered four experienced and influential women broadcast journalists. Presented here is the roundtable discussion and their answers to the above questions.

When ABC asked Diane Sawyer to jump from CBS last February, the big question was, how high? That is, how high was the network willing to bid to lure Sawyer away from her post as sole female correspondent on *60 Minutes*? The answer turned out to be around $1.5 million, a salary which no anchorwoman has commanded since Barbara Walters (who takes home $2 million for asking the rich and famous what kind of tree they'd like to be) left NBC for ABC in 1976.

Barely a month later, though, CBS struck back, wooing—and winning—Connie Chung, NBC's heir apparent to anchorman Tom Brokaw, for an estimated $1.8 million; that very same day NBC announced that CNN's Mary Alice Williams would step in and fill the void for a less astronomical but still estimable $500,000. All three women will now anchor high-profile magazine

Peggy Orenstein is managing editor of Mother Jones *magazine.*

ABC's Barbara Walters (photo courtesy Capital Cities/ABC, Inc.).

shows—Diane Sawyer, who will share the limelight with White House correspondent Sam Donaldson, will launch an as-yet unnamed show in August; Mary Alice Williams, along with co-anchor Maria Shriver, will debut on a show called *Yesterday, Today, and Tomorrow* over the summer; and Connie Chung will head up a revamped *West 57th*.

The fast and furious battle for female talent might seem to be good news for women broadcasters, indicating a turnaround in the networks' commitment to hiring and promoting women. Or it might simply be another attempt by network executives to win in the Nielsen war without sacrificing the bottom line (news shows cost significantly less than entertainment shows to produce, so they turn a profit faster). To find out, we gathered four of television's top female journalists—independent producers Linda Ellerbee and Marion Goldin, *NBC Nightly News* correspondent Ann Rubenstein, and Meredith Vieira, who is expected to replace Sawyer on *60 Minutes*—for a discussion of women in television and the future of the news.

Ann Rubenstein spent 13 years as a correspondent for network affiliates in the Midwest. Since 1986, she has been the general correspondent in New York City for the *NBC Nightly News*. "The big question has always been, is there life after network news?"

Marion Goldin, formerly a producer at *60 Minutes,* won a Peabody Award for an independent project, *C.E. News Magazine,* in which young people interviewed the political candidates. "Rather than just a gender issue, there is a kind of person who doesn't fit in network news anymore. There are men who won't play the old-boy network and women who play it more beautifully than the most seasoned men."

Linda Ellerbee has been a writer and correspondent for such shows as *NBC News "Overnight"* and ABC's *Good Morning America* and *Our World* (for which she won an Emmy). "Speaking as a viewer, there is more to us than meets the Nielsen box. Yes, we'll watch trash television. But I never went to a murder that didn't draw a crowd."

Meredith Vieira served as the CBS Midwest Bureau Chief before taking a correspondent spot on the magazine show *West 57th*. "I really am in this business because I was there at the right time. They desperately needed women at CBS. Had I failed, it would have been proof: 'Well, see, you get a woman and that's what happens.'"

Orenstein: What would you tell a young woman fresh out of college, 22, 23 years old, who wanted a career in television journalism? What would she need to have the right stuff now?

Rubenstein: I can tell her some things she ought to do, morally and ethically, once she's in. Hang onto her own code of ethics. Do not depend upon those of her employers. They'll ask her to do things that you shouldn't do. You must really decide for yourself what you're going to do and not do. And what price you are willing to pay for whatever they're offering. Otherwise you're going to find yourself one day standing out in the snow with a microphone and sticking it in the face of a woman who's just had her son killed and asking her how she feels about it. Because somebody told you that's the way to get to the top.

Goldin: Mike Wallace once said to me about a high-ranking CBS executive, "The problem with so-and-so is that he has no moral compass." I've never forgotten that. My advice would be to make sure you have a moral compass before you get into this business, or any other.

Ellerbee: A good sense of humor. And a good, strong sense of self-worth. The minute you begin to let them define you you're dead.

Vieira: They start defining you the first day.

Rubenstein: That's hard. But *you* begin to define yourself based on your job, too. That's a real trap.

Ellerbee: Stand up for yourself from day one. I know we've all seen the people that come in and think, well, I'll do it their way to get there, then they'll do it my way. Do it your way every single day. It's the only way you'll ever continue to do it your way. Because there's never a place you can stop and rest and then suddenly turn around. Besides that, if you're a woman and you're the least bit aggressive, then somehow or other they're going to call you a troublemaker anyway.

Goldin: I think maybe when all of us got into the business, we—at least I—thought of CBS News as a lifetime career.

Vieira: I thought I'd grow old at NBC.

Ellerbee: I wanted to.

Goldin: Exactly. I don't think even for people who want to that that's in the cards anymore. So to the extent that you would be afraid to do what Linda and others have said—stand up, keep your ground—so what if you're a little crazy?

Ellerbee: David Brinkley told me this years ago, and it's the most helpful advice I ever got in this business. It was the first time I ever anchored a show, and it was co-anchoring with David Brinkley on a political show. Just before we went on the air I turned to him and said, "I'm scared to death." And he looked at me and said, "Well, I don't know why you'd be scared; all they can do is fire you." And you know what? He's right! They can't put you in reporter jail. All they can do is fire you.

Rubenstein: The video police won't come get you.

Orenstein: Meredith, what do you think of all that, of "maintaining the moral compass?"

Vieira: I think it's very hard to do. I really do. Especially when you just begin, because you're unsure of yourself anyhow. You're taking baby steps. It's easy to say, "Stand up for what you believe." And that is the right position to take. But when you know you might lose your job, and it's the first one you have, it's frightening. But I think as you gain confidence...

Ellerbee: Well, if you can take baby steps, you can take little baby stand-ups.

Vieira: That's right, that's right. I think that's what it amounts to.

Orenstein: What are some of the battles you remember?

Vieira: I wouldn't go out and say "How do you feel?" after a fire. I remember that specifically. I was out doing a piece on a funeral where they wanted me to basically hang around the widow. And I said, "I just will not do that."

Ellerbee: First of all, you *know* what the answer is to that question, "How do you feel?" Not good.

Orenstein: The Gannett Center for Media Studies recently examined the status of women in television. Their report said that more women are executive producers than before, there are a few more women in front of the cameras...

Ellerbee: What? Two?

Orenstein: ...there are salary disparities between men and women, between 15 and 81 percent, with the highest being at the level of executive producer. The real power is still pretty much with the men. Given those data, how much do you think the situation has changed for women?

Vieira: I think it's very distressing that a network like CBS has only one woman overseas. After all these years?

Rubenstein: NBC has none. I don't think women are doing better in any respect, frankly.

Ellerbee: Not at all. Ed Joyce [former president of CBS News] used to brag, "By God, 70 percent of our researchers are women. We hire women."

Rubenstein: And just think, Howard Stringer [president of the CBS Broadcast Group] started out as a researcher.

Ellerbee: I thought you were going to tell me he started out as a woman.

Rubenstein: Yeah, started out as a woman. Trapped in a woman's body.

Ellerbee: At most networks, I think there are fewer of us than there were when I started.

Orenstein: But there was a time in the '70s when the Federal Communications Commission made a lot of noise....

Rubenstein: It wasn't the FCC. Let's not give the FCC that much credit. It came through the FCC. It was the civil rights movement in this country and the women's movement that did it. It was pressure. The FCC didn't wake up one day and say, let's put women on the air.

Vieira: Yet I really am in this business because I was there at the right time. I've worked very hard, but they desperately needed women on CBS. I was in Providence, and I had an interview, and I was on the air in a week! And I had never done television. Had I failed it would have been proof: "Well, see, you get a woman and that's what happens." I saw women fail who hadn't had the proper training, but that was the attitude. That's just not fair. And that's happened to minorities.

Ellerbee: Most of us got hired originally because we're women.

Vieira: Right.

Ellerbee: The question is, how do you stay hired? Because you're a woman or because you're good?

Goldin: But I think also part of the responsibility for the low numbers that we see now has to be taken upon ourselves. As a group I think women got very quiet over the past ten years.

Rubenstein: I think we stopped saying things. The stakes were too high, and the jobs were too scarce, and you don't make waves when you've got a good job.

Orenstein: Ann and Meredith, what do you two do to flourish at the networks? You're obviously both doing very well.

Rubenstein: I try to get lost in my work, because I find that it's when I'm not busy enough, or sitting in my office day after day, that I tend to get bogged down in the politics of the operation and all the extra things that distract me from what it is that I love, which is the work.

Goldin: But Ann, you just said that one of the things that's happened to make women's position in broadcasting not any better, and perhaps worse than it was, is because women got quiet. Isn't that what you're now describing as the...

Rubenstein: Yes.

Goldin: ...prescription for survival?

Vieira: I'm one of the quieter women. I just do my job, basically. I'm very proud of what I do, I focus on that. Within my own little world, I want my work to be a true reflection of good journalism. But I think it leads to a real identity crisis somewhere along the line. I'm not sure that I've come totally to grips with mine. But talking back and really standing up is a hard thing to do. And you have to understand that you could lose it all. For all of the right reasons. Because they're a bunch of shitheads. It's very tricky.

Rubenstein: I'm not making the waves and the noise that I think we all feel guilty about not doing. On the other hand, I'm remaining on the air. I'm remaining as a statistic that NBC has so many women, and that has its value and merit as well.

Ellerbee: Well, I don't think that's a good enough argument for us women to make. There are good reasons for remaining quiet, probably because you want your job. But under their little quota system that probably does exist, they're just as likely to replace you with another woman. It is hard to speak up, you're right. Marion and I are older than you all...

Goldin: Speak for yourself, Linda.

Ellerbee: ...as you get older you find you speak up more. For whatever reason. The bullshit rises and rises until at some point you have to just shout to get out of it. But I would like to see the younger women coming into it have some sense that the battle is not over. That the battles are not won. I just get the feeling, "Hey, we graded it! You pave it!" And I don't see any road paving going on out there.

Goldin: One of the saddest things is to see a good measure of the younger women back at square one. I mean, they do everything but wear Little Bo Peep dresses and hair bows.

Orenstein: I've noticed that a number of women who are the most visible right now—Faith Daniels, Maria Shriver, Kathleen Sullivan—are, on average, about 20 years younger than their male counterparts, with much less experience. Obviously youth and looks still matter.

Vieira: My boss would never have come in to me during my pregnancy and said, "Hey, 40 pounds you've gained there, honey—you look like dog doo to me." But I certainly sensed it. They've been trained to think that their anchorwomen are beautiful. It's very hard to get around that. I don't believe it's changed. Barbara Walters still looks great. I'm not sure that she'd be on very long if she didn't.

Goldin: What woman looks like Charles Kuralt or Morley Safer...

Vieira: ...or Irving R. Levine.

Ellerbee: But the minute you begin to talk about that, people are going to say that's just sour grapes on your part. It's not. The issue should not be how good-looking you have to be on television. It ought to be how smart we have to be as well. And that gets lost a lot of the time.

Orenstein: Meredith and Ann, are you concerned about aging?

Vieira: I am.

Rubenstein: Absolutely.

Vieira: If I'm right in my assumption that they want young people on the air, the next one who comes along who's younger and smarter and can articulate well may find herself in my job. I think it's also debilitating to obsess on it. You know, that's not how I should be wasting my time—worrying oh my God, I have a wrinkle, instead of studying the next question. So, it's a dangerous thing.

Rubenstein: Stock up on that Retin-A.

Orenstein: It also seems that youth and beauty can be a limitation, depending on how it's used. I'm thinking about the *Vanity Fair* shots of Diane Sawyer.

Rubenstein: Meredith is probably best equipped to talk about that. I don't know whether you all saw that *Esquire* piece on her a while back.

Ellerbee: We all saw it.

Goldin: Meredith can say categorically she would not pose that way now.

Vieira: Well, I can say I did it for the fun of it.

Rubenstein: Did you know what he...

Vieira: I knew it was going to be a flattering piece. I knew it was done in fun. I see myself as a lot of different things. I didn't question it. In retrospect maybe I should have. It was interesting—the reaction that I got was basically from women, not from men. I got reactions from feminists on both sides. Feminists who said, "Right on, finally you're allowing yourself to be what you are, and that's how far we've come." And others who said, "You have just set back our movement a long way." People look up to you as somebody in the business, and here you are posing in these pictures. The one in the pink taffeta dress was certainly suggestive. And that's been detrimental. I suppose if I had it to do over again, knowing me, I probably would. But I certainly didn't mean any harm, and I assume a little bit did come out of it.

Orenstein: If Meredith had called the rest of you up in the night before that shoot and said, "I'm thinking of doing this, what do you think," what advice would you have given?

Goldin: I could have argued both sides of the case.

Rubenstein: The professional side of me would have said don't do it. The other side of me as a person would say you've got to do what you've got to do.

Ellerbee: My first reaction to the Diane Sawyer cover on *Vanity Fair,* quite frankly, was it was unimportant as an issue. They were beautiful pictures, and she looked beautiful. It would be nice to look like that, wouldn't it? Feminist that I am, I was not bothered by it. I think I was persuaded by women friends of mine in the business that I should have been bothered by it, and that we have come a long way, and that this is not the image we want to give off. I agree. It's not. But I also agree with Meredith. Look, I am also a woman, I like looking good. So I wouldn't have given you any advice.

Vieira: Just let me hang myself.

Goldin: Well, until this morning, I would have come here to criticize you. And to criticize Diane. But what you and Linda have said has made me think. And I suppose that in the ideal world...

Ellerbee: ...it would be OK. You know what it is? It's the limits of society that make it dangerous.

Goldin: But because that is the way we are perceived in so much of what we do I think it can be detrimental, because it just feeds into that stereotype.

If we were taken seriously and as equals, and not called cunts and other horrible things, then fine.

Ellerbee: I thought you had great legs, though.

Orenstein: Well, clearly, the kind of feedback you get on your looks is different than men get, but what about the feedback on your work?

Vieira: It depends. I mean, I'll seek feedback a lot of times. Positive and negative. But I don't find people in the networks are gushers. I mean, you don't exactly walk down the hall... "Hey, great job, Meredith. Way to go on that story."

Goldin: Maybe I'm romanticizing, but I seem to remember a day when it was more collegial. When people did help and did compliment you, and didn't look at you as a worse competitor than somebody from another network. And now that doesn't exist. Now there is that sense, sometimes overt, certainly covert, of that old Hollywood phrase: Better my colleague here should fail than my worst enemy.

Orenstein: Does that have something to do with the new ownership and the shift in management of the news divisions?

Goldin: It was as soon as news became part of big business, as soon as news was made into ratings, as soon as you could never come in the next day or the next week and have what you did honestly critiqued, because if it got super ratings, then it was good, and if it got dumpster ratings, well, then it couldn't be very good.

Vieira: A lot of these executives are extremely insecure human beings who are very nervous about the guy at the top themselves. And they change so quickly from one attitude to the next that one day they're on your side, and the next day it's whatever is politically wise for them.

Goldin: The networks have been taken over by bigger corporations and the only thing they care about is the bottom line. What's so hypocritical is they'd ask you to save money on a crew or on your own salary or on a staff person who maybe was going to make $15,000 or $20,000 a year while Larry Tisch [president of CBS News] is giving caviar and champagne parties at the Democratic and Republican conventions and every other place you look. And where is the investigative reporting from a network that pays Connie Chung $1.8 million? If that's where your resources are...

Ellerbee: At NBC a couple of years ago they actually sat down and took all of the correspondents and how many minutes they were on the air that year, and prorated the cost—What's this correspondent worth to us? How much does he produce? Here's his salary; here's the number of minutes he's on the air. Then you have a list. And you slice off the ones at the bottom. That doesn't take into account that some of the stories take a long time to produce. What a foolish way to look at the news!

Goldin: I've come to the conclusion that the TV news networks are divided into two categories: the few great celebrities and the rest of the sycophants.

Ellerbee: Those tend to be men, the sycophants.

Goldin: Oh, really? I find it in a lot of women, too.

Ellerbee: Really?

Goldin: Oh, yes. They're certainly of both sexes. There's a line from *The*

King and I: "Yes, Your Majesty; no, Your Majesty; tell me how low to go, Your Majesty." Why, I've seen middle-aged women who've talked to executive men in baby talk.

Ellerbee: You know, we all had daddies. We were all little girls who wanted the approval of daddy. And we add that to everything else that society and our parents put into us about little girls. And you get out there in the business world, and your boss is "daddy." We're conditioned. I mean, even these days, people will say, "Did you have a mentor?" I hate that word. They mean a daddy. They mean ... we used to say a rabbi.

Rubenstein: Do you have a tormentor ... not a mentor, a tormentor.

Ellerbee: I think women have to work harder to get out of that mind-set. I had to make conscious efforts to do that.

Rubenstein: I've never talked baby talk to a man. How do you do it?

Vieira: You end up talking sort of like a child to a parent. And in the "star system," if you're "talent," male or female, you're treated like a child. So, that's built-in. I mean, they're always stroking you. Always, you know, you're the good little kid. But you know, I think in terms of your network staff, they still do care about their work.

Ellerbee: The people that do the work—the writers, the editors, the producers, cameramen and women—they care. Because their jobs are made much more difficult if they have to work with "talent," who's actually an airhead. But the people who hire them? I don't think they care that much. They say they do.

Goldin: As the only person here behind the scenes, I think it would be grossly unfair to our readers for any of us to leave the impression that it's just on-air talent who are airheads. The fact is that the same people who are doing the hiring of on-air talent are doing the hiring of behind-the-scenes talent. And I am here to tell you that many, if not all, of the same characteristics that are desirable for on-the-air talent—sycophancy, baby talk—they want behind the scenes as well as on the air.

Ellerbee: I worked at one network, which shall go nameless, where there was an executive producer who had a real cadre of women producers...

Rubenstein: Oh, do we have a lot to talk about afterwards.

Ellerbee: ...a real cadre of women producers. Some of whom he'd slept with, some of whom he hadn't. It was sort of interchangeable. But, of course, that was the impression if you were in that cadre. The terrible part of being accused if you're a woman in this business, whether you're behind the scenes or not, is sometimes people think you've slept with the boss to get where you are. Now the terrible part is that there are some who did. And do.

Orenstein: How has that affected your careers? You've obviously all rebelled against the standard expectations—and you've survived.

Goldin: I'm very proud of what I did for 25 years at the networks—22 of them at CBS and two and a half at ABC. It also speaks for itself that I'm no longer with the television networks, and don't want to be. Again, this may sound self-serving—you'll decide. Somebody asked me whether NBC had called me when I left ABC, and I said no. You've got to believe me. If they did I'd be a bag lady before I'd consider it.

Ellerbee: I remember a day, it was the summer that I was 40 years old. I was working on a show that was in some disarray. It was chaos. I was rushed, and I was writing. My boss came into the room with yet another "Have I got an idea!" And it was a dreadful idea. It was a dreadful, dreadful idea. And he wanted to know why. Sometimes a lot of things can go through your mind very fast. I started to open my mouth and do what over the years you get in the habit of doing, which is break it to him gently. Find ways to get him out of that idea without him losing face.

Rubenstein: It's called creative deflection.

Ellerbee: That's right. I didn't have the time. I was under the gun, and I didn't have the time. I turned around and I said, "That is an awful idea. I don't have time to tell you why now. It is a terrible idea. I don't want to hear about it." And he said, "Well, what's the matter with you?" And I blew. I don't know where it came from. But I started to yell at the man, "I am tired of babying you all." We talk about us doing baby talk—I'm tired of mothering little-boy executives. Grow up. Take my word for it, it's a bad idea, and get out of my office. I'm busy.

Goldin: And get your adulation somewhere else.

Orenstein: Are there stories that went the other way—stories that you originated and believed in that were spiked, that never made it on the air?

Vieira: Bits of pieces. I remember doing a piece on a deaf student who wanted to make it in the movies. And I wanted to say, here we are doing this story on CBS, which doesn't even have closed caption. She wants to make the next step, and they can't even go that far. And they said, "Absolutely not, you can't say that." I said, "Why not? It's true." And they were just adamant about it, because they were negotiating some deal for their closed caption. That decision was from very high up. My boss said fine, I think it's right to do it. But then it went up a few more steps. But never has a whole story been spiked.

Rubenstein: Yeah, mine haven't been either.

Goldin: One of the most stunning stories I've ever been involved with was for ABC. It was about Charles Wick, for eight years head of the U.S. Information Agency and a very good friend of Reagan's. He owned a string of nursing homes. Rarely if ever had I seen such good documentation, not only in terms of reports, but in terms of pictures. I wanted to call them inmates. That's what these old people looked like lying in these beds in this nursing home in Visalia, California. To the highest levels of ABC—this is before Capital Cities bought them—there were meetings with different versions: eight minutes, three minutes, two minutes. The story never aired. Nor did it air anyplace else. It was political pressure: Wick's attorney in Washington calling Ev Erlick, executive vice president at ABC. Good, classic spiking.

Vieira: I can think of one other thing that happened to me at the local affiliate: a story on sexual harassment in the workplace. We were going to do it on CBS Records, because we had received so many calls from employees there. And we could not do it. Networks are notorious for this. Pointing the finger at someone else, and not just really raking the company over the coals for something like that. But never can you point the finger at CBS or NBC or ABC. And we really had a good story there. And that was definitely denied. We ended up doing it on a cosmetics firm. And it destroyed them.

Orenstein: Let's shift to the way the format of the news has changed, how that affects what you do. Over the years certain trends have been established — starting with the opening up of the happy-talk format in local news, the first infiltration of entertainment news into the business. Eventually news magazines come along. Then Donahue. And then Oprah. And now Geraldo. How have these changes affected what you do and what we see?

Vieira: I think the talk shows lowered the common denominator. Everything's becoming info-tainment in a way.

Rubenstein: The networks are covering...

Ellerbee: ...fewer stories.

Rubenstein: And the honest-to-goodness hard news stories are the stories coming out of Washington.

Goldin: And overseas.

Ellerbee: There isn't that much hard news covered at all anymore. What they call hard news very often isn't. And more and more it's in the back half of the evening newscast. On all three networks.

Rubenstein: We're not a program of record. We're not covering breaking news now. When I was in Chicago from '84 to '86, we covered lots of big breaking stories. We were really covering news of the day. With the technology advancing the way it has, the network mentality is, well, by the time we get on the air at night the locals have covered everything that's broken. We better give them something different. Marion's theory is that everything should become trash TV. Everywhere you look, trash tabloid television. And then people would have their fill of it. Then maybe everything would swing back the other way.

Ellerbee: Meredith is right. It does lower the common denominator. But Marion is right, too. It is not going to eat our babies. Speaking as a viewer, we are not what we watch. There is more to us than meets the Nielsen box. Yes, we'll watch trash television. But I never went to a murder that didn't draw a crowd. Wars draw a crowd. So do fools and burning buildings. But it's not all you watch. I find far more objectionable those of us in the business who'll do it. I don't think it's nearly as sinful to watch it as it is to do it.

Goldin: We were talking about where there is going to be an outlet for what we call quality kind of programming. And my sense of it is that there aren't going to be those outlets until trash TV runs its course.

Ellerbee: You're right. I get at least one offer a month. My most recent was a large-operation offer, to anchor a game show about murder. But I think in fact the boredom factor will get there. It's very encouraging that already the advertisers are beginning to worry about it. WNBC canceled Geraldo. Morton Downey, Jr., is having trouble finding sponsors.

Vieira: I didn't realize WNBC canceled Geraldo.

Ellerbee: Yeah — he's going to WCBS. [Film director] Joe Mankiewicz said that television is nothing but auditions. If that's the case, we're going to look back on trash television, at least I am, as an infinite number of chimpanzees marching across the stage playing an infinite number of accordions. A little bit of "Lady of Spain" goes a long way after a while.

Orenstein: But the programmers argue that the American viewing public gets what it wants.

Ellerbee: That is the biggest fallacy in our business. That's the argument that people on our side use to put dreck on the air. "Well, we're just giving them what they want." The American public didn't ask for trash television. They'll watch it the same way we go out and watch a fire. It's not all they want. What happens is when something's hot like that it drives out everything else.

Orenstein: When you look back over the years, though, what are the pieces you've done that you're proudest of?

Goldin: Well, I guess I've done, oh, around 70 pieces for *60 Minutes*. Not to mention other broadcasts. And there was certainly a percentage of clinkers. But I'm very proud of a body of work that stretches from Watergate—when Nixon resigned *60 Minutes* was able to do a retrospective on Watergate, because we had taken every opportunity to do Watergate stories—to a piece in 1978 on Murrieta. That was an exposé of a clinic purporting to cure cancer, arthritis, heart disease, narcolepsy. It preyed on the infirm and the elderly. And we went undercover as wealthy people with a Rolls-Royce and wigs, which was fun. But it also had its serious side. It really helped people understand charlatans and quacks.

Ellerbee: *NBC News "Overnight."* Now, that's the piece of work I'm most proud of. And I'm going to use that instead of a story. I could pick some *Our World* shows that I'm real proud of. Real proud of. But I think *NBC News "Overnight"* is the thing. When I look back it's probably the best work I've done.

Orenstein: Ann and Meredith, what about you?

Rubenstein: It's probably the stories that go relatively unnoticed. Not the stories about the big stars or the Raisa Gorbachevs coming to town. It's one that I did about deaf children in St. Louis graduating from the Central Institute for the Deaf, where they learned how to speak. You could see how hard those kids were trying, and it really touched me. So it's not, did my piece change the world, or how many people out there did I reach? It's what it did for me. What did *I* learn from it. It's the smaller ones that escape all of the hoopla.

Vieira: I would agree with Ann. My favorite was about a kid as well. A little boy named Anthony in Chicago, who'd spoken of poverty as only someone who lives it can. And someone without pretenses, because he hadn't formed those yet. And I have a buddy for life. I mean, we talk every week. I see him. So that's something that I'm going to take with me. CBS could fire me tomorrow, and it doesn't matter. I have that.

Orenstein: With cable broadening its appeal and more and more independent stations on the air, isn't the field for good programming opening a bit?

Ellerbee: That's the good side. Marion and I are out there in that world of independent production.

Goldin: The record should show that, particularly recently, men are opting out of network television, too, because they don't fit either. Rather than just a gender issue, there really is a kind of person who doesn't fit in network news anymore. There are men who don't want to play or can't play the old-boy network. And there are women who play it more beautifully than the most seasoned men.

Orenstein: Linda and Marion, when did you know that it was time to quit the networks?

Ellerbee: I didn't quit because they canceled *Our World*. I had a contract that said they had to pay me for another two and a half years whether I did a lick of work or not. But I think I was coming closer to it and closer to it. There's a moment that drives you over the edge. I did a little thing on *Good Morning, America* called "TGIF" that I had done on the *Today Show*. And the executive producer of "TGIF" came to me and said he had three changes that he wanted to make. I said, "What are they?" And he said, "I want to change the title, because I'm afraid we're offending Christians." So I asked him, "What do you mean?" And he said, "Thanking *God* it's Friday." And I asked him who he thought we ought to thank. Thank Allah it's Friday? He had no answer. And I said, "What is the second thing?" And he said, "Do you have to play this 'TGIF' theme song?" And I said, "Yes! What is the third thing?" He said, "Does it have to run on Friday?" At that moment inside I said, I'm outta here. I'm gone.

Goldin: Well, I'm going to be flip, because it was really a process. The short flip answer is standing in my kitchen one night saying to my husband, "I can't think of a name for my company." And he stood there for no more than two minutes, and said, "Marigold." And then I knew that I had to do it.

Ellerbee: I quit because I wanted something else. I wanted to work for myself. And because I was tired. I was tired of the bullshit. Real tired. One thing we've not brought up today, which is so true, and should be brought in here: I love the work! And that's true of all of us. We haven't brought up that side of it. I love it! Some of my happiest moments in the whole world are spent in editing rooms. And I didn't want to give up the work! I just wanted to give *them* up.

Rubenstein: You love your work. You don't always love the environment in which you practice it.

Goldin: I want to second, third, and fourth how much we all love the work.

Orenstein: Throughout this discussion there's been a kind of division and maybe a tension between two independent producers who have been around a little longer, and two women who are on the networks and are a little younger. What do you see when you look across the table at each other?

Rubenstein: I'm encouraged. I mean, the big question has always been, is there life after network news? I think it's very encouraging to see people going off on their own and succeeding. And more important: they're happy. Enjoying their work again.

Vieira: It's hard to get off that merry-go-round, though. It really is. Especially when that brass ring is there, and they keep telling you, you almost got it!

Ellerbee: Don't get off until you're ready.

Rubenstein: Or until they throw you off.

Vieira: I find myself sitting here, part of me wanting to scream in terms of the inequities that I see, and the other part going, oh, God, someone's going to read this. CBS xeroxes all these articles, and they hit everybody's desk. And the most outrageous thing I've said is probably what will be in the article, and, oh, shit, you know. That's what I feel.

Ellerbee: There was a question earlier about ... you talked about worrying about growing old. The reason I didn't and the reason I don't is because I never intended to grow old as a network correspondent. I think if we have a message, the two of us to them, it's that there's a wonderful world outside the networks. And that for all of the bad times for networks, these are good times for television.

Putting trash television aside, because I do believe that will pass, there are a lot more places to show your work these days. And there is a lot of freedom. You can make money. I make more money than I made at the networks. You can have a lot more control. You can even have networks come and buy your product. I am a freelance producer and TV journalist. I couldn't have done that ten years ago. I have just begun doing commentary three days a week for CNN, but I don't work there. We're producing documentaries for PBS, for cable, and, we hope, eventually for the networks. You can do this. You can do your work outside of them in ways that weren't possible for us when we were your age. So I think you have a lot to look forward to in a much broader sense than the networks. I mean, it's time to stop thinking "the networks" and think television.

Orenstein: Marion, what about you?

Goldin: During the presidential campaign I covered George Bush and Dan Quayle with a 13-year-old and an 11-year-old.

Ellerbee: Was that *Children's Express*?

Goldin: Yes, *C.E. News Magazine*. And we made more news with the 13-year-old and the 11-year-old than the whole pack covering Quayle and Bush. There were dozens, if not hundreds, of adult reporters in the pack, but here was a vehicle where persons of original cast of mind could do what no one else did in the campaign. At the end, we had a meeting, and one of the children said, why don't we just show the candidates against a plain backdrop? Forget the balloons. Put them behind a plain backdrop and let's just listen to what they have to say.

Rubenstein: That's a perfect example. I think network executives are so afraid to be different. Every year they say, we're going to do it different this year. No balloons. No photo opportunities. We're not going to be used like we were before. And then every year it turns out to be the same story. And it raises the question: Are there no executives at any of these networks who have the courage and the balls to stand up and say, "No, I don't care what CBS or ABC does, we're not going to do it that way. We're going to do it our way"?

Vieira: Look at the Bush inauguration. That was terrible coverage, a virtual love fest for Bush—no insightful reporting.

Orenstein: Well, let's say you had all the power at the networks or outside of them. What's the biggest change you'd make right now to affect what viewers see?

Vieira: I'd like more international coverage than I think there is.

Ellerbee: You know, South Africa made a great case, and Israel followed them up immediately: Throwing out the press does work. News coverage went away.

Vieira: Absolutely. I'd like to see an investigative unit back. And a documentary unit back with a real commitment to that. I'd like to see a commitment to women in executive positions.

Rubenstein: I would like to see us get back to the business of news. And do more stories that reflect what went on in the United States that day. More harder news stories.

Ellerbee: I'd put *Our World* back on the air.

Rubenstein: That's true. I mean, you laugh, but I would put shows like that back on the air. And get rid of the rating system. Replace it with what? I don't know.

Goldin: These TV executives have asked us people who program to do the impossible. Why should we have to attract 30 million people to anything? A million people is the *New York Times* readership on a daily basis.

Ellerbee: *Our World* was canceled for having only 12 million viewers a week.

Rubenstein: That is amazing, isn't it? *Only* 12 million.

Ellerbee: PBS wants to put that show on the air. If they get 12 million viewers a week, it'll be one of the highest-rated shows in the history of PBS. There was a compact that was broken. When God made the airwaves, the federal government said, "We will give you this license to use something that belongs to the people of the United States, for personal profit. In return you will give back to the people of the United States a lot of public-information programming, public-affairs programming. You will give back to them things that are good that do not depend on your making money." We simply have to stop applying ratings to that side of the compact.

"Blurred Lines: TV Network News Is Making Re-Creation a Form of Recreation"

by Kevin Goldman

In Anchors: Brokaw, Jennings, Rather and the Evening News, Robert Goldberg and Gerald Jay Goldberg write:

Kevin Goldman is a staff reporter for the Wall Street Journal.

"*Re-creations. Reconstructions. Reenactments. Simulations. They are all just different words for the same thing: faking it. If there is no footage, create your own (using technology, or more often, actors).*

"*Proponents say that if a network has done all the reporting, if it has the facts, if all that's missing are the images, what's wrong with re-creating them? What's wrong with simply illustrating the facts that are known?*

"*Opponents say that TV news has a unique contract with its viewers. By showing actual footage, TV news allows viewers themselves to be eyewitnesses to events. That's the contract. If you see it on the evening news, you know the events really happened. But with are-creation, who knows? It's not so much that producers will utterly fabricate a whole story although that could happen, but that, in a quest for extra drama or pizzazz, all sorts of subtle changes can creep in that distort the story. And then, how can anyone tell what's fact and what's fiction? These issues were widely debated through much of 1989. Some producers called recreations 'a natural step in broadcast news.' Others called the notion a travesty.*"

These are the last words Abbie Hoffman ever uttered, more or less, before he killed himself. And You Are There, sort of:

ABBIE: "I'm OK, Jack. I'm OK." (listening) "Yeah. I'm out of bed. I got my feet on the floor. Yeah. Two feet. I'll see you Wednesday? . . . Thursday."

He listens impassively.

ABBIE: (cont'd.): "I'll always be with you, Jack. Don't worry."

Abbie lies back and leaves the frame empty.

Of course that wasn't the *actual* conversation the late anti-war activist, protest leader and founder of the Yippies ever had with his brother. It's a script pieced together from interviews by CBS News for a re-enactment, a dramatic rendering by an actor of Mr. Hoffman's untimely unsuccessful struggle with depression.

The segment is soon to be broadcast on the CBS News series "Saturday Night with Connie Chung," thus further blurring the distinction between fiction and reality in TV news. It is the New Journalism come to television.

Ms. Chung's program is just one of several network shows (and many more in syndication) that rely on the controversial technique of reconstructing events, using actors who are supposed to resemble real people, living and dead. Ms. Chung's, however, is said to be the only network news program in history to employ casting directors.

Abbie Hoffman in this case is to be played by Hollywood actor Paul Lieber, who isn't new to the character. He was Mr. Hoffman in a 1979 Los Angeles production of a play called "The Chicago Conspiracy Trial."

Television news, of course, has always been part show-biz. Broadcasters have a healthy appreciation of the role entertainment values play in captivating an audience. But, as CBS Broadcast Group president Howard Stringer puts it, the network now needs to "broaden the horizons of nonfiction television, and that includes some experimentation."

Character Studies. Since its premiere Sept. 16, the show on which Ms. Chung appears has used an actor to portray the Rev. Vernon Johns, a civil-rights leader, and one to play a teenage drug dealer. It has depicted the bombing of Pan Am flight 103 over the Scottish town of Lockerbie. On Oct. 21, it did a rendition of the kidnapping and imprisonment of Associated Press correspondent Terry Anderson, who was abducted in March 1985 and is believed to be held in Lebanon. The production had actors playing Mr. Anderson and former hostages David Jacobsen, the Rev. Benjamin Weir and Father Lawrence Jenco.

ABC News has similarly branched out into entertainment gimmickry. "Prime Time Live," a new show this season featuring Sam Donaldson and Diane Sawyer, has a studio audience that applauds and that one night (to the embarrassment of the network) waved at the camera like the crowd on "Let's Make a Deal." (ABC stops short of using an "applause" sign and a comic to warm up the audience. The stars do that themselves.) NBC News has produced three episodes of an occasional series produced by Sid Feders called "Yesterday, Today and Tomorrow," starring Maria Shriver, Chuck Scarborough and Mary Alice Williams, that also gives work to actors.

Call it a fad. Or call it the wave of the future.

NBC's re-creations are produced by Cosgrove-Meurer Productions, which also makes the successful prime-time NBC Entertainment series "Unsolved Mysteries."

The marriage of news and theater, if not exactly inevitable, has been consummated nonetheless. News programs, particularly if they score well in the ratings, appeal to the networks' cost-conscious corporate parents because they are so much less expensive to produce than an entertainment show is—somewhere between $400,000 and $500,000 for a one-hour program. Entertainment shows tend to cost twice that. Re-enactments have been used successfully for several seasons on such syndicated "tabloid TV" shows such as "A Current Affair," which is produced by the Fox Broadcasting Co. unit of Rupert Murdoch's News Corp. That show, whose host is Ms. Chung's husband, Maury Povich, has a particular penchant for grisly murders and stories having to do with sex—the Robert Chambers murder case, the Rob Lowe tapes, what have you.

More Imaginative News. Gerald Stone, the executive producer of "A Current Affair," says, "We have opened eyes to being a little less conservative and more imaginative in how to present the news."

Nowhere have eyes been opened wider than at CBS News. At 555 W. 57th St. in Manhattan, one floor below the offices of "60 Minutes," the most successful prime-time news program ever, actors wait in the reception area to audition for "Saturday Night with Connie Chung."

CBS News sends scripts to agents, who pass them along to clients. The network deals a lot with unknowns, including Scott Wentworth, who portrayed Mr. Anderson, and Bill Alton as Father Jenco, but the network has some big names to contend with, too. James Earl Jones is cast to play the Rev. Mr. Johns. Ned Beatty may portray former California Gov. Pat Brown in a forthcoming episode on Caryl Chessman, the last man to be executed in California, in 1960.

"Saturday Night" has cast actors to appear in future stories ranging from the abortion rights of teenagers to a Nov. 4 segment on a man named Willie Bosket, who calls himself a "monster" and is reputed to be the toughest prisoner in New York.

CBS News, which as recently as two years ago fired hundreds of its employees in budget cutbacks, now hires featured actors begining at $2,700 a week. That isn't much compared with what Bill Cosby makes, or even Connie Chung for that matter (who is paid $1.6 million a year and who recently did a guest shot of her own on the sitcom "Murphy Brown"). But the money isn't peanuts either, particularly for a news program.

Getting Out of Middletown. CBS News is also re-enacting the 1979 Three Mile Island nuclear accident in Middletown, Pa., with something less than a cast of thousands. It is combing the town of 10,000 for about 200 extras. On Oct. 20, the town's mayor, Robert Reid, made an announcement on behalf of CBS during half-time at the Middletown High School football game asking for volunteers.

"There was a roll of laughter through the stands," says Joe Sukle, the editor of the weekly *Press and Journal* in Middletown. "They're filming right now at the bank down the street, and they want shots of people getting out of cars and kids on skateboards. They are approaching everyone on the street and asking if they want to be in a docudrama."

Mr. Sukle says he wouldn't dream of participating himself: "No way. I think re-enactments stink."

Though a re-enactment may have the flavor, Hollywood on the Hudson it isn't. Some producers seem tentative about the technique, squeamish even. So the results, while not news, aren't exactly theater either, at least not good theater. And some people do think that acting out scripts isn't worthy of CBS News, which once lent prestige to the network and set standards for the industry.

In his review of "Saturday Night with Connie Chung," Tom Shales, the TV critic of the *Washington Post* and generally an admirer of CBS, wrote that while the show is "impressive . . . one has to wonder if this is the proper direction for a network news division to take."

'No Longer News.' Re-creating events has, in general, upset news traditionalists, including former CBS News President Richard S. Salant and former NBC News President Reuven Frank, former CBS News anchorman Walter Cronkite and the new dean of the Columbia University Graduate School of Journalism, Joan Konner. Says she: "Once you add dramatizations, it's no longer news, it's drama, and that has no place on a network news broadcast. . . . They should never be on. Never."

Criticism of the Abbie Hoffman segment is particularly scathing among people who knew and loved the man. That includes his companion of 15 years, Johanna Lawrenson, as well as his former wife, Anita. Both women say they also find it distasteful that CBS News is apparently concentrating on Mr. Hoffman's problems as a manic-depressive.

"This is dangerous and misrepresents Abbie's life," says Ms. Lawrenson, who has had an advance look at the 36-page script. "It's a sensational piece about someone who is not here to defend himself."

Mrs. Hoffman says that dramatization "makes the truth flexible. It takes one person's account and gives it authenticity."

CBS News interviewed Jack Hoffman and his sister, Phyllis, as well as Mr. Hoffman's landlord in Solebury Township, Pa. Also Jonathan Silvers, who collaborated with Mr. Hoffman on two books.

Doing 'Some Good.' Mr. Silvers says, "I wanted to be interviewed to get Abbie's story out, and maybe talking about the illness will do some good."

The executive producer of "Saturday Night with Connie Chung," Andrew Lack, declines to discuss re-creations as a practice or his show, in particular. "I don't talk about my work," he says. The president of CBS News, David W. Burke, didn't return numerous telephone calls.

One person close to the process says it would not be in the best interest of CBS News to comment on a "work in progress," such as the Hoffman re-creation, but says CBS News is "aware" of the concerns of Ms. Lawrenson and Mr. Hoffman's former wife. Neither woman was invited by CBS News to participate in a round-table discussion about Mr. Hoffman that is to follow the re-enactment.

Mr. Lieber, the actor who plays Mr. Hoffman, says he was concerned at first that the script would "misrepresent an astute political mind, one that I admired," but that his concerns were allayed. The producers, he says, did a good job of depicting someone "who had done so much, but who was also a manic-depressive."

CBS News spares no expense on these re-enactments. It even spent $2,500 on a beard for Mr. Lieber, the actor says. To re-create the speech Mr. Hoffman gave in 1987 at Vanderbilt University, in Nashville, Tenn., CBS News went to the New Jersey Institute of Technology. To attract the 400-odd students it needed for its mock audience, the news division hired a free-lance casting director, Cynthia Hildebrand, who heads New Jersey Talent Works. She distributed fliers on the campus and at Rutgers University across the street. Prizes were offered in lieu of cash, specifically compact-disk players, cameras, cassette tapes, record albums and kegs of beer.

Offering beer to college kids in a state where the drinking age is 21 upset school officials. "When the dean of students found out about beer, she ordered the posters down and CBS News to stop," says Sol Fenster, the president of the technology institute, which was paid $1,000 for a day's use of its theater.

"It was my mistake, not CBS News's," Ms. Hildebrand says. "As soon as it was pointed out to me, I stopped. We gave cash to the fraternity that delivered the most students." And the fraternity, Theta Chi, bought its own beer, according to brother Jim Sullivan.

To re-enact the kidnapping of Terry Anderson, CBS News went to the Chelsea area of Manhattan and put up posters of the Ayatollah Khomeini. Thus, presto-change-o, it became a street in Beirut. No greater authenticity was needed for a scene that lasted a mere 20 seconds.

Voice to the Thought. That CBS News intended to re-enact part of Mr. Anderson's ordeal took former hostages interviewed by the network rather by surprise. They weren't informed until months after the fact that actors were to impersonate them and breathe life into their recollections.

"You mean an actor is playing Terry?" Father Jenco asks a reporter. "You mean an actor is playing me? They didn't tell me," he says, more puzzled than angry.

Mr. Jacobsen, whose part in the hostage drama was played by actor Jim Weston, says he doesn't mind that CBS News didn't clue him in to its plans. CBS News won't comment officially, but people there say it didn't confide its plans in people interviewed last summer but that it was going to have to tell the former hostages eventually because they were slated to take part in a discussion after the re-enactment.

"There's no better way to suggest the sheer hell we went through," Mr. Jacobsen says. Now president and chief executive officer of Mercy Medical Center in Durango, Colo., he says he is concerned that Mr. Anderson's captors will "see or at least hear about the CBS show, and I hope if they take offense..., they don't take it out on poor Terry."

A Promising Expedient. CBS got interested in using re-enactments last year, after Mr. Lack, the executive producer of "West 57th," made a pilot for a prospective new show called "True Stories" that was to use actors. The show didn't fly, but the idea of using actors in TV news pleased CBS's Mr. Stringer. The former president of CBS News wanted to get more news shows on the schedule.

So far, re-enactments haven't produced the audience. On Oct. 21, Ms. Chung was seen by 6 percent of all television households, opposite "Hunter" on NBC, which had 16 percent of the audience, and a made-for-TV movie starring Burt Reynolds on ABC, which garnered 8 percent. Indeed, on Oct. 14 and 21 Ms. Chung's show was last in the ratings among network television shows, according to figures compiled by the A. C. Nielsen Co. The highest rating Ms. Chung has had so far was on Oct. 7, the night she interviewed Marlon Brando, the man himself, and was seen by 9 percent of TV households.

But news programs, with rare exceptions such as "60 Minutes," have traditionally suffered in the ratings against entertainment programming (which is one reason the genres are merging in some of the new shows). And despite their poor ratings, news programs still can make money for broadcasters. The CBS program "48 Hours," for instance, is seen by less than half the audience that sees "The Cosby Show" on NBC at the same hour. But the CBS News program regularly finishes second in its time slot, and a CBS executive says it earns about $900,000 a week for the network. "West 57th," the show replaced by "Saturday Night," always came in second too, and it too was profitable.

So why was it canceled? No one contacted at CBS News will say for the record, but some believe it was because Mr. Burke, who joined CBS News about 15 months ago from ABC News, where he was the executive vice president, wanted to make his own mark on the news division. Also, CBS had lured back Ms. Chung from NBC News with the promise she could have her own prime-time news show, and "Saturday Night" was to be it.

In Underwear and Chains. One executive at CBS Inc. says the show's re-creations are "at least classy, not sleazy." But some re-enactments cast some doubt on that. The script for one scene in the Terry Anderson re-enactment, shot on a sound-stage on West 61st Street, has Mr. Wentworth, the actor portraying the hostage, in "his underwear, shackled and chained by wrist and ankle," arguing with a guard about a radio.

"What happened to the papers? What happened to our radio? Why can't we have the radio?" the actor says after "pounding on the door." The guard replies, "Because, Mr. Terry, we don't want you to hear bad news." Actual characters in the Anderson saga see the playacting as a good thing. "The exposure Terry will get is worth its weight in gold," says Peggy Say, his sister.

Certain re-enactments have been real bombs. In July, ABC News got a critical drubbing when its "World News Tonight" showed an impersonation of Felix S. Bloch, a senior American diplomat, as he allegedly handed over a briefcase to a Soviet intelligence agent. The word "simulation" was accidentally left off the screen, and the *cinema verité* technique was real enough to fool viewers into thinking they were witnessing a clandestine film of actual espionage. Besides that, this was on the evening news, where the audience expects to witness events, not theatrical productions. Anchorman Peter Jennings apologized for the omission on a later broadcast, but the damage had been done. In an interview, Roone Arledge, the president of ABC News, says, "This was a violation of our policy, and the people involved have been reprimanded. Maybe they should have been fired, but they weren't."

Special Dispensations. However, as a result of the incident, Mr. Arledge says, the ABC News policy has been changed. Now, if anything out of the ordinary is going to be done, permission must be sought from the president of ABC News or his designee, he says. "Before this, an executive in charge of the program could give permission."

Apologies notwithstanding, ABC News hasn't put a stop to re-enactments. Earlier this month, its magazine show "20/20" videotaped a private detective rummaging through a trash can as he had previously done in fact, searching for documents. Mr. Arledge says the piece was screened by executives and approved before broadcast. "It didn't confuse anyone," he says. "Everyone knew we weren't actually there when he was first going through the garbage. I don't know if I would have it done that way, though."

NBC News has taken its licks, too. One segment of "Yesterday, Today and Tomorrow" depicted a home for the mentally retarded that looked to some like a 1940s Hollywood version of an insane asylum, complete with howling and muttering. The moral here presumably is: If you are going to do this sort of thing, at least strive for verisimilitude.

Obviously, much more is involved than making acting look realistic. "It's OK for 'Unsolved Mysteries' or 'A Current Affair' to do these re-creations," says Mr. Frank, the former president of NBC News. "But it undermines the one thing a news organization can offer: credibility."

The Cronkite Distinction. Walter Cronkite was the host of "You Are There" from 1953 to 1957 and again for one season in 1971. The network show, which wasn't a production of the news division despite the loan of Mr. Cronkite, re-enacted historical events, complete with dialogue nobody was there to transcribe when it was uttered. He suggests establishing a separate broadcast unit within CBS Inc. to handle any historical re-creations. The technique "has no place in a news division," he says.

David Nuell, the executive producer of the syndicated show "Entertainment Tonight," distributed by Paramount Communications Inc., says he has used re-creations because "we're an *entertainment* news show." But Mr. Nuell, who will leave "ET" in December to join NBC's "Today" program as senior executive producer, says he would "never" allow re-creations on a news broadcast. "Some of the things on 'Unsolved Mysteries' are wonderful, he says. "But the viewer does not differentiate. ... It isn't for a network news division to do re-creations because it's confusing."

In the end, playing fast and loose with reality is likely to become even more common in prime-time news programs, while remaining unwelcome on the evening news itself. CBS News, for one, is rewriting its standards and practices handbook to allow for the technique.

Says Mr. Salant, who was president of CBS from 1961 to '64 and again from 1966 to '79: "I don't mind. As long as they get an actress to play Connie Chung."

"CNN at the Front Line of News"
by Jonas Bernstein

Upstart CNN has taken the lead in reporting the war from the Persian Gulf. Its live broadcasts have become a key factor in the war's diplomacy. But along with its influential coverage from Baghdad, there has been some queasiness over how the stories have been handled. Critics say that the cable network is putting vital information at the enemy's disposal, even playing into enemy hands. CNN argues that it is simply providing raw data on the war without judgment.

With the stellar performance of their smart bombs and cruise and Patriot missiles, defense contractors have had good reason to be popping the champagne corks. The Gulf war has also been very, very good to another U.S. corporation: Cable News Network. According to a survey released Jan. 31 by the Times Mirror Center for the People and the Press, six in 10 Americans feel the 10-year-old, Atlanta-based upstart is outdoing its more established competitors in covering the war. That is double the number who picked CNN as top of the heap three weeks earlier, just before the war started.

Jonas Bernstein is a staff writer for Insight *magazine, which is published by* The Washington D.C. Times.

But if the blow-by-blow descriptions of Baghdad's bombardment by the now-famous trio of Shaw, Holliman and Arnett won CNN new respect with the viewing public (along with more advertising clout: It has just jacked up its fees for prime-time ads by 400 percent), there is also a distinct sense of unease on the part of many Americans with the cable network's reporting from the enemy capital. If it grows, say some analysts, this unease could start to undo all the gains CNN has made over the past month. "This is their moment in the sun," says S. Robert Lichter of the Washington-based Center for Media and Public Affairs. "And they have to make sure they don't get burned by it."

It is not only the general public that has been turning more and more to CNN since the start of the Gulf war. The network's 24-hour-a-day news reports can be heard echoing down the corridors of power the world over. "Everyone is tuned in to CNN, it's on in the background all the time, like Muzak," reports one White House staff member. An American journalist on a recent swing through the Middle East found Egyptian President Hosni Mubarak and Turkish President Turgut Ozal watching CNN in their offices.

The reason the main actors in the Gulf crisis are glued to their television sets, say media analysts, is that CNN, with its global reach and live reporting, has itself become a key component in international diplomacy. "We know that it's being watched by those heads of state, and we know they're making decisions based on what they see," says Patrick O'Heffernan, assistant to the director of the Center for Strategy, Technology and Policy at the Georgia Institute of Technology. "So one of the fallouts of all this is that what CNN is doing and has done for the past 10 years has tremendously accelerated diplomacy and decision making."

Indeed, international media outlets like CNN may even be superannuating traditional governmental sources of information: The media have become "the primary source of information during crises," says O'Heffernan, because they are "there faster than the CIA or the [National Security Agency]." One story has it that CIA Director William Webster phoned President Bush to inform him of a Scud missile attack; the president replied that he was watching it on television.

The attitude of CNN's executives, basically, is that it is up to world officialdom to catch up with this brave new world of information. During a recent discussion of the press and the war on PBS's "MacNeil/Lehrer NewsHour," former *Wall Street Journal* correspondent Ellen Hume recalled President John F. Kennedy's "being able to take his time during the Cuban missile crisis and decide which cable to answer from the Soviets." She added: "We don't have that luxury anymore; today, Khrushchev would be on CNN announcing that he's taking action." Ed Turner, CNN's vice president for news programming, responded: "CNN, and the technology that helped create it, is not going to go away, nor is it going to be disinvented. And therefore, perhaps, we need a different kind of diplomat to deal with the new reality."

Critics argue that in the case of its coverage of the Gulf, CNN (which after all is a U.S. company) has a duty not to place these new technologies at the disposal of America's adversary. This case was stated perhaps most forcefully by Rep. Lawrence Coughlin in the House Jan. 30. "Since the initial courageous

CNN's John Holliman (left) and Bernard Shaw (right) as they reported from Amman, Jordan, during the war with Iraq (photo courtesy CNN News).

days of reporting from Baghdad by Bernard Shaw, John Holliman, and Peter Arnett," the Pennsylvania Republican said, "the reporting from Baghdad has not been free. Though not by his own wishes, Peter Arnett has been reduced to being the Joseph Goebbels of Saddam Hussein's Hitler-like regime."

The congressman is apparently not alone in his outrage. The Times Mirror survey that showed CNN the choice of six in 10 Americans for Gulf war coverage indicated much less enthusiasm for the cable network's reports from Baghdad. Arnett, CNN's remaining correspondent in the Iraqi capital, was described as having done "a particularly good job in reporting the war" by only 5 percent of the respondents—the lowest rating among the television news reporters and anchors. And a 45 percent plurality said that they disapprove of networks broadcasting news from Iraq that has been censored by Saddam's government, a practice CNN and Arnett are becoming increasingly identified with.

There is also anecdotal evidence of anger at CNN. On a recent MacNeil-Lehrer broadcast, Cynthia Tucker, assistant editorial page editor of the *Atlanta Constitution*, noted: "I do know that there is a lot of suspicion and hostility toward the press out there. As you know, CNN is headquartered right here in Atlanta; in fact, it's only about a block from the newspaper building.... When people who are angry can't get through to CNN, they often call the newspaper to complain. So we've got lots and lots of complaints about Peter Arnett's coverage from Baghdad."

Critics charge that CNN's favorable treatment by Saddam's regime has come with a price. Although the network has been allowed to broadcast virtually without a break since the start of the war, long after other Western journalists were expelled (Baghdad recently allowed European print and television journalists back in), and even to bring in its own satellite dish, Arnett has been on a tight leash. And his reports, vetted by Iraqi censors, have stirred controversy Stateside.

The first was Arnett's Jan. 23 dispatch that began: "Yesterday military information ministry officials took me on a two-hour visit to a powdered milk factory that actually makes infant formula. This was on the Western outskirts of Baghdad. They said it was destroyed by American bombing." Arnett went on to note that "the sign board at the entrance to the factory read 'Baby milk plant' in both English and Arabic." Some of his defenders have interpreted this observation as an attempt by Arnett to signal his doubts about the veracity of what he was being shown. But he concluded by saying the plant was "innocent enough from what we could see."

Arnett's report was immediately denounced by the White House, Joint Chiefs of Staff Colin L. Powell and allied commander Gen. Norman Schwartzkopf, all of whom assured the public that the plant actually produced biological warfare weapons. (Since the report was aired, a company in Northern Ireland has said that the putative packages of infant formula shown by the Iraqis were in fact its dry milk powder, sold to Baghdad prior to the international embargo. They said that their product is not usable as infant formula.)

Indeed, CNN itself had earlier reported on the "baby milk factory" and expressed doubts about its authenticity. "When CNN's Richard Roth covered that 'baby milk factory' last August, he expressed skepticism about it," says Reed Irvine, chairman of Accuracy in Media, a press watchdog group in Washington. "Arnett didn't qualify it. You left that broadcast with the impression that we had bombed a baby milk factory that was supplying the only supply of infant formula to all the children of Iraq under the age of one."

Other controversial CNN reports have included Arnett's 90-minute interview with Saddam, during which the dictator ranted about Zionist plots. Another was with an American peace activist named Anthony Lawrence, who described Operation Desert Storm as "an imperialistic attempt to wrest the oil resources of this region for a bloc of Western nations that don't own them." Additionally, a recent Arnett report of civilian vehicles damaged by allied bombing conspicuously failed to address the question of whether military vehicles were in the vicinity. Arnett also recently referred matter-of-factly to a discrepancy between Iraqi and U.S. figures for downed allied planes, giving equal credence, in the view of some, to both.

Irvine, among others, argues that Arnett, a veteran war correspondent and Pulitzer Prize winner, is himself part of the problem. "His record in Vietnam was horrible," he says, adding that his dispatches from Vietnam for the Associated Press tended to be critical of the U.S. war effort and included some reports of dubious credibility. It was Arnett, he notes, who, after the U.S. forces took the town of Ben Tre from the Viet Cong, quoted an unnamed Air

Force major as saying: "We had to destroy the city to save it." Says Irvine: "To this day, Peter Arnett has never told who this guy was."

Arnett has described his position in Baghdad as similar to that of Harrison Salisbury in Hanoi during the Vietnam War. This worries some media critics, who believe that the prize-winning *New York Times* reporter was used by the North Vietnamese as a conduit for propaganda. Others say it is wrong to second-guess Arnett's motives, given the constraints and pressures under which he is operating. "This really is unfair to Arnett, who is getting out what he can," says Lichter. "But he can't provide editorial judgment, so CNN needs to take responsibility for the gray areas involved in this kind of reporting."

In its own defense, CNN argues that viewers are warned of the constraints that Arnett is operating under. "We constantly label everything very clearly, describing beforehand that Mr. Arnett is not free to go wherever he wants to in the city," says CNN spokesman Alyssa Levy. "That he's escorted, that everything that comes from him has been censored, and that he has very limited sources of outside information aside from what he's told by the Iraqi government. And that's clearly described every time something's on the air from Baghdad."

Says Charlie Hoff, managing director of CNN Newsbeam, the network's domestic satellite service, "We're better-off having a source there, having someone there telling us something, showing us something than if we were cut off totally. It's that simple. The media is a propaganda tool for the world. We're used by our country and by other countries. I don't know what the Pentagon or White House reaction will be to our reporting live out of Baghdad. They may react very negatively, but regardless of what they say, they will certainly monitor everything that comes out of there with a great deal of interest and their intelligence people will pore over that.

"We're not making judgments. All we're doing is providing information from this point and this point: the raw data. The problem is we're censored on every front, so the information we're getting from both sides of the Saudi border is less than 100 percent naked truth. That's not to say it's lies — we don't know if either one of them is lying — but it's not naked truth, and that's a shame."

Some media watchers say they are not concerned about the effect of Iraq's ham-fisted propaganda and disinformation on the American public. "I don't worry about Arnett broadcasting anything back to the States," says Peter Braestrup, who was the *Washington Post*'s Saigon bureau chief during the Vietnam War and author of "Big Story" and "Battle Lines: A Study of Military/Media Relations in Wartime." "I think CNN has that pretty well handled. There's time for rebuttal. The thing I worry about is the Third World."

Indeed, says one expert, a fabrication like the baby milk factory story tends to take on a life of its own, particularly in the Third World, even if it is accompanied by warning labels during its original CNN appearance. "CNN has a tremendous reputation worldwide for being the source of raw, breaking news: the unvarnished truth," says Todd Leventhal, a specialist on disinformation at the U.S. Information Agency. "And it has a very high reputation for integrity and high journalistic standards. If they put a disinformation or propaganda story on Radio Baghdad, it's going to be discounted worldwide. If they can manage, through clever manipulation, coercion or whatever means they have at their disposal, to get some of their propaganda or disinformation themes broadcast by CNN, this gives them tremendous circulation worldwide."

Critics also question CNN's equating of censorship by the Iraqi regime, which has executed journalists, with that of Israel or the allied military command. One such critic is Vice President Dan Quayle, who recently complained, the White House staff member reports, that "when you have a report from Saudi Arabia about American troops, it will say, 'Cleared by military censors,' a report from Israel will have the same thing and so will a report from Iraq. He said this implies a kind of equivalence and that this is outrageous."

Leventhal agrees: "Iraqi-style censorship is more than just wielding a heavy pencil. The Iraqis have no moral qualms about applying any sort of coercion or trickery and deception to achieve their aims. Censorship in the Iraqi context means something far different than military censorship by the coalition forces. If someone were to compare the two, it would be like saying assault with a deadly weapon and jaywalking are both against the law, so therefore they're roughly equivalent."

On the other side of the ledger, CNN's coverage has been beneficial to the allied side in certain ways. "During the first two days of this war, it became clear that the allies were not carpet bombing Baghdad," says Braestrup. "CNN and the other press—but particularly CNN, ... because it broadcasts worldwide—preempted Iraqi claims of carpet bombing and also certified as to the serious damage to military installations that the raids caused." In fact, says Leventhal, the Iraqi regime from the beginning has charged the allies with deliberately bombing residential areas. "Some of the television reporting helped knock that down, there's no doubt about it," he says.

Some argue that Arnett's reporting continues to have intelligence value to the allied side. "Even though he's reporting and showing what the Iraqis want him to, there are still little nuggets of intelligence that our side can pull out of his reports," says O'Heffernan. "You can bet that every inch of that tape that he broadcasts over here is being gone over frame by frame by somebody in the Pentagon, to identify that so-called baby milk factory and where it is and how much damage we did and whether or not our bombs are being set right and should they be a little more powerful, etc."

There is evidence that CNN is becoming more sensitive to the charge that it is acting as an arm of Iraqi propaganda. The network has begun to read critical letters on the air: A recent one lambasted Arnett for not challenging some of Saddam's more outrageous claims during his interview with the dictator. Additionally, the network recently started to air a statement by Perry Smith, one of its military consultants. In it, the retired Air Force general notes that many viewers have complained about the reports emanating from Baghdad concerning civilian casualties and goes on to point out how U.S. air bombardment has become increasingly accurate from war to war. Following the statement, the anchor says that the views are those of Gen. Smith, not CNN. Nonetheless, it is clear that the network is starting to react to the criticism.

But some media watchers think it could do more. Lichter says that since CNN continues to have the jump on its competition, it should not feel impelled to broadcast live or unedited segments from Iraq, like the Saddam interview, the statements of allied POWs or antiwar activists, or guided Iraqi tours of civilian bomb damage. Appearing on CNN's "Larry King Live!" *Los Angeles Times* television critic Howard Rosenberg said of some of CNN's coverage, "It's almost as if it goes in the ear and comes out the mouth without hitting the brain."

"I would pick it up and think of it as the raw material for journalism, rather than journalism itself," Lichter says. "Do a 'surround story' on the nature of propaganda, on how believable this is, rather than getting the material out, just as Saddam wants, and then relying on somebody else to come back and evaluate it. I mean, news judgment is what separates journalism from just pointing a camera and a microphone.

"To say 'This is cleared by censors' is not the same as saying 'Here are the various interpretations that can be put on this; here are the various problems.' That's what they normally do with American government reports, for God's sake. You get critics who say, 'You can't take this at face value.' So all I'm saying is grant Saddam Hussein the same degree of skepticism that you have for the American authorities."

Also recommended: "A Little Network Plays Giant Role in Gulf Coverage" by Glenn Emery; "The War Turns in Cable TV's Favor" by Susan Dillingham and "Press's Mighty Pen Dulled" by Tom Dunkel, all in the Feb. 18, 1991, issue of *Insight* magazine.

The Present: Faces

We welcome them into our living rooms and dens as if they are old friends. In truth, we often spend more time with them than we do with relatives and neighbors.

But how much do we really know about the faces on our television screens? What do these articles tell us about them?

Ultimately, viewers like them because they believe them and think they know them. "Basically, I think I'm a decent person, I think I'm a good person. If I live by my own principles that will be a good example for any one who wants to look at me as a symbol."—Ed Bradley in Mary Corey's article "Ed Bradley's Two Muses: Work, Music."

"He's one of those people who succeeds and lasts in television precisely because there is no 'behind the scenes.' There's no difference between the Brinkley on camera and the Brinkley off."—George Will about David Brinkley in Maria C. Johnson's article "Journalist David Brinkley Has Seen It All and Reported It Well." Walter Cronkite was repeatedly cited as "the most trustworthy man in America," during his tenure as anchor at CBS. The same can be and is said about many of the other anchors and reporters seen everyday.

They are prodigious workers. Tom Brokaw has been nicknamed "Duncan the Wonder Horse" by colleagues astonished by his "legendary work ethic" as James Kaplan writes in his article about Tom Brokaw. Many of the others have also achieved national recognition for their work.

They are driven by desire to be the best in the business and to be on top of any breaking story. They are all captivated by how the world works. Many are insatiable readers.

The travel which their careers demand has cost them the normal lives most families lead. Ed Bradley, Sam Donaldson, Charles Kuralt, Harry Reasoner, and Peter Jennings all have divorces in their background; their marriages often became casualties of their careers away from home.

An exceptional college education does not make a significant difference in broadcast news. In the column "Intelligence Report," in *Parade* magazine, Dec. 30, 1990, Lloyd Shearer wrote:

> It is interesting to note that there is no correlation between this nation's three highest-paid TV anchormen and their educational backgrounds. Dan Rather, 59, who pulls down about $4 million a year at CBS, was graduated from Sam Houston State Teachers College in Huntsville, Tx., in 1953 with a B.A. for secondary school teaching. Tom Brokaw, 50, after a slow start at the University of Iowa, attended the University of South

Dakota at Vermillion, from which he was graduated in 1962 with a B.A. in political science. His salary at NBC is reportedly $2.7 million annually. And ABC's Peter Jennings, 52, the most popular of the news stars, dropped out of high school in Ottawa, Canada, at 17. Today he earns a yearly stipend of nearly $2 million.

Many instinctively see "the big picture"; how world events interlock. Peter Jennings' years of experience as a foreign correspondent are an example. They understand media and political events world-wide. They understand the subtleties of their craft. (Ted Koppel's use of sensory deprivation on his guests in his "Nightline" show is a clear example. He is a clear master of "manipulative psychology.") They understand the power of television news—and they acknowledge its weaknesses, especially its ephemeral nature. They understand how to play hardball with politicians and opponents. The articles about Sam Donaldson and Dan Rather are particularly instructive in this regard.

They are aware of the problems of prejudice in their industry and are acutely aware of the inequities in salaries and prestige among white men and women, blacks, Hispanics and other minorities (even though some privately acknowledge that addressing old inequities may be a long-term effort). They are aware of the celebrity status of their careers and acknowledge that this often gets in the way of covering a story without making it a "celebrity event." They are aware of all the other instabilities in their profession.

We might forget they carry the emotional baggage of aches, hurts, and regrets just as the rest of us do.

Above all, they love what they do.

Here are the friends you invite into your living room or den everyday. Perhaps, through these articles, you can know them even better.

Roone Arledge

"Rooneglow"

by Judy Flander

What inspired ABC News to corral top anchors, drive ratings steadily up and enter the '90s as the most dominant network news team ever? It must have been ... Roone Arledge.

There's a baby blue Bentley double-parked just a few doors down from the ABC News offices on New York's West 66th Street, the chauffeur, in civvies, curled up cozily in the backseat reading a book.

He's waiting for his boss, ABC News President Roone Arledge who, in a couple of hours, will come charging out of the building and off to a meeting, two assistants in his wake. "It's a used Bentley," explains Arledge's own boss, Capital Cities/ABC Chairman Thomas S. Murphy, with an indulgent chuckle. "Roone told me he bought it at a good price." With a No. 1-rated evening news broadcast, a strong bench of correspondents and producers and a stable of star journalists — and the top-rated programs in which to showcase them — Arledge, a robust 59, is riding high.

"Nightline," "This Week with David Brinkley" and "20/20" are all part of the Arledge era that began in 1977. Prestigious foreign coverage, which includes investigative documentaries such as Peter Jennings' recent exposé on the ramifications of U.S. support of the Khmer Rouge in Cambodia, has added a dimension to ABC's reputation as a serious and committed news operation. And, most important, profits, according to an impeccable source, are crowding a hundred million dollars a year.

"Probably Roone's greatest accomplishment politically," says a former ABC associate fondly, "has been in getting Cap Cities to love him."

"Roone's a ferocious power player," says another former ABC executive. "He fits into the CEO mentality, playing Cap Cities cautiously and adjusting his centers."

Just four years ago, when Cap Cities took over ABC, Murphy may never have known that Roone Arledge kept a chauffeured car at his disposal. In those days it was a Jag with a liveried driver, and it was parked discreetly on side streets or over at nearby Tavern on the Green. "ABC World News Tonight" was in third place in the ratings, and the thrifty, new, buttoned-up management was checking out all the network's operations and personnel.

Judy Flander is a Washington, D.C., freelancer and a Washington Journalism Review contributing editor.

158   The Present: Faces

"When Cap Cities came in," says a former Arledge associate, "everybody was on shaky ground." Roone Arledge, particularly. With his opulent style of getting around and unorthodox style of getting things done, the atmosphere at ABC News had to have been a bit of culture shock for Murphy and Cap Cities President Dan Burke. According to one former executive, Arledge was really afraid that Cap Cities would fire him.

But he was hardly taken unawares. Before Cap Cities' arrival, Arledge says he "saw what was coming" and took steps to make the operation "more efficient." This translated into reported reductions of 200 positions, mainly by attrition, $25 million slashed from ABC News's annual budget and temporary belt-tightening [by] Arledge, known for his flamboyant excesses. And, of course, the Jag, the most conspicuous consumption symbol, was out of sight.

These days, Tom Murphy says expansively, "Roone has always gone first class." In fact, Murphy, accompanying Arledge and the "Prime Time Live" staff for a broadcast from the Kremlin in January of 1989, took a day trip to Leningrad with him to visit the Hermitage Museum. He's a "big fan" of "Prime Time," considered by many critics to be Arledge's only clinker. "It's doing 40 percent better than other shows in that spot did," says Murphy. ("Prime Time" is in a killer time period Thursday nights, up against NBC's "L.A. Law" and CBS's "Knots Landing.")

Of the three network news divisions, only ABC has so far weathered the recent corporate takeovers without demoralizing personnel reductions and the kind of ratings that rattle staff and make executives turn pale.

"The danger is for the news division to be the weak sister financially," explains Arledge. "It's hard enough to do solid journalism in a culture where anything controversial alienates advertisers," he said in a rare press interview late this spring.

His staff and colleagues say he's reluctant to do interviews. They frequently use the word "shy" to describe a man who is also outgoing and friendly, and who loves to dance at ABC parties. But when you have his attention it will be focused 100 percent on you—everyone at ABC will tell you that. Nancy Dobi, Arledge's assistant, while walking down the hall to his office, explains why she's worked for him for 10 years. "Roone is the most interesting and funniest person."

It's going to be a one-on-one interview. No flacks. Dobi slips out but not before asking me, laughingly, if I expect to uncover the "Roone mystique."

The corner office has a wall of television screens—all three networks, CNN, ESPN, C-Span and others. Another wall is lined with shelves groaning under the weight of Arledge's sports and news trophies, 36 Emmies among them. His crowded desk is brightened by a few big Russian dolls-within-dolls. But these aren't the usual babushka dolls, they're depictions of dead Soviet leaders. "Imagine having a Stalin doll, a Brezhnev doll, making a joke about the head of the country and selling them in the airport," Arledge says with a small smile.

Arledge cuts a handsome figure in a superbly tailored suit. He long ago traded his aviator glasses for contacts. People predicted he would be charming. He is. Also disarmingly forthright.

"I was probably not involved as I should have been in 'Prime Time' even though I started the concept, getting in Diane Sawyer and all that," he says.

Any one of ABC's precious few women correspondents (19 out of 105) would have killed to be on that program as coanchor with Sam Donaldson. But Arledge was after Sawyer. "The thing about Diane is, she is a hard-working, dedicated journalist and she happens to be attractive," he says. "Beautiful women attract people." He knows it sounds "sexist," but he's also convinced it's a fact.

So the man who, on taking over the presidency of ABC News, raided CBS for additional talent and created a market that made NBC's Tom Brokaw and CBS's Dan Rather millionaires, struck again.

Sawyer, a CBS "60 Minutes" correspondent, was already in the million-dollar bracket, but she succumbed to the Arledge charm after months of being courted with roses, lunches and dinners, signing on for a reported $1.6 million a year. "I found out about three great Italian restaurants," says Sawyer, delightedly replaying the courtship. She says she now sees him for an occasional lunch at the nearby Cafe d'Artistes.

Like other network news chiefs, Arledge has always had an eye for beauty. Some of his women correspondents reportedly turned green when he hired Kathleen Sullivan, who was then what he calls a "'CNN newsreader," as coanchor of "World News This Morning" in 1982. Arledge says he wasn't concerned about Sullivan's lack of experience because he had veteran correspondent Steve Bell as coanchor to take over during breaking stories. Her departure in October of 1987 to become coanchor of "CBS This Morning" pained Arledge, who was known to have been very fond of her. But he looks startled when asked if he'd take Sullivan back now that she's been bumped by CBS for still another ABC defector, Paula Zahn.

"I haven't thought of it," he says, adding that he expects she'll find a berth in CBS's sports division. As for Zahn, another dazzler, "We could have matched CBS's offer, but it wasn't worth a million dollars for us to have her do two five-minute news cut-ins" for "Good Morning America." (Except for the news cut-ins, GMA has always been controlled by the entertainment division.) Zahn, he says, "was making $200,000 from us."

Zahns and Sullivans are out there waiting to be discovered. Prizes like Diane Sawyer are few.

But even with Sawyer, something went wrong with "Prime Time Live," forcing the program to resort to hype and titillation and pander to pop personalities in a battle to hold its own. Ratings zoom when the show snares tabloid targets like Marla Maples and the racially provocative Louis Farrakhan. At times Donaldson and Sawyer seem visibly uncomfortable. Rick Kaplan, the executive producer who was moved over from Ted Koppel's groundbreaking "Nightline," doesn't want to talk about it at all.

"I think we got a little carried away with the live element," Arledge admits. But he believes the show will evolve. "It's a much better program than people have given it credit for," he says. It's the time period that bothers him most. "We're having a difficult struggle," he says. "I can't understand why news shows have to prove themselves in the worst time periods even though they're profitable."

You would think they would want to nurture them. It puts us under great pressure even though we have a two-year commitment."

Except for a recent pep talk to the "Prime Time" staff, Arledge keeps his distance. "If you get too involved," he says, "all the ideas come from you. People have to grow up on that program looking to the senior producers. It's a little delicate when you should get involved and when you shouldn't."

"Arledge believes you put good people in key places and let them breathe," says Sam Donaldson.

It's a management style for which Arledge is both praised and faulted. An admirer says, "It's pretty shrewd of him to stay away from that show. To put it bluntly, the man on the top doesn't necessarily get blamed for the bad stuff, and he gets credit for the good stuff. This is about power. Roone is master of masters when it comes to maintaining his role."

Associates, past and present, talk about a chief who doesn't delegate explicit authority, who lets people have the temporary power and the opportunity for success or failure. "Some people can thrive with that, some go nuts," one of them says. Arledge is also extremely deliberate in making decisions, sometimes letting things drag on for weeks, even months. "I call it doing the Roone ponder," says Frank Gifford. "He has an incredible mind, and he looks at every facet; he can see farther ahead than anyone."

However maddening his methods to some, Arledge's success as the reigning news chieftain is indisputable. "World News Tonight" holds a steady No. 1 rating, often a full point above CBS. "20/20" has established a profitable evening newsmagazine in an area where NBC's wheels keep slipping. "Nightline" occupies virgin territory unexplored by other networks. "This Week" has revitalized the Sunday morning interview format. And the combined star power of Peter Jennings, Barbara Walters, Hugh Downs, Ted Koppel, David Brinkley, George Will, Sam Donaldson and Diane Sawyer has no parallel in the history of television news.

How has he pulled it off? A lot of people will tell you it's done with mirrors, an explanation reinforced by Arledge's image as a Wizard of Oz who operates from behind a screen, seldom seen by the rank and file.

"Roone has a unique, eccentric style, but it works," says Brit Hume, an Arledge favorite who took over Donaldson's spot at the White House. "He is a recluse, but at the same time when you come in contact with him he is affable and astonishingly shy. There's an aura of mystery about him. That's part of his mystique." But for most news staffers Arledge is only a voice on the red "Roone Phone" installed in every ABC News control room. From the moment he signed on at ABC in 1960 as a sports producer, he has exhibited an eagle eye for detail and is likely to call any show at any time. "He's definitely a presence in the control room," says a lower-run Washington bureau staffer.

"It is the difference between having a producer running a news division instead of a newspaperman," says Dorrance Smith, executive producer of "Nightline." "There's not a typical reason for Roone calling a control room. It could range from lighting to telling you one of the guests is boring, so focus on the other. Or, he calls and says, this is a bit long in tooth. So we go to a commercial."

Arledge often calls "World News Tonight" Executive Producer Paul Friedman during a broadcast. "It drives producers crazy, by the way," Peter Jennings laughs, "but no producer would want to say that." What Friedman does say is that Arledge is "a superb editor," and "the remarkable thing to me is he doesn't meddle more." Arledge is also very much a presence at his Monday morning staff meetings with executive producers and anchors. "It's his agenda," Jennings says. "The mythology is that Roone sits at a mighty Wurlitzer and whips out a tune," says ABC News Vice President Dick Wald. "The truth is he leads the team."

A lot of the time, though, many people don't actually know where Arledge is. He'll go off to a golf game with his pal, Frank Gifford, or to a lunch or a dinner and get involved in hours-long conversations and be completely out of touch. He is notorious for not returning phone calls, and while he is known to "roam the halls on the fifth floor," he does not maintain an open office door policy. He has, on occasion, even left his own vice presidents, like Wald and Irwin Weiner, cooling their heels in his hall. "Sometimes David Burke couldn't even get in the door," says another former ABC executive referring to the Arledge first deputy who jumped ship to become president of CBS News in 1988.

"I have seen a lot of people get emotionally bent out of shape by believing they could engage Roone in some kind of friendship or constant dialogue," says Jennings, who has been friends with Arledge for 20 years. "I decided long ago you just don't invest that emotional currency to get him on the phone. If you really have to talk to him, you can get to him." As close as he has been to Arledge, Jennings says he never forgets their essential employer-employee relationship.

Arledge is often backstopped by ABC News Senior Vice President Joanna Bistany, who is known as "The Lion at the Gate." Even executive producers don't always get past her. Since Burke's departure, Bistany seems to have taken over many of his duties. "I inherited David's title," she explains.

Bistany, who came to ABC News in 1983 as director of news information from the White House, where she was David Gergen's special assistant in the press office, is known to have a close relationship with Arledge. A number of women correspondents at ABC who have tried for years to get some sort of parity with ABC males, speak of her disparagingly because, as the woman most strategically placed to help them alert Arledge to their plight, they believe she has done nothing. "She's the Nancy Reagan of ABC News," says one observer. "David Burke once told me Joanna got where she is because she's one of the boys," says a former member of ABC's inner circle. Not all ABC women agree on these assessments. "I've found Joanna to be an ally," says Diane Sawyer.

People at ABC News, including the stars, often wait a long time for that golden moment when Arledge concentrates his undivided attention on them. "It's like a lover relationship," observes a former staffer. "Every once in a while you get it, and it is so strong and powerful you wait for it to happen again."

"Roone is wonderfully engaging," says Jennings, "but don't expect to have another six-hour lunch."

One striking fact about Arledge's presidency is that he no longer has any powerful successors. "After Roone, there's nobody," a colleague remarks. Dick Wald, an Arledge classmate at Columbia and a former NBC News president, is considered "charming on the cocktail circuit" but lacking in any real power. He has never been as close to Arledge as David Burke. Those two men remain good friends. Admitting it was sometimes "hard" working with Arledge, Burke says the difficult moments were "minuscule" compared to the quality of their overall relationship. "He taught me everything I know about the business."

Probably the only serious contender was Av Westin, a former vice president and executive producer of ABC's evening newscast and, subsequently, of "20/20," who made no secret to colleagues that he resented Arledge's management style. When Cap Cities came in, Westin made a politically fatal end run about Arledge in a highly publicized memo to the new management in which he outlined his own ideas for running the news department. "At Cap Cities, you just don't break the rules like that," says a former ABC staffer close to the scene. Cap Cities backed Arledge, who put Westin out of harm's way until his contract run out. "Another person would have fired him outright," says a colleague.

Arledge, it seems, can't fire people outright. "He is like a child, like a boy, a dear spirit," a former ABC associate says, with affection. "He has his own way. He makes them miserable until they go away."

The people who have had this treatment call him "icy." "If Roone wants to pretend you are not in the room, he is as good at doing that as anybody else," says a former colleague. "It's his way of avoiding contact and confrontational situations. He's the classic example of an extremely talented creative person who has problems being a manager." One ex-ABC staffer complains that "the only feedback you get from him is criticism."

While some people talk about Arledge's elusiveness, or his remoteness, or his coldness, he is also described as charismatic, brilliant and fun to be with. "Roone's a Renaissance man," says Ted Koppel. "He's as much at home with opera or ballet or professional boxing." It's a "paradox" that's always amazed and delighted his second wife, Ann, from whom he's been divorced for seven years.

Roone and Ann Arledge keep in touch, checking on each other's well-being, she says. "The best part is, we're good friends. He's just awfully busy. But there is deep love there. There always will be."

Their parting caused both of them a great deal of pain, friends say. Arledge was deeply affected and was more unavailable than usual. No one knows why the marriage failed. But Arledge has never had much time left over for family, either for Ann or for his first wife, Joan, or their four children.

His position has given him entré into high society, and he cuts a swath on the haut dinner party circuit. Ethel Kennedy and Eunice Shriver are long-time friends, and he has hobnobbed with socialites like Marietta Tree and Brooke Astor. Some of his critics call him "a social climber," and George Bush, who invited him to a White House dinner (Arledge took along Joanna Bistany), dubbed him "my new best friend," according to *Newsweek*.

At least once keeping such company brought on accusations of conflict of interest. In 1985 Arledge axed a "20/20" story about rumored affairs between Marilyn Monroe and both Bobby and John F. Kennedy. It was assumed — and still is by many — that he killed the piece because of his friendship with the Kennedys.

It's a motivation Arledge has always denied. "The original purport of that piece was that there was a connection between [the alleged liaisons] and either organized crime or intelligence and the White House," he explains. "I thought all they proved was that there might have been a relationship between Bobby Kennedy and Marilyn Monroe, and I don't think they totally proved that."

The episode gave the press fodder for months. Everyone on the "20/20" staff from executive producer Av Westin to coanchors Barbara Walters and Hugh Downs protested.

"We had three sources on everything. Roone tried to find fourteen reasons why there wasn't enough information. But I knew all along he planned to kill it," says a former "20/20" staffer.

"After they got through dramatizing their unhappiness," Arledge says, "it turned into a big flap."

Whatever he does, Roone Arledge has always had a press following accorded more to celebrities than to network executives. Sportswriters were the first to give him extensive coverage. Before he transformed the face of network news, Arledge literally invented modern sports television. His brainstorms included technical wonders like instant replay and creative programming — notably that of showmanship, "Monday Night Football," with its prescient three-anchor format — Howard Cosell, Don Meredith and Frank Gifford. He was elevated to president of ABC sports in 1968, a job he held for 18 years before Cap Cities finally had him relinquish it in 1986.

As sports chief, Arledge loved to hang out with star jocks, jetting off to far-flung golf courses with his close associates, staying up half the night carousing, affecting their macho attire which, at the time, was heavy into safari jackets, unbuttoned shirts and gold chains. "He was a big lug of a guy, a sucker for a skirt," remarks a former ABC woman correspondent.

It was an image he had to live down — along with his P. T. Barnum reputation — when he became president of ABC News. "There was a time when I think any number of us were not particularly thrilled at Roone standing up to represent our organization," Jennings says. "The polish, and sense of how important what we do is [that] he has acquired over the last 10 years is really considerable."

When Arledge made his move to head the news division, his main obstacle was then ABC News President Bill Sheehan, a 20-year veteran of the network. "There was a change of management, and Fred Pierce became president of ABC," recalls Sheehan, who is now director of information for NASA. Arledge, he says, "was talking to the right person in Freddy, not my favorite guy. He decided Roone could do the job better than I."

Arledge may have had to shove Sheehan aside to get the job, but when he took over the presidency of ABC News it wasn't a prize. You couldn't tell the difference between the network's third-place nightly news show and "Family Feud." Sheehan's legacy was the odd-couple anchoring team of Barbara

Walters, who had been hired away from the NBC "Today" show for a milestone one million dollars a year, and long-time ABC correspondent Harry Reasoner, who made no effort to hide his distaste at being paired with Walters. "It was painful to watch," Arledge says.

"One of the most difficult jobs I had to start with was finding a graceful way of getting Barbara out of a situation where she was going to be destroyed. I knew from the beginning that it was Harry who would have to go. Barbara was just too valuable to this organization." Arledge says he still has a residue of guilt "for never even giving Harry a chance."

His ultimate solution was a recycling of the three-anchor ploy with Max Robinson in Chicago, Peter Jennings in London and Frank Reynolds in Washington.

Because of Walters' delicate position, Arledge at first named the men to "desks" rather than designating them as anchors. Although he says he talked to Robert MacNeil (of PBS's "MacNeil/Lehrer NewsHour") for the New York "desk," he decided to leave it "empty," also in deference to Walters. Eventually everyone but the principals began referring to the troika as anchors.

"The main driving force behind the three anchors was that we were competing with Walter Cronkite, and we didn't have a Walter Cronkite," says Arledge.

"Oh, is that what he says?" laughs Jennings when told this illuminating comment. "That was my quote. Roone denied it for years." Yes, he says, amused, Roone does rewrite history.

Whatever—the move worked. For 11 weeks in 1980, ABC News was actually in second place, on the heels of the seemingly invincible Cronkite. "For us to move into second place was really more exciting for us than when we moved into first place," Arledge says with that disarming boyish grin.

Then disaster struck. "Frank was suffering from cancer, and he never told us," Arledge says. "He was off the air for a long time, and we were trying to find out what was wrong. Ratings were going down. I doubt if any other organization would go as long with an anchor sick and not knowing why. I'm not sure we could do that today."

Reynolds died. Max Robinson, uncomfortable as a black role model and convinced ABC was not doing enough for blacks, was to self-destruct.

It was August of 1983, and Arledge had two "equally qualified persons" to go solo, Ted Koppel and Jennings. "It was a dilemma," he says, "one that was solved when Koppel graciously decided to stay with 'Nightline.'"

Arledge's next hurdle was to talk Jennings into returning from London and going it alone. "Peter was reluctant to take it on as solo anchor," Arledge says. And it was at least a year before Jennings decided he'd made the right decision. It took six years of slow, steady growth for "World News Tonight" to make it into first place.

Arledge turned next to Sunday morning, where ABC was producing a half-hour children's show, "Animals, Animals, Animals," followed by a panel interview show, "Issues and Answers." According to Dorrance Smith, a former "This Week with David Brinkley" executive producer, "Roone had felt for a long time that the formats of all three network Sunday shows—where panels grilled one guest for a half hour — were dull and boring." Arledge shelved both programs, came up with a new hour format and looked about for a "heavyweight" anchor. He was "eager" to have George Will as a regular panelist, "but George said he didn't want to do it every week — he had to go to church or something."

Arledge, who needed a strong, proven anchor in Washington, asked Dick Wald, who had been president of NBC News, to set up a meeting with David Brinkley. "David loved the format from the beginning," Arledge says.

"This Week with David Brinkley," which began airing in 1981 includes a summary of the week's news, a viewer fill-in on the subject at hand, and George Will and the feisty Sam Donaldson as regulars. "After I got David," Arledge says, "George Will came immediately aboard. Sam was obvious from the first as a good candidate for the program." Arledge, apparently, has left Brinkley on his own. "I almost never see him, never talk to him," Brinkley says.

Arledge also cornered the late-night news market, giving Johnny Carson real competition. It was the dream of all news divisions to have an hour news program, and ABC was least likely to get one, Arledge explains. His original idea was an hour of news from 11 to midnight, local news followed by a half-hour of network news.

"'Nightline' was Roone's inspiration," says Koppel, who has been anchoring the acclaimed broadcast since it debuted in March of 1980. Arledge, who had been waiting for a way to show affiliates that an 11:30 newscast could make it, seized on the time period in late 1979 to run updates on "The Iran Crisis: America Held Hostage." Frank Reynolds was the first anchor, but midway through the prolonged hostage crisis, it became clear that the two shows were more than he could handle. Koppel, Arledge's choice as a replacement, proved to be a natural anchor and demonstrated his brilliance as an interviewer.

Arledge has always had his producer eye on the show, says Koppel. "It's enormously difficult to watch people do something different than the way he would choose. More often than not he would let go unless the program ran into some trouble." The only area where Arledge does not hold sway is weekday mornings. "When I first took over, quite frankly, I thought about taking on 'Good Morning America' from the entertainment division. I could have done that easily at the time."

What stopped him cold was a program regular, Hollywood gossip columnist Rona Barrett, who expected to be ABC News entertainment editor. "I felt we had to establish ourselves as a serious news division," Arledge says.

Does Arledge have any new worlds to conquer as ABC News chief? Yes, once the problems surrounding "Prime Time Live" are solved, he'll turn his attention back to Sunday mornings. "I want to do a companion piece to the Brinkley show," he says. ABC News has two half-hour Sunday morning shows preceding Brinkley: "Business World," anchored by Sander Vanocur, and "The Health Show," for which correspondent Keren Stone has been acting anchor since Kathleen Sullivan's departure. "I'd like to take business and health and combine them into an overall news program." Would that call for another heavy-duty anchor? "Yes, it will," Arledge says with a laugh, closing down a discussion as to who that would be.

Whatever negatives some people harbor about Arledge, part of his mystique is a sympathetic concern for colleagues in crisis, especially for those he has known for a long time. In a recent interview, the first thing Howard Cosell noted about Arledge was how concerned he was when Cosell's wife had surgery for lung cancer two years ago. "Nobody was more attentive than Roone Arledge, sending her flowers every day, phoning her as soon as she was able to talk." (Cosell was somewhat harsher on the ABC News president in his book, *I Never Played the Game*. He called Arledge "Machiavellian" and expressed anger over how Arledge handled his exit from "Monday Night Football." "I had broken my back for him for 13 years on 'Monday Night Football,' and he never even called or dropped a line to say goodbye.")

Even Geraldo Rivera, one of the few people whom Arledge has actually fired outright—he took public umbrage when Arledge killed the "20/20" piece on Marilyn Monroe and the Kennedys—has mellowed. "My feelings for Roone now are as an old friend who took incredible chances with me, withstood the critics and allowed me freedom even though I didn't fit the mold."

Neither does Arledge. And that's probably what's made him network news' longest running president and, as Washington Bureau Chief George Watson puts it, "the most powerful and interesting force in network television today."

Meanwhile, five floors below Arledge's office, the blue Bentley is warming up.

Ed Bradley

"*Ed Bradley's Two Muses: Work, Music*"
by Mary Corey

Ed Bradley has been a key member of the "60 Minutes" team since 1980. But who is he, what is he like off camera and what has he accomplished? Mary Corey offers a brief look at the other sides of Ed Bradley.

For the past three years, Mary Corey has been a reporter for the features section of The Baltimore Sun. Her work also has appeared in The Los Angeles Times, The Philadelphia Inquirer and The Houston Chronicle.

In 1985, she was a magna cum laude graduate of The College of Notre Dame of Maryland, where she majored in communication arts and minored in English and political science.

She is single and lives in Baltimore.

You can call him Ed, or you can call him Teddy.

When it comes to CBS News correspondent Ed Bradley, two separate identities emerge.

First there's the seasoned "60 Minutes" journalist in the double-breasted pinstriped suit who spoke to 500 people at Towson State University Sunday. The man who is rumored to make more than one million dollars a year, the veteran who has covered everything from the Vietnam War to the White House.

And then there's the footloose Teddy, his self-professed "alter ego," who loves to rock and roll with New Orleans soul groups like the Neville Brothers, who got his ear pierced for his forty-fifty birthday and who skis "hard and fast" down powdery Aspen slopes every chance he gets.

Just who is Ed Bradley?

"At times he's quiet and reserved, removed and difficult," says the 47-year-old newsman during a ride to the airport after the speech. "And at other times, he's Teddy — the easiest person in the world, outgoing and gregarious and loads of fun."

But his colleagues don't always appreciate his less serious side. "I'm not sure they understand it or even like it," he says. "But they accept it because it's me. I don't think anyone can question the job that I do. I show up and I hit the mark."

Jeanne Solomon Langley, a London-based producer for the show, sees a symbiosis between these two identities. "It's not like he's a broadcast journalist for the fame and the money so he can lead this other life. There isn't a conflict," she says. "I think when he goes to Aspen to relax he comes back with a renewed vigor for the '60 Minutes' side of things."

On this night, if he had his druthers, he'd be watching his show in the privacy of his Manhattan co-op. Instead, he's catching the tail end of the program in a limousine, en route to the airport. "Most of the time I watch it by myself, almost never with strangers," Mr. Bradley says impatiently during a commercial. "I don't like to watch it with a lot of people because people talk.... What are you supposed to say, 'Shut up'?"

Slouching against this plush seat, his face illuminated only by the eerie glow of the TV and an occasional street lamp, there's no doubt he's a handsome man. Flecks of gray that have crept into his beard and hair make him appear distinguished. And his custom-tailored suit, pocket scarf and tortoise-shell glasses complement the picture of Ed Bradley as worldly, sophisticated, urbane network correspondent, albeit one who sees himself as someone who can "just sort of go out and meet people and try to get them to talk to me."

In his nine-year career with the show, some of those more memorable people have included Lena Horne, Sir Laurence Olivier and George Burns. He's won three Emmys for his work on the show, along with several other awards for various segments on "CBS Reports."

Ms. Langley has watched the newsman hone and refine his talents. "The longer he's on '60 Minutes,' the more assured he's become," she says. "People imagine he's going to be very aggressvie. But he's a good listener. He makes it as informal as possible.... His is a relaxed style."

168 The Present: Faces

To the audience at Towson State, he displays that easy confidence when explaining the dynamic behind the show. "I often think that at '60 Minutes' we're very much like the storytellers of centuries ago who traveled to the farthest corners of their world to stop at villages and the great cities of their day exchanging stories. I often imagine them returning home and having people gather around a fireplace to hear one of the storytellers say, 'You can't believe what I saw' or 'Wait till I tell you about this guy I met in Marrakech.' Well, imagine that that television set is the fireplace of the 20th century and there we are each week, current day Marco Polos saying to you, 'You can't believe what happened last week when I went to...'"

Islamabad, Pakistan. Mr. Bradley just returned Thursday ("or Friday, I can't remember," he says) from interviewing Prime Minister Benazir Bhutto. The week before he was in London, and his itinerary for the coming week includes a quick trip to Florida. There are estimates that Mr. Bradley, who has been divorced twice, travels 100,000 miles, often visiting more than 50 cities a year.

"I'm afraid to add up all the miles I travel," he says. "It might make me want to think about getting another job.... But I think I'd go crazy if I had a 9-to-5 job in one place every day."

But a yearly salary that a source says exceeds one million dollars helps repay Mr. Bradley for the rigors of the profession. Speaking dates such as the one at Towson State can bring $5,000 and up, according to Janet Cosby, whose agency books Mr. Bradley's talks.

He attributes much of his success to the fact that "people believe I'm fair and sense that I'm honest about what I'm doing," he says. "I'll give [interviewees] a fair shake [and] that makes them feel comfortable sitting down saying, 'OK, Ed, here's my story.'"

His parents separated when he was an infant, and Mr. Bradley was raised by his mother in a lower-middle-class neighborhood in Philadelphia. "It wasn't a storybook American childhood," he says. "But I survived."

Basic to that survival was his mother's outlook on life. "I was always told you can be whatever you want to be," he says. "All you have to do is work hard at it. And I believed 'em," he says and laughs at his own naivete. "It's not really true. But if you're going to succeed you almost have to believe it."

While he doesn't relish his image as a role model for minority youngsters, he's learned to accept it.

"It's not something that I wake up every day and say, 'OK, let's put the role model out there.' I have to live my life for me. I accept the fact that I am a role model. I used to not like it. ... Basically, I think I'm a decent person, I think I'm a good person. If I live my life by my own principles that will be a good example for anyone who wants to look at me as a symbol."

He majored in education at Cheyney State College, near Philadelphia, but his life took a dramatic turn after he met a disc jockey during a lecture. "I went out to the radio station, took one look at it, and I knew that I was put on this earth to be on the radio," he says. After volunteering at the station for a year, he was hired. But with a starting salary of $1.50 an hour, he taught elementary school during the day to meet expenses.

In 1967, he was hired by WCBS radio in New York but resigned 3½ years later and moved to Paris. Although he told friends and colleagues that he was leaving to write the Great American Novel and poetry, he says, "The major reason I did it was [because] I didn't want to work every day.... I never had the luxury of free time, to do what I wanted to do, to answer my own bell."

But by the fall of 1971, he was back in broadcast journalism, working as a stringer for the Paris bureau of CBS. Subsequent assignments for the network included serving as a television correspondent during the Vietnam War, covering the 1976 presidential campaign and becoming a White House correspondent during the Carter administration. He also was the anchor of "CBS Sunday Night News" and a principal correspondent for "CBS Reports" before being named as a co-editor and correspondent on "60 Minutes" in 1980.

Despite his success in journalism, he says, "I'd still love to be a musician. I just don't have that kind of talent."

Being on stage for an upcoming HBO/Cinemax special was a highlight of his life, he says. "For me to get up there ... [singing] with someone like the Neville Brothers — a world class, multitalented band — it's just fantastic, it's the greatest fantasy come true."

David Brinkley

"A Touch of Wit: Journalist David Brinkley Has Seen It All and Reported It Well"

by Maria C. Johnson

William Whitworth profiled David Brinkley in the article "An Accident of Casting" in The New Yorker *in 1968. Here Maria C. Johnson of* The Greensboro *(North Carolina)* News and Record *updates Brinkley's life, as he nears retirement.*

Maria C. Johnson, 30, is a features writer for the Greensboro News & Record, Greensboro, N.C. A native of Lexington, Ky., she holds a bachelor's degree in communication from the University of Kentucky. She joined the News & Record in 1983. She worked as a bureau reporter, a federal courts reporter and a general assignment news reporter before joining the features staff in 1987. She writes about a variety of people and subjects.

CHAPEL HILL—He started out writing about activism at his Wilmington high school—what students were wearing, what they were eating, who was buying sodas for whom.

"Just junk, trash," ABC newsman David Brinkley remembers. Eventually, he covered other subjects—political conventions, things like that.

"I am a very good reporter," he says flatly.

He has come to Chapel Hill, from cherry blossoms to dogwood blossoms, to be inducted into the N.C. Journalism Hall of Fame at the University of North Carolina at Chapel Hill—never mind that he never took a class here. He may be the only dean without a college degree.

Brinkley's name became a household word after he and a Montana cowboy-turned-reporter named Chet Huntley started television's first hit news program.

"The Huntley-Brinkley Report" won eight Emmys in 14 years on NBC. Huntley reported the news from New York, Brinkley from Washington. The show ended with the now-famous salutations:

"Good night, David."

"Good night, Chet."

After the show ended in 1970, Brinkley stayed with NBC for 11 years before going to ABC, where he happily presides over his Sunday morning news review, "This Week with David Brinkley."

Last year, his book "Washington Goes to War," an insider's tale of how Washington lost its innocence during World War II, camped out on the bestseller lists.

He is a very busy man.

He arrives for an interview promptly, dressed in tweed blazer, open-collar shirt and casual slacks. He offers a hand, mutters something about the quality of the hotel, and takes a seat in the lobby. He sweeps his eyes from one end of the room to the other. He looks bored. Its the same I've-seen-it-all look that has been satirized on "Saturday Night Live."

He's never seen the imitiation, nor any done by comedians of the 1960s who found material in his terse style and deflating wit, his enduring trademark.

When Soviet Premier Nikita Khrushchev's statement, "Your children will live under socialism," was altered to "Your grandchildren will live under socialism," Brinkley commented, "We've saved one whole generation," says a profile of Brinkley in "Current Biography."

Witty, yes; cynical, no, says daughter Alexis, 19, a freshman at Chapel Hill.

"He definitely is warm and caring," she says. "I'd say he's a little bit shy, which you wouldn't think by seeing him on TV. Obviously, in the position he's in he can't be shy asking people questions and things, but as for personal things ... he's not forceful."

She says her father leaves his work at the office but brings his humor home.

"One thing he always does is, if you come home and say, 'I've had such a bad day' and the whole world seems to be crashing down, you'll look over and he's like he's playing the violin. He's very funny."

Brinkley looks rested and every bit of his 68 years. He is slightly stooped;

he just had a back operation. The hand that picks a loose thread on the sofa is covered with age spots, but the blue eyes catch a spark when he starts talking about news.

After high school, he took a job with the Wilmington *Star-News,* where he worked for two years until the draft for World War II started. Brinkley signed up and served for 1½ years before he was given a medical discharge for kidney problems he insisted he didn't have. He returned home.

Brinkley grew up in downtown Wilmington. His mother, Mary, had him when she was 42, an embarrassment for a proper Southern lady. His father, William, a bureaucrat for the now-defunct Atlantic Coastline Railroad, died when Brinkley was a child.

Young David, named for a Scottish king, spent long hours in the public library.

"My friends kidded me a lot about it, saying that I would read every book in the library," he once told an interviewer. "If I'd had more time I might have. It wasn't a very big library."

Brinkley still has a sister, Mary Nelson, who lives in a rest home in Wilmington. His other three siblings are dead; he was 12 years younger than the closest.

"I was a mistake," he explains.

Back from the Army, Brinkley returned to the *Star-News* as a reporter. He remembers covering the opening of a shipyard that built "liberty ships" to carry troops, ammunition and supplies. The first boat was named after a former North Carolina governor, Zebulon Vance.

"That was a big thing," Brinkley says, chuckling. "That was really a big deal."

He left Wilmington for the last time to take a job with the United Press, which sent him to several Southern cities, including Charlotte.

"It was a very dull city, very conservative," Brinkley says. "I never found any news there."

But he did find connections. He worked in a building that was home to a CBS radio affiliate. Radio staffers raved to their bosses about what a hotshot Brinkley was. He lined up a job with CBS and quit United Press.

When he reported to the Washington bureau, he didn't get the reception he expected.

"They claimed they'd never of me, so I told them to go to hell and went to NBC, where I beat their ass, and took great pleasure in it and have ever since."

Brinkley went to work writing scripts for radio announcers.

"The trick was to write it in such a way that they could not screw it up," Brinkley says. "That's really where I learned to write for broadcast."

Soon, he was on the air with a news program at noon. He'd drop by the White House and Congress to gather his news.

"Washington was much quieter than it is now," he says without a hint of sarcasm. "It's just gotten to be choked on itself. I stay there because there's nowhere else I can go and do my work."

The big break. His big break came with television. The big-name radio announcers, including Lowell Thomas and H. V. Kaltenborn, wanted nothing to do with television, so the network put young Brinkley in front of the cameras.

"The big stars later—after TV became what it became—tried to get back on and failed," Brinkley says. "They all failed."

Television was harder than radio. Your tie had to be straight. Your hair had to be combed. You couldn't bury your face in a script. You didn't have writers.

Brinkley always wrote his own material.

"Most of what I do now is ad-libbing. In fact, it's all ad-lib."

While television networks were still experimenting with their new medium, Brinkley contributed stories to John Cameron Swayze's "The Camel News Caravan."

"It was so bad, it was a joke," Brinkley says.

In 1956, the network replaced Swayze's show with Huntley and Brinkley. America liked them, and they liked each other.

"He was very nice, very nice, very unpompous," Brinkley says of his partner, who died in 1974. "He never learned what you don't do in a big city."

Brinkley remembers one Sunday afternoon he and his wife dropped by to see the Huntleys in New York. The telephone rang. It was a fan from Dayton, Ohio—Huntley's phone number was in the book—who wanted to know if the Huntleys could have dinner with him and his wife.

"He said, 'Yes!'" Brinkley says between snickers. "I couldn't imagine! I don't have my number in the book. I can't. You get calls at three in the morning from drunks in Dallas who want to argue about something."

With no model, Huntley and Brinkley did their show the only way they knew how.

"You use pictures when you have them and words when you don't, and stop once in a while for a commercial," Brinkley says. "There's no other way to do it."

Television magazine. From 1961 to 1963, Brinkley also blazed the trail for television news magazines with "David Brinkley's Journal." Every week, he did two or three stories, making caustic observations as he went. The show won critical acclaim—two Emmys—but few viewers.

Meanwhile, "The Huntley-Brinkley" report was going strong. A poll in 1965 showed that more adults recognized Huntley and Brinkley than the Beatles.

The show ran until 1970, when Huntley decided that he wanted to get back to his cattle in Montana. For the next dozen years, Brinkley worked as a nightly co-anchor with John Chancellor, then in documentaries, and finally in a news magazine opposite "Dallas," then the nation's top-rated television show.

"The night they said, 'Who shot J.R.?' I was on the other network against it," Brinkley says. "It was a death sentence. The electric chair."

He quit NBC when Bill Small became president of its news operation.

"He kept trying to tell me what to do and how to do it, and he didn't know anything." ABC contacted Brinkley to see if he would be interested in a Sunday morning program they had in mind. He was.

Doing "This Week." Today, "This Week with David Brinkley" is the most popular news discussion program on Sunday morning. Each week, the show focuses on a topic in the news. Brinkley rides herd as his lieutenants, Sam Donaldson, George Will and a guest journalist, grill guests.

Often, Brinkley, Donaldson and Will can be heard snickering off-camera. Brinkley says he loves working with the duo.

"They're both good friends, very bright, and we all get along very well."

Donaldson, who joined the show shortly after it started in 1981, has high praise for Brinkley.

"He's in a class all by himself," Donaldson says. "There's the Brinkley level, then there's people like me."

Donaldson thinks there are several reasons for Brinkley's success: He has been blessed with a distinctive voice and cadence that makes what he says sound significant; he also has an instinct for what's interesting and important.

Several weeks ago, Brinkley received an Internal Revenue Service brochure explaining rules for collecting taxes in a nuclear disaster. He used the item at the end of his show, when he usually closes with an anecdote.

"David spotted that as something that would be of interest to the public," Donaldson says. "That's ahead of the curve."

Will says there's another reason for Brinkley's success.

"He's one of those people who succeed and last in television precisely because there is no 'behind the scenes.' There's no difference between the Brinkley on camera and the Brinkley off."

Will agrees with Donaldson on Brinkley's reporting ability: "He's the best."

Like a great baseball player, Brinkley seems to perform without effort, but the ease comes from years of hard work, Will says.

"He's been around for a very long time. He knows a lot. Knowledge requires judgment, and jugment requires time."

On the show, Brinkley sets the tone, then lets others ask most of the questions. Occasionally, he jumps in, pointed but never eager. A few weeks ago, he twiddled his thumbs as he questioned Israeli Prime Minister Yitzhak Shamir.

Sometimes, he takes off on one of his pet peeves; which include Japanese imports, the United Nations and Congress, Donaldson says.

"I think David has a lower respect for Congress than I do."

A Look at Washington. These days, Brinkley gathers most of his information from newspapers, wire service reports, and by socializing with political figures, often in his home. He doesn't pound the pavement as he did in the early days. His book includes references to a "young reporter"—him.

Brinkley borrowed the idea for his book from "Reveille in Washington," a 1941 volume by Margaret Leech that told the story of Washington during the Civil War. If Leech wrote that using second-hand information, Brinkley thought, he could do a book about wartime Washington based on his own experiences.

Most of the book is just that: his remembrances, although he also used news accounts and interviews with Washingtonians to reconstruct scenes.

Brinkley wrote the book as he speaks; unvarnished, in an undulating beat, punctuated with humor.

The book starts with pre-war Washington and closes with the death of Franklin Delano Roosevelt and the transfer of power to Harry Truman, who was Brinkley's favorite president.

"His crowning accomplishment, to me, was that he always did what he thought was in the country's best interest and never game a damn what anyone thought about it. I'd like to see that again."

It's time for the interview to end. Television person that he is, Brinkley has been sneaking peaks at his watch. His second wife, Susan, is standing nearby in a full-length mink coat, waiting for her husband.

"Hello, honey," she greets.

"Hello, honey," he responds.

While they are here, they will buy a condominium for their daughter. Brinkley will also visit his son, Alan, a history professor on leave from City University of New York for a fellowship at the National Humanities Center in Research Triangle Park.

Brinkley has two other children from his first marriage, which ended in divorce. Joel is the Jerusalem bureau chief for the *New York Times,* and John is a reporter covering Washington for Scripps Howard, a news service.

"I'm proud of all of them," he says.

Brinkley says he'll get around to writing another book when he thinks of a topic. He spends most of his leisure time reading or writing. In the summer, he and his wife get away to a home in the mountains of Virginia. In the winter, they live in Florida, and he commutes to Washington.

When it comes to hinting at his plans for the future, he is worse than FDR before the Democratic convention of 1944.

"I don't have any plans," he says. "I've never had any plans."

Tom Brokaw

"Tom Brokaw: NBC's Air Apparent"
by James Kaplan

Tom Brokaw "has neither Peter Jennings' urbanity nor Dan Rather's intensity, but he has something—something that for better or worse, carries an immense weight in America today," James Kaplan writes. Who is Tom Brokaw; what is he like? Kaplan suggests, "Ordinariness is Brokaw's bulwark against the chaos of the world and against the extraordinariness of his position in it."

On a reasonably ordinary Tuesday morning, Tom Brokaw sits in his office in Rockefeller Center and prepares to contemplate the verities of network news. James Brooks's movie *Broadcast News* has recently come out to wide interest and acclaim; and Brokaw himself appears to be at the center of something — having lately conducted both a mass debate among the Presidential candidates and an interview with Mikhail Gorbachev, which, if nothing else, thoroughly scooped his two competing anchors. Maybe he's even the state of the art. Who is Tom Brokaw? What is the art he's the state of?

His small corner office gives no clues. It could be the engagingly messy office of any engaging young executive. There are many books on many surfaces. There is a glass case full of mementos. There are knickknacks (among them a small statue of Mikhail Gorbachev as a gnome with big red lips) on shelves along the wall. A computer terminal flickers wire-service headlines. Photographs line the shelves — photographs of Brokaw's parents; of his attractive wife, Meredith, and their three attractive daughters; of himself climbing a sheer rock face; and again of himself in a cowboy hat, sitting on a Western fence, against a bright-blue sky.

Brokaw looks exactly like what he is: an ex-jock who has stayed in good shape. He is tall and lean, and this morning he has a winter suntan. His face is boyish, somehow open and closed at the same time, with an air of quiet mischief (tempered by a certain sadness) playing around the eyes. Tom Brokaw could play Tom Sawyer.

Ordinariness is Brokaw's bulwark against the chaos of the world, and against the extraordinariness of his position in it. He is an anchorman on network television news in the United States in the waning years of the twentieth century. "Anchorman": the term originally referred to a team's last runner in a relay race, the strongest athlete. The phrase took on its current meaning in the late 1950s, when it was conferred upon Walter Cronkite, first among equals in a team of crack CBS television news correspondents. Over the years, though, thanks largely to Cronkite and the epic events of the sixties over which he presided, the title has slowly risen into another realm, an atmosphere both higher and thinner. Gone is the sense of a team player. A new connotation has arisen — something close to "figurehead."

The position is notable for the level of fame it confers: today's anchorman is a world-class media superstar in a world where the boundary between reality and the media that attempt to represent that reality grows ever more indistinct. The position is also notable for its compensation: Brokaw reportedly earns two million dollars a year. The position is also remarkable for the fact that it is difficult to say precisely what an anchorman is.

James Kaplan is a free-lance writer.

Tom Brokaw folds his hands behind his head and leans back in his chair. The watch on his wrist, a nondescript black diver's watch, is a cheap Casio. "I grew up in a working class family in South Dakota," he says in his pleasant baritone. He has a slight speech impediment: he can't say his Ls. He manages—this man who speaks to some sixteen million people every weeknight—to make the flaw winning, part of the boyish ordinariness, like a cowlick that won't stay down. "My dad was a highly skilled migrant construction worker—moved from job to job. After the war, he ran heavy equipment for the Army Corps of Engineers, in the civilian branch. So we lived on dams on the Missouri River in South Dakota.

"We moved to this little town called Yankton when I was in high school," Brokaw says. "And by the time I was a senior, there was just no disciplinary framework around me. I was not a great athlete, but I was a letterman in three sports. I was very active in student politics. I could do whatever I wanted to do. And I thought that's how life was.

"I came out of high school with the hopes and dreams of everybody, including my family's. And then I went off to the University of Iowa, and fell off the edge of the world. I was bedazzled by all the big-city girls from Chicago and Des Moines. Had a whee of a good time.

"But I didn't do well, obviously. So I enrolled at the University of South Dakota. And continued this nosedive. Through my sophomore year. Nineteen-sixty was a watershed year for America, because John Kennedy was elected; it was also a watershed year for me, because I bottomed out.

"I quit school, and went off to work at a succession of small radio and television stations. When I was twenty years old, I was working in Sioux City, Iowa, at a television station with people who had no futures. And I came face to face with a certain amount of hard truth about myself and life—that it required hard work, and discipline. So I started driving back and forth from Sioux City to Vermillion, South Dakota, and finished my degree. Repaired my relationship with my wife—who was not yet my wife; we were married when we graduated.

"I wrote newspaper stories when I was in college, but I really was drawn to television: It seemed very exciting. It was new, and it was explosive: the space shots, and the *Today* show, and Huntley and Brinkley, and Cronkite, and the conventions.

"So I went to work for a very good television station in Omaha. And then to Atlanta. And, when I was twenty-five and working in Atlanta during the civil-rights period, I did some in-the-middle-of-the-night kinds of things for NBC. When all hell would break loose in Americus or Selma, I would get on an airplane and fly down there until they could get a correspondent in place.

"I had some pretty good runs. So NBC said, 'Why don't you go to work for us in California?' I turned them down. I really wanted to go Washington. I was happy in Atlanta. Civil rights was a big story. But then, networks being networks, they upped the ante a lot.

"So I went to California, and worked there for seven years, for the whole crazy-tilt time. Saw it all. Then I went to Washington, to the White House, and then came here to the *Today* show. And then, *Nightly News*."

"Tom Brokaw: NBC's Air Apparent" 177

Here is a handsome (but not too handsome) young man, winningly imperfect (that hell-raising past; that slight speech impediment), from America's heartland. A young man whose career ascent has been smooth and ever steeper, whose path has conveniently followed the contours of our recent history—the civil-rights marches, the counterculture, the political conventions. And now the media culture. Here is a great American archetype. And a great American target.

In *Broadcast News,* James Brooks posits a not too dissimilar young man, who rises along a curve not dissimilar to Tom Brokaw's and becomes a network anchorman. The problem is that Tom Grunick (played by William Hurt) is all glitz and no wits: deep down, he's a hollow man, none too smart, and immoral to boot.

But, Brooks says, it's the system that does it to him. By continually emphasizing style over substance—by passing over smarter, more talented reporters in favor of good looks and convincing delivery—the ratings-greedy network elevates Hurt to stardom, and (yes) demonhood. Tom Grunick is the embodiment of all that is wrong with television, and therefore of all that's wrong with our society—even, by implication, the Presidency.

Is James Brooks right? Is Tom Grunick Tom Brokaw?

The answer is a firm no—and yes. Tom Brokaw is very far from a stupid or shallow man. He reads widely; he uses the language well even in informal conversation. He has a passion for news, and he understands how the world works. By all accounts, his family life is happy. He has been married for twenty-five of his forty-eight years. (His wife has her own career as the owner of a New York City chain of toy stores.) His credentials as a reporter are solid. His work ethic is legendary. Some say that Dan Rather beat him out when both men were White House correspondents, but nobody denies that Brokaw did a fine job there. He went to the *Today* show with a kind of genteel reluctance, stipulating in his contract that he wouldn't hawk products on the air. During the Presidential campaign of 1980, Brokaw worked an amazing double shift, covering the conventions and the primaries and holding down his *Today* post at the same time, leading *Today*'s then-executive producer Steve Friedman to nickname him "Duncan the Wonder Horse." ("He walks! He talks! He does late-night, he does early-morning, here, there, and everywhere.")

When Brokaw went to the *Nightly News* in 1982, he was teamed at first with Roger Mudd: NBC was hoping to get the old Huntley-Brinkley magic back again. It didn't click. The network yanked Mudd and left Brokaw solo, raising charges that it had chosen the pretty boy over the seasoned old hand. Even if these were unfair (and even if they contained an element of truth), the charges soon died down: people were watching Tom Brokaw.

At CBS, Dan Rather replaced Walter Cronkite in 1981; at ABC, Peter Jennings, who had anchored from 1964 to 1967, would take over again in 1983. A three-man race was on, with the teams in the far background. Never before had the competition among the networks crystallized in just this way. At the same time, the news divisions of all three networks had been undergoing profound changes. They still are. Each of the networks was bought by a giant conglomerate in the mid-eighties—ABC by Capital Cities, CBS by Laurence

Tisch's Loews Corporation, and NBC by General Electric. Network news divisions, which had often been run as loss leaders, became cost-accountable. Budgets and staff were cut; promotional campaigns were stepped up. The three anchors became, willy-nilly, corporate symbols. Stars. All three men had been ace reporters, and proud of it; all at once they weren't exactly reporters anymore. What were they?

"What is an anchorman? Is he a reporter?" I asked Reuven Frank. Frank, who was president of NBC News from 1968 to 1972 and again from 1982 to 1984, is, at sixty-seven, an odd combination of *éminence grise* and *enfant terrible*: he no longer holds titular sway, but his opinions—most of which are sharp, and sharply expressed—still swing weight in the broadcasting world. These days he's producing documentaries and writing his memoirs.

"No. In no sense," Frank said. "Most of them are trained as reporters, and have been reporters, and good reporters. Brokaw covered Watergate for us. And well. And competitively. But he is not *now* a reporter, and when he goes out to report, there's something artificial about it. It's known as 'Bigfooting': when the big shot arrives in somebody's territory, and takes the story away. It's very common in the networks news. And all three of them do it.

"The anchorman is the point of communication," Frank said. "All this stuff funnels through him. To the viewer, he is the news. So we hear a lot of talk about *interpretation*. And we are now getting a lot of emphasis on 'live.' And live is usually somebody who figured in a medium-to-major news story of the day being available to comment on it, and to ignore the anchorman's question, and make his point, in a minute thirty.

"The anchorman is the vector. He's both a professional and an artifact. And he gets paid what basketball players get paid. But," Frank continued, "the star-anchorman thing is coming to an end. One of the reasons the *People* magazines are so prominent is that there's no news. When you think of the news of the sixties and seventies you're talking about civil rights and Vietnam. You're talking about things that books are now being written about. What the hell is news now? The summit meeting? The two biggest stories of 1987 were AIDS and South Africa. Neither of them is a frivolous story, but they're not stories that shake everybody.

"One of the reasons that news audiences are drifting away is that they don't care what the news is. Because it's not worth caring about. And the public is always right."

What did he think of *Broadcast News*?

"As a movie, I found it tedious," Frank said. "But it was remarkably accurate physically. I mean, the way that control room was set up.... The business with Hurt being a dumb anchorman was pretty exaggerated. But he was a good broadcaster. That's not to be sneezed at."

Tom Brokaw is a good broadcaster, and more. He is managing editor and chief of correspndents of the *Nightly News*: he has ultimate control over what is said on his show, and who says it. The power is enormous. Not only can he hire and fire (and there are those who charge that since Brokaw is in a position to snuff competition—whether he does so or not—the conflict of interest is patent), he determines the world view of those who turn to the network news for their world view. He can sweeten the world. He brings order to chaos. He is, for sixteen million people or so, a kind of god.

"Brokaw seems as acceptable to me as any of the other anchormen," says Neil Postman, Professor of Media Ecology in New York University's Department of Communications, and author of a critical study of television, *Amusing Ourselves to Death*. "My complaint would be that the network news is not done seriously. Maybe they think they do it seriously, but that's because they accept a framework that defeats, at the start, any attempt to be serious.

"Commercials have the effect of trivializing what has been spoken about," Postman says. "The whole context in which news is done says to the viewer, 'We're not gong to do more than ninety seconds on this, and we don't want you to be weeping for the ten thousand people who lost their lives in the Mexico earthquake, because that's not the condition we want you in when we get to the United Airlines commercial.'

"Second: because television is, after all, a visual medium, the first question, I'm sure, Brokaw and all the others want to know when they prepare for each day is, what sort of film footage do they have. And if they don't have film footage, for the most part, it's not news.

"Obviously, not all of the important things that happen are visualizable. David Halberstam did a piece for *TV Guide* in which he made this point, and gave as an example the story that was developing for ten years or more about the Japanese taking charge of the world economy, and surpassing America. It wasn't really covered much, because there was no film footage to be used with it. The absolute dominance of the visual image tends to eliminate certain subjects from being treated altogether, and to amplify certain subjects that are not that important but which have good film footage accompanying them.

"In the end, I think people watch television news more to see the teller than to hear what is told. Which is why it's no coincidence that Brokaw is so attractive, and why both Dan Rather and Peter Jennings, as well as Brokaw, could be movie stars. I'm sure they also have what is called credibility — a term usually used in reference to actors, when you say someone gave a credible performance.

"Television, no matter how you slice it, is a performing art. Thinking is not a performing art. Which is why you rarely see anyone thinking on television."

Is Tom Brokaw merely a performer? Is his credibility simply a studied performance? Postman, it would seem, is advancing the Tom Grunick argument. On this ordinary Tuesday, Brokaw arrives at the office about ten o'clock in the morning. He works in his office for about two hours, listening in on a conference call among the NBC domestic news bureau chiefs, reading his mail, talking on the phone, beginning to decide on the stories for the evening's show. At noon, he tapes headlines to be broadcast later in the day, as well as a couple of promotional announcements. He takes his gym bag and leaves for his workout and some errands. He rarely eats lunch.

At 2:30 P.M., he returns. He moves from his office to a waist-high cubicle in the bullpen of the newsroom, facing a bank of eleven TV monitors and surrounded by the cubicles of his colleagues. He speaks on the phone to bureaus;

he discusses stories with his producers, writers, and editors; he writes, rewrites, and edits. (He walks! He talks!) At three o'clock he goes to a small studio next door to broadcast NBC *News Digest,* a one-minute summary.

At about 3:45 P.M., he goes into a closed-door line-up meeting with executive producer Bill Wheatley, senior producer Cheryl Gould, and much of the production staff. During the twenty-minute meeting, Brokaw and staff decide which stories will run that evening—and at what length, which correspondents will do them, who will write what. Brokaw has chief authority and veto power, but his colleagues are strong persuaders.

From shortly after four o'clock until just before broadcast time, Brokaw is back in the bullpen, writing, discussing, bantering. At 6:24 P.M. exactly, he puts on his blazer and goes down to the third floor. The broadcast lasts a half-hour, eight minutes of which are commercials. It is rerun at seven for the stations that show the news then. Brokaw watches the rerun, then has a brief talk with his producers. Shortly after 7:30 P.M. he goes home.

It is a longish day but not a laborious one. Duncan the Wonder Horse has certainly worked harder in the past. But the stress is there. And the argument could be made that since all Tom Brokaw's years of reporting inform every decision he makes throughout the day, and since these decisions shape every broadcast, his credibility is not merely the result of a boyish face and a pleasing, slightly flawed baritone delivery.

But whatever else Tom Brokaw may be on or off the tube, he *is* a performer. And he is a performer of a certain kind: an affable, reasonably relaxed presenter of the news. He has neither Peter Jennings' urbanity nor Dan Rather's intensity, but he has something—something that, for better or worse, carries an immense weight in America today. Brokaw is actually curiously diffident in his *Nightly News* persona, as compared with his offscreen personality. Maybe that's no accident. It may be that, as Tom Shales, TV critic of *The Washington Post,* said, Brokaw "was not particularly tough" in his interview with Gorbachev. But then look at Dan Rather and George Bush in their nine-minute set-to on the *CBS Evening News* in January, a bout that had more punch than Tyson/Holmes. Rather was widely criticized for being too tough on the Vice President. Granted, Bush isn't Gorbachev, but the astounding moral seems to be that we focus as much attention on the men who interview the leaders of the world as we do on the leaders themselves. And—the world leaders may have it easier here—we're not sure just what those anchormen should be. Tough? Friendly? Cool? Warm? Suave? Folksy? A little of everything, we say; each thing at the right time.

Should an anchorman (as Brokaw has) conduct a promotional "interview" with the President of the United States in the middle of the Super Bowl? Should he (as Brokaw has) read Longfellow's "Christmas Bells" on an NBC special? "I call Brokaw the new NBC peacock," Shales says. "He doesn't know how to say no. He'll appear on any documentary; he'll do whatever he can to increase his visibility."

This seems harsh. Nobody denies that a network anchorman *is* its anchor, its strongest runner, its symbol. And businesses promote themselves, and no one is naïve about that in this great land.

And the business is heating up. The network news shows watch each other carefully. The result is, perhaps, a certain homogenization. And as the differences among the three broadcasts shrink, the importance of the anchormen, and of the head-to-head rivalry among them, grows.

At the same time, from another side, the very institution of the network news broadcast—and, by extension, that of the anchorman—is being threatened. There may be less news, but there's more competition for it. "We're under siege," Brokaw admits. The local affiliates, with ever more access to work events and taped reports of those events, joust with the networks for news time. As do game shows and reruns. Cable continues to chew away at TV market shares across the board. "But we continue to believe that the audience looks to us—and all the surveys indicate that—for the important stories of the day," says Brokaw. "We're going to survive."

And what did he think of *Broadcast News*? Tom Brokaw gives a wistful smile. "Very entertaining," he says.

Catherine Crier

"'The Revolution Will Be Televised': A Year in the Life of Catherine Crier"
by Kevin McHargue

CNN's Catherine Crier was trained as a lawyer and has been a judge in Texas. She says her role as a lawyer and judge is "not all that different from the role of journalist. From the time I got out of law school, first as an assistant district attorney, then on the bench, I was hitting the streets, interviewing witnesses, writing reports, if you will, and presenting a story to a judge or a jury."

For Catherine Crier, the only transition was, writer Kevin McHargue says, "from a jury of 12 to an audience of millions."

When this article was published, Kevin McHargue was editor of The Daily Texan, at the University of Texas at Austin. He has since graduated.

To some traditional journalists, former Dallas judge Catherine Crier's sudden rise to media stardom last October was a cause for alarm. But to Crier herself, it was a chance to participate in a "tele-revolution."

"Timothy Ash said 'At the end of the 20th century, all revolutions are tele-revolutions,' and I think that's very true," Crier says. "During the fall of Ceausescu's regime, there was a battle over the Bucharest TV station, and it centered on there, because the message was not lost on either side how important access to those airwaves was."

Because of the nature of the medium, television news gives the people access to powerful visual images as well, whether it's a wall or a Chinese student standing up to a tank. Crier believes those images, even more than the events themselves, helped change history.

"When those people who for so long had such limited access to information, all of a sudden were able to hear the cries of their brothers and to see events that were happening across their borders, where people were taking their future in their hands and making a statement about it," Crier says, "it spurred them on to come forward and make their own changes at home."

Explaining how she feels about being part of that televised history, Crier falls back on her favorite adjective: "Tremendous." The past year on CNN, and Crier's role in it, has been tremendous indeed.

When she was hired to anchor CNN's evening newscast, the University of Texas graduate was unknown to most media professionals, and she drew her share of unfavorable reviews from the good-old-reporter network.

"'Fair' is not a term that I think can be used in talking about that sort of coverage," Crier says, still sounding a bit more like a public official than a journalist herself. "They have columns and they're free to interpret it how they choose."

What bothers Crier is the background left out of those columns that dismissed her as an unprepared pretty face, the triumph of style over substance.

"Sometimes it's frustrating when the headline says, 'CNN hires unknown,' then way down in about the fifth paragraph, it says, by the way, a judge, a lawyer, an author, a speaker," she says. "There was some experience back there." In the world of TV journalists, in fact, Crier says she has more than her share of substance.

"I didn't turn in a 250-word story to an editor, I turned in briefs to the court. I didn't do a standup in front of the courthouse; I was arguing in front of the jury," she says. "I didn't cover the political conventions because I ran for office, was an elected official and *participated* in the political conventions. I don't think that having the direct experience in any way diminishes me."

The coverage of Crier's hiring also carried tinges of sexism. In the words of that irritating commercial, many critics hated her just because she was beautiful. Journalists couched their reaction in terms of experience and background, but those same journalists have failed to voice similar criticisms of Pierre Salinger or Bill Moyers, two men who jumped from politics into broadcast news.

Some publications just lumped Crier in with other women — including Connie

CNN's Catherine Crier (photo courtesy CNN).

Chung, Diane Sawyer and CNN alum Mary Alice Williams—and decried the "star system" in TV news. Granted, part of that undue attention can be attributed to the relatively small numbers of women in broadcast journalism, a situation Crier says will be slow to change.

"Women are still slowly making gains and slowly being perceived as capable and qualified in more of an equal capacity," she says. "As more and more fill the ranks, more and more will rise through those ranks. You see the gains being made very slowly, and I think that's still a frustration for most women."

Whether the criticism was subtly sexist or just reporters protecting their turf, Crier says she knows why she was hired, and it wasn't for her looks. "I know in talking to CNN what they were interested in," she said. "They were intrigued, as I was, at the parallels between the two positions. There are an awful lot of parallels that many don't see at first glance."

The role of a lawyer and judge "is not all that different from the role of a journalist," Crier says. "From the time I got out of law school, first as an assistant district attorney, than as a civil trial lawyer, than on the bench, I was hitting the streets, interviewing witnesses, writing reports, if you will, and presenting a story to a judge or a jury."

For Crier, the only transition was from a jury of 12 to an audience of millions. "The more technical aspects were the newest elements," she says, "trying to modify my interviewing skills to this particular medium. No longer do you have two days to cross-examine a witness, but you might have two minutes to interview a guest."

Given the time constraints, Crier concedes that television has to be "more superficial."

"In newsprint, you might be able to spend an entire page talking about one story," she added. "[In] a basic 30-minute newscast, once you take out the commercials and the downtime, you have the equivalent of two-thirds of a single page in print journalism. You have more territory to cover in a limited amount of time."

What television lacks in depth, Crier argues it makes up for in breadth, scope and, most of all, speed. "Particularly with the crisis in the gulf now, you see the effect," she says.

"World leaders, when they want to deliver a policy statement, so much of the time it's via the press conference, and it's only moments later that you are going to Baghdad or Washington or Kennebunkport to get the response. It used to be that world leaders might have months or weeks to evaluate and respond. Now it's almost momentary."

Television itself began that trend toward faster news, but Crier says CNN is "stepping up the pace of the entire world."

"I think it's amazing," she says. "I think CNN has had a tremendous effect on the newsgathering process. We truly are in the information age and CNN, more than any other newsgathering organization, print or radio or television, really exemplifies that new age. Things are delivered almost instantaneously now."

The rest of the press, Crier argues, cannot hope to match that flow of information. "When you pick up a newspaper today, you're reading basically yesterday's events," she says. "On CNN you're finding out what happened ten minutes ago."

Crier, an admitted "news junkie," admits that the pace of CNN has left her somewhat breathless. "It's been the most incredible year imaginable," she says. "My second day on the air was the San Francisco earthquake, and it hasn't stopped since. My love is international relations and international affairs. The events in Eastern Europe and the Soviet Union have held me spellbound, watching the entire character of the globe change."

Watching the aforementioned "tele-revolutions" in those countries has impressed Crier, but she expects the revolutions to take different forms in America.

"I think the whole environmental movement is going to pick up steam," she says. "I notice that one of the networks is coming out with an environmental entertainment show. You're going to see more and more of that, and as you do, I believe the movement will pick up steam again. Television can play a tremendous role in those issues."

Looking again at international relations, Crier sounds like her boss, Ted Turner, when she describes the role of television in forging a "global community."

"People look at others and see each other and begin to identify with each other, and we're not so different," she says. "When people begin to realize that, the preconceived notions and the fears crumble away."

Television news, however, can only mobilize those who watch it, and the figures on that front are somewhat depressing. A recent poll found that only 45 percent of Americans under 35 surveyed had watched TV news the day before, down from 52 percent in 1965. Asked the same question about newspapers, only 30 percent could say yes. Crier finds that survey "very disconcerting."

"Unfortunately, as information is becoming more and more accessible, young people are turning away to an extent and not absorbing," she says. Citing the old maxim that "knowledge is power," Crier concludes that Americans are tuning out at their own risk. "It used to be property was power, but information is what seems to be governing growth and opportunity and development today."

On Crier's side of the camera, information seems to be flowing pretty well. As she continues to hone her skills as an anchor and correspondent, she hopes to branch out into more field reporting and possibly a political issues show along the lines of *Crossfire* or *The Capital Gang*. "I find that fascinating," she says. "It's one thing to receive information, but it's another thing to understand it."

In the meantime, Crier seems determined to enjoy her job. "I am tremendously enjoying the process," she says, invoking her reliable superlative one last time. "Each day is a learning experience."

Note: Catherine Crier announced November 16, 1992, that she would be joining ABC's "20/20" as a correspondent in January 1993, joining reporters Tom Jarriel, Lynn Sherr, Bob Brown and John Stossel. ABC had long looked for a fifth correspondent for "20/20," which is hosted by Hugh Downs and Barbara Walters. Previously, Mary Alice Williams, also a CNN anchor, left for NBC. —ed.

Walter Cronkite

"Rolling Stone *Interview*"
by Jonathan Alter

Following the cultural perspective and questions of Rolling Stone *magazine interviewer Jonathan Alter, Walter Cronkite admitted (in 1987) he missed the Woodstock generation as a significant story and much of the music that* Rolling Stone *readers would appreciate. How different in tone and style is this interview from the Ron Powers 1973* Playboy *interview? How is it similar?*

When you look back over the last 20 years and all of the many, many important events that you covered, which stand out as most significant? Are there certain things that you think will be remembered 100 years from now as being of outstanding importance?

I would think that the most important event of our 20 years has got to be the walk on the moon [in 1969]. In future history books, this will be comparable to Columbus's discovery of America, and our political and economic concerns will fade into memory and will scarcely be an asterisk. On the other hand, in contemporary history, there are many major events to be remembered. I would think that the counterrevolution by the Reagan administration in foreign policy and in domestic economic policy will have a great historical impact. A great deal will depend on the election coming up as to whether that counterrevolution is continued. I call it a counterrevolution to the Roosevelt revolution of the thirties and forties.

What do you think the major events of that counterrevolution are? The size of government isn't smaller than it was; in fact, it's bigger.

Well, scaling back the philosophy of what government should or can do for the people, the scaling back of major social expenditures; the tax structure, which has permitted this buildup of an incredible deficit that will impinge upon history down through the next century; and in foreign policy, this image of the United States in a more macho vein than since, probably, World War II. These things will be considered important.

In looking over some tapes of your broadcasts, I noticed that the evening Nixon resigned, you said, "The system worked," in the case of Nixon. Now we have a president who has been caught lying about the contras, and yet nobody seems particularly interested. Is this a case of the system not working?

I think that would be a little hard on the system. I think that what's happened is that having gone through the trauma of the Nixon resignation and the

---

Jonathan Alter is a senior writer covering the media for Newsweek.

Walter Cronkite today. Note "CBS eye" cufflinks (photo courtesy Walter Cronkite).

Watergate fallout, the public, and hence the Congress, really has no stomach for going through that again, for seeing another American president forced from office. And this would be additionally difficult now because the president has been so popular. It would destroy the last vestiges of any confidence we have in ourselves.

So we just have to live with the lawbreaking?

I think the attitude is, Why not ride it out?

You've thought a lot about the notion of public trust, and for many people you're the definition of that. Is it surprising or disturbing to you that the polls show that the majority of American people believe that the president is lying about all this but nonetheless don't particularly care?

Well, yes, I think it's very disturbing. I think it's part of the whole disturbing atmosphere today in regards to public opinion and public reaction—that Vanna White should be, suddenly, this popular figure, this cult figure almost. I guess she's never said a word on television, as far as I know. I'm not objecting to Vanna White's extreme beauty; I'd be glad to entertain her for dinner any time—if my wife would let me. But I think the idea that you can gain national fame through this kind of a performance is indicative of the same kind of values that permit us to accept presidential behavior of this kind without greater reaction. It goes on in all walks of life today, in everything we do. We have debased the cultural currency.

Does that debase your own fame and honor?

As I've always said, to take a newsman and claim he's the most trusted figure in America—they must not have polled my wife. You say "most trustworthy newsman," all right. But then to translate that into national trust, well, how do the people know? I may cheat on my bank account, I may cheat on my wife, I may cheat at cards. They don't know that. I don't do any of those things, you understand—he said with a smile on his face.... I hate to criticize those wonderful people out there who voted for me as most trustworthy, but at the same time, I think it's indicative of the kind of headline thinking that we all do today. It's without any really in-depth analysis of what it is we're saying, thinking or doing. We seem to be an almost entirely incognitive kind of a population, and I don't know whether that's a world symptom or whether it's limited to our country.

Is it that much different from what it was 20 years ago, when Tiny Tim was married on the "Tonight" show?

Oh, no, I don't think it's a lot different. I mean, we've had this series of blows to our presumably long-held beliefs in the purity of our politicians and our religious leaders and so forth. All of that collapses around our shoulders suddenly. Even the sexual habits of movie stars are suddenly revealed as being vastly different from how they've been portrayed on the screen. You begin to wonder if anything is what it seems. We're living in some kind of miasma of perfidy.

Is part of that because the reporting wasn't as detailed 20 years ago? A lot of people in Hollywood knew that Rock Hudson was gay but didn't write about it. They knew about politicans' sexual peccadilloes and didn't write about them.

Well, they're not writing about them today. I mean, Hollywood knows a lot of other people who are gay. I think these cases that we're speaking of were exceptions. Rock Hudson was the first star to succumb to AIDS. Gary Hart was clearly a rather special case, because it was so flagrant. It's almost a matter of propriety, of social graces, of diplomatic skill, political savvy. You've got to say, "Gosh, if he can do that, does he have the balance to be president of the United States?"

Let's return to this notion of trust. Do you think that if you had been an anchorman in a less contentious era—when your soothing quality wouldn't have the same effect on people—that you might not have been so popular?

I hope this doesn't sound as immodest as it probably is, but if I had some secret back then, I think it was the fact that I really was dedicated to trying to tell the story and make it understandable. I never really had any sense of trying to perform. I wouldn't say I didn't worry about ratings, but never did anybody suggest to me how to perform on the air. A generation has come up in which the consultants, the station managers, the news editors, everybody, is telling the young newsman and -woman how to look on the air. They tell them how to cut their hair, tell them whether to wear a mustache or not, tell them how to dress. They build in a consciousness that they're performers. You can see it in their eyes, you can see it in their demeanor. They're reading something off a prompter that I think they really don't understand completely.

I'm not talking about every one of them, by any means. I'm talking about the fact that a generation has come along that has been molded in that fashion. I don't think local stations hire anchorpeople because they are great news writers or because they're superb reporters or even good editors. I think they hire them because they're performers.

Do you think that news-writing quality makes a big difference?

I think that news-writing experience is terribly important to a person in television. I don't think it's important that a person necessarily write all his or her own material on the air as long as they know how to write it. There is a problem of getting just enough facts to get by on and of not examining the story very carefully as to where the lead might really be or what might need further investigation. We don't really have enough strong editorial control or direction in the news rooms in radio and television.

After the Tet Offensive, in 1968, you publicly expressed serious doubt about the war in Vietnam. Do you regret not going public with those doubts earlier?

No. I don't think it would have had a lot of effect earlier, and I'm not sure that earlier there was proof that it was hopeless. In the early days of our involvement, I thought it was an exemplary use of force to try to preserve a ground for planting democracy in an area where there wasn't any, where there was a vacuum. It seemed like it was worth taking the small risk of advisers. Then, after that, a few protective troops. But with that buildup, it got obviously way out of hand. My disenchantment began when I made my first visit to Cam Ranh Bay, which might have been '65. That was when I had my first suspicion that maybe this wasn't quite what it was made out to be — which was helping the Vietnamese — and that we were taking over the war. I still didn't think it was my role to say anything about it. I was saying things about it in speeches, but I separate what I do there from what I say on the air. That's why I never did a commentary on the air. So anyway, I went on for two or three years, trying to be impartial on the air but getting more and more unhappy and disenchanted with the war.

You say that if you had gone public earlier, it wouldn't have had any effect. Does that mean that you believe that even somebody as trustworthy and popular as you can't tell the American people something they are not ready to hear? That you can't be too far out in front of public opinion?

Yes, I think that's right. I think that timing is important. This does not mean that I do not appreciate and believe that we need the courageous leaders who will speak out on their convictions from the beginning. I believe that we desperately need them in our political life, but I wasn't in politics.

190   The Present: Faces

Well, it certainly had a major effect. President Lyndon Johnson said later that if he'd lost you, he'd lost America. Why didn't you try to speak out on some of the other major issues of that time?

I'd hate to think that a popular newscaster could turn around American public opinion on anything. Nothing could be more dangerous than that for a democracy.

Twenty years ago you did a documentary on the Warren Commission report on the assassination of President Kennedy. You said that the report was flawed, but the most plausible that could be expected, and that CBS News concluded that Lee Harvey Oswald was the sole assassin. In the years since, have you had any reason to doubt that?

Yes. We did not know, at that time, a rather important, salient matter: the CIA plot to assassinate Castro. An additional little fact was that Lyndon Johnson thought there was a conspiracy. I'm assuming that what he knew probably was just what we learned later about the CIA's involvement in Cuba.

As you look back on the late sixties, do you think there's a connection between the trauma of the assassination of President Kennedy, and the doubts about the circumstances of it, and so much of the trauma and disenchantment that took place in this country after that? Did it manifest itself in the streets?

I wouldn't say that the Kennedy assassination alone could have triggered that, but I think the series of assassinations — Martin Luther King, then Robert Kennedy — had a cumulative effect, which, I think, broke down our natural resistance to violence and kind of set loose hysteria. It manifested itself in the streets.

You did a three-part series in 1968 on crisis in the cities. Twenty years later those problems are infinitely worse than they were then. Drug use is an epidemic instead of a problem, and the underclass is permanent instead of being a persistent problem. Why is it that these issues no longer get the kind of attention that they did in 1968?

I hate to say out loud what I think the reason is, because I think that what some people say is true. Unfortunately, you've got to throw a brick through a window to get any attention. The reformers have had to march and threaten authority. I think that's, unfortunately, the lesson of history.

This is one of the things that is puzzling: Why hasn't leadership learned the lesson?

The lesson being...

That we should be doing something about these problems, not waiting for them to explode. In the name of humanity, we ought to be tackling this problem with all of our resources — perhaps some of those resources that are going into making nuclear weapons, which aren't going to do us a darn bit of good if the inner structure is so rotten that it can't sustain the democracy we want to defend. I must say that I wonder why people put up with what they have to put up with in our society.

What is television's role in this? The events of the late sixties were much more visual than problems like the budget deficit, the trade deficit. Isn't it true that the extremely serious problems that we have now don't engage the public's attention because television has such a hard time figuring out how to make them compelling?

Television has let us down, to an extent, by not staying with these hard-to-depict problems; at the cost of a more interesting broadcast, they should be addressing the issues. This has been my complaint for years.

At the 1968 Democratic National Convention, in Chicago, you made a famous comment when Dan Rather was being roughed up on the floor by Mayor Richard Daley's security forces. You called them "thugs." Then, later on, you interviewed Mayor Daley and were inexplicably easy on him.

That was probably the worst interview I ever did in my life, and I have nothing but regret over the way it was done. I can explain why it happened that way, but it's a poor excuse. It happened because I had in mind when Daley got there that I was not going to say anything, I was going to let Daley explain himself. Give him some air time. Well, it turned out that floor developments gave us more time, and Daley was perfectly willing to sit there. I had him there, and I should have done the interview that any half-reasonable, trained newsman would do. But I had this damn thing in the back of my mind of letting him talk, thinking, "Well, he'll hang himself." It was just a nutty idea. That, combined with the fact that he barged into the room before I was ready for him. I was planning on taking some time to get my thoughts together as to how I would lead him into hanging himself. But the whole thing was an absolute disaster; that's all I can say.

What else stands out from that week in Chicago?

What stood out to me that week in Chicago was something that never happened; I am convinced to this day that Johnson [who had chosen not to seek re-election] expected Daley to create a draft for him.

You're kidding.

I was sure they had Johnson tucked away somewhere. I kept waiting for this scenario to develop. Then we heard that Johnson had *Air Force One* waiting down at [his Texas] ranch. I was confident that that was the plot.

What did Johnson say when you interviewed him later at the ranch?

He denied that he would have accepted a draft. What else could he say? The airplane was there in case he felt it was necessary to address the convention. What he wanted was an invitation to address the convention, of course, but it never happened. The whole of that convention was such an incredible shambles. God, nobody knew what was going on, there was no cohesive leadership. Daley expected to have a leadership role. The riots in the streets denied him that and carried over onto the floor.

How much importance do you attach to the political underpinnings of the youth movement of the late sixties and early seventies, what they used to call the New Left? Do you think it's just a little blip?

I think you've got to say it was a blip, because we extended the vote to 18-year-olds, and they didn't go out and exercise it. I thought we had going— with George McGovern and others, Eugene McCarthy—a movement of youth that would have an important impact on our politics. And a healthy one. I'm terribly disappointed that they didn't follow through when they got the vote. Now, I don't entirely blame them for that. They were led down the garden path, in a sense, and then old-fashioned politics kind of came in and turned them off. And I can see that this might create an early cynicism. I think it was unfortunate and probably unjustified. As a matter of fact, I've always blamed Senator McCarthy for helping turn them off in that election. I thought he acted very irresponsibly in not supporting Hubert Humphrey [after the latter got the Democratic nomination] with everything he could do. And that would have been a lot—playing the Pied Piper.

Right before the 1972 election, you ran a two-part series on Watergate. What was your thinking, doing that?

The election obviously played a part in our thinking, because it was felt that the people ought to know what Watergate was about before the election. This sounds like a politician's answer. It wasn't to influence the election. I really mean that seriously. It wasn't meant to be an editorial saying, "Don't vote for Richard Nixon." It was meant to lay the facts out. So the people could make a judgment, at least. And nobody was pulling it together to look at what this whole thing added up to. And I felt that this was required at some point.

Didn't White House aide Charles Colson call CBS and try to squelch the second part of the report?

This was the only time in my entire years on the *Evening News* that there was interference from either the political or the commercial interests in a broadcast. And I think [then CBS news president] Dick [Salant] was trying to protect me when at first he denied to me that there was any. I don't blame him for fibbing to me. I wouldn't call it a lie; I'd call it a fib. Because I think he was simply saying, "Well, I've got to do it. I don't want Cronkite to have to bear the responsibility for yielding to political pressure. If I tell him, he's guilty, and there'll also be an explosion and a bigger amount of problems. It's better the way I'm handling it."

I think, in other words, he was assuming the guilt.

And preserving your deniability.

Yeah, that's right.

Was anything of any importance taken out of that second broadcast?

No, but it lost a lot of impact. Part of the impact was the fact that we gave so much time to it the first night. And also the fact that we were able to lead people through the process very carefully. All the connections, drafts and drawings and things. We had to drop some of their graphic presentation.

Was that the opening salvo of the war between CBS and the Nixon administration that developed in the next couple of years?

I guess it was.

Do you think that one of the reasons for the aggressiveness of the press over Watergate was that Nixon and Agnew had beaten up so much on the press, so reporters didn't like Nixon personally?

Oh, no. I don't think so.

So you don't think the president's personality has that much to do with the way some of these things got covered?

No, I wouldn't say that entirely. I think that a pleasant personality can deter the press over a period of time. But not forever. I don't think that major transgressions are going to go unreported because of friendliness.

But you've been watching from the sidelines during the Reagan administration. Don't you think that the press, until relatively recently, was pretty easy on him?

I don't know. I'll always have a problem with making judgments of that kind. The outstanding example, to me, of that kind of judgmental approach was during the Vietnam War, when I was catching it from both sides, the Establishment and the students. And at almost every student gathering I tried to talk to, the students would say, "Why don't you ever tell us the truth about the Vietnam War?" And then they would cite an incident, such as My Lai. And my answer always was, "Well, where'd you hear about that?" And that would stop them. Frequently they'd be belligerent and say, "Well, not from you." Well, that's all right, it wasn't from me, but somebody is reporting it, and he's out there.

In 1980, at the Republican convention in Detroit, you played a pretty major role in the decision not to invite Gerald Ford onto the ticket with Reagan.

I played the major role because Gerald Ford opened up. I asked the question he shouldn't have answered. It's as simple as that.

That was to ask under what conditions he would accept vice-president.

Yes, and then I said, "Sort of a copresidency," and he said yes. Or he said, "Well, not exactly," or something—I forget what he said—but that was the word that kind of stuck: "copresidency." So...

The year before that, you were in a similar situation in the Middle East, where you essentially played the role of shuttle diplomat in setting up Egyptian president Anwar Sadat's historic visit to Jerusalem. How comfortable are you with that circumstance?

Well, I'm perfectly comfortable with that, because that's a fallout of reportorial practice and nothing more than that.

Have you ever felt in retrospect that you underreported the extent of the domestic opposition to Sadat?

I think we probably did. It was very hard to get a handle on, however. I think Sadat still had a pretty good popularity rating among the Egyptians, generally. The religious fanatics were getting more and more upset about Sadat's performance. He told me one time. I said, "They cite the Koran on this and that." And he said, "I know the Koran better than any of them. Don't worry about them."

Do you still believe, as you've been quoted saying before, that he was the most courageous, impressive leader that you've ever met?

No question about it in my mind. No question about it. As it turned out, courageous perhaps to the point of foolhardiness. But, damn, he was. I think he was sensational. I think most of the Israelis think so, too.

In terms of walking into a room and feeling the presence of greatness, of true historical greatness, when you look over all the people that you interviewed in all of the years, who did you most get that sense from when you talked to them?

Most of the people who have achieved a public image have that. That's part of it. They don't achieve that fame and stature unless they began with that characteristic and capability. That's part of leadership.

In 1979, the American embassy in Iran was seized, and Americans were taken hostage. A lot of people say that by signing off saying, "This is the thirty-sixth, the thirty-seventh day," and so on, "of captivity for the American hostages," you focused unfair attention on the failures of the Carter administration.

I did not intend to bring pressure on the Carter administration. We did not intend it as a political gesture. This was a patriot sort of a feeling toward these unfortunate Americans who were caught there. And I said, the second day of this, third day maybe, you know, there's gonna come a time when this thing is going to move off the front page. And then there's going to come a time when it's going to move off the back page. And I'm not going to let that happen. I'm going to start reminding people that they're still there. And not let censorship by the Iranians keep us from reporting anything.

We still have hostages in the Middle East. Do you think that Dan Rather and Peter Jennings should be saying the same thing now?

Well, I have just as much sympathy and feeling for anybody held against their will anywhere in the world as I did for those in Iran. But I think the situation is a little different journalistically. The people who are being held now recognized the danger of the situation and elected to remain where they were or go where they were in danger. Whereas that was not the choice of those who were doing their duty in the embassy in Iran.

How did Jimmy Carter stack up as a president?

I think he's got one of the best brains of anybody I've known. I also think that his heart was in the right place on most of his moves. I think he had the great misfortune of not being a very skilled political operator on the national level. We got what we voted for: he ran against Washington, and he continued against Washington, and that poisoned his relationships with the Hill and the bureaucracy.

Do you think history might treat him more kindly?

Well, I doubt it. Because I don't think that much happened there. I think one of the things he is frequently maligned for today is his human-rights policy. I think it's one of the greatest things he did. I think the idea of trying to put America's actions where its words are—the Constitution, the Declaration of Independence, that we're all created equal—was a marvelous thing.

How about an assessment of Reagan?

I think that Reagan is a man of great convictions given to simplistic answers. Which is typical of a great number of us Americans, and therefore the key to his popularity—giving complex problems simple answers, that are totally impractical in execution and in many ways dangerous. I think that our macho foreign policy is dangerous and not helpful. It frightens our allies and certainly must frighten a lot of our enemies. I think that the tax policy has been disastrous. I have profited greatly from his tax policy, but I still say it's wrong. I should be paying more taxes.

Do you think in the long run he's worse for the country than Nixon?

Well, I would certainly be more concerned about the fallout from his programs than Nixon's. I thought Nixon was pretty good on foreign policy, not so bad on our domestic policy. I'm sorry that Nixon lost the political courage to follow through on the welfare reform that he came up with at one point. I thought there were a lot of good points in it.

So on balance, Reagan is a worse president than Nixon.

Oh, gosh, that's awfully hard to say. I'm trying to think of a nice, diplomatic answer. I think that history will put those things into balance.

So the reverence toward Reagan will fade with time?

Well, people may say that perhaps he was the most buoyant, cheerful and comforting president we've had.

How do you feel about the way the counterculture of the sixties and early seventies was covered?

The generation gap?

Yeah. The whole cultural change that took place.

I don't know. From time to time I thought that we were guilty of cheating an important story by giving it a headline name. And I sort of feel that way about the generation gap. Generation gap in a sense that most of those who were disenchanted with the Establishment, our society, our politics and economics, our social structure, were the younger people. Although they were joined by a considerable number of sympathetic older people who were active demonstrators and a lot of others who joined them in their attitudes.

But there were manifestations in that period that were a little unusual for a generation gap, which exists at all times. This one that developed in the sixties, seventies, with the narcotics, with the dress habits, the real rejection of society—adding that all together, it was more a virulent generation gap than we have normally, I think.

Did you ever wish that you had maybe gone to Woodstock or something like that?

I wish I'd gone to Woodstock, of course. Oh, gosh, I thought of that many times. I really missed a story there. One of my two daughters was there. I thought I got a fairly full report. I learned later that there were a lot of things that weren't fully reported about that.

What did you miss?

Oh, I think probably the almost universal marijuana smoking at the time. She obviously didn't report that one to me. She was in school at the time. In fact, she called and said that they were going from school over to Woodstock on a school project. And I believed it. I knew so little about what Woodstock was that I thought, well, it was a rock concert and a school project to go and listen to some modern music.

Here's another example of the older generation completely missing the impact, the important story. I was on vacation when Elvis Presley died, and I called the office in midafternoon to see how things were going. And they said Elvis Presley had died. And I said, "Well, no kidding, that's too bad." They said, "We're thinking of leading the program with it." And I said, "Leading the program with it? Good God, you must be crazy."

So what did they lead with?

There was a pretty good other story, fairly significant. I've forgotten what it was. The Congress passed the tax law—one of those big stories.

Is this area of cultural history something that you feel like you just missed the boat on? I mean, you never interviewed John Lennon, for instance, did you?

Yes, I would say that's right. I missed the boat on the rock generation, if you please. And that's just one of my failings. It didn't excite me. I really looked down on it. The music bothered me; I didn't like the music. Still don't. And I'm not a great music lover. I don't pretend to be an opera buff. I go occasionally, but I'm certainly not an egghead musically. I'm a Dixieland fan, as a matter of fact. My father-in-law was a fine-music lover, played the violin. And I remember his criticisms of Bing Crosby for that crooning. My gosh, he said, that's terrible music. And of course we all loved Bing Crosby in my generation. And I realized when my kids were growing up with rock that I was an old fuddy-duddy in that regard. Just like my father-in-law.

Well, how much importance do you attach to it in the larger sweep of world events? Do you think that the Beatles changed the world or were more of a cultural phenomenon?

Oh, I think [they were] obviously important to our cultural history. It's music that has had great influence on a whole generation of people. I don't think it has any more importance than probably swing, Dixieland and other musical fads of the moment.

The only thing I would kind of suggest—and I'm treading on dangerous ground here, becuase I don't even pretend to know much about it—but I gather that an awful lot of rock music consisted of lyrics that extolled the use of narcotics. I would think that perhaps had an influence far beyond what music normally would. But I am hesitant to go much further with that, because I just don't know that much about it. It's part of the boat I missed.

I noticed something interesting during your coverage of the first moon landing. I think you waited for two minutes before they were going to touch down, you didn't say anything, you just decided you weren't going to intrude in that. After the module touched down, when you were still exhilarated by the moment, you said you were speechless, then you said, "I'd like to know what those kids who are kind of pooh-poohing this thing are saying at this moment. I'd like to know what they thought in those moments when our [hearts] were in our throats."

I think it was probably a window into the innermost recesses of my consciousness. I felt that this was a marvelous moment that we could all rejoice in, that we could put all this other stuff aside. It probably crossed my mind that, now, damn it, can you really get up and say this is not a great moment?

Sam Donaldson

"ABC's Television Tiger: Sam the Man"

by Jane F. Lane

Sam Donaldson is not "a philosopher king of broadcast journalism" like Ted Koppel (his characterization), nor is he a "cerebral academic" like George Will, nor is he a "gent" like David Brinkley. His idea of the truth is "elemental and visceral...."

Picture CBS's pretty blond Lesley Stahl diving into the men's room after Sam Donaldson and John Dean, hysterical that her ABC archrival might extract some scoop on restricted turf. Isn't all fair in love and television journalism?

Not on your life. Donaldson threw her out.

Sam Donaldson may not be the meanest reporter in Washington, but he's the most aggressive, a one-two punch pugilist who feels it in his gut when he rains the big questions, the right questions, in the White House and on Capitol Hill. It's combat, not conversation, that this guy wages in front of a camera.

"My axiom is get the mouth in gear; hope that the mind will follow," says the 56-year-old Donaldson, feet propped up on the table of the seventh-floor conference room at ABC's Washington bureau. He's just finished "This Week with David Brinkley," an experience that left him irritable and contentious. The subject was George Bush's clean air bill, about which Donaldson knows (and possibly cares) little, despite the stacks of briefings littering the conference table. Donaldson doesn't like it when somebody declares with perfect aplomb that air is 70 to 96 percent cleaner, and he can't bash him right back with an opposing figure. Aaargh! Sam Donaldson growls with vexation. His one gambit to blast the discussion out of obscurity by introducing the incendiary—and seemingly irrelevant—subject of Lee Atwater clicked, but only tantalizingly briefly.

"You work off the top of your head, interacting with the thoughts of others," says Donaldson. "At the White House, I felt I had an obligation to ask a germane, front-burner question. I've got to start with a threshold question. If you don't discuss the five mandatory top-drawer subjects, then you haven't done your job. The time requirements are such that you can't indulge in verbal diarrhea; I MUST ask you about X."

The question of whether Donaldson—with his thunderbolt eyebrows, his

Jane F. Lane is a free-lance contributor to M *magazine.*

menacing bark, his "sneer, the shit-eating grin," as he lustily describes his favorite facial expression—can make music with Diane Sawyer is the question of the moment at ABC. Roone Arledge, a "genius," Donaldson says, whose brilliance for production far outweighs his lust for celebrity, and a crew of news warriors put themselves on the line with "Prime Time Live," a weekly show at 10 P.M. Thursdays.

This journalistic rendering of Beauty and the Beast—a news show about timely events with Sawyer and Donaldson as hosts, and Chris Wallace as chief correspondent—Sam threatens, will "blow 'L.A. Law' out of the water."

"Diane and I are not gonig to work with a script. We are going to ad lib every word we say," says Donaldson with gusto, for this—live television—is his passion. "We are going to touch on everything people are interested in. I've never seen a politician who's said, 'Well, I don't know if I can win but my mother wants me to run, so maybe you should vote for me.' I KNOW we are going to be successful. Fact IS stranger and more interesting than fiction."

For a man who believes in the one-minute exchange, Donaldson does have a way of going on. He harangues his listener, blocking and fading, seducing with irresistible interviewer's gimmicks or slamming the rhetorical door. Much of this exercise serves the purpose of winding himself up to performance level, as when he delivers his homily on the wonders of Her Dianeness.

"Diane is very reserved, far more than I am—some people call her an ice queen—and elegant. I can't compete with her in the looks department. I was worried about it at first," he says, fraying a raveled end on his shoelace. "You know, here is this monster beating up on our Diane. But she gives it right back. We're seen as two people arguing a point. One of the reasons the show will work is because we work well together. We like each other, and we respect each other. She is not Barbara Walters, but Barbara and I are the same people—aggressive, pushy, hot people. Barbara wears a dress, I wear pants.

"But let me hasten to add that my first love at the moment is Diane."

Donaldson sports his heavyweight belt if not with pride then with a sense of justice. He denigrates the lumbering, desultory tactics of newspaper reporters and glorifies the acid-test truth of the single, ultimate question. There is a ruthless veracity to the confrontation between a television reporter and his opponent, Donaldson believes, a gladiatorial one-on-one that can be fatal.

"You get what you see," he says. "I'm a reporter. I think the press is fair. I'm not going to defend anything I've said, or any story I've done. We all get what we deserve in the press, as we all get what we deserve in life."

The question of whether reporters, as potentially influential people, should be vulnerable to the identical personal scrutiny as those they cover provokes Donaldson. "I've answered that 50 times before," he snaps, disputing the implicit assumption of jounalistic hegemony.

"I have power as a reporter if I can bring information to you," he says. "People think we can persuade people to think as we do—I don't believe that for a minute. I don't change votes because I argue strongly for or against a proposition. It's television that has power. But it's not a personal ability to influence or persuade; I have influence because I have brought you information."

A personal attack, he emphasizes, would likely be designed to destroy his

Sam Donaldson of ABC News (photo courtesy Capital Cities/ABC, Inc.).

credibility as a news reporter, and that practice, most assuredly, he opposes. As for his professional strategies, he maintains their honor, and dignity.

"I'm not for wiretapping and I've never," he observes respectfully, "filched a document from someone's office. Which is not to say I won't take a little peek if I'm in there with somebody."

And which is not to say he won't use any available edge to vanquish an opponent, including throwing Lesley Stahl out of the men's room into which she has dogged Donaldson and Dean.

"If I didn't like her so much I wouldn't have used so many examples in my book of her aggressiveness," says Donaldson, referring to "Hold On, Mr.

President!," a memoir Random House published in 1987. "Does Lesley cross the line occasionally? Yes. But which of us doesn't? Lesley came into a man's world, the old boys' club of Dan Schorr [then CBS Washington correspondent]. Lesley is often all over the lot, but she can ask the killer question. I think of George Shultz admitting to her that he could speak for himself, but not the entire government, on the Iran arms deal."

All the better, then, if the opponents are matched in weight class.

Filtered through retrospect, the notoriously confrontational relationship between Donaldson and Ronald Reagan seems pale and even trivial. Reagan was a president, Donaldson says, who rode in like John Wayne and then had his wife do his dirty work for him, a president "who usually did what the last guy who got to him said." In arms control, the President's greatest accomplishment, Donaldson observes that Gorbachev was the leader and Reagan the follower.

Donaldson narrates a story from Reagan intimates of arduous policy meetings where chiefs of staff, after elaborate preparation and presentation, would turn hopefully to the President for a decision.

"He'd get that big expectant smile, push his chair back,"—here, Donaldson stands up to his full six feet, far slimmer, however, and less imposing than Reagan's—and with perfect intonation, impersonates the former president. "'Well, fellas,'" he imitates with an ingratiating charm, 'work it out.'

"He was one of the most passive people you'd ever meet. When George Bush makes a mistake, it's miscalculation. With Reagan it was willful ignorance," Donaldson says hotly, striding over to a world map on the wall and striking it angrily. "He saw something Norman Rockwell painted."

Bush strikes a more genuine, if not necessarily substantive, chord. But for a "pretty sensible, moderate, decent, intelligent politician," he is too anxious about reaction to his ideas, Donaldson says, and too inconsistent in projecting a persona.

"Of course, we elect politicians to follow the popular will," Donaldson says. "Bush is NOT a wimp, but he pays too much attention to gauging public mood before he makes a statement. His coverage has been erratic."

Donaldson slams GOP national committee chairman Lee Atwater for low-blow slugging during the Bush-Dukakis fracas, for playing on racial prejudice, particularly in the South. As for Roger Ailes, who ran Bush's campaign, "I denounce his practices, but I like him personally," Donaldson says. "He's yet to go over the line where I think there's a flaw in his character."

"Still," he stresses unsympathetically, "the election could have been winnable for a Democrat, some Democrat," but obviously not Dukakis, a man who didn't have "the wits to throw it back in Bush's face before the sun went down."

For Bush's confederate Dan Quayle, however, Donaldson reserves his most severe criticism.

"You get what you see," he says flatly. "If Quayle is using this facade to hide a steel-trap mind, you could have fooled me. Basically he is a lightweight; basically he is good to his wife and kids. I don't dislike Dan Quayle or wish him ill, but he is basically unqualified to be the president of the United States, which is the qualification for being vice-president of the United States. George Bush picked Dan Quayle because he wanted a nonentity that would not threaten him in any way, shape or form."

Donaldson delivers these aperçus without a trace of enmity or prejudice, but with the rich resonance of his "what you see is what you get" tenet. He is not, as he characterizes his friend Ted Koppel, "a philosopher king of broadcast news," a cerebral academic like his "This Week" colleague George Will, or a gent like David Brinkley. His idea of the truth is elemental and visceral.

"Carter was a very combative, essentially humorless problem-solver," Donaldson reflects. "He had the best mind — he could take in information and come out with a solution that on paper was the right one. But Carter didn't understand that the best book solution wasn't the best political solution. Presidents can only have one fight at a time, one and a half if they're powerful. Carter wanted to fight with everybody. As I get older, fewer and fewer things appear to be principles that you can tack up on the church door. Ev Dirksen (the late senator from Illinois) is the politician I admire: He did his deals; he made his compromises. The Newt Gingriches of this world — hmmm, they have no friend in me."

So inside the master of the one-minute miracle question is a spiel-meister of fairly extravagant proportion. The fact is — and they will only reveal this in rare moments of confidence — journalists cling to the security of objectivity, of distance, of contest as they would to a tattered blanket. They are, in the best cases, wildly self-protective people who get their voyeuristic kicks from exposing others. Donaldson, happily, goes beyond this little ritual.

Unremarkably for such an utter professional, he catches the shortcomings in a colleague and suggests a question about his private life. The issue, had been considered and rejected as moot. What private life?

He concedes there has been a deficiency.

"I am not a well-rounded person, not a man for all seasons. Everyone in this business who amounts to something is the same way. It's not a part of their life, it IS their life," says Donaldson, who generally has a maximum of one full day off a week — Saturday. "I like this business; I LOVE this business. Why am I here on a Sunday? Why are YOU here?"

"I regret I didn't balance better my personal life and my family. My ex-wife is my ex-wife because she wanted a life of her own, somebody who came home and didn't use home as a pit stop. You're no use to your wife when you come home limp, and I use that word deliberately.

"I don't mean to sound like I'm longing for something I lost. My life has turned out well. I'm married to a woman I love very much."

Donaldson on the Press

All the News Is *Not* Fit to Print

With a degree in telecommunications from Texas Western in El Paso, Sam Donaldson, who was born in New Mexico and grew up on his father's dairy and cotton farm, is pretty much of an electronic news fundamentalist. He's worked at ABC since 1967. His first love was radio, and his first job was radio, and his first job as a college freshman was as a disc jockey at the 250-watt KELP in El Paso. By his senior year, he was an announcer at KROD-TV. He missed radio.

"Ask anyone who has worked in both, and they'll tell you the real freedom and romance in broadcasting is to be found in radio," Donaldson writes in his memoir, "Hold On, Mr. President!"

"I read the newspapers when I can," he admits grudgingly. "If I can confess to the days I barely skim them, you would destroy me."

Print and television stories are structured differently, he says, with an obvious emphasis on the grab in the latter. "Howard K. Smith, who was almost like an idol to me, told me the greatest sin in television news is to be dull. A story is interesting intrinsically, but then the structure is the important thing, with the use of the pictures. A television spot does not begin with a lead sentence; you depend on the anchor for that, although today some of them want to do tone poems."

So, what DOES he read?

- "The *Washington Post* is an indispensable first read. It far eclipses the *New York Times* for national news and political news. I love Meg Greenfield [the paper's editorial page editor], we all love her, but Meg, God love you, when the *Post* didn't endorse a presidential candidate because it couldn't make up its mind..."

- "I skim the *New York Times* because I have to, not because I enjoy it, with the exception of Safire, Wicker and Tony Lewis. It is the dullest major newspaper I have ever seen. You have to sit there and—dammit!—READ through it."

- "I love the *Washington Times*. Wes Pruden, the managing editor, writes a column that's my kind of column. Pruden always says 'Bang!' That's a name to watch."

- "There are two *Wall Street Journals*. The editorial page is not so capable, run by people who simply have axes to grind, and they grind them seemingly without any consideration intruding in the process. If it's a Democrat under fire, the *Wall Street Journal* loves it; if it's a Republican, it's huffing and puffing. That's not consistent. The rest of the paper is absolutely first class."

- "I occasionally look at *USA Today*, but I don't read it, unless I'm traveling."

Douglas Edwards

"CBS' Original News Anchor Signs Off"

by Mark Schwed

Douglas Edwards was the first broadcast journalist to have his own by-lined news show: "Douglas Edwards and the News," for CBS in 1946. Here, Mark Schwed offers a portrait of Edwards as he retired from CBS, in April 1988. Edwards died in Sarasota, Florida, October 13, 1990, at the age of 73.

About 40 years ago, Douglas Edwards sat behind a plain desk next to the Dione Lucas cooking show, looked into the eye of the camera and delivered the very first evening television newscast for CBS.

It took some convincing to get him to take that hot seat. Radio was king then, and most people thought that was the only place for news. Television was little more than a freak show conceived by weird engineers. Radio was paying the freight.

Little did he know he was looking into the eye of the future. Tomorrow, after more than four decades doing TV and radio news for CBS, the most senior journalist at the network is signing off with his last broadcast, at the age of 70. He will start like this: "Good evening, everybody, coast to coast." He couldn't say that in the old days because TV news wasn't coast to coast. In 74 seconds, Edwards will sum it up—the kings, the queens, the wars, the presidents, the shootouts, the news of four decades—and then he will say goodbye.

"I don't want to take any more than a minute and 14 seconds. There is still news to deliver, you know."

Edwards' final CBS radio show will be on KNX (1070 AM) at 6 P.M., and his last TV apperance will be CBS "Newsbreaks" at 10:56 A.M. and 2:40 P.M. on KCBS—Channel 2.

And then Edwards will hit the lecture circuit and write that book—and he and his wife, May, are building a house in Florida, where they will retire.

"I'm going to miss it," Edwards said from his office in New York.

It was May who convinced him to step aside after a CBS career that began when he joined the network as a radio reporter in 1942. "My wife nudged me," Edwards says. "She wanted to spend more time with me."

Mark Schwed was a staff writer for The Los Angeles Herald Examiner. *This article was published before the* Herald Examiner *closed.*

Before Rather, there was Cronkite, and before Uncle Walter, there was Douglas Edwards. Indeed, the news was named after the anchorman. "Douglas Edwards and the News" aired from 7:30 to 7:45 P.M., the program was in black and white, and when there were no pictures, which was often, Edwards would simply talk viewers through.

"My first appearance on television was in May of 1946, about 42 years ago," he says. "It was rather difficult following (Lucas') cooking school. Everybody's mouth watered. She always left the food on the set, though. I was never hungry when I did the news."

That savory broadcast first hit New York and nowhere else because CBS had only one station. As CBS founder William Paley and chief executive Frank Stanton bought more TV stations, Edwards' influence spread. Within two years of his debut, Edwards was seen in five major cities, with an estimated audience of ten million people.

CBS records May 3, 1948, as the start of the 15-minute, Monday-through-Friday network newscast that Edwards anchored for 14 years before turning it over to Cronkite.

And CBS presented the first gavel-to-gavel coverage of national political conventions in 1948 — Republican, Democratic and the Henry Wallace Progressives. Politicians were quick to recognize the power of that little black-and-white set.

But if politicians knew a good deal when they saw it, others were not so sure.

"I didn't exactly want to do it at first," Edwards recalls. "Frank Stanton, the Number 2 man at CBS — I had a long conversation with him. He took me by the hand and led me into the future and pointed toward what television would ultimately be. He was absolutely correct. He said it would be an astounding new medium that would have greater potential than radio because it carried pictures along with the sound."

And CBS executives set a precedent they may not regret. They offered Edwards a ton of money just for making the switch.

"They took my radio contract and tore it up," he says. "Then they doubled my salary. In the first year of television I was probably making $800 a week. It was a lot of money back then. It's not what Danny Boy (Rather) gets today. In other words, I peaked out too soon."

In the early days, the newscast had no commercials; CBS News could find no sponsors for the show. So Edwards delivered the news uninterrupted. But even then, ratings meant everything.

Edwards' co-producer was Don Hewitt, now executive producer of the most successful prime-time news show of all time, "60 Minutes."

"Don and I would follow the ratings with great interest. Even back then there was ratings pressure. We latched onto a sponsor in February 1949 — I think it was Oldsmobile — and went three days a week.

"CBS kept adding stations. They added more until they stretched from border to border, coast to coast. I remember that first time I said 'coast to coast.' It was a big deal. I said, 'Good evening, everybody, coast to coast.' I left that in the act. We beat everybody broadcasting from coast to coast."

And what of today's TV industry?

"There has been a melding of news and entertainment. TV is a medium which entertains, which sells and I believe above all, which informs. It is absolutely magnificent as an education and information medium when it is used best. When you, for instance, take it to a national political convention, you simply cannot beat TV."

It has been a long enjoyable haul for Edwards. Born in Ada, Oklahoma, he got his first real job at a tiny radio station in Troy, Alabama, where his family had moved. As a 15-year-old junior announcer, he would spin records, read poetry and even sing some songs. All for the highfalutin' salary of $2.50 a week. The Big Apple is a long way from Troy, or is it?

Linda Ellerbee
"And So It Has Gone"
by Michele Stanush

Linda Ellerbee is sitting in the waxed cavern of the Radisson Plaza Hotel lobby, smoking Merits, uncomfortable in the lipstick and other colored goop she's put on to get her picture taken.

"I hate wearing makeup," she grouses. "The older I get, the more I hate it because I've had to wear it for years."

For years, Ellerbee's mug—every pore and pucker—was scrutinized by millions of television-viewing Americans, some of whom paid more attention to her weight than to her wisdom.

But most saw Ellerbee as a controversial yet acclaimed newscaster and writer. She and her throaty voice talked to America on award-winning (though later cancelled) shows such as *NBC News Overnight* and ABC's *Our World*.

These days, however, Ellerbee is talking about others things. About Life-After-the-Networks and leaving a $500,000-a-year (more or less) job, about her fledgling production company, about tackling a drinking problem, about someday wanting to move to the Austin area.

Ellerbee, 46 and a native of Bryan, was back in Texas for a few days to speak at a University of Texas women's conference and to roam the Hill Country, communing with mesquite trees and pondering a return to her home state.

Michele Stanush is a staff writer for The American-Statesman.

"Kinky Friedman, who is a pal of mine, tells me that I'll never write anything seriously worth a damn until I come back," she says.

Ellerbee's laugh is lost in the expanse of the Radisson's lobby. But it's a strong and bawdy laugh. A barroom laugh. The laugh of someone who'd be fun to drink with.

And she was.

During her keynote address at the University of Texas women's conference (during which she thumbed her nose at fashion by wearing what resembled baggy sweats), Ellerbee slipped in an unexpected confession.

"I'm a recovering alcoholic," she said, "and I've been sober now for almost two years."

The crowd of 3,000 started clapping, rising in a standing ovation. Privately, Ellerbee wondered what that meant. Publicly, she just smiled. "This is the first time I've ever said that in front of a large group of people," she told the group.

If it was a startling admission, it isn't unusual for Ellerbee to get candid and controversial.

Her best-selling 1986 book, *And So It Goes: Adventures in Television*, talks about everything from shortcomings in network television to an illegal abortion she got in the years before Roe vs. Wade.

This month, Ellerbee has a new book coming out—*Move On: Adventures in the Real World*—which promises to be just as revealing, including a chapter on her alcoholism.

In an interview with the *Austin American-Statesman*, Ellerbee talked about her past, present, and possible Texas-bound future.

Q: Why are you thinking about moving to Texas, and the Austin area in particular? Would it be a part-time move?
A: I really don't know. I would love to have a vacation house here. The problem is finding enough time to vacation.

Like most Texans, I never really left. Yes, I want to come back. Now, whether it's going to be next year or five years from now, I don't know. But I sort of think about finishing up my life here.

If and when I come back to Texas, the Austin area is where I'm going to come. I've never lived here. But I've always loved this area. I went to camp in the Hill Country when I was a little girl. And my best friend had a house in Wimberley.

In high school, I had friends who went to "The University" and we would come visit on weekends. And I have a lot of indirect family here. My children's father's family.

Q: Would you consider moving your production company here?
A: Sure. Not immediately. Who knows? One day we may be so big we have offices in New York and Austin. But I have no plans to move the company down here at this time.

Q: Why did you start the company and how is it doing?

A: It seemed the networks were less and less interested in experimenting, and certainly less and less committed to doing documentaries.

We've had our rough times. There's no question that an independent production company is not the easy way to go. There were times when I thought we wouldn't make it. But we are over that hump. We've got business now into 1993.

(A contract with) Nickelodeon just happened last week. Nickelodeon is interested in how you produce news for children. All the attempts used for children have failed because they don't take into account certain things — that children want and need for a story to have a beginning, middle and ending.

We have a deal with *Forbes* magazine and WQED in Pittsburgh (which produced *National Geographic* specials) to produce four American Heritage specials a year, which are documentaries. One of them under consideration right now is the Texas nation.

And we have little pet projects that we want to do. We'd still like to put *Our World* back on the air. It was a good show.

Q: What made you decide to leave network television after *Our World* was canceled in 1987? Was it because you had to?
A: I didn't have to. That's a total mistake. When I left the networks, I had two years to run on a contract with ABC and had offers from another network. In fact, I could have — if I'd wanted to — sat on my behind side for two years and gotten paid an amazing amount of money.

But what I didn't want to do was to sit around and wait until somebody decided I was too old, or too overweight, or too uppity, or too something.

Q: What is *Move On,* which is scheduled for release this April, about?
A: It's a lot of short stories that are true. Stories about myself. Stories about other women that I know. About my family. About growing up in Texas. It's stories about the changes that we go through, especially growing up and living in the last half of the twentieth century.

There is a chapter in there about what happened when I left the networks, but it's just a chapter.

At one point, in part of the book, I went back to the places that had been pivotal or important in my life, and interviewed people. Talked to people. Walked those same streets, looking for answers.

Q: Is your alcoholism discussed in the book?
A: I really wasn't sure I wanted to write about this at all. At first I didn't. I had written down on a piece of paper a whole list of arguments about why I wasn't going to include that chapter.

My publisher said, "Well, you do what you want. But you have written what amounts to a very honest book about change, and I don't see how you can call this an honest book about change if you don't include one of the biggest, if not *the* biggest, change in your life."

And that was such a compelling argument that I looked down to see which argument was going to refute that. And there wasn't one.

Q: How did your drinking problem develop, what made you try to kick it and how does it feel to go public with it?
A: My father was an alcoholic. It runs in the family, and I was one of those people who said, "Of course it will never happen to me because I've seen it." But it did happen.

It grew. You'd cover a story, and then you'd go out and drink because that's what the big kids were doing. And you don't realize how much it's sneaking up on you. Toward the end, I'd work all day and then I'd go drink. I'd get up feeling awful, then I'd work and I'd drink.

I got frightened I was going to kill myself. I don't mean commit suicide. But the slow, sure suicide of alcoholism. I didn't want to die. I hated my life that way. And I didn't want to become Jessica Savitch.

Ann Richards gave me a lot of courage to be that open about that. I kept a very close eye on this campaign. I thought it said a lot about how Americans deal with redemption. Whether they want to make room in their hearts for redemption. And obviously, they do. That gives courage to a lot of recovering alcoholics.

Q: What writing projects do you plan for the future?
A: Fiction is next. In fact, I'm blocking out a novel. My publisher wanted me to write fiction this last time, but I wasn't ready. It's very tough. Although *Move On* is not fiction, it's written more in a fiction form.

Linda Ellerbee

Born: August 15, 1944, in Bryan.
Education: Dropped out of college after a year and a half at Vanderbilt University.
Family: Two children: Vanessa Veselka, 22, and Joshua Veselka, 20.
Current occupation: Owns New York-based Lucky Duck Productions; writes a syndicated newspaper column.
Notable achievements: Eleven years at NBC, including anchor and writer for programs such as *Weekend* and *NBC News Overnight*. Writer and anchor of ABC's historical series, *Our World*. Won Emmy for best writing. Book about television, *And So It Goes,* on *New York Times* best-seller list five months.
Love interest: "My partner and I. We worked together for years. He was a cameraman for ABC in Washington when I was a Capitol correspondent, and then we started a company together. And then we fell in love."
Favorite place to travel: "The Hill Country. When I moved from Texas, I missed the yellows, the golds, the tans. Most of all, I missed the big sky. That's why I live in Greenwich Village. The buildings are short. I can see the sky and I don't feel like I live in a canyon." *[cont.]*

Wisdom worth clipping: "I read a line in a review of a book about Agatha Christie which I taped to the computer where I write. It was something to the effect that Agatha Christie was an adventurous, daring young woman who turned into a cheerful, overweight, happy, elderly novelist. And I thought, what's wrong with that?"

Influences on her writing: "Over time, that changes. There was a time when I tried to write like Tom Wolfe. This was very early. There was a time in my life when I think I wrote stories about good and true fish."

On good-health regime started at age 45: "Obviously, I still put on weight, so I don't keep up with it entirely. (But) I walk lots and lots of places, and, like every middle-class, middle-aged woman, I have my little exercise bike in my bedroom. And I get on it and feel like a fool riding to nowhere."

Least-favorite question by reporters: "Any question that begins, 'What are our favorites.' I hate that because suddenly I can never think of any of them."

Peter Jennings

"The ABC's of Peter Jennings"
by Norman Atkins

Peter Jennings is a living paradox: a native Canadian, he's a master of American television; a news anchor, he's proudest of being a reporter; the anchor with the most urbane and international image, he's the least educated of the major network anchors; he is the living logo of ABC News and its "World News Tonight" and his potential is unlimited.

Why is Peter Jennings crying? Why is the cool medium's coolest anchor, the steadiest commander manning Info Central in times of crisis, getting all misty eyed during this quiet moment of repose? Surely the Nielsen numbers

Norman Atkins is a free-lance writer.

210   The Present: Faces

bode well, as *World News Tonight* is now regularly winning the weekly ratings wars. *The Washington Journalism Review* poll brings just cause for sanguineness, having awarded Jennings Best Anchor for the third year in a row. Demographic surveys of this spring's graduating college seniors rosily predict an ever-burgeoning young audience for Jennings, whom ABC News president Roone Arledge calls "the anchor of the future," whatever that means. Even the obituaries in this morning's paper deliver good news, to the extent that they are filled with the names of Dan Rather's loyal viewers.

Jennings is sitting in an easy chair in his office, which is tucked away on ABC/Capital Cities' cozy midtown–Manhattan campus. He's down on himself for deciding to air a religious broadcaster's handout videotape of the final preexecution interview with mass murderer Ted Bundy. He's afraid he was seduced by a compelling video moment and thus failed to scrutinize the journalistic methods used in packaging the interview, but he's not crying about that or anything. And he's got a hockey injury bandaged up on his right arm, but he's not in any excruciating pain. After all, he got the better of those kids on the ice in that pickup game near his East Hampton weekend home.

When Jennings leans over the office coffee machine, you can see a round bald spot on the back of his head, which the camera obscures, making him look younger than his 50 years. His tie is loose around his neck, his sleeves rolled up, his jacket off. Despite his reputation for being Mr. Sophisticate, a patrician dresser, he buys most of his suits off the rack at London's mass-middle-class store Marks and Spencer, and no, he doesn't keep a stash of freshly pressed shirts in his closet, à la Tom Grunick in *Broadcast News*. His thriftiness is legendary — Arledge still ribs him for purchasing a pair of secondhand shoes, and the major impact of his reportedly $1.8 million annual salary on his lifestyle seems to be splurging for $12 bottles of vino, up from two dollars. Banging out copy around the rim of the news room, Jennings dons glasses, not his contacts, which he's loath to wear. In fact, unless he's reminded in the frenzied moments before the 6:30 feed by assistant Charlotte Taylor ("my den mother"), he sometimes forgets "to put in my eyes" in time for the news, in which case the cameras, with their teleprompters, have to roll up close and personal.

What happens once those cameras capture his image and transmit it to what he calls "the box," or "the cube," in 12 million homes across the nation is what makes Jennings profoundly uncomfortable and what has led him to a few tears this morning. It all started when I tried to praise the warmth and sensitivity of his coverage last December of the bombing of Pan Am flight 103. He recoiled at this characterization, adamantly maintaining that he's a portrait of neutrality and detachment on the air and confessing perplexity at what members of his audience graft upon his televised image. By way of example, he showed me a letter he received from the parents of a kid who'd died aboard the Pan Am jet, along with one of the last letters the kid himself sent stateside from London, where he'd been studying. The kid wrote, in essence, that the American political establishment was a sham, with the exception of one true shining light, namely Peter Jennings, for whom he'd decided to cast his absentee ballot in the 1988 presidential election.

Ironically, the Canadian-born anchor is constitutionally disqualified from making a run at the White House. Jennings seems to understand the letter is bizarre, but that isn't stopping him from shedding a few tears for the fan to whom he now feels retroactively attached. He may repress his disciplined emotions on camera, but right now they're pretty much out of control. Still, reaching for a Kleenex on his desk, he says he could turn off the tears in a snap. "If we were going on the air, you'd see nothing."

But what really wigs Jennings out, and may be the real source of his weeping, is how he's been transformed from a simple news reporter into the Face of the News, a nightly image onto which viewers project their dreams and nightmares about world events. He's freaked by how this kid's notion of a Jennings presidency could be so out of whack with reality. And he gets choked up again when, later in the interview, he discusses a five-year-old cancer patient who thought he saw a halo over the newsman's head—a Jennings archangelship.

During the second of our two interviews, Jennings is in considerably better spirits. On this morning, his wife, Kati Marton, walks him to work from their nearby Central Park West co-op. She's a former ABC correspondent who's working full time on a book (about the mysterious death of journalist George Polk), and so the couple is searching for an *au pair* to look after their two kids, ages six and nine.

Over the course of the interviews, Jennings is repeatedly interrupted by phone calls from the far-flung field, for which he still harbors a flame and from which he sometimes feels cut off in the New York anchor's chair. He peppers a phone conversation with ABC's Damascus stringer with bits of Arabic, a vestige of his years as a Middle East correspondent. He helps orchestrate a surprise birthday party for Barrie Dunsmore, ABC's man in London—calling friends "mate" and letting an "eh" slip in every so often—and plans to jet over for the day. One study, which otherwise praised his news writing over that of his rivals, did note his penchant for "Eurocopy," and his Euroconversation is even more pronounced. In casual talk, however, he loses the rhythmic head tilts, bordering on neck exercises, that he uses on the air to punctuate sentences and that Tom Hanks did a wicked parody of on *Saturday Night Live*.

Jennings himself can be deadly serious, as when he confides—as if revealing some major scoop-in-progress—that Broadway director-choreographer Jerome Robbins is going to be ABC's Person of the Week, a segment of the show that happens to be his baby, his little innovation. But at the same time, he possesses the requisite antidote of self-mockery, posting in his makeup room a blowup of a Mike Peters cartoon in which a psychiatric patient announces, "There must be something wrong with me, Doctor ... I just don't care who ABC's Person of the Week is."

It has been said that as an anchor you excel in covering disasters—for example, the explosion of the space shuttle 'Challenger' in 1986. Do you see it as your mission, in part, to bring together the American village in times of crisis?

No, I do not see it as a mission. But Don Hewitt, executive producer for *60 Minutes*, at CBS, has taught me to understand that *that* television set [*points to the one in the upper-left-hand corner of his office*] is sometimes a chapel. And I didn't realize that until the *Challenger* explosion, when we had been on the air for about 11½ hours. When I got the bulldog edition of *The New York Times* and found that they had devoted 13 pages to this story, I said, "God, what a story!" I had to look at a newspaper to measure the impact of what I had done. Then the reaction began to build, and thousands of people said to me, "Do you realize what a service you provided on that day?" The answer was no. But what television had done was it had been there as this electronic link for all of us to mourn together.

That would make you the facilitator of this chapel.

I must say, once I was aware of it, I became very self-conscious. After three or four days of this, I remember going up to Capitol Hill to talk to Dan Boorstin, who was then the Librarian of Congress and a great historian, and saying, "Dan, this is quite heavy-duty stuff. Give me some sense of context." Which of course he did, quite brilliantly, by reminding me that when American pioneers pushed west across the country and someone in the wagon train died, they would all stop, gather the wagon trains around and have a collective experience. Which is what I think television does for us in the modern age.

If you regard me as someone who is more involved, I'm not really pleased about that in some respects, because I see journalists working at that involvement in some cases. *Identifying with the grief-stricken.* I find that awful. I don't think I have ever seen tragedy unfold in front of me, electronically, and then said to myself, "I had better identify with tragedy."

What about when ABC correspondent Charles Glass was taken hostage in Lebanon or when former ABC anchor Max Robinson died of AIDS?

Charlie is a friend. I was best man at his wedding. When he was kidnapped, I was devastated. And spent every waking hour when I was not on this broadcast trying to get him free. When I was on the air for a half an hour every night, Charlie was a news story. And I hope I comported myself accordingly.

At one point when Charlie was a hostage, they released some videotape of him confessing he was a CIA agent. I was on the air, doing live coverage of the Wall Street collapse. And somebody in the system made a mistake and put the piece on live. As a general rule, I don't think we should put on pieces that are unscreened. So it suddenly popped up on the air. And there was my friend—with a pistol to his head, as I later learned—acknowledging he was a CIA agent. Which was absolute bullshit.

Did you almost lose it on the air?

That, I think, is the closest I've ever come to losing it on the air.

Let's get back to your roots. Your father was a bigwig in the Canadian Broadcasting Company. Did he have a chance to see you on American TV?

Oh, very much so. He came to New York once when I was knee-high to a grasshopper, and I have this wonderful recollection—I had an old second-hand Porsche 911, and I brought it to New York, which was a terrible mistake, but I have this wonderful image of driving down Columbus Avenue one night with Walter Cronkite and my father in the back seat of the car. *Yahhhhhh...*

The news clipping on your wall says he wore English suits and was "quite the imperialist." What does that mean?

Probably that he was anti-American.
And yet he almost went to work in American TV himself.
That's right. In 1933, my father got offered a job at NBC radio. I mean, times were tough, and there was no money in Canada, and he came down here, and some guy stopped him at a place called Black Rock, outside Buffalo, where the immigration check was. And asked all these questions my father didn't like — it had a lot to do with coming and taking the job of an American at the time of the Depression — and he said, "Geez, then I'm going to go home."
Could he have schmoozed his way past the immigration check?
Probably. And then I'd have been American born.
You obviously have a green card. Will you ever become a U.S. citizen?
I don't know. First of all, it's a very private decision, a decision which has an impact not only on my own emotions but on my mother's and my wife's and my children's. It has also been used as a bit of a club occasionally, and I've become offended by that.
Some yahoo complained you weren't standing when they played the national anthem at the Democratic convention, not realizing that you couldn't hear it from behind the glass booth.
That's right. In fact, I was just thinking of that the other day. Neither David Brinkley nor I stood up, and my superiors got this outraged letter from some retired brigadier general who accused me of being nothing but a "guest in the country." I wrote him back, and we resolved it. I get offended when people say, "How dare you . . . because you're not an American." So I've just decided it's a private matter. Moreover, the country may not want me.
Growing up in Ottawa, you never finished the tenth grade. What prompted you to drop out of school?
I have no idea. First of all, I was bad in school. I was bone lazy. I didn't really understand the value of hard work until I was about 19, and then I'd already been working two years. It was of far greater interest to me to get out and play hockey or football than to study literature or, God forbid, math and chemistry.
So you went off to work as a bank teller and then got into radio. You were even a crooner at the Miss Canada Pageant.
Once, I was. There is, in fairness, a little history to that. The pageant song was meant to be sung by Gordon MacRae, who was the guest host, but he was loaded at the time. So somebody said, "Can you sing, Jennings?" I said, "Of course I can sing." I wasn't very aware in those days of the impact one could have on television, or how it might haunt me 30 years later [*laughs*].
At the time, when you were singing or when you were hosting 'Club Thirteen,' the Canadian equivalent of 'American Bandstand,' did you think you might end up as a Dick Clark or a Casey Kasem?
No, no, I was just having a good time. I worked at a local television station. There were only six of us anyway, and if you didn't sweep the floors in the morning they wouldn't get swept, and if you didn't do the dance party, you wouldn't get on the air. It never occurred to me to say no. It has been embarrassing later on, but not in any serious way.
You don't wish that you hadn't done it?

I don't wish that I hadn't done anything, except, perhaps — I was married twice before, and I wish I had been a kinder, more thoughtful person, and more mature on both those occasions. That's about all I regret.

You were first hired by ABC when you were 24 years old. How did that come about?

[ABC reporter] John Scali just reminded me of this the other day. I met him in Ottawa at a NATO conference, and ABC didn't have very many employees in those days. Scali apparently watched the reporting I'd done on Canadian television and called his boss here. And shortly thereafter [another reporter] and I did the reporting for ABC on a Canadian-government crisis, and ABC took our feed. And shortly after that, they offered us jobs. And I said no.

Why?

I was terrified of coming here. I just didn't think I was ready to come. America was enormous. I'd only been here once before, to go to a Broadway show. I'd never seen buildings so tall, and that was sort of symbolic for the overpoweringness of it. And so I said no. And about six months later I woke up and said, "Holy Jesus, that was a mistake." And I wrote Elmer Lower, who was then the president [of ABC], and said, "Excuse me, could I reconsider?" And he wrote back and said yes.

Then after two years of working as a national correspondent, management came to you and said, "Peter, you're only 26 years old, but we want you to anchor ABC news."

I mean, it was *ludicrous.* I look back now, and I wonder to myself what *they* must have been thinking. At the time, ABC was really into kids' programming. *Gidget* . . . I honestly don't remember what the programs were. And we didn't have any news tradition here like CBS and NBC. And I think somebody said, "Let's go KIDS across the board [*laughs*]. And so let's get this kid Jennings — he can string two words together, he has all his teeth — and ask him to be the anchor."

They figured they were so behind they had nothing to lose.

Yeah. And you know something, we didn't do a bad news program in those days. I've looked at the old programs.

You don't wince when you look back?

Oh, I wince at my own performance! Oh, my God, there's a picture in one of the next rooms here of me when I was doing it. *Ahhh, awful!* I don't think it harmed my career in the long run, but it was really silly.

Did Walter Cronkite, Chet Huntley or David Brinkley ever pull you aside during those days to give you pointers?

Well, Walter Cronkite was always very supportive. He used to take me to lunch at a Danish smorgasbord place, and he would give me advice. But I don't know what they thought.

Only once, at some meeting of the International Radio Television Society, were the three anchors — which even to say seems ludicrous, doesn't it? — together in one place. And somebody in the audience stood up and said, "You guys are really in show business." And Huntley took great exception and said, "That's not true. My only concession to show business is on the way to the studio I stop at the makeup department and have these bags painted out [from under the eyes]." And Cronkite said [*in deep, stentorian Cronkite imitation*], "Yes, yes. And Jennings stops in and has them painted on."

So Cronkite didn't say at the Danish place, "Peter, go back to reporting."

No, the one person who was quite influential, other than my father, was John Chancellor. He was Chancel*ler* in those days, not Chancel*lor*. And I remember him saying to me constantly, "You're going to do very well in this business, but you have to spend more time at the face of the mine." And he was absolutely right.

So you quit. They didn't fire you.

They would have fired me very shortly. There's no question that my string was getting shorter and shorter and shorter. But I'd been in the Middle East, in Israel, at the end of the '67 war, and I just fell in love with the region. And I fell in love with the story. And it all sort of came together: Get out of here! And off I went. They were so relieved.

First you did two years of reporting in the States for ABC. Then you went abroad for 16 years, as if journalism were the ultimate ticket to see the world.

Absolutely. Absolutely. And, to finish the phrase, on someone else's money. And in my case it's enhanced by the fact that I was getting my first honest-to-God education.

Were you the kind of foreign correspondent who was at the bar at midnight telling great stories of the day's adventures?

I think it's endemic to foreign correspondents to lie to one another about how brave they were on any given day. Two of my very best friends were my direct competitors overseas, CBS correspondent Tom Fenton and Garrick Utley at NBC. There is something very collegial about being a foreign correspondent. You can beat each other's brains out all day, but it is inexcusable not to have a good time together at dinner in the evening.

In addition to a reputation for drinking cheap wine, one thing that seems to dog you from your years as a Middle East correspondent—and you see this creeping into parentheses in 'The New Republic' from time to time—is the perception that you are anti-Israel, or biased toward the Arab countries.

You could at least take note of the fact that any time anyone is accused of being anti-Israel in *The New Republic,* it's the old story: If you're not 99 percent in favor of Israel, you're anti–Semitic. That's *The New Republic.*

I was the first television correspondent to formally open a bureau for an American television network in the Arab world [in Beirut in 1969]. It was really the first regular exposure that the Arab world was getting. It was in the wake of the 1967 Arab-Israeli war, in which the press corps had altogether gone overboard in *cheering* for Israel, in terms of defeating the Arabs. And I felt very strongly—and I still do—that there is much more than the Israeli side to the Middle East story. There are 19 countries in the Arab world, and I worked in them all. And I did a lot of stories in those days which said, "Hey, hold it, folks, Arabs are *people.* They don't just ride camels, they don't all live in tents. They drive Mercedeses...." And, of course, as we went through the seventies, we found that they had a considerable amount to do with our economic destiny.

You were also married to a Lebanese woman—your second wife.

Yeah, but I don't think that has the slightest bit ... I'm presently married to a Hungarian woman. That was occasionally used as a club—you know, "*He was married to a Lebanese woman.*" Expletive deleted to that one!

When you moved to London in 1977, you served as chief of correspondents and then as coanchor with Frank Reynolds and Max Robinson. It was said that your feeds were taped, even though they gave the impression of coming across live.

Well, sometimes they were taped. In fact, most often they were taped. Because, quite frankly, I was buggered if I was going to stay around to the middle of the night. I was already working longer hours than anybody who was working here. It was midnight [London time] when *World News Tonight* went on the air.

Did you have a sense in London that you were being groomed to take over as sole anchor?

No, not the vaguest idea. I thought I had the best job in the business when I was in London. I didn't think the broadcast worked as well as it could have. It was logical for Reynolds to be in Washington and for me to be in London, but it was illogical for Max to be in Chicago, *the way* Max was in Chicago. Max never approached the Midwest as if it were a real nation-state. And therefore what Max ended up doing a lot of the time was floods and snowstorms and traffic jams. And Frank and I had very defined jobs.

It wasn't Max Robinson's fault that he was covering snowstorms.

No, no, I think it was New York's attitude. The one-dimensional attitude New York had, and to some extent still has.

When Frank Reynolds died, they called you and said, "Peter, we want you to be the sole anchor."

My first instinct was to say no altogether. And Kati, my wife, was the one who convinced me this was a very important job, and you didn't just say no idly. We had a long, very difficult time in deciding to come.

I think at some point we'll go back to a multianchor system. I hope I'm not too old to run around some more. If I were to put together a multianchor system today, I would indeed have one overseas, and I would have one in Washington, and I would have one or two rove. One thing I've managed to convince them of here is that when I now go on the road, as in the Far East, we subanchor. For goodness' sake, let's not spend all our time doing the American stocks and snowstorms from Tokyo.

I sense that if you had your druthers, you'd air 'World News Tonight' from a different foreign capital every night.

Yes, yes, and probably from a street corner, too. Never standing in front of a national parliament. Yes, and it's important to me that we maintain that edge at ABC that we've had for some years, which is saying to our audience, "We're not alone in the world."

During commercial breaks, are you tracking Rather and Brokaw?

Yeah, sure.

It doesn't mess you up at all?

No, not unless they have something we don't [*laughs*]. And then, yeah. It happens at all three networks. If we, for example, led our broadcast with an exclusive story, rockets would go off at CBS and NBC: Can we match it?

When you saw Tom Brokaw in Armenia, did you get on the phone with Arledge and say, "Why can't I be there?"

I'll tell you what happened when I saw Tom Brokaw in Armenia. I phoned around and said to my colleagues, "They kicked the living expletive deleted out of us!" I was furious, furious at myself. I was livid. I saw that one as a pure journalistic beat. That's an imaginative use of one's resources.

So why weren't you there?

We didn't think of it in time.

Did you watch Rather's controversial interview with Bush?

Oh, that I saw. It was compelling. It was indeed a political event, and therefore it became part of the campaign. And people all across the country made judgments about whether or not Bush won or Rather won. People sometimes ask me, "Would you have behaved like that?" and the answer is no. Which is not condemning Dan. It's just not the way I operate. And I could even defend Dan on this particular subject.

What's the Dan Rather defense?

The Dan Rather defense is that what you're seeing in the Dan Rather interview—put aside the substance of his questions for a second—is the kind of interview that *you* might do with a subject with whom *you* were having a fight. Only you'd have to leave all that stuff in your typewriter. And somebody taping it might leave it on the floor. But that was live. That was a knock-down-drag-'em-out *Rolling Stone* interview on live television.

Was George Bush taking advantage of Rather, manipulating the fact that they were live?

I think it is a mistake to do live interviews with politicians on the evening news.

You've done them.

I've done them, but not very often. I did George Bush and Michael Dukakis at the end of the campaign because we had never done them and I was under some pressure to finally do them. Not pressure from them but from my own shop. And I just kept saying to myself, "This is going to be *deadly* boring. These men are like machines at this point. There is nothing I can ask them which is going to elicit an original thought." And I was so resentful of that. And as you noticed, I work for management, and so I did it. And they were boring. Boring.

On election night at about 6:30, when you came on the air, you said, "It looks like we're going to have a real old-fashioned night." And three hours later, when you looked behind at the board and saw 271 blue electoral votes for Bush, you sheepishly announced that he had won, embarrassed that it was so early in the evening.

[*Smiles*] Yeah. Yeah, I didn't have a good election night, I must say. I totally screwed up calling the presidency. First of all, we were correcting our one and only mistake of the night in trying to call the presidential thing based on our key precincts. But there was a part of me which was saying, "Jennings, you're screwing it up for people in California." I had recently been in

Washington State, and I was very self-conscious of the remote possibility that we might be impinging on the voting franchise. You see, as a matter of personal principle, I do not like projecting elections. My personal principle. I do not run this news division, so I play by the rules.

During the campaign season, you broadcast a piece about the Canadian prime-minister debate, in which candidates John Turner, Brian Mulroney and Ed Broadbent were filling up socks full of shit and heaving them at one another, toe to toe, no reporters in between. And you smiled at that, as if you wished the American electoral process were more like that.

We were the first to put that story on the air. I had been talking to someone—either my mother or my sister, I guess, both of whom live in Canada. And they said, "You should have seen these guys last night!" And so we quickly checked, and I think when everybody saw the spot that night and read about it in the newspapers the next day, it then became quite a feature of our own elections campaign. It was the symbol for us to take out all our frustration on the control that had been imposed on us and the debate system here. Aside from the fact that it was rock 'em, sock 'em, it made us feel, I think, more manipulated.

All right, let's talk about how the networks and ABC might do better in the 1992 campaign. First of all, refuse to cover a debate in which the candidates are allowed to give just their canned speeches. Let them swing it out like Mulroney and Turner.

Well, I think it's an ideal circumstance, but I'm not one of those who thinks that even a debate as contrived as they were in the '88 campaign should be ignored.

But look, the networks are playing a game of chicken. You know chicken, with cars?

Sure. You ever played it?

No. Have you?

A little bit, yes. We used to play up back roads at night in Canada. Another car would come, and we would turn our headlights out. That was scary.

Ever get hurt?

No, I never kept my lights off *that* long.

So, you know, the networks are playing chicken. None of you wants to pull out of the debate because you're afraid the other two networks would cover it and you'd miss out. But if all three pulled out, the candidates would have to follow your rules.

Yes, I think that's right. I take your point, that we could, all together, say, "Look, guys, the only way you're going to debate on national television is if you're prepared to have a freewheeling and open debate à la Turner and Mulroney."

But maybe it wouldn't work. Because there are so many ways to have access to television now that the candidates could do without the networks. They could put together their own independent networks at the drop of a hat. They don't really like to be on network television anyway. The political candidate would much rather be covered by local reporters. Also, I don't believe in cooperating with the other networks.

If you don't buy that scenario, ABC can promote itself this way: "We're the network that will not show canned speeches. We're the network that will show no bogus photo opportunities. No spin doctors will you see on ABC."

Well, you didn't see any spin doctors on ABC.

No, not after the second debate, which was appreciated.

Yes, I felt very good about that. Yeah, I think that's a reasonable position to take. I mean, but for me to set that down in concrete—to your benefit at this point [*laughs*]—is really rather foolish.

First of all, it's not going to be my decision to make; it will be my management's decision. Arledge is the kind of guy who might just take that position. There's no question in my mind that [of the network-news executives] Roone is the most avant-garde thinker.

You talk about "management." You don't see yourself as management.

Hell, no! Hell, no. [CBS News president] David Burke once asked me, "Why do you hate management so much?" I said, "Because it keeps me sharp." It's always worked to my personal benefit all my career to have an antimanagement attitude. I don't have an antimanagement attitude now at all. My management is very good to me.

If you had pulled the right lever, could you have become managing editor rather than senior editor of 'World News Tonight'?

It was offered to me, and I declined it. Because I think it's pointless.

Brokaw and Rather obviously think it's important that they are managing editors.

I gather. I think that for me to have that title would have made a kind of political statement that I really didn't want to make. Look, the strength of ABC News is in its collectivism. I have one of the absolute best producers in the business, Paul Friedman. It is impossible for an anchorperson, given the demands that are put on him, to make all of the editorial decisions which are required. Ergo you can't be the managing editor.

Is it a coup for ABC to have picked up Diane Sawyer from CBS and Chris Wallace from NBC?

I personally think the word *coup* should be reserved for governments. But I'm very pleased they're here. I think it sends a very important message. It says that broadcast journalists of the stature of Sawyer and Wallace want to work here.

Do you read all your viewer mail?

When I first got this job, I not only read all my mail, I *answered* it all. And I'd sometimes leave here at the end of the week saying, "I can't stand it anymore."

I kept on my desk there for a long time a picture of a young boy, five years old, who had cancer. He had been in the hospital for months. His parents could do absolutely nothing to give him any light in his life. His mother called me to tell me about this. They tried books, comics, games, toys, clowns. And they tried television. And one day they'd gone out for dinner, and by happenstance they left it on, and *World News Tonight* came on. And this kid saw me, and his parents came back and found him smiling. His mother was convinced that he had seen something around my... She thought he'd seen a halo. [*Jennings gets weepy and blows his nose.*] What really finished me was that she wrote me to say that he had just died in the middle of *World News Tonight* with a smile on his face.

Well, those days I think it would have been a lot easier [selling] hardware. That is the closest I've ever come to appreciating that some people sometimes see things about you on television that you are totally unconscious of. I don't know how to explain that, but it does seem to go with the territory. And my own view is, here is someone doing this job — me, Brokaw, Rather — we should be totally intimidated by that thought. And the most important thing in this job is to know that.

I'm good at my trade. I'm good at my trade as you are at your trade. I can go and cover any story, anywhere, and do a credible job for my news station, but I never thought I would have to deal with that.

But you make it sound as if doing a good story means repressing genuine feeling. Maybe that warmth and feeling that come from a life experience are what allow you to do the story well.

Look, maybe I'm a television correspondent with a newspaperman's mentality. I think a lot of us in television or broadcasting have spent altogether too long envying those of you who know how to push pencils. I do. I am an unabashed victim of pencil envy. My wife is a writer, and I am in awe of her abilities. Similarly, I think the most honorable thing I've ever done in my life is to be a reporter.

Television is a pretty evanescent medium. You can't Xerox a TV news story.

No, it's immensely frustrating. It's made somewhat better by the advent of VCRs. But it can be so fleeting, television.... I remember writing a piece for *The Christian Science Monitor* about three or four years ago, and I virtually framed it and sent it to my mother. She'd been watching me on the box for years, but I was able to preserve this thing in print that I wanted her to have.

You have strong feelings about the educational benefits of television, that it should focus on issues, foreign affairs, economics. So the preoccupation with the girl trapped in the well...

No, not my favorite story. And the whales come along every so often and really grab all of our attention. And I hasten to make the point that we can afford to do the whales and the homeless, but it's more important in the long run that we do the homeless. I went to a homeless conference shortly after that story, and the first three speakers said they wished they'd come dressed as whales because they might have gotten our attention.

Many people believe the trash TV shows — Morton Downey, Jr., Oprah Winfrey, Phil Donahue and Geraldo Rivera — are changing the dimension of the news so that it's becoming infotainment.

In fairness, Downey and Rivera belong in a different category than Winfrey and Donahue. I don't know Winfrey's broadcast well, even though it's on ABC. But Phil Donahue's been doing this for ten years, and I think he's done some of the best information programming that we've seen in the country.

As a consequence of Geraldo and Downey, Phil's been forced to get into the mud-wrestling ring.

That's right. I think we're immune from that at this point. And I'm inclined to think that the Riveras and Downeys are a passing phenomenon. While we all may be titillated by Satanism, that passes. Our lives are not made up of preoccupations with Satanism.

The evening news is designed to make us comfortable. Although the stock market may crash, although the ship may go down in the Persian Gulf, in the end, we're basically being reassured.

You know, there are a lot of people in this business who believe that part of our job is to reassure the public every night that their home, and their community, and their nation, is safe. I don't subscribe to that at all. I subscribe to leaving people with essentially — sorry it's such a cliché — a rough draft of history. Some days it is reassuring, some days it is absolutely destructive.

But take your reactions at the end of a broadcast. If you end with a story on the Ethiopian famine, you have a worried look on your face, to show this is indeed a grievous problem. But there is something reassuring even in the manner of your worry, Peter.

Let's talk about "the look" for a second, and only because "the look" gets attention. Some jackass did a study last year — somebody actually gave this jackass money! — in which he concluded that ABC News was pro-Reagan in 1984 because I *smiled* after Reagan stories and didn't smile after Mondale stories.

I did not waste my time going back and reanalyzing all of this. But I acknowledge that there are people out there who take how I look quite seriously sometimes. I think it would be in plain bad taste to conclude a broadcast on a story from Ethiopia saying, "See you tomorrow," smiling broadly.

But if the stock market were to crash tomorrow, you wouldn't show a panicked look on your face.

If the stock market collapses, I suspect I will not show panic, because [*laughs*] I'm not extended very far into the stock market.

No, you'll probably end the broadcast just as you would if we were involved in World War III: "We will see you here tomorrow." Like Walter Cronkite, always reassuring, even during Vietnam....

You see, I never liked the Cronkite tag line. "*And that's the way it is.*" Never liked it. Because it's telling people that television is doing something that we're only doing a little bit. In fact, I've often wanted to go on the air and conclude a broadcast by saying, "And that's part of the way it is." Or "And that's a little bit of the way it is."

Tom Johnson

"Tom Johnson: Q & A"
Interview by Patricia Villarreal de Macias

For Tom Johnson, serving as publisher of *The Los Angeles Times* was a lifetime dream come true. But, after 13 years it was time for a new beginning, and when Ted Turner approached Johnson about heading the Cable News Network—he seized the opportunity.

Taking the helm of CNN just one day before Iraqi tanks rolled into Kuwait, Johnson received a baptism by fire. But he came out of it on top of the world, as his network virtually decimated the coverage of the Big Three. CNN's ratings soared as viewers in millions of homes, most notably those in the White House, got their first reports of action in the war zone from CNN's army of correspondents.

Last Saturday, Johnson mulled over the lessons the global network learned from the war, predicted the network's future and contemplated the emotional trauma of sending reporters into a combat zone.

Images: What is the future of CNN?
Johnson: I think the future is very bright. I think there's an opportunity for us to grow more—globally. We're already in 105 countries and I think by the end of the century perhaps even earlier, I would like to see us serving every single nation on earth. There is a tremendous demand for information. We presently provide it in English and in Spanish. Longer term—I would hope perhaps we could even find a way to provide CNN in the languages of the regions we serve.

Images: Are you expanding your bureaus?
Johnson: We are expanding. We are looking at new bureaus in areas such as Johannesburg, Mexico City and New Delhi. We haven't made decisions on those yet, but I hope that we will be able to expand more this year. CNN has demonstrated the importance of international news. There's a tremendous awareness of international news, particularly if you look today at the situation within the Soviet Union. So, I think we need to continue to expand and that expansion has the full support of Ted Turner.

Images: When you went in to CNN it was the day before the war, that must have been crazy. How did you do it?
Johnson: I went to Atlanta to start work on August 1 and Iraq invaded Kuwait August 2. It was a wonderful, almost total, immersion into CNN. I

Patricia Villarreal de Macias is a student at the University of Texas, Austin.

expected I would have some time to go through it quietly and carefully, but instead, I was tossed into all of the turmoil that took place. But CNN was prepared for all of this. CNN had been covering such global issues as Tiananmen Square, the San Francisco earthquake, the collapse of the Berlin Wall and many other hot news events. It was ready for this. It had been in preparation for the last ten years. So, with or without Tom Johnson, CNN would have done this very well, but it certainly was wonderful to be there for this experience.

Images: The coverage of the war sent the ratings skyrocketing, and you may have spent as much as a million dollars a day—but was it worth all the money you spent on the coverage?

Johnson: The final costs are not yet in. We're still out there with a staff because a formal cease-fire has not been signed. We were prepared to spend as much as $35 million to cover that in 1991. Because the war ended much sooner, the costs will be somewhat less, perhaps in the range of $20 million for 1991. However, CNN's revenues grew, and I think we are one of the few news organizations that can say that our revenues grew more than our expenses during this period of time. We were actually able to cover the war, cover it well and do it in an economically sound way.

Images: Now that the war is over, have you lost cable subscribers?

Johnson: Well, we've lost no subscribers. In fact, we have significantly more cable homes subscribing to cable services as a result of CNN's coverage. The audience is back to more normal levels, although we are still ahead of where we were before the war. I'm very optimistic about it. We have more advertisers. We have a number of advertisers who actually came on to CNN during the war to reach this large audience. We are the one network that can reach a global community.

No other network is reaching 105 countries. I think you'll see more and more advertisers coming to CNN—more and more of an audience coming to CNN. It's also interesting to know that we can't really measure the audience outside the United States. There are not the same sort of measuring services that exist here.

Images: Your revenues were high, even though you went about $12 million over budget at the end of 1990?

Johnson: Yes, that's right. We went over budget on our expenses for the coverage of the war, but fortunately, the sales and marketing people went over budget in their sales of advertising and ... we are really emerging from this in a very strong position economically, and journalistically with audiences. I think it cuts back to very good journalism can also be very good, very good business. One of the remarkable things about CNN is it took Ted Turner a lot of time and a tremendous commitment of money, and it worked.

Images: How did you make the decision to allow Peter Arnett, Bernard Shaw and the others to stay in Baghdad?

Johnson: It was an easy decision.

Images: But I understood that, for you, it was difficult.

Johnson: It was difficult from the human side for me, but it was easy from the news side. Clearly, that was where the war was. Clearly, we wanted to be in Iraq and in Baghdad. I had some quite specific warnings from the White House, from the State Department and from the Pentagon — warnings that we should move our people out. I considered moving them to the outskirts of town. I considered even moving them temporarily to some other location. But Arnett and Robert Weiner, the senior producer, wanted to stay. And we decided, with Ted Turner's mandate, that those who wished to stay could stay, and those who wanted to come out could come out.

We even provided a $10,000-a-day charter plane out of Amman to take those in and out who wished to until the war actually hit.

I agonized a great deal about the human side of it. I had lost two correspondents: one in Tehran, Joe Alex Morris, the other on the Nicaraguan-Honduran border when I had been publisher of *The Los Angeles Times*. I mean, I helped unload the body bag of the correspondent who had been killed on the Nicaraguan-Honduran border. So I was concerned particularly during night one when there was a great deal of euphoria about our ability to continue to cover. I knew with those bombs falling, those Tomahawk missiles coming in, some within a mile of the hotel, that at any moment those lives could be snuffed out and I agonized quite a bit.

Images: Do you ever intend to hire bigger name anchors to draw bigger crowds?

Johnson: No. At CNN, news is the star. We do not intend to get into the big-name megabuck business. We have some very fine journalists and correspondents who are paid within a CNN context. There are people who are better known than ever before, such as the Wolf Blitzers . . . as well as people like Bernie Shaw.

But we will not get into the megabuck business. We will offer very attractive competitive salaries. But I think about how many correspondents we were able to field in the Persian Gulf — for the cost of a few anchors' salaries on some of the other networks we were able to put dozens of people into the field. So, we'll stay with that policy. CNN will be a lean and mean news machine, as it has been described, and we don't expect to deviate from that.

Images: What if these guys come to you and say, 'Hey, we're stars now, and we want a raise?'

Johnson: To the extent we can improve their compensation, we'll do it. But it is unrealistic to expect — we simply aren't. One of the problems with some of the other networks has been exceptionally high salaries provided to a very few, compared with the need to staff the newsroom with people who are paid in the context with the rest of the world of journalism, print and others.

The other networks are moving to cut back on costs at a time when CNN is building. CNN is one of the greatest news places to work around. There is an enormous amount of enthusiasm. There is a great deal of "psychic" income in working at CNN.

Images: You have spoken of a global network. Today, you have said your correspondents, such as Arnett and Shaw — people who did a lot of work on the war — knew some military secrets. But if you plan to be a global network, what will you do if you find out some secrets about an "enemy" of the United States?

Johnson: I would never put lives at risk unnecessarily. We didn't provide military information that could jeopardize troop movements. Our job is to report the news, and we reported the news as completely as possible. We were not permitted to talk about military troop movements, SCUDS moving up and down highways, mobile field missiles — we did not report that. We were not permitted to report that. We had some very good information about how the allied ground assault would be handled. The media have a responsibility to deal very sensitively with matters such as this, not publishing information that would needlessly jeopardize lives.

Images: Even if you had information about Iraq's tactical movements?

Johnson: You look at it on a case-by-case basis. We are in a position where we wish to present as fully as possible the news. Certainly, we did everything we could to open up the story from all angles. We were under strong censorship in all of these areas. We were restricted in our travels — all media, not just CNN. We fought for more and more access, but certainly if we came across information that would jeopardize lives on all sides, I don't see that that is something we should do. But you examine each case in a very selective manner. You must look at it case by case. My instincts are always to publish, but you have to balance that against your responsibilities, particularly to the lives that are at stake.

Ted Koppel

"Ted Koppel's Edge"
by Marshall Blonsky

Ted Koppel, the "philosopher king of broadcast journalism," in Sam Donaldson's phrase, is a master of behavioral psychology. Read carefully how Koppel and his "Nightline" crew psychologically isolate his interview subjects, under the guise of electronic split-second control, into a "foreign perceptual world where the guest no longer has the benefit of two dimensions — spatial/instantaneous as well as temporal/sequential."

Koppel controls. "By removing his person from you," Marshall Blonsky writes, "Koppel cunningly deprives you of your

Marshall Blonsky teaches communication courses at New York University.

animal instinct, of the will you could muster in an eye-to-eye, mano-a-mano exchange."

Ted Koppel has just surprised me—it's two hours to show time—by telling me he doesn't have a clue how he's going to start his program. It's 9:30 P.M. on Thursday, June 30, in the ABC "Nightline" conference room in Washington. Koppel and I, alone, are eating a typical "Nightline" dinner. Last night it was pizza, tonight it's Chinese delivery. The host asks perfunctorily if I'm enjoying the meal. "It's not so good," I tell him, to elicit something beyond the niceties. "Marshall, as we age our taste buds deteriorate," Koppel, 48, ripostes. Later I found out that he smokes heavily.

I recently spent three weeks, intermittently, at "Nightline," watching and listening as Koppel reported on the Soviet Communist Party conference, on Angola, on the downing of Iran Airlines Flight 655; as the "bookers" lined up some experts, and in their language "blew" others off the show; as Gov. Michael S. Dukakis and then Attorney General Edwin Meese 3d "blew" Koppel, refusing to come on his program. During my tenure, I watched as Koppel fashioned, night by nightline, a smooth electronic image.

He let me into his meetings and thoughts by fits and starts. He measured out welcome. He never put anything off the record, playing Dr. Jekyll while letting his staff play Mr. Hyde: "You've got to *get off our conference calls!*"

I had come to Koppel's Washington headquarters to get my own reading on the man five to seven million American households tune to every weekday night for their final reading of what happened that day. Ted Koppel of the curious haircut, the man straight out of the Archie comic books, Alfred E. Neuman without the tooth gap (as he is often perceived by his audience) is the day's last decoder. He sends his viewers off to sleep, as the Romans recommended, examining their consciences and probing those of their leaders.

He managed to bring South Africa's Minister of Foreign Affairs, R. F. Botha, and Archbishop Desmond M. Tutu into American homes on the same program, if from different cities, Johannesburg and Capetown. He startled the country with a new objectivity and nightlight on the Israeli-Palestinian nightmare when, in April, he spent a week broadcasting "Nightline" live from Israel, giving both sides a forum in which to present their case.

He was the first to get Jim and Tammy Bakker, after their fall from televangelism's pinnacle, because, as Jim told Koppel on the show: "I guess we had invitations just to about every program ... but I felt that you're not only tough but I felt that you would be fair...." Later, Koppel cut through their pietism, challenging Jim, who hoped to return as the head of the Praise the Lord ministry, with, "But you know, you're a lousy manager." To which the Reverend admitted, "Yes."

It's Thursday, June 30, and Koppel is briefing me on tonight's "Nightline." Jonas Savimbi, the Angolan rebel leader, will be Koppel's live guest in two hours and Ted, as everyone calls him, hasn't yet figured out his opening salvo. He tells me he's going to look into Savimbi's face on a studio monitor as his guest watches the five-minute background report—it will show an atrocity, protestors—that will precede the questioning. "He may frown, he may scowl,

ABC's Ted Koppel, anchor of "Nightline" (photo courtesy Capital Cities/ABC, Inc.).

he may smile, he may shrug his shoulders," Koppel says. "That will give me my first clue as to where the points of vulnerability are."

How does he read a face, revolutionary or otherwise? Koppel won't say. So I say, "Read my face, read my physiognomy." Show me how you do it.

"Look, you want me to read your physiognomy?" Koppel's voice is tenser, tough.

"Yeah."

At last I have a chance to find out what lies behind the screen, behind the questions Koppel asks. I want to do nothing that he himself doesn't do to his guests, to break through the mask of the person many people consider to be the greatest interviewer/inquisitor on television.

"You had a predisposition," Koppel begins. "I think that's a dumb way to do a story. You came in and you told me, 'Look, I regard you as the most intellectual among the television journalists.'"

As I sit there wounded, he continues. "At the moment, I've challenged you. You're a little bit hurt. Not much, but a little bit. It's all going through your head right now—does he think I'm a fool? That's all in your body language. Attention: rigid, not wavering, not moving, trying to be in absolute control of yourself, wanting to know where your head is, where your eyes are, where your hands are, steepled, no fluidity, none at all. Now I've got your attention because I'm talking about you. And if I were interviewing you, I'd know that I had you *right now;* I got you off balance.

"That's when I'd move in, and that's when I'd hit you with two or three hard ones."

So that's what it's like to be a "guest" on "Nightline," the rubber clown who's punched and (sometimes) springs back for more. It is a breakthrough, not of communication, but of aggression, in which I accept the punch.

Koppel is telling me: "Please don't misunderstand. You asked me to engage in a parlor game with you"—he's pulling back—"and do something I don't normally do." He's telling me he doesn't demonstrate and analyze his method for interviewers. He *does* use it to edge out his guests every week night on television.

Throughout my "Nightline" stay, Koppel tries to hold Governor Dukakis to a promise made on the night of his New York primary victory. Dukakis later conditioned his appearance on a face-to-face interview with Koppel. Appealing to fair play, Koppel refused to grant him a privilege that Vice President Bush, appearing just after the California primary, had never made a condition. (Bush had asked for, and received, a return monitor—rarely permitted—on which to see Koppel; Dukakis would have been given the same privilege.)

Why the struggle? What is the advantage of appearing face to face with Ted Koppel?

When you're interviewed on "Nightline," normally you sit in a studio, in Washington or anywhere else in the world, a listening device in your ear, facing a camera. You don't even have the comfort of seeing the image of Ted Koppel. The producers do not provide a monitor for you to watch the likeness of your inquisitor. Richard N. Kaplan, "Nightline" executive producer, explains: "If you watched that monitor, you would see yourself a second later than you speak. Let's say you're a guest in Cincinnati. The signal comes from Cincinnati to New York. It's fed down to Washington, where Ted sees it. He talks to you. The signal is mixed in New York and fed out to the network, and that's what you see coming back on the monitor. That takes a second. You would see yourself coming back a second later. You ... would ... start ... talking ... like ... this. To watch yourself talk out of synch is mind-boggling. You can't do it."

Or "Nightline" won't let you.

Kaplan suggests another reason for the absence of a monitor: "When people are real comfortable, that makes them more easily able to ignore the questioner. When everybody's listening to an earpiece [and] all of a sudden a voice cuts through and says, 'Wait a second!' it stops you. Ted maintains control because they're dealing with an earpiece and not seeing the other guests or Ted."

And Koppel needs this edge, Kaplan says. "Most people who come on the program certainly know more about the subject than Ted does. They've been picked because they're experts. So Ted needs any edge you can give him."

"We do Bush," Kaplan continues. "Bush doesn't do very well." Several times he called Koppel "Dan," referring to CBS's Rather. Soon after the Bush interview, Kaplan says, "We get a call from the Dukakis campaign saying: 'Now, you know, with Dukakis, Dukakis wants to sit in the room with Ted.'" For if Dukakis can sit next to Koppel, he can gain eye contact, "and eye contact means gaining control," Kaplan explains. But if your "umbilical cord" (his phrase) is the earpiece—not a physical presence, not your eyesight and your ears hearing an unmediated voice—then, Kaplan says, "you are going to be real sensitive" (shall we say, subordinate?) "to any voices that come across that earpiece."

So there is no eye contact, not even your eye to image-eye, no instantaneous recognition of the interlocutor; rather, a sequential passage of words through your ear. In fact, it places the interviewee in a foreign perceptual world where the guest no longer has the benefit of two dimensions—spatial/instantaneous as well as temporal/sequential. Using language, you still possess the power of analysis, but you cease to react automatically, as the human animal. By removing his person from you, Koppel cunningly deprives you of your animal instinct, of the will *you* could muster in an eye-to-eye, mano-a-mano exchange.

The months of tug and pull between the man who would be President and the Alfred E. Neuman who worries a lot seemed only to be about fairness. In fact, the struggle was also over power, the power to impose the potentially lethal "Nightline" format.

Koppel refused to concede the edge.

"Governor Dukakis wanted to do 'Nightline'," says Leslie Dach, the candidate's communications director, "but it's better to do it with him sitting across from you, to see each other without any artificial separation, instead of being asked to go down the hall." The nominee of his party would be uncomfortable obeying ear logic, weakening still further his noncharismatic image—uncomfortable being edged. As moderator from 1971 to 1973 of "The Advocates," a show pitting contentious sides against each other on issues of national concern, Dukakis had learned how to incite and manage controversy, and to appreciate the advantages of direct confrontation.

During the Democratic Convention, Richard Harris, a "Nightline" producer, approached Loen Kelly, a Dukakis liaison, offering the Governor a face-to-face interview with Koppel "any night that week"—not a substitute for the long-sought hour-long companion to the Bush interview, but a separate opportunity.

Dukakis's people declined. When asked why, Leslie Dach answered, "We were making a lot of news and we were happy with it."

Earlier, Kaplan had stressed that Dukakis would be offered the chance for a "Nightline" appearance again, under the usual ground rules. And so would Bush. "You know," said Kaplan, "you can certainly be elected President without appearing on 'Nightline.' But we have very high standards on this program—we intend to always live up to them."

A muffled version of the struggle leaked to the press. *Time* magazine reported that "Dukakis aides wanted their man seated next to Ted Koppel, as Gary Hart had been"—a rare exception, granted for his first interview after his initial withdrawal from the Presidential primary race.

Also an exception was Jesse Jackson, who on the night of his triumphal speech at the Democratic National Convention sat next to Koppel in the ABC booth.

"Forgive me, I got a little distracted," said Koppel.

"I didn't know you could get distracted, Ted."

"I didn't either," said Koppel, and then reached out to touch Jackson's arm.

Jackson had the advantage not only of a face-to-face interview, but also of the tactile dimension Koppel had surrendered more than his edge.

Four days earlier, when Jackson was still en route to the convention, Koppel had interviewed him long distance on the question of the hour: "What does Jesse want?" Addressing Jackson, Koppel said, coughing: "Just before you left Chicago, you put it in very bitter terms. You referred to yourself and your followers like the field hands out there, you know, bringing in the harvest while Massuh Dukakis and his aides are sittin' up there in the Big House...."

"Now, Ted, wait a minute," Jackson interrupted. "I, I think it's a bit unfair. I did not say 'Massuh' Dukakis."

"No," Koppel said, effectively admitting he had exaggerated.

"You, you, you are suggesting..." Jackson seemed about to define, and reject, the racial issue. But again Koppel interrupted:

"I said *like* that."

"No, but you see, even to say that," said Jackson, "is to suggest a racial issue as opposed to the basic arrangement. I am expected to register more Democratic voters than any other Democrat. And I have."

Jackson had seized the monitor edge from Koppel and answered as if he were face-to-face, piercing and nullifying Koppel's technological advantage.

A couple of hours after demonstrating his face-reading technique on me, Koppel puts it into practice.

It's 9:10 P.M., Thursday, June 30. Jonas Savimbi is in Washington, doing public relations for his Angolan rebel cause, and I ask Koppel, "What will you look for in his face?"

"Have you met Savimbi?" he asks. "He's going to be in the studio tonight because he's attending a dinner here in Washington." Koppel suggests I meet him. "He's a very tough piece of work. I mean, you will have no trouble looking at Jonas Savimbi and imagining Jonas Savimbi killing a man."

Two hours later, Koppel, having put on his makeup and his earpiece, its wire running down his back, goes into the greenroom to greet Savimbi, who is waiting to go on camera.

"Marshall, come on over." Koppel, now friendly, summons me inside and introduces me to Savimbi.

Koppel: "Marshall is only masquerading as a journalist — he's normally a professor. Journalists don't look this distinguished."

Koppel is looking into Savimbi's face and I am, too. And I look at Koppel, who is gathering an impression that will generate his first question. Savimbi could kill, Koppel could wound, and I am the wide-eyed pedant.

It's almost air time. Koppel is behind a desk on a stage at one end of a vast, almost empty ABC newsroom. His scuffed tan briefcase is at his feet, off camera. He brings it from his office every night; maybe it's a security briefcase, for he never opens it on the air. From my vantage point below and behind him in a chair at an unused desk, I can see his jaw working and his left hand toying with his fountain pen. His cough, continual while he smokes, is mastered now, and I grasp the duality of the man. He is powerful but alone. He seems to control his guests but lives on the edge of rejection. He appears smooth but he is rough. All is being masked now.

On air:

Koppel: Mr. Savimbi . . . as you know, Governor Dukakis has already indicated that if he's elected, then U.S. aid . . . to you and your forces will end. Would it be fair to conclude, therefore, that you are here in kind of a last-ditch effort to change as much public opinion as you can before the elections?

Savimbi: We are here in order to present our program of peace. . . . What is . . . at stake now, it is the peace in the country."

He never wavers from the peace line.

After the show, Koppel dismisses the staff — "I need ten minutes with Marshall." — fills a paper cup with ice to use as an ashtray, and asks me, "Well, what did you think?"

Before I can fully formulate an opinion, he treats me to self-critique and a critique of Savimbi: "The show never really caught fire, but you know that's really up to them [the guests]. My job is not to be pouring gasoline on it until finally something ignites."

Koppel is generous in his post-mortem on Savimbi's lack of fire. "From Savimbi's point of view, banality is exactly the protective cloak that he needed. All he had to do was come across as a man of utter reasonableness, committed to the peace process, reacting more in sadness than in anger to these ridiculous charges that his troops engage in atrocities or plant land mines."

Ordinarily, Koppel crowds his guest. When I first met him, he told me, "Once you recognize that the person has just handed you two or three really disingenuous answers in a row, than you have been authorized, in a sense, to say 'bull.' But you've got to say it in another form. There is another code for that. And that code can be the raised eyebrow, the look of astonishment, the 'Do you mean to tell me that . . . ?' or 'Maybe I haven't really understood what you, you've been telling me, but . . . .'"

But the "but" didn't seem to come for Savimbi. Not only had Koppel been unaggressive and Savimbi unforthcoming, but Koppel also felt he had made a wrong choice for the night's subject matter. He said he felt blindsided (by whom, I didn't learn): the big story of the day wasn't Savimbi, it was, Koppel said, the first Soviet Communist Party national conference in 47 years, where on the third day a delegate had stunned the session by calling for the dismissal of President Andrei A. Gromyko.

Koppel's only coverage of the conference had been on the first day, when Pierre Salinger, ABC's chief foreign correspondent, had appeared from Moscow with 27-year-old Artyom Borovik, foreign editor of *Ogonyok,* a Soviet weekly, and, commenting from Washington, Stephen Sestanovich of the Center for Strategic and International Studies.

For tomorrow, the last day of the conference, Koppel hoped to get high-level Soviet bureaucrats who could decode the events of the day. He had to settle for Salinger from Moscow, and only by telephone; Vladimir Kozlovsky, an émigré Soviet journalist with Novoye Russkoye Slovo in New York, and Robert Legvold, director of Columbia University's Harriman Institute for Advanced Study of the Soviet Union, commenting from Boston.

Koppel had told me at the beginning that *he* would close only one door: that of his private life. Ted Koppel's basic biography, nevertheless, is in the public domain. Edward James Koppel was born in Lancashire, England, in 1940. His father, an industrialist, had fled the Nazis in '38 with his wife. Koppel went to a boarding school. "It was all considered part of toughening you up, learning self-control and becoming more self-contained."

At 13, he came to New York with his family. He went to Syracuse University, later earning his master's in communications at Stanford, where he met his wife, Grace Anne. He became a United States citizen in 1963. He got his first job at ABC at 23 and has never left. He covered the Vietnam War and was the network's chief diplomatic correspondent from '71 to '80, during which time he met and fell under the influence of Henry Kissinger. "As much credit as I'm willing to give him for having taught me things," Koppel has said, "I'm still more liberal than he is, but I'm much more of a pragmatist when it comes to foreign policy than most of my colleagues."

"Nightline" evolved out of "The Iran Crisis: America Held Hostage," the late-night 1979 Koppel show that helped keep the hostages in the American conscience after the Iranians had captured the United States Embassy in Teheran and boosted ABC's then-low ratings for that time slot. From the outset, Koppel earned the admiration of his peers.

All of this is part of Koppel's growing marble monument, even his reticence in talking about his wife and four children, his year as a part-time house-husband while Grace Anne studied law, Koppel working occasionally as an anchorman and on special assignments. Whenever his wife called during my stay, he always took the call, and whoever was in his office scuttled out.

Koppel attributes part of the success he has attained to what he calls the "Vanna Factor," a reference to Vanna White, the letter-turner mannequin on "The Wheel of Fortune."

"Vanna leaves an intellectual vacuum, which can be filled by whatever the predisposition of the viewer happens to be," Koppel told me. "The viewer can make her whatever he wants." And so, too, make Ted Koppel. "In theory, I am equally tough on everyone; therefore viewers can project on me their own politics, their own views, their own predispositions. That makes me the beneficiary of a certain public acceptance that I would not have if I were, let's say, a commentator who expresed his own views on subjects, or a politician."

Vannafication is a fundamental principle of the understanding of political and media success—and failure. Koppel believes the Vanna Factor now exists in all aspects of American public life. "Mike Dukakis is using it; George Bush is using it," Koppel said. "And the more successful you are in leaving a certain uncertainty in the mind of the voter. . . . You would think that the voter would be frustrated by that, but on the contrary he has become acclimated to the notion that you just fill in the blank. He watches me and he chooses to believe that I believe what he believes."

On Jackson's night at the convention, Koppel applied the Vanna Factor to the detriment of Jesse. "It's the very level of passion generated by Jesse Jackson that carries a price," Koppel says. "It is the dullness of a Dukakis or a Bush that contributes to their acceptability across such a wide spectrum."

So Koppel, in his own view is a void, a vessel, filled with millions of viewers' questions and concerns.

Every morning at 11, the "Nightline" producers, whether at home, in their offices or in their cars, participate in a conference call to hear and discuss the day's bulletins and decide on the night's story. You get on the call by dialing a special ABC Washington line, as I did for three weeks; you ask the network operator to put you on the "Nightline" bridge, giving the unchanging password. Although ABC News's headquarters and main technology are in New York, Koppel dislikes the city; hence, he and his staff have to be bridged from Washington to New York, and to London, the show's European link. As each person joins in, a chime sounds, as if a magic wand had brought another fairy onto the ethereal bridge. No matter how grim the content, the conversation is pleasant, like a brunch of angels. And always:

"Is Ted on yet?"

"Good morning."

"Hi, Ted."

Let the conference call begin.

It's Wednesday, July 6, three days after the United States cruiser *Vincennes* downed Iran Airlines Flight 655. As they talk, Koppel decodes his producers' discussion about both sides' anger: "Behind all this breast beating I sense they're still trying to continue a diplomatic discussion."

Later, at 9 P.M., as we tackle another Chinese call-up dinner, he elaborates. "The immediate expectation is that a devastating accident like this can only lead to disaster. Not necessarily. It all depends on how the leaders of both countries use it. They can be screaming bloody murder about each other on one level and still be dealing on another level to establish contact. This town specializes in balloon floating, and that's what you're seeing right now."

The program topic decided, the only thing left to do after the conference call was to fill in the content, which was to have been Jimmy Carter, the Iranian Ambassador to the United Nations and the "Baby Shah," the son of the late Shah of Iran.

But Jimmy Carter is off on a book tour, the Baby Shah is blown away and the Ambassador declines.

"Put yourself in the position of a poor Iranian diplomat who doesn't even know who's running the show back home now," Koppel explains as we eat.

Earlier, the "Nightline" bookers had scrambled for substitute guests. They ended up with Representative Les Aspin, head of the House Armed Services Committee, and Senator John Warner, senior Republican on the Senate Armed Services Committee, plus a taped interview with Abolhassan Bani-Sadr, former President of Iran.

The episode made me viscerally realize that no matter how conceptually dramatic Ted Koppel is, he cannot control events. People come on "Nightline" to serve their own ends, not Koppel's. He is always having to struggle to get good guests.

The day before, Koppel hadn't been available until late afternoon. The entire "Nightline" staff seemed at a loss, unable to advance the night's program. The program was suddenly headless. The staff, mostly in their 30's and heavily augmented by college interns, can follow orders, but as Koppel becomes more of a self-centered star—one of his staff has said it used to be that you had a 70-30 chance of winning an argument with him, now it's nil—it can contribute less to "Nightline."

There is excessive talk in New York and Washington of a Koppel-turned-public-servant. Henry Kissinger has suggested that Koppel could have a high-ranking position in the State Department. Koppel himself has talked about the limits of his "Nightline" tenure, of the possibility of choosing a different course. He has already made his mark on television by adding depth and range to news coverage. For seven years, every weekday night at 11:30 P.M. he has put his skills on the live line and often as not has emerged victorious.

His most dramatic recent success occurred when he convened a town meeting in Jerusalem between Israelis and Palestinians. Koppel was able to humanize a fence the Palestinians insisted be a barrier between the two sides. He sat on it, swinging his legs side to side. He succeeded in standing—or sitting—for American fairness, and that was his edge over his emotional combatants.

Now he has created his own, independent production company, which should considerably augment his reputed one million dollar-plus annual income. This will guarantee his freedom to introduce new ideas in a medium that he considers a victim of the Vanna Factor.

In an address to the 1987 graduating class at Duke University, Koppel warned of "false gods of material success and shallow fame," saying "their influence is magnified by television." His hero that day was Moses. "Our society finds truth too strong a medicine to digest undiluted. In its purest form, truth is not a polite tap on the shoulder. It's a howling reproach. What Moses brought down from Mt. Sinai were not the Ten Suggestions. They are Commandments. Are, not were."

So a man who invokes Moses would prefer not to be muffled by television, not to be Vannafied. Behind the screen, Koppel is not impartial. He has a strong moral bias, a position on politics and life, but knows he must mask it to to survive as an electronic journalist. He must resign himself to being not Moses but a television priest. That is why he is tough and smooth, principled and self-effacing, restless and content, successful and dissatisfied.

Charles Kuralt

"*Kuralt Finds Serenity on the Road Less Traveled*"
by Jean Marbella

All reporters pride themselves on their ability to cultivate—and maintain—contacts and sources. But as broadcast reporters climb into the rarified air of the top anchor posts, their ability to maintain contact becomes limited, as a consequence of their time in the network studios and as a double consequence of their own celebrity status. But Charles Kuralt is different. He has chosen not to only maintain but to nurture his contacts. By working the small towns and by-ways of America, he has carved his own niche in television journalism.

If ever there was a Sunday morning kind of guy, Charles Kuralt is it. He's everything a perfect Sunday morning should be—soft around the edges, warm through and through, another cup of coffee in bed with a puffy quilt and a couple of cats tucked all around.

Imagine instead if the jangly, vid-cool reporters of "West 57th" (appropriately relegated to Saturday night) or the intense Dan Rather (best saved for harried weekday evenings) were to shake you out of your slumber.

But mercifully, CBS for the past ten years has sent the roly-poly, rather rumpled Mr. Kuralt to gently rouse loyal viewers with "Sunday Morning," an easily paced one and a half hours of some of the most engaging and amiable TV around.

"We figured we ought to speak softly and not shout at anybody," Mr. Kuralt, in Baltimore earlier this week, said of the news-and-features show over which he presides with a calm and poetic touch.

Jean Marbella is a staff writer for The Baltimore Sun.

Indeed, you won't ever hear the kindly, multi-chinned Mr. Kuralt bellowing, "Hey, Mr. President!" above the chop-chopping sound of the helicopter on the White House lawn. More likely, he'll quietly take you to visit a craftsman out in Pennsylvania or to see some egrets flying over the Florida swamps.

Which are the kinds of places he's spent much of the past 22 years as perhaps the country's best back roads and largest-balls-of-twine kind of TV reporter. Those behind-the-headlines glimpses characterize both "Sunday Morning" and his popular "On the Road" pieces, stories that Mr. Kuralt happened to run into while roaming the country in a van with a camera crew and sent back to "CBS Evening News" and his own specials.

But what brought him to Baltimore Monday and yesterday was not the usual Kuraltian adventure, but rather a speech sponsored by the Maryland Chamber of Commerce, which wanted to highlight the business community's interest in restoring Chesapeake Bay.

There wasn't an overall or a wheat stalk in sight in what he called "the most elegant hotel room I've ever stayed in." Glassy, chromy and with an indecipherable (to Mr. Kuralt, at least) heating/cooling system, the suite at the Stouffer Harborplace Hotel, where he gave an interview, seemed a deserved payback for all those less-than-plush motels that Mr. Kuralt has pulled into after another day of reporting from Somewhere, U.S.A.

But wonder of all wonders to this roadside reporter, the best feature of the suite is that, common-sensibly enough, it has an extra phone on the desk in addition to the usual one on the night stand.

"Long ago, I learned at Holiday inns and motels to sleep on the side of the bed away from the phone because the mattress was broken down on the other side by fat guys like me sitting on the bed and talking on the phone," Mr. Kuralt said with a laugh.

The suit-and-tie crowd of some 750 businessmen and women that came to hear his talk in one of the hotel's ballrooms aren't typical of the kind of people he rubs elbows with on those blue highways.

Yet his appeal is such that fans are found even in this button-down crowd. This state legislator wants a note for his preacher, explaining why he's always late for church on Sunday mornings. This businessman reminisces about a mutual friend, someone Mr. Kuralt went to high school with in his native North Carolina and, indeed, remembers.

And everyone seems to want to point out on a map where they're from, the map being the natural medium of communication with this roving reporter. Peering over half-glasses, Mr. Kuralt runs his own beefy hands over the map as well, showing where he rode a skipjack, demonstrating that, yes, he does know where Smith Island is.

He is surely one of the more accessible celebrities around. And that is the grace of his reporting—he actually seems to *like* people and doesn't patronize or exploit his subjects for the amusement of urban sophisticates tuning in on their stereo TVs and sipping decaffeinated espresso.

"He's a friend. He's not just a reporter," says Roger Welsch, a Nebraska folklorist who met Mr. Kuralt about 15 years ago and has since become one of the highly idiosyncratic contributors to "Sunday Morning." "I was running for the weed board on a pro-weed ticket. He was here in Nebraska asking about what sorts of bizarre characters there might be. We just struck it off real good.

"He's generally interested when he asks a question: he really wants to know the answer. He's the kind of person, if you saw him in the bar here, you'd want to ask him, 'How much rain did you get?'" Mr. Welsch adds.

"Sunday Morning" is off the beaten TV track in many ways—it's outside the competitive, prime-time slots, and Mr. Kuralt is convinced hardly anyone knows it's even on the air. [Not true—it usually gets a respectable 4 rating and 16 share, outdrawing NBC's "Sunday Today."] But, true to form, Mr. Kuralt likes being out of the loop even if it means his show took a disproportionate share of cutbacks when CBS started slashing its budget a couple of years back.

Instead of budgets, stories are the measuring stick for his success.

One of his van trips took him down a road, gravel at the time, to Prairie, Miss., and to one of his favorite stories ever.

In Prairie, he found Norman and Gloria Chandler—a sharecropper and his wife who raised nine children in conditions so impoverished that they had to go to town and borrow the $2.50 bus fare it cost for their eldest son to go off to college. They managed, through sheer hard work, to send all of their kids to college.

The couple's fiftieth wedding anniversary in 1978, which coincided with Thanksgiving and drew all nine children back to their roots, became an "On the Road" classic.

"He sort of became accepted as part of the gathering," recalls the oldest son, Cleveland Chandler, who now is a Howard University economics professor and lives in Baltimore. "He has this sense of humor, he's very approachable. No one put on a front, nobody was sort of subdued by him being there with the gear and the camera. I don't know how he did that, how he gained the acceptance of people who didn't know him before."

It's what he does best—people, rather than People, stories. A guy in Iowa who just got tired of farming one day and started building a yacht even though he'd never even been in a rowboat before. A guy in North Dakota who thought, dang, there ought to be a highway between Duluth, Minnesota, and Fargo, North Dakota, and started building it himself.

Despite the kind of fame that makes him instantly recognizable in hotel shops, the 54-year-old Mr. Kuralt still calls himself just a reporter, not a "talent" as on-air personalities are referred to, nor an "anchor" or even a "journalist," but a reporter.

"That's the funny thing about TV, the dichotomy of TV. What I do ... meeting people, taking notes, is why [I] got into this business. That's where the fun of it lies," he says. "By becoming an anchor, you sort of give that up. That's why I felt I didn't want an agent. I've never had an agent—it's really agents who do that, try to stir things up. My career has just sat there all these years.

"I wanted to stay on the road. The joy of wandering down the highway, not entirely sure of where you're spending the night—I didn't want to give that up. This weekend, I was watching Allen Pizzey, a correspondent. He does some pretty swashbuckling stories. He was in Afghanistan, and I thought, that's real reporting! Telling what it was like, the struggle between the two sides. That's why I got into this. Allen Pizzey is the guy having all the fun. But everyone knows Dan Rather, not Allen Pizzey."

Mr. Kuralt has found himself overseas a lot in recent times—CBS made him go to Russia with former President Reagan last year, Rome for the pope and Japan for Emperor Hirohito's funeral—but he'd just as soon stay stateside. In his book, that's where the real exotica is. (And speaking of books, he's the author of five, actually, including a 1985 best seller titled "On the Road with Charles Kuralt.")

But before Mr. Kuralt became the chronicler of the common man, the 32-year CBS veteran did the foreign correspondent route—the Vietnam War, tours of Latin America—and the "big" stories like civil rights and presidential campaigns, like the 1960 Kennedy-Nixon face-off. Along the way, he picked up eight Emmys, three George Foster Peabody awards and all sorts of other accolades large and small.

But he wearied of what such big events draw—packs of reporters. "I saw crowds beginning to gather," the former newspaperman notes in mock horror. So he turned to the roads less traveled.

"In 1967, I took to road for a three-month trip, to see what I could find," he says. "When three months were up, no one ever said stop. I just kept going."

Now he's rubbing his eyes and sniffling in yet another hotel room. (But don't blame the hotel suite's mysterious heating/cooling system, jet lag or a cold. Rather, this grandson of a tobacco farmer says, it's his enthusiastic smoking that's wreaked sinus havoc.)

If the avid fly fisherman ever retires, he'll have a hard time picking just one spot in which to settle down.

"My parents live in Kitty Hawk [N.C.]. That's where I thought I would end up once," muses Mr. Kuralt, who lives in New York with his wife and has two grown children. "I love the mountain west—Idaho, Montana. It's sort of Alpine America. But I feel at home about anywhere now."

Jim Lehrer

"The Secret Life of Jim Lehrer"
by Hap Erstein

What do broadcast anchors do when they are not "working a story" or in front of the cameras? Jim Lehrer, one half of PBS's

"MacNeil-Lehrer NewsHour," is a playwright. Ultimately, whether he is on the PBS network with Robert MacNeil and his broadcast colleagues, or crafting the script for a play, his universe is the word. And, somewhat like Charles Kuralt, he maintains contact with nostalgic America, by collecting bus company memorabilia.

Scratch a comedian and you often find someone who wants to play "Hamlet." Within many a journalist is a man who yearns to be a playwright. Jim Lehrer, the Emmy and Peabody Award-winning co-anchor of public television's "MacNeil/Lehrer NewsHour" has stuck out his neck and done something about it. Tonight, a staged reading of one of his first scripts, "Chili Queen," is in the spotlight at New Playwrights' Theatre.

"I make my living on television and I don't have any negatives about it," the 52-year-old ex-newspaperman drawls. "I've got a bird's nest on the ground as they say in Texas. And yet it's not enough for me. Now I realize that may sound stupid to people, but that's just gonna have to sound stupid to people. It's not enough.

"It's also a part of what my function is in journalism," he suggests. "Maybe if I was one of our essayists, or if I was writing a column or I was a critic. But my job, and I'm not frustrated by it, is to keep that out. But there's something building up. I want to express it in journalism so much, but I do want to tell these stories."

In college, his goal was to become what he calls "one of the two Ernies, [war correspondent] Ernie Pyle or [novelist] Ernie Hemingway." He took a playwriting course to learn about crafting dialogue, but "I didn't have any master plan. I was not stage-struck."

Mr. Lehrer wrote a couple of plays, but put them aside to become a reporter and then editor in Dallas. Along the way he wrote the novel "Viva Max!" which was turned into a so-so movie with Jonathan Winters. In the 1970s, he moved to Washington and segued to television, leaving the theater far behind until a personal setback reopened the stage door.

In December 1983, the newscaster suffered a heart attack. During his recuperation from double-bypass surgery, he returned to writing plays. "After I was sick, when I was recovering, it focuses the mind on many, many areas and your life priorities. I kept thinking, 'Now wait a minute, if I've got three days, three years or three decades left, how do I want to spend them?'"

His soul-searching led to no major changes, but a small one began to gnaw again. "I really realized that the desire to write fiction was still there and it hadn't been completely satisfied, probably never will, no matter how much you write," Mr. Lehrer says, relaxing in his Arlington office at WETA-TV, where he broadcasts each weeknight. On his walls are part of a whimsical collection

Hap Erstein is an award-winning theater critic for The Washington Times, *where he has covered the drama beat on a local and national basis for the past eight years. He is a regular panelist on "Around Town," an Emmy Award acclaimed cultural roundtable program on public television. He is a regular contributor to "Museum and Arts Washington" magazine and is working on a book about the history of the nation's capital as a theater center.*

of bus depot signs, memorabilia from the days when he worked for his father's independent bus line in Wichita, Kansas.

"The problem was I just didn't think I had the energy to write a novel," he admits. His novelist wife, Kate, suggested plays, which he tackled with the gusto and naivete of a beginner. "I had an awful lot to learn and I did an awful lot of reading. We went to every play that we could possibly go to, and I started playing with it."

Writing for the theater was in the back of his mind the day he drove up to a roadside Dairy Queen in Emory, Texas, for an ice cream sandwich. He observed an argument between a waitress and a customer over how much change was due, quickly bought his ice cream and drove away. Most people wouldn't have given the incident another thought. To Jim Lehrer, it was the kernel of a play.

Originally called "Dairy Queen," this comedy of confrontation with occasional serious overtones was workshopped and refined for a year in New York. When it came time for a full showcase production, the fledgling playwright made a courtesy contact to the Dairy Queen company, sending along a copy of the script. What he got in reply was what Mr. Lehrer calls "one of those letters that give lawyers such a bad name" — a threatened lawsuit. Thus, "Chili Queen" was born.

The title change was a boon, for he added in a subplot about a pie-in-the-sky invention by the diner's owner — frozen chili on a stick. "It really was a godsend," he laughs, "because I put all that chili stuff in there and kicked myself for not having it in there in the first place."

Mr. Lehrer has learned that plays are not so much written as rewritten. "Let's say that I was stupid enough, or new enough, to say, 'Here is my play. You take my play and you go produce it and call me when you're ready. Call me on opening night.'

"Number one," he ticks off on his fingers, "it probably would never have happened, and shouldn't have happened. But number two, it wouldn't have been as good a play. I mean the process of playwriting, I have discovered, is taking plays up there in these workshops and around in these staged readings as much as it is in anybody's typewriter and anybody's mind."

Perhaps the most refreshing thing about Jim Lehrer's attitude on playwriting is his understanding that he still has a lot to learn. "The hardest part, and this is lack of experience on my part, is to keep the action on the stage and not have the characters stand up and say, 'Well, now, let me tell you what just happened,'" he comments.

"I wrote a play that I had a reading on called 'Cedar Chest.' It's not a bad little play, but it'll never make it because there's an awful lot of action . . . referred to," he laughs, "and damn little on the stage. I ought to put that one aside and come back to it when I develop a little more skill."

Among the many ways that his journalism background has helped him as a playwright, Mr. Lehrer reports, is knowing not to grow too fond of the first draft you write. "If you're in journalism more than about three days and you don't like to be rewritten and edited, get out. So I don't mind saying, 'Well, all right, let's try it another way. Let's fool with this a bit.'

"Sometimes, you know, we're all a little bit in the granite school of journalism. Take it directly from my word processor or typewriter and put it in granite. They're pearls and it'll never get better, you think." So far, his speed has astonished the theater veterans he has worked with. "I very quickly can rewrite something and try it out. That made the process go much quicker and a little more flexible than it might have been otherwise."

His experiences as a newspaperman also have filled his head with plots. "I keep running into friends of mine who are writers. A few of them will say, 'I don't know what I'm going to do next. I'm fresh out of ideas right now.' Well, I mean, after my years, I've got enough things to write about that are just stored up in my brain that would last me ten lifetimes."

The playwright's bane—writer's block—is simply unfathomable to him. "I can't imagine not having something to write about," he grins. "And that's because, see, journalism keeps you engaged. You're not an active participant, but you're present at an awful lot of things. Particularly the kind of journalism that I practiced, which was very local. When it comes down to writing plays, the fact that I wrote something about a Dairy Queen, it's something that just happened."

In "Chili Queen," the irate customer holds the obstinate waitress hostage at gunpoint and local television starts covering this standoff of "The $10 'Odd Couple.'" Here, too, Mr. Lehrer has an insider's view of media exploitation.

"I didn't want it to be a media play," he insists, "where it's 'Oh, Lehrer's on television and he's writing about television.' I realized though when I was doing it, once I set up the situation, I couldn't do it without dealing with the media. Because it's just a natural plug. But there's a little flavor there of how things can get distorted and how it can influence people to do things they might not otherwise do. The 600-pound gorilla syndrome."

Still, his colleagues in the media have been very supportive of his new career. "They love it," he beams. "My friends were so nice to me about it, and they're envious, quite frankly. They'd be the first to say, 'My God, I wish I could do something like that.'

"A lot of people say something about my guts to try this, a man like me trying something as public as this. And I tell them it's not guts at all. As I was telling you a minute ago, it's just a natural thing for me to do. I have to do it."

Mr. Lehrer is reluctant, though, to discuss his work with other playwrights. "I mean, I don't consider myself yet a playwright," he says shyly. "I'm a beginner yet. I'm still learning. And to sit around and talk about this in the club, I don't rate that yet, I don't rate membership in that. Because I don't have anything to contribute. I have a lot to take in. I wouldn't mind listening to some people, but I can't talk play theory yet."

By now, he has written a handful of plays, often linked by his Southwestern roots and his curiosity about ordinary people. His next play, however, will be a change of pace—an inside Washington tale.

"Simply put, it's about a man who's been in public life and becomes obsessed with what his obit's going to say in *The New York Times*," Mr. Lehrer says, clearly enjoying spinning his yarn. "It's the story of what he does to try and influence it before he dies. He's been in Washington and held high public office. Not the president, but pretty close. I've written a lot of it already and it's kind of fun, but it's not really political. Maybe when I'm through with it."

Although he allows that it is very difficult to juggle his writing with his television work, Mr. Lehrer adds, "It's like anything else. If it's important, you find the time." So he gets up early in the morning and writes before he goes to the studio, as well as at night and on weekends.

Because his television show originates from two cities, that affords additional flexibility for his theater career. "For instance, when [Robert] MacNeil is gone, I have the option of going to New York to fill in. And I would just opt to do it in New York." Nightly, he would do the "NewsHour" program and then head to the theater. "It wasn't easy, but it worked."

The showcase production of "Chili Queen" last November generated the usual new ideas for revision and an unusual amount of interest from producers. "Not only inquiries," Mr. Lehrer says with evident pride, "but definite offers to produce from about five or six regional theaters from around the country." Playwrights Preview Productions, the group that provided the showcase, has created a for-profit subsidiary to run the play Off-Broadway. And there is talk of a full production here in Washington in the fall, possibly at New Playwrights'. "There's some things being discussed as far as Washington is concerned," Mr. Lehrer notes, "but the deal isn't set. I've also learned that about this business. Television looks almost stable compared to the theater. 'Til the curtain actually goes up, don't buy your popcorn."

Still, it looks like Jim Lehrer, Playwright, may be on the verge of a breakthrough to success. The thought is more than a little daunting. "For me, I've got to tell you, a lot of these things are wonderful, but if nothing else happens—literally nothing else happens—I'd be fine.

"I have seen my play on a stage done by superb actors, as well as I think it can ever be done. I've had the cake and I've had the frosting. We're talking about the à la mode now. We're talking about putting ice cream on it."

Certainly one such scoop of tutti-frutti would be awards for his playwriting. Isn't that somewhere in the back of your mind, Jim?

He grins sheepishly. "I joke with my wife all the time," he admits. "When I finish something, I immediately start drafting the Pulitzer Prize acceptance speech. But everybody does that. If you're writing something, particularly a play or a novel where you're writing something that becomes very personal, and you're doing it for public consumption, that means public acclaim and all the things that go with it. Oh, heck, I'm not going to kid you."

Yes, playwriting is fulfilling by itself, Mr. Lehrer concedes, but the reaction of an audience is very intoxicating. "I mean, I want people to laugh when I have a funny line. I'm hooked on all that," he says with a who-wouldn't-be shrug. "It's a wonderful thing. And I love the applause and the whole bit. I love being a playwright. I would love for every play that I write to be hugely successful and for me to be acclaimed and all of that." Jim Lehrer pauses, and drops his voice into a whisper. "What I think I'm saying to you, and I hope it's true, is that I don't need it. But I would love to have it."

Robert MacNeil

"MacNeil Says 'NewsHour' an Ideal TV Anchor Job"

by Todd Hegert

Robert MacNeil, of the "MacNeil/Lehrer NewsHour" is, like Peter Jennings, a Canadian. But, unlike Jennings, MacNeil, at PBS, works without the constant pressure of ratings points compared to the competition. How does MacNeil describe the "MacNeil/Lehrer NewsHour"? "...thoughtful, quiet, and thorough, resolutely devoid of flash and hype."

It was divine intervention, says Robert MacNeil, that saved him from a life of obscurity on stage and left him free to make his mark on camera as one of America's most respected purveyors of TV news.

MacNeil, executive editor and co-anchor of public television's "MacNeil/Lehrer NewsHour" (which airs at 5 and 10:30 P.M. Monday-Fridays on KTSC, Channel 8), set out from his childhood in Halifax, Nova Scotia, to become an actor and playwright.

"I was very lucky to have a voice speak to me out of the heavens when I was about 21 and say, 'You would be a lousy actor. Go and do something else,'" said MacNeil from his New York office.

Something else turned out to be broadcast journalism. And, for heeding that advice, heaven seems to have granted Robert MacNeil a rare dispensation from the strictures of network news.

While Rather, Jennings and Brokaw race through their half-hour network newscasts, MacNeil and partner Jim Lehrer spend an hour exploring the issues and events of the day. They interview newsmakers, scholars, artists. They choose their own stories and attire. They don't jump in fear at variations in the Nielsen ratings.

"Imagine it. We have an hour of televsion time, five nights a week, that is being carried on 256 stations, which a few million very devoted viewers watch every night, and nobody's telling us how to do it. There's nobody saying, 'Your

---

Todd Hegert graduated from the University of Nebraska in 1978 with bachelor's degrees in journalism and English. From 1979 to 1982 he worked for various weeklies in California. From 1983 to 1985 he worked for the Times Call *in Longmont, California, first as a news editor, then as Sunday/Features editor. He joined the* Gazette Telegraph *in 1985 as a deputy features editor, spent two years in that position, then went back to writing for a year. In June 1989, he became features editor.*

ratings went down a half a point last week, we better put a sleeveless sweater on you....' None of that kind of crap," explained MacNeil, who will speak in Pueblo on Saturday at the dedication of new studios at public television station KTSC.

MacNeil describes the "NewsHour" as thoughtful, quiet and thorough, resolutely devoid of flash and hype. It's an approach that has brought MacNeil and Lehrer more than 30 awards for journalistic excellence, including a George Foster Peabody award and a Television Critics Circle award.

MacNeil traces his career in broadcasting back to a Shakespearean production he was in as a sophomore in college. A producer for the Canadian Broadcasting Corp. saw the play and asked MacNeil to do some radio acting. MacNeil paid his way through college with various jobs in radio, including some news announcing.

But, after graduating from Carleton University in Ottawa, he was still determined to make a name for himself in theater. With $2,000 he had saved from his radio work, he moved to London, intending to become a playwright. When the money ran out, he took a job as a reporter for Reuters News Agency.

"No voice ever told me to go into journalism. I just did that because I needed a job. No, I fancied myself as a writer. A writer of plays and novels," he said.

His early desire to be an actor went into MacNeil's mix of talents and ambitions in London and, in 1960, after five years with Reuters, he took a job with NBC News as a London-based foreign correspondent. That, said MacNeil, was "great fun." But things changed when NBC transferred him to the United States—first to Washington as a White House correspondent, then to New York, where he joined NBC's lineup of junior anchormen.

"It was quite terrific and exciting in a way, but it was also very empty. It was not something that I wanted to do or was particularly good at," he said.

MacNeil found network television's preoccupation with entertainment and audience size at odds with his ideas about quality news coverage. He asked NBC to send him overseas again, and when the network refused, he quit his job.

"It was frustrating enough to write a book about, which was a basic critique of television journalism as I saw it practiced then." The book was called "The People Machine."

MacNeil was given a chance to put his theories into action in 1975 when the Public Broadcasting Service agreed to broadast the "MacNeil/Lehrer Report," a half-hour news program generally devoted to a single issue. In 1983, the show was expanded into the "MacNeil/Lehrer NewsHour."

"Both those shows are, in a way, in reaction to what is done on commercial television," he said.

Now in his third decade as a journalist, MacNeil said experience has changed his attitude and approach to the news: "I find my historical patience increasing, which is probably in a way fatal for a journalist. I am increasingly content to wait to find out what happened."

MacNeil says he is becoming increasingly critical of what he feels is an overly narrow view of the news by the media.

"How we define news has become, in my mind, more arbitrary and in a sense emptier.... We define the news, the events of the day, in a very sort of formulistic and arbitrary manner," he said.

MacNeil's own interests and projects range far beyond the "NewsHour" — from hosting a PBS dramatization of the John Le Carré novel "Tinker, Tailor, Soldier, Spy" to co-writing and narrating "The Story of English," a nine-part series on the history and evolution of the English language.

But, despite a reputation that would allow him to pursue his other interests and ambitions full time, he remains committed to the "NewsHour."

"We would be crazy — Lehrer and I — to lose energy for something that we really have just begun to imprint on the national consciousness."

Roger Mudd

"Association with PBS Is Still Good News for Roger Mudd"
by Michele Greppi

It has been said that you get "a better guarantee with a Die-Hard battery than you do as an anchor in broadcast news." And who can vouch for this better than Roger Mudd, who carries scars from years of competition for this anchor chair or that desk?

A month before he will join the throngs covering the Democratic convention, Roger Mudd was prowling the Georgia World Congress and CNN centers, asking a panoply of questions and looking at floorplans, storing away information.

He had spent parts of the day rehearsing for Saturday night's Georgia Emmy Awards ceremony and sharpening some points in opening remarks that proved a savvy newsman can be more entertaining than entertainers (Rep. Pat Swindall, in his loan-sting press conference Friday, had hiked the confessional stakes, Mudd said, by "admitting he never wanted to be laundered, just dry-cleaned").

When this was published, Michele Greppi was a staff writer for The Atlanta Journal.

Mudd also made time for a trip to the Old New York Book Shop, where he found nothing to add to his collection of twentieth-century Southern fiction first editions.

He was back in the state where, as a serviceman fresh out of a Washington, D.C., high school, he learned to drink moonshine, shoot pool and eat fried poundcake. In 1945, the Army stationed Mudd in Dahlonega, Georgia. He recalled the students from nearby Brenau College were "the prettiest women north of Ecuador."

The 60-year-old Mudd also was back in the state where, fresh out of Washington & Lee University, he coached a Rome prep school's junior varsity football team to a respectable, if short, season.

In 1950, he taught English and history at Darlington School, where his "modest little team" tested single-wing plays for Clemson and ran up a "4-1 or 4-2 record."

But coaching was a sideline and teaching was a brief detour, although one he still muses about. Mudd intended to go on to a doctorate that would expand on an arena he delved into while working on his master's degree at the University of North Carolina: the press and New Deal government intelligentsia.

He thought he ought to get a working understanding of the press before he climbed into an ivory tower to study it, so he landed a job on the rewrite desk of the Richmond (Va.) *News Leader*. By the end of the summer, he recalled, he had begun to get some bylines, but "I wasn't very good." And "they didn't offer to keep me."

He didn't want to leave Richmond, so he took a news director job at the paper's sister radio station, which was beefing up its coverage. With a three-year stint at WRNL, he was off on a broadcasting career that would find him cast as a young elder statesman, elder elder statesman as well as two-time wallflower in network shuffles.

In 1981, he left CBS News an "extremely disappointed" man. During 20 years with the network, he had done standout work on Capitol Hill and the campaign trails that led to it and the White House. He had won two Emmys for reportage and a Peabody Award for "Teddy," a tough, prime-time, 1979 interview that many said marked the beginning of the end of Ted Kennedy's presidential aspirations.

For eight years, Mudd had been Walter Cronkite's vacation fill-in and presumed successor. But when the time came for the grandfather of news anchors to announce his retirement in early 1980, the perhaps too complacent Mudd found himself elbowed aside by a fevered Dan Rather. Mudd learned about it less than two hours before the public did, made an immediate exit from the Washington bureau and took a leave that lasted until NBC News put him on the air after the elections that year.

This contract had an heir-apparent clause that gave him first option on succeeding John Chancellor as NBC anchor, but he volunteered to share the duties with Tom Brokaw, the one-time Atlanta anchor whose "Today" show stint had provoked a lucrative bid from ABC.

The two manned twin helms of NBC's "Nightly News"—Brokaw from New York, Mudd from Washington—for 16 months before NBC weighed anchors and dropped Mudd back to senior political correspondent, leaving Brokaw in a solo spotlight in mid-1983.

In early '87, after NBC had canceled "1986," one of a number of awkward attempts at a credible and watchable newsmagazine show—Mudd's pairing with Connie Chung inspired parodists—an again disheartened Mudd left network news. That March, he signed on as special correspondent and essayist with PBS' "MacNeil/Lehrer NewsHour."

Although he still may be able to reach into pockets of disappointment and find reminders of old bitterness, he voices no wish for what was, because what was network news is no more, he said, thanks to influences in and out of electronic journalism. "It was and it remains an interesting life," he said, "but I had come to the conclusion that it had changed so much since I had gone into it."

The priorities for his post-Murrow generation were to cover the news, do it well, do specials at 11:30 and do significant prime-time documentaries without regard to profit in the ratings.

Competition for audience and the resultant merchandising of anchors' "images, reputations and vanities," deregulation of broadcasting, and network ownership by "fast-food people," Mudd said, have shifted the emphasis "from substance to shadow."

"They spend as much promoting a scoop as covering it," said the man who prohibited his Rather-era agent from "hustling because it was somehow unseemly," and who for years avoided interviews with print reporters because it smacked of a celebrityism that made him uncomfortable. He finally decided he was being sort of silly. "If you believe in what you're doing, at some point you have to talk about it."

He believes in the hour-long, weeknight "MacNeil/Lehrer NewsHour" as "the televised handbook for political ballplayers and fans."

The PBS news program, which will broadcast out of Atlanta during the Democratic convention that begins July 18, extends Mudd's string. He has covered every convention since 1960 (in 1964, CBS supplanted Cronkite in favor of a Mudd-Robert Trout team).

Next spring, when a new administration is still settling into Washington, Mudd will anchor an assessment of the state of American education, a co-production of MacNeil/Lehrer Productions.

This five-hour, $3.9 million report will have him thinking again about the short detour that 38 years later still raises a question of whether this father of four and husband of 31 years might have made a greater contribution to a few as a teacher than he did to many as a journalist.

Jane Pauley

"In Wake of 'Today,' Jane Pauley Learns America Loves Her"

by Diane Holloway

> *Not every broadcast journalist has Roger Mudd's discouraging record of second-place finishes. Jane Pauley has turned replacement on the "Today" show into her own personal victory ... with the public.*

If you believe everything you read in the magazines, Jane Pauley is just about perfect.

TV Guide recently dubbed her one of the most beautiful women in television. *People* magazine hailed her as one of America's most beautiful people. And *Esquire* rated her high on its list of 100 best wives. Pauley's husband, Garry Trudeau, reminded her that Blondie was also on *Esquire*'s list, so she shouldn't take the best-wife tribute too seriously.

"But I have to say that the one that was the most preposterous, and that I enjoyed the most, was the most-beautiful-people issue of *People* where I followed Michelle Pfeiffer," Pauley said with a chuckle.

How does Pauley feel about the media madness surrounding her?

"It's an embarrassment of good publicity," she said. "Somebody congratulated me last January after the *Life* magazine issue came out for achieving '60s-style publicity in the '80s. Now it's the '90s, and it continues apace. I'm bracing for the backlash, because, quite frankly, I am making myself sick."

Pauley's husband teases her mercilessly about the fuss being made over her, and Pauley's sister told her she now views Pauley as something of a mythological person.

"I'm afraid I can only sustain this level of goodness for a few more hours," Pauley said with a sigh.

The funny thing about all the beauty polls and celebrity rankings is that

---

Diane Holloway is television critic for The Austin *[Texas]* American-Statesman. *She writes daily television columns consisting of reviews, interviews and analysis. She also writes feature articles for the Sunday magazine section and other television-related features. She is a former officer and current board member of the national Television Critics Association. She previously worked for the National Endowment for the Arts, as a program specialist, and the American Film Institute, as an editor.*

Pauley is a far cry from glamorous, especially compared with other network newswomen. Maria Shriver, Barbara Walters, Connie Chung and Diane Sawyer are designer-dressed with perfect coiffures and manicures. Many of them, Shriver in particular, sport diamond rings big enough to break a finger.

Pauley, on the other hand, is wholesome and unassuming both in appearance and demeanor. She looks and sounds more like the 39-year-old wife and mother of three young children that she is than a million-dollar anchorwoman, which she also is.

When she talked with reporters in Los Angeles recently about her new show, *Real Life with Jane Pauley,* Pauley wore a simple skirt and jacket, flats, a plain gold wedding band, no nail polish and only a little bit of makeup. Her hair looked as if she had just pulled the hot curlers out herself.

It is precisely because Pauley is so down-to-earth and easygoing that Americans loved waking up with her. Even when she was pregnant with twins, she was perky and charming. She was a popular fixture on *Today,* a refreshing complement to the brashness of Bryant Gumbel. But after she was replaced by the younger, blonder Deborah Norville, Pauley's popularity suddenly turned into adulation.

"There was a perception that I was in danger in some way last fall, and I think that probably accentuated people's feelings of wanting to protect me," she said. "Other than that, I couldn't begin to explain it, and I've never seen the likes of it."

Whether she left of her own accord or was forced out by Norville is still unclear. Pauley will say publicly only that she felt the timing was right for her to leave.

"All arrows were pointing in the same direction simultaneously," she said. "That, and other factors as personal as the fact that I was sending children to kindergarten for the first time that fall, and I was about to celebrate a thirteenth anniversary.

"While I sometimes feel like I'm quoting myself, the fact of the matter is I was starting to feel like a one-trick pony. Won't she ever leave? Is this all she can do? So, it was a confluence of events that all seemed to point to the same direction."

Viewers were convinced that their beloved Pauley was shoved out by Norville, and they turned away from the venerable morning show in droves. Soon after Pauley's departure, *Today* fell behind ABC's *Good Morning America* in the ratings and has remained there ever since.

The outpouring of love and concern for Pauley was so strong that NBC made her Tom Brokaw's primary substitute on *NBC Nightly News* and also gave her her own prime-time magazine, *Real Life,* which in its previous two outings stomped the competition flat. The third installment airs tonight (at 9 on KXAN-TV, Channel 36 Cable 4).

Unlike *60 Minutes, 20/20, Face to Face with Connie Chung* and *Prime Time Live,* Pauley's show does not deal with headline stories or go after celebrity and newsmaker interviews. As the title implies, the show focuses on issues that relate to everyday lives. The only celebrity involved is Pauley herself, and she is determined to keep a low profile.

"I wanted to do a show that was about mainstream people, that was about everyday people, dare we say even ordinary people," Pauley said. "My premise was that in the '90s, as blessed relief from the '80s, people are hungry to know more about people like themselves. We had become, in our exceptionally busy lives, isolated from each other on an everyday basis."

NBC has not given *Real Life* a permanent spot on the prime-time schedule, but Pauley is convinced that will happen, probably sometime in January. And she has high hopes for what her show could accomplish.

"In a very humble way — and I stress a *very* humble way — I think our program in its heart and mission hopes to establish little data points, little tiny dots that on a cumulative basis will give you a better sense of what it is like to live in America today," she said.

In the meantime, she keeps a cautious eye on her heightened celebrity status, wondering when the glaring limelight will fade. Although she won't admit it — because, as she says with a wry smile, "I'm also one of the most polite people in America" — Pauley must be pleased that her bumpy ride last fall has catapulted her to the brink of prime-time stardom.

Dan Rather

"*Bushwacked!*"

by Richard Stengel

No anchor ever stepped into a more volatile situation when Dan Rather replaced Walter Cronkite at the helm of the "CBS Evening News" in 1981. And Rather never taped a more tempestuous show than in late January, 1988, when he interviewed George Bush, running for president and running to shed his wimp image. The following Time *cover story implies that Rather trapped Bush, but Bush came out ahead. But not everyone believes that. In* Anchors: Brokaw, Jennings, Rather and the Evening News, *Robert Goldberg and Gerald Jay Goldberg write:*

> "At first, the story seemed clear. A liberal newsman had tried to ambush the Republican Vice-President, and had gotten his comeuppance. The CBS team had asked for a general straightforward interview, but then tried to pull off a sneak attack by focusing solely on the Iran-Contra issue. Bush had fought back and won. Or so it seemed.

> "Actually, it was the Bush team that mounted the sneak attack. Both executive producer Tom Bettag and senior political producer Richard Cohen had sent clear signals to Bush's staff that this would be a 'tough' interview. Far from surprised, Republican media advisor Roger Ailes saw such an interview as the perfect opportunity for Bush to shake his 'wimp' image. George would come out swinging, and the rich, East Coast, namby-pamby Vice-President would be transformed into a macho guy, the perfect heir to Ronald Reagan. 'It was the most amazing bit of Ailes black magic I ever saw,' said Marty Koughan, the CBS producer who crafted the Bush profile that led to the Q & A session.
>
> "While George Bush claimed all along that he had been set up — 'a misrepresentation on the part of CBS' — that he had come in expecting a straight-ahead interview and had been suddenly forced to fight for his life, in fact it was CBS and Rather that were bushwacked. 'George Bush,' says Bettag, 'was lying through his teeth.'"
>
> Did Rather trap Bush? Did Bush and his Republican campaign team sandbag Rather and CBS? You decide.

In the curious, often unruly marriage between politics and television, there are certain charged moments that flicker in the national memory. Richard Nixon tense and sweaty debating an unruffled John Kennedy. Ed Muskie's frozen tears in the snows of New Hampshire. Ted Kennedy groping for meaning and a verb in an interview with Roger Mudd. Ronald Reagan squaring his jaw and asserting, "I'm paying for this microphone, Mr. Green!" Who cares that the man's name was actually Breen? It was great television.

Such moments supposedly provide insight into a hidden reality. In a flash they divulge the inner self, the man behind the mask. They are video epiphanies, what media wizards call a "defining moment." The viewer does not so much receive information as he does an impression. From that impression an opinion may be formed, and based on that opinion, a vote may be cast.

One such moment occurred last week. Like most of the others, it came upon the viewer unawares. Unlike others, it was staged, self-generated, almost ceremonial: a media event. Dan Rather was interviewing George Bush on the CBS *Evening News* — live. Unusual, but not unprecedented. But what could have been just another conversation between two familiar talking heads turned into a collision with a resonance far out of proportion to the intense nine minutes of airtime. Their contretemps was not just a conflict between men but between two institutions, two symbols: the Vice President and the anchorman, the loyal emissary of the Reagan establishment taking on the embodiment of the East Coast liberal press.

At first, what happened seemed blindingly clear. A powerful TV journalist hectored the Vice President, who had been lured into the interview expecting that it would focus on his presidential campaign. Eager to combat his wimpy image, Bush came to shove, denouncing Rather's tactics and counterattacking

Richard Stengel is an associate editor of Time *magazine.*

by recalling the evening last September when Rather stalked away from his anchor duties and left the network blank for more than six minutes. The tightly coiled anchorman, a combustible character in the coolest of mediums, seemed almost to spring out of his chair, unsettling his audience with high-voltage intensity. It was video High Noon: Bush had shot down the legendary media gunslinger from Black Rock. It was the *new* George Bush. Not Bush the perpetual stand-in, but Bush the stand-up guy. Bush Unbound. Bush Unwimped.

The timing was almost perfect. His dustup came only two weeks before the Iowa caucuses, where he is trailing Bob Dole in the polls. For a candidate seeking to generate support from conservatives, getting mugged by Dan Rather and then beating him off was the political equivalent of winning a Purple Heart. "I can't really explain it, but a chord was hit," Bush said during a swing through South Dakota two days later. "I suppose people saw a guy up there by himself, standing up for what he believes."

Yet as the heat began to fade, people wondered about the light. Yes, Dan Rather had been brusque, even downright rude, but just what had George Bush stood up for anyway? That he has the right not to be dogged by questions he claims already to have answered? That he should be judged by more than just his murky behavior during the Iran-*contra* fiasco? Yes, but what had he been doing all that time? In rebutting Rather, Bush was not delivering a message, but beating up the messenger.

Rather's aggressive interrogation of Bush was an ambush that backfired. But the Bush people had planned a sally of their own: the Vice President was eager to launch a crowd-pleasing counterattack on live television. Within days, however, there were signs that Bush's strategy might also boomerang. Once the applause ended, Bush's testy rebuttals to Rather raised nagging qualms about his dubious involvement in the most misguided and sordid policy of the Reagan Administration.

In a poll for *Time* by Yankelovich Clancy Shulman, 42 percent of those who saw or read about the exchange said they believed that Bush came out ahead, while 27 percent said Rather did. (Republicans split 59 percent to 16 percent in Bush's favor, but Democrats split 40 percent to 31 percent in Rather's favor.) Yet when asked whether it was right for Rather to push Bush on his role in the Iran-*contra* affair, 59 percent replied that it was (including 46 percent of the Republicans and 72 percent of the Democrats). Moreover, 79 percent said they believed the Vice President knows more about the arms-for-hostages deal than he has told the public.

The nine minutes that shook the wimp image were not nearly as spontaneous as they seemed. For both sides the encounter had been meticulously planned. By the middle of December CBS News had already aired a series of political profiles. Richard Cohen, senior political producer of the *Evening News,* lobbied for a different approach to Bush, one that centered on the Iran-*contra* affair. Rather and the other producers agreed. In early January Cohen sent a letter to the Bush campaign requesting a lengthy taped interview for a campaign profile. "Part of our early coverage of the 1988 presidential election has been a series of candidate profiles," he wrote. "We purposely saved your profile for last ... Dan Rather is very interested in your profile and has decided to do it himself." Then, as well as later, CBS never came out and said they planned to focus exclusively on the Iran-*contra* affair.

But from the moment the Bush campaign received Cohen's letter, they suspected that this was more than a run-of-the-mill interview. Multiple copies of the letter circulated to the campaign's wise men. Unlike those in other organizations, the Bush staff members are not gluttons for publicity; they can afford to be discriminating. If they sniff a hatchet job, they steer clear. On his copy of the letter, Bush wrote, "I feel comfortable with Rather. Make sure this guy gets reply soon." Campaign Manager Lee Atwater was dead set against the interview. He was wary of Rather, but he was in the minority.

Bush spokesman Peter Teeley began negotiating with CBS over the ground rules. In further discussions Roger Ailes, Bush's noted media consultant, contended that the only way to assure that the Vice President got his message across was to do the interview live. Eventually the Bush campaign insisted the interview be live or not at all. Take it or leave it. Says Teeley: "There was every indication from the beginning that the interview would be highly confrontational."

CBS was uncomfortable. Live interviews, particularly on the *Evening News*, are unpredictable. A taped interview allows for editing and shaping; a live interview gives the subject a chance to manipulate the conversation. The subject can filibuster, deftly evading a probing question. CBS had already produced a hard-hitting five-minute introduction examining Bush's contradictory claims about his Iran-*contra* role. Executive Producer Tom Bettag saw three options: run the five-minute intro on its own, kill the story or accede to Bush's conditions. Finally CBS agreed to do the interview live, and warned Bush's staff that Rather's questions were going to be tough and pointed.

On the weekend before the broadcast, CBS began airing promotions for the Bush-Rather interview and calling political writers to flag for them the "first interview on Iran-*contra* that Bush has done with any network." The day of the interview Rather had three one-hour rehearsals with the six people involved in the broadcast. He was coached as if he were a candidate preparing for a debate or a pugilist preparing for a fight, rather than a journalist going into an interview. Howard Rosenberg, a producer from CBS's Washington bureau, played Bush. "We knew it was going to be a brawl," says Cohen. "We prepared with that expectation." In the last of the three rehearsals, Rather was warned that Bush might bring up what Rather calls "the Miami thing," the blackout last September when a bristling Rather stomped off the *Evening News* set to protect CBS's decision to allow the U.S. Open tennis match to cut into the broadcast.

Though CBS never directly informed the Bush camp that the interview would focus exclusively on Iran-*contra*, its intentions were hardly a secret. "We kept getting reports that it was going to be an ambush," said Bush's chief of staff, Craig Fuller. "CBS was leaking so badly that if they'd been Dutch they'd have been under water," said Teeley. On Monday Teeley telephoned Bush to inform him of the rumors about a potential on-air confrontation, suggesting that Bush have a briefing for preparation. "I don't need a briefing," Bush replied. He had just returned from a day of campaigning in New Hampshire. "I want to relax," he said.

The cameras were set up in Bush's vice presidential office on Capitol Hill. In New York, CBS staff members watched Bush walk into his office accompanied by Ailes and Fuller. CBS had set up a monitor in Bush's office so that he could watch the five-minute introductory report. "You may want to see this," said one technician. As he watched the first teaser for the interview— "Still to come, a live interview with Mr. Bush on arms to Iran and money to the *contras*"—Bush got steamed. "If that's all it's about," he announced to the technicians in his office, "they're going to find themselves with a seven-minute walkout on their hands."

When Rather began the interview with an Iran-*contra* question, Bush came out firing. He quickly accused CBS of bad faith: "I find this to be a rehash and a little bit, if you'll excuse me, a misrepresentation on the part of CBS, who said you're doing political profiles on all the candidates."

CBS staffers claim to have been flabbergasted by the Vice President's gambit, suggesting that he was being disingenuous. But Bush was genuinely angry. He was also primed. When Rather noted that many Republicans believed Bush was hiding something, Bush played it deftly. "I *am* hiding something," said the Vice President. Rather: "Here's a chance to get it out." Bush: "You know what I'm hiding? What I told the President, that's the only thing."

At the best of times, neither Rather nor Bush are relaxed, easygoing TV performers. This time, both became agitated, developing an uncanny facility for speaking at precisely the same time. From the start, Rather was peremptory, as though time were running out even before the clock began ticking; he seemed on the edge of an explosion. Bush never relinquished his tone of tinny, aggrieved militancy; Rather never departed from his badgering, bulldoggish questioning. Before too long, he had crossed the line between objectivity and emotional involvement. Rather: "I don't want to be argumentative, Mr. Vice President." Bush: "You do, Dan." Bush, edgy and frustrated, deployed his tactical nuclear weapon. "It's not fair to judge my whole career by a rehash of Iran," he said. "How would you like it if I judged your career by those seven minutes when you walked off the set in New York? Would you like that?" (Who cares that it was only six minutes, and Rather was broadcasting from Miami? It was a great television moment.)

The format was flexible. Rather had anywhere from three to about nine minutes to grill Bush. Through his earpiece, Bettag had been counting down the time to Rather. After eight minutes, he announced one minute to go. Bettag had already killed several stories. With 30 seconds left, he began telling Rather to cut. Ten. Nine. Eight. Rather: "There are clearly some unanswered questions. Are you willing to go to a news conference before the Iowa caucuses, answer questions from all..." Seven. Six. Five. Bush: "I've been to 86 news conferences since March..." Four. Three. Rather: "I gather the answer is no. Thank you very much for being with us, Mr. Vice President." Two. "We'll be back with more news in a moment." One. Cut. All that was missing was the squawk of the game-show buzzer signaling that the contestant had lost the last round.

Bush indulged in some all too familiar locker-room swagger. He told campaign aides and CBS staff members in his office after the show, "The bastard didn't lay a glove on me... Tell your goddamned network that if they want to talk to me to raise their hands at a press conference. No more Mr. Inside stuff after that." Then, as he put it afterward, he went over to his wife and said, "I just had the darnedest interview." Later he apologized for taking the "Lord's name in vain."

The postshow atmosphere at CBS was grim. Some 6,000 people called CBS's New York headquarters that evening, most crying foul. Howard Stringer, the president of CBS News, came somewhat belatedly to Rather's defense. "The public doesn't often see aggressive journalism on television," he explained. "This is not the time to be careful how we address the people who want to be President of the United States." Stringer says the episode reinforced the need for live television on the evening news. "If we want to sanitize the evening news all the time, where all the edge is taken off for fear of what the audience thinks, we run the risk of going back to the least objectionable programs."

The next night, Rather departed from the customary *Evening News* format to offer a personal word. Along with a kind of primer on journalism—"Trying to ask honest questions and trying to be persistent about answers is part of a reporter's job"—he served up a tepid mea culpa on having cut Bush off at the end: "Ending live television isn't done as gracefully as we hope or intend, and last night was one of those times."

The incident seemed to revivify Bush and galvanize his campaign. "We're getting phone calls now from fence sitters we've been after for weeks," said Bill Cahill, a Bush staffer in New Hampshire. At a campaign stop in South Dakota, Bush found dozens of his listeners wearing lapel buttons with a diagonal slash across "Dan Rather." At Bush's national headquarters, an aide scurried

Whom do you trust more to tell the truth?	Total	Republicans
George Bush	22%	41%
Dan Rather	49%	33%
Do you think Rather was rude to Bush in the interview?	Total	Republicans
Yes	51%	60%
No	38%	28%
Was Rather right to push Bush on his role in the Iran-*contra* affair?	Total	Republicans
Yes	59%	46%
No	32%	47%
Do you think Bush's response shows that he is not a wimp?	Total	Republicans
Yes	55%	60%
No	31%	28%

From a telephone poll of 612 adults taken for *Time* on Jan. 27 and 28 by Yankelovich Clancy Shulman. The sampling error is plus or minus 4%.

through the lobby with a long memo draft titled "Reaping the Benefits of the Rather Interview."

Yet as Bush basked in the afterglow of victory, he once again diluted his p.r. triumph with remarks that would be more appropriate for an overeager Boy Scout who had just won a survival-hike merit badge. At a chili lunch in Worland, Wyoming, he told an appreciative audience, "I need combat pay for last night, I'll tell you." To a high school chemistry class in Cheyenne, he described live television: "You know, it's Tension City when you're in there."

By Friday, however, Bush seemed eager to avoid the impression he was dwelling on the matter. "I don't want to go into it," he told *Time* Correspondent David Beckwith as they flew across Iowa. "I don't want to dwell on it. I don't want to discuss it. I've said it was an event, a powerful event, and you've seen the reactions from around the country. But there's no benefit for me to dwell on it. I was amazed at the response everywhere we went this week—Wyoming, South Dakota, Iowa—but there's no point in my trying to capitalize on it." Did Bush feel his judgment or integrity has been called into question by his Iran-*contra* role? "I think most people think it's been exhaustively looked into, that I haven't done anything wrong, though they might question my judgment. But the record speaks clearly on all that. So let the people decide it."

Bob Dole, who had the most to lose by the Bush-Rather dustup, took the long view. Advisers counseled him to maintain a judicious silence, but he could not resist a barbed comment about Bush's born-again aggressiveness. "If you can't stand up to Dan Rather," he said sharply, "you've got to deal with Gorbachev and a few other people." Dole also noted that the affair was another indication that the Iran-*contra* issue will not go away.

Bush's ripostes to Rather were the capstone to a month-old "get tough" campaign orchestrated by Media Adviser Ailes and other staffers. "If somebody hits him," says Lee Atwater, "Bush is going to try to hit back harder." In recent weeks, Bush has jabbed at Alexander Haig, tweaked Bob Dole, and lit into James P. Gannon, editor of the Des Moines *Register,* for what he claims was unfair reporting about his role in the Iran-*contra* affair. Two weeks ago, at an "Ask George Bush" gathering in Cedar Rapids, Iowa, Bush waded into the audience, seized a piece of Jack Kemp campaign literature from a 15-year-old girl and dramatically ripped it into pieces.

Bush insists that his macho attitude will not translate into a campaign of press bashing. "I feel much more relaxed with the press now than I ever have," he says. But in attacking the press, he is joining the club; the time-honored sport of press bashing is a growth industry in 1988. Gary Hart, upon reentering the race, abjured the media as part of his campaign to "let the people decide," and he has not let up since then. Gephardt's new populist approach lumps "editorial boards and writers" in the "Establishment" that he has suddenly decided to decry.

While the episode may have squelched doubts about Bush's fortitude, it seems to have revived doubts about his role in the Iran-*contra* affair. A reading of the confrontation's transcript suggests that Bush was evasive, while Rather seemed knowledgeable and persistent. In television, style overwhelms substance, image replaces information. But as the sense of a showdown between Bush and the evil anchorman began to subside, perceptions began to change.

Paradoxically, television's "defining" moment is not usually defined at the time. The moment gains resonance through hindsight. The original memory is adjusted and tinkered with by what comes afterward. Reviewing the Kennedy-Nixon debates reveals that Kennedy was almost as nervous and stilted as Nixon. In the end, the benefit Bush can draw from his tangle with Rather will depend on whether viewers recall it as a moment of justified indignation or as a peevish attempt to avoid coming to terms with the Iran-*contra* affair. It could go either way, for in fact it was both.

Dan Rather
"*I Was Trained to Ask Questions*"
by Richard Zoglin

No anchor has ever presented a television image quite as quixotic as Dan Rather. Inheriting Walter Cronkite's faithful, but demographically aging following in 1981, Rather's first few weeks and months were an attempt to find himself as anchor. Tom Brokaw is blander, Peter Jennings more urbane, and ultimately with a demographically younger and more educated following, Rather's tenure as CBS anchor has been marked by: the 1986 New York incident in which he was beaten by two unidentified assailants who repeatedly demanded "Kenneth, what's the frequency?"; and on September 11, 1987, Rather stayed off the air for six minutes in a black fury after a CBS tennis match ran late (leaving the CBS network with "black"—no picture). The "Bushwacked" episode is only one in a number of episodes no other anchor would dare match.

Who is Dan Rather? Goldberg and Goldberg, in Anchors, *write:*

> 'This complex character, so ambitious, so hard-charging, so full of self-doubt, so driven by contradictory emotions, has always seemed more intense, more passionate than either of his competitors, Jennings and Brokaw. Dan Rather has always ap-

peared a little larger than life. Any small event about him is news. Whether he wears a sweater or not, whether he stands or sits, the event gets reported. This personality—with his demons and his many accomplishments—often seems bigger than the small screen. That's Dan Rather's power, his draw. It's also his undoing. He's a high-voltage personality, on and off the tube. This is what people in the industry mean when they talk about Rather as a "lightning rod." He's the kind of guy who braves a hurricane, who gets slugged at a political convention—who makes things happen around him. He's also the kind who often travels with a bodyguard, ex-secret service man Toby Chandler, and keeps a shotgun in his house.

The scene on the floor of the 1968 Democratic Convention in Chicago was chaotic, and Dan Rather, naturally, was in the middle of it. When CBS cameras located their roving floor reporter, he was involved in a shoving match with security guards. "Take your hands off me unless you plan to arrest me!" Rather shouted just before disappearing behind a mass of bodies. He popped back up seconds later, trying, between gasps, to explain the incident to Anchorman Walter Cronkite. "I'm sorry to be out of breath," said Rather, "but somebody belted me in the stomach during that."

Even then, Dan Rather had a nose for trouble. But it was the sort of trouble that was good for the career of an ambitious young TV reporter climbing steadily up the network ladder. Rather, at 56, is now at the very top of that ladder, anchorman for the CBS *Evening News* and possibly the most powerful TV journalist in America. But his emotional, frequently combative style has also made him the most controversial. Rather's heated encounter with George Bush last week was just the latest in a barrage of storms ... that seem to engulf him with the regularity of spring squalls on the plains of his native Texas.

No TV anchorman has ever aroused such passion. For conservatives who remember his days as President Nixon's nemesis, Rather is the very embodiment of what they perceive as the media's liberal bias. When Senator Jesse Helms, the right-wing Republican from North Carolina, launched a campaign in 1985 to take over CBS, he urged supporters with pointed glee to buy up CBS stock and "become Dan Rather's boss." Many TV news traditionalists are no fonder of Rather: he is too high-pitched, too image conscious, too well paid.

Even Rather's fans frequently find him mystifying—never more so than last September, when he became broadcasting's most famous missing person. Miffed that CBS coverage of a U.S. Open tennis match was cutting into his evening newscast, Rather abruptly walked off the set just before the network switched to the news, inadvertently forcing the CBS nationwide signal to go black for six minutes. The incident renewed dark suspicions that Rather is too high-strung and emotionally unstable to be running a network newscast. Asked the London *Times*: "Is Dan Rather, bishop of the nation's news business, losing his marbles?"

A bit of British overstatement, to be sure, but Rather does seem oddly prone to bizarre scrapes both onscreen and off. In November 1980, while still

Richard Zoglin is an associate editor at Time *magazine.*

"I Was Trained to Ask Questions" 259

a correspondent for CBS's *60 Minutes,* Rather hopped into a Chicago taxicab and headed for an interview with Studs Terkel. When the driver couldn't find Terkel's house, an argument ensued, and, according to Rather, the cabby held him hostage while speeding recklessly through the city streets. Rather filed a disorderly conduct charge but subsequently dropped it.

Six years later, Rather was walking along Park Avenue on Manhattan's Upper East Side when, as he told police later, a pair of strange men attacked and beat him. One of them asked the unfathomable question: "Kenneth, what is the frequency?" The incident—still unexplained—provided grist for talk-show wisecracks for weeks.

Rather's behavior as an anchorman too has sometimes seemed inexplicable. In an interview during last summer's Iran-*contra* hearings, he peppered former CIA Chief William Colby with questions about the rumor—taken seriously by almost no one else—that the late CIA director William Casey was not really dead. In August, when former ABC Newsman Charles Glass escaped from terrorists holding him hostage inside Lebanon, Rather sounded a jarring note of skepticism, referring to Glass as a "young American who says he was a hostage." ABC *Nightline* anchor Ted Koppel called the characterization "beneath contempt."

Rather has never seemed comfortable in the anchor chair. A courtly and painstakingly polite man in person, he seems stiff and tense on camera. Even his attempts at spontaneity and good humor look programmed. One week he tried ending his broadcast with the sign-off "Courage"; widespread derision forced him to drop it after three nights. Walter Cronkite, Rather's predecessor, was calm and reassuring, an avuncular figure to the nation. Rather seems tightly coiled and uneasy, an eccentric cousin capable of almost anything.

The Bush flare-up was hardly in the same category as Rather's more embarrassing gaffes. At worst it was a case of a reporter getting carried away in the heat of an admittedly intense encounter. With Bush on the attack from the outset, and the clock ticking away on the live interview, Rather pressed hard, and legitimately, for answers. Although he appeared agitated, his questions were informed, coherent and to the point. Even his response to Bush's remark about the six-minute walkout was deft under pressure. "I think you'll agree," he said after a few seconds, "that your qualifications for President .. [are] more important than what you just referred to." Only with his abrupt ending did Rather appear snappish and rude.

The shock waves set off by the interview seemed magnified simply because Rather was involved. "Dan leaps out like a tiger, and some people don't like that," says ABC Correspondent Ann Compton. "He is a lightning rod for the American people who believe the press is rude." CBS stations around the country were besieged by phone callers criticizing Rather (though pro and con opinions became more evenly divided as the week went on). A *Times-Mirror* Gallup poll conducted Wednesday showed that Rather's favorable rating among viewers—already lower than that of either of his two network rivals—dropped to 66 percent, from 73 percent last fall. Many journalists too criticized Rather for losing his cool during the session. Even Sam Donaldson, the pit bull of network correspondents, contended that Rather went "too far."

Buoyed by the midweek backlash in Rather's favor, CBS executives stood by their man. "There is no question that what Dan portrayed on the air was not the sort of gracious Southern gentleman that he is in person," said News President Howard Stringer. "What we got was a journalist in pursuit of a story." CBS Chairman Lawrence Tisch, who was traveling in the Far East on business when the episode occurred, was briefed on it by telephone and, according to Stringer, was "very supportive." CBS staffers, though shaken by the initial barrage of criticism, were also upbeat by week's end. "This is one of the first times in recent years that people have rallied around Dan," said one producer. "What we saw was the old Dan Rather—the tough journalist."

Rather was "pretty chagrined" immediately after the interview, according to one associate, but he quickly gathered his spirits and strongly defended his performance. "I never felt the interview was out of control," he told *Time*. "I couldn't get answers, but I did not get mad." Aides who briefed Rather before the interview say the anchor was fully prepared for a heated exchange. "We knew Bush would attack, and we knew he wasn't going to answer the questions," said Producer Martin Koughan. "The trick was, how does Dan keep control of the line of questioning? Better rude than cowed."

Rather's emotional commitment to the story was clearly high. "In 1983, 241 Marines were murdered in Beirut by terrorists mounted by Iran," he says. "Most of them were 17 to 21 years old. They were our sons; they were our brothers. That burned in my memory. Then the incredible thing happened: over the dead bodies of those Marines, the United States of America sent our best missiles to Iranians who sponsored the killing. I never got that out of my head. How could that happen?" For a journalist, such fervid personal involvement might seem overwrought, not to say unprofessional. "People say I'm not cool," Rather responds. "Well, I am not a Buddha. I am not a robot. On my best days, I am a thinking reporter."

Colleagues agree that Rather is intense and fiercely competitive. But few have many more clues to his elusive personality. "Dan is a man of many moods, a complicated man, hard to figure," says one who has worked closely with him. Rather, who lives with his wife Jean in an East Side Manhattan co-op, avoids the city's social scene. A workaholic who usually gets by on four hours' sleep a night, he spends his spare hours reading, watching sports on TV and fly-fishing in the Catskills during summer vacations.

The son of a West Texas pipeline worker and a waitress, Rather began his journalism career with a part-time job at the Houston *Chronicle* after graduating from Sam Houston State Teachers College. He moved to a local radio station, then to KHOU-TV, the CBS affiliate in Houston. His intrepid coverage of Hurricane Carla, which swept over Galveston in 1961, caught the eye of CBS executives, who soon hired him as a correspondent.

Rather first gained nationwide attention when he happened to be in Dallas on the day President Kennedy was shot. His aggressiveness almost got him into trouble. Based on unconfirmed reports from the hospital, Rather told his bosses in New York City that Kennedy had died, leading CBS radio to report the news more than half an hour before the official announcement was made. The bulletin turned out to be correct, much to Rather's relief, and he covered himself with glory as coordinator of CBS's Dallas coverage during the assassination aftermath.

His success led Rather to stints in London, Saigon and Washington, where he served as chief White House correspondent during President Nixon's Watergate days. His combative reporting had already drawn the ire of Nixon supporters when, in March 1974, Rather rose to ask a question during an appearance by the President at a National Association of Broadcasters convention. The TV executives in the audience greeted him with a mixture of boos and cheers. "Are you running for something?" asked Nixon. "No sir, Mr. President, are you?" shot back Rather. The smart-alecky reply solidified Rather's position as Nixon's least favorite TV reporter.

Rather later spent six years as a correspondent on *60 Minutes*; his pugnacious style fitted well in the show that invented confrontation journalism. But Rather's sights were set higher. As retirement approached for *Evening News* veteran Anchorman Walter Cronkite, Rather and Roger Mudd emerged as the two chief contenders to replace him. Though close to the same age, the pair seemed to represent different eras of TV journalism. Mudd was cerebral and low-key, the well-connected Washington insider. Rather was the brash, high-profile network terrier—and an undeniable star. Sometimes too much the star. For one well-publicized *60 Minutes* story, Rather traveled into Afghanistan disguised in native garb. He introduced himself to a rebel leader with the memorable line "Hello, my name is Rather." Critics hooted at the stunt and dubbed him Gunga Dan.

Nevertheless, Rather beat out Mudd for the anchor job, rankling some TV traditionalists in the process. In an effort to keep him from jumping to ABC, CBS gave Rather a record $22 million ten-year contract, a quantum leap in the pay for network journalists. The network also had to ask Cronkite politely to move up his retirement date to accommodate Rather's new contract. Cronkite agreed, but some insiders claim he was never happy about it.

Once he took possession of Uncle Walter's chair, Rather experienced a rough ride. Ratings began to dip, and CBS's image makers began tinkering with Rather's dress and demeanor. Early on, they put him in sweaters in an effort to soften his intensity. For a while, Rather tried hard to be warm and homespun, his writing full of purple prose and corny puns. (Before the start of the Reykjavik summit, he announced, "Ready, set, Gorbachev.") Later he reverted, with equal strain, to a straitlaced, sober, almost glum delivery.

CBS News executives admit that Rather is not a natural anchorman. "He tries his damnedest to look relaxed, but it is not in his nature," says *Evening News* Executive Producer Tom Bettag. "He tries to run through walls. He does clumsy things at times." Yet for all Rather's problems, the CBS *Evening News* retained its hold on first place in the ratings until last summer, when it dropped to third place. Staff morale had already plummeted after a wave of layoffs in the spring initiated by Chairman Tisch. Rather tried to rally the troops, appearing on a Writers Guild picket line and attacking the staff cutbacks in an op-ed column for the New York *Times*. But his own morale was sinking as well, and viewers could see it in his lethargic demeanor on screen.

Then came the evening last September when a U.S. Open tennis match threatened to run past the newscast's scheduled starting time of 6:30 p.m. Rather, in Miami for coverage of Pope John Paul II's visit, argued with network executives that if the match did not end on time, the newscast should be delayed instead of shortened. The match ended at 6:32, but when the network switched to Miami, Rather had left the studio. Six minutes passed before he could be rounded up and returned to his chair. Rather later apologized for the incident, but critics saw it as further evidence of his petulance, and also his power. (In addition to anchorman, Rather is managing editor of the evening newscast.) Even Cronkite, in an uncharacteristic rebuke, told an interviewer that he would have fired Rather for the transgression.

Rather's volatile behavior and the drooping ratings sparked rumors that his anchor job might be in jeopardy, or that a co-anchor might be foisted on him (prime candidate: Diane Sawyer). Though Tisch publicly expressed support, associates say he was growing disenchanted with his temperamental and decreasingly popular news star. "If Rather had been the manager of a Loew's hotel, Tisch would undoubtedly have fired him," says one source close to Tisch.

What may have saved Rather was a timely switch in ratings methodology by the A.C. Nielsen Co. When the company's new electronic People Meters went into operation in September (replacing viewer diaries), the CBS *Evening News* was suddenly and inexplicably back on top in the ratings. Rather, meanwhile, was given even more visibility as anchor of *48 Hours*, CBS's new prime-time documentary series. Even after the Bush brouhaha, no one is seriously predicting that Rather is in trouble. "Dan is the franchise of the CBS *Evening News*," says one former CBS executive. "He might make them nervous, but nobody is going to fire the man who is bringing home the ratings."

Still, last week's incident seemed to galvanize the journalistic community into a spirited debate over Rather's behavior. His chief rivals, ABC's Peter Jennings and NBC's Tom Brokaw, would offer no comment. But ABC's Ted Koppel, speaking at the DuPont–Columbia University awards for broadcast journalism in New York City, asserted that the problem was not Rather's questioning but that CBS had allowed Rather "to serve as high priest in the ceremonial de-wimping of the Vice President." Marvin Kalb, the former CBS and NBC correspondent who is now a professor at the Kennedy School at Harvard, was among those who defended Rather's tough tactics. "I thought Dan was assertive and aggressive in pursuit of questions that have gone unanswered for weeks," he said. Many others seemed offended. Los Angeles *Times* TV Critic Howard Rosenberg compared Rather to Captain Queeg in *The Caine Mutiny* and attacked his prosecutorial style: "There was no excuse for him assuming the roles of judge and jury in a newscast. ... Who appointed him America's shrieking ayatullah of truth?"

Clearly, Rather is suffering from the dual, and sometimes contradictory, demands that viewers and critics make of their TV anchormen. On one hand, they are expected to be seasoned reporters, not just newsreaders; Rather, Brokaw and Jennings all pride themselves on their occasional forays "into the street" to report stories. On the other hand, they are expected to be, in a sense, *above the fray.* ... But good reporters are not necessarily reassuring, and Olympian gods are not necessarily good reporters.

Rather's skills as a reporter, in short, are the very ones that seem to get him into hot water as an anchor. TV viewers were far more comfortable with Tom Brokaw's interview with Soviet Leader Gorbachev in December—deferential, dignified, comforting. Says Rather, "I was trained to ask questions, and to ask again until they are answered or it is clearly demonstrated that they aren't going to be answered. I didn't grow up as a reporter believing that my job was necessarily to be popular." That attitude may not be a prescription for success as a network anchor in 1988. But it does ensure that Rather's tenure, however long it lasts, will not be dull.

Max Robinson
"Tragic Fadeout"
by Marilyn Milloy

Max Robinson fought for blacks in television news, even after becoming the first black anchorman on network TV. Then his career crashed, for reasons that lie scattered like wreckage on the media landscape.

It was TV news but it wasn't really television. Twenty-five-year-old Max Robinson read the daily news briefs, true enough. But viewers saw only the word "News," flashed in bold letters across their screens. This was the way things were done in 1964 at the UHF station in Portsmouth, Virginia. People knew Robinson's mellifluous voice, but nobody knew his face.

That is, until one day when the eager young man persuaded a cameraman to remove the sign. Then, in violation of station rules, Max Robinson read the news for all to see.

The next day, he was fired.

Robinson's audacious act had startled the station brass. It also had ignited a firestorm among white viewers enraged that one of "those" people was allowed to work in the studio.

This, Robinson decided, was not how things should be. Always rebellious and given to self-indulgence, he set out on a dual and sometimes conflicting mission: to perfect his skills and to combat the TV industry's racism—his way.

Marilyn Milloy is Atlanta Bureau Chief of Newsday.

Fourteen years later, Max Cleveland Robinson became the first black anchorman on a TV network newscast, with nine million households around the country tuned in nightly to ABC. With this achievement he clearly had scored a coup, for in many ways Robinson had not changed since his Portsmouth days. Not only did he retain a capacity for breaking rules, he [was] still able to needle a system that was pitifully slow in bringing blacks into responsible positions.

Thus it was vintage Robinson who, in this hypersensitive job, one paying about $300,000 a year, suggested publicly that his own bosses were racists. It was a not-so-transformed Robinson, either, who occasionally left his colleagues wondering whether he would make air time, so angered had he become over the permeating scourge of racism.

Robinson served as a lightning rod: highly visible, crackling with electricity, an easy target. To this day, he remains the only black to have regularly anchored a weeknight newscast for an over-the-air network (Bernard Shaw has been anchoring for the Cable News Network since its debut in 1980). But the depth of Robinson's concerns and his gall were largely lost on the people who watched the smooth and gifted newsman. So were the details of his life.

It was no wonder, then, that when Robinson succumbed to AIDS shortly before Christmas, his death, at 49, seemed to have nothing of the context demanded by the public when high-profile personalities contract the stigmatizing disease. Here was a man who seemed so together, so *normal,* people said. What went wrong?

The answer is as complex as was Robinson himself.

Before he died, Robinson told friends that it was a woman, not a man, from whom he'd contracted AIDS. And at his memorial, the Rev. Jesse Jackson seemed pressed to make this point, what with homosexuality and dirty drug needles still believed the most common ways of acquiring the disease.

To a hushed crowd of more than 2,000 people who had jammed a Washington church to pay tribute, Jackson recounted Robinson's telling him, "Jesse, on this bed and on this Bible, it was not homosexuality. It was promiscuity. I'm not sure and know not where, not when, even on my dying bed — if it is my dying bed." He urged that his "predicament" be a lesson for his people.

To many who knew him, Robinson's affliction was not totally incomprehensible, given his racy style of living. Yet it was a lifestyle not far different from those of many of the rich and famous in the media.

He drank heavily, and while he strongly denied it, there were persistent rumors that he used drugs. The first marriage ended after five years, the second was annulled after two months, the third lasted a decade. He seemed never to go wanting for companionship, as women swooned over him.

Just how much Robinson's freewheeling lifestyle was fueled by his rage over race remains open to question, for even during those times he was said to be most content, this restless pace was often his way.

What seems somewhat more clear, and far more relevant, is *why* he railed so against the status quo and, in a strange way, against himself. Indeed, what seemed to distinguish Robinson was his stubborn refusal to play the insider's game, his propensity for going against the grain, his tendency to flirt with self-destruction.

In some ways, friends said, the reasons were apparent. Robinson had been a pioneer much of his life: as the first black reporter at one Washington station and as the first black anchorman in the capital, then nationally. And he knew he was having to reckon with emotions that were alien to his white counterparts: guilt over his meteoric success, the pressures of "representing the race," frustration over blacks' lack of power and under-representation in the media, anger over race conditions generally.

But, his friends say, the support he needed to negotiate the emotional maze was simply not evident. Instead, the higher he climbed professionally, the more alone he found himself — a problem that plagues many high-achieving African-Americans. Robinson found, to his torment, that his status was of little help in the drive to make things different.

There was resentment and friction from white colleagues who felt he hadn't paid his dues. Having "skipped some steps in his climb to the mountaintop," as a friend put it, Robinson already had bouts of self-doubt. But the hostility came as a surprise and, though few would know, it devastated him.

"We really had been dreamers and had such hopes," said Jewell Robinson Shepherd, one of Robinson's two sisters, and the one with whom he lived for a short while in the '60s. "We were always talking about how everything was going to work out, how black people would be given a chance, would be thought equal and worthy and how skin color wasn't going to be a measure of anything."

But with the '80s upon him and those dreams still, to him, mere dreams, Robinson began to withdraw. At times he would not show up for work, or arrive late. He would rail publicly against discrimination in his workplace, complain that what the white establishment wanted was not a black journalist with a different cultural and political sensitivity, but a clone.

He was a challenger, as Professor Shelby Steele, in *Harper's* magazine last year, labeled those blacks who tell whites, "If you're innocent of racism, then prove it." In refusing to simply be grateful for his prestigious job and go with the flow, Robinson "held [whites'] innocence hostage."

Any other course, Robinson seemed to be saying, would be selling out. And "the terrible thing about selling out," he told an audience of students a few months before he died, "is that you'll have nothing left to sell. . . . And believe me, I know in this country that once you have nothing left to sell, you are absolutely dispensable."

Challenging created a paradox: Robinson's unsolicited noises set him apart from many blacks who'd made it. At the same time, "Max lived in most successful black people," said Grayson Mitchell, a journalist friend, now a Chicago businessman. "What makes others different is that we manage to suppress all of that — the guilt, the anger — and compromise in ways Max would not compromise in order to make it in white America. . . . Max wanted to be dealt with on his terms."

It was in a lower-middle-class household in segregated Richmond, Virginia, that Robinson grew up in the 1940s and '50s, the second of four children. His father, Maxie Robinson, is a legend to many in Richmond: a star athlete in college, then the tough, no-nonsense and very successful coach of football, basketball, track and baseball at all-black Armstrong High School. He was also a history teacher, a strong-willed man with a dignified gait who demanded a lot from his students and, by most accounts, got it. Robinson's mother, Doris, who now lives in Norfolk, was a widely adored woman of great Christian fervor who taught school before her marriage and later became known as a spellbinding speaker in appearances at Richmond churches.

Young Max's was a snug and nurturing environment, despite the segregation he later says left an indelible mark on his psyche—the time he was seven and drank at a whites-only water fountain, only to be stared down by a mean-looking white man; riding by the whites-only swimming pool and wondering what it would be like to play in the water there. Not only were his teachers always encouraging him to do well so he could "give something back," his parents made sure he and his siblings were exposed to all manner of culture for, in their view, the sky was the limit.

"There was this whole community of people telling us we were special and important and wonderful, and that we were destined to be the leaders, if you will, of our race," said Shepherd, now an actress in Washington. And so in school Robinson reveled in discussions about the contributions blacks had made through time, particularly taking to a black history class where he studied such greats as W.E.B. DuBois and historian Carter G. Woodson.

At Armstrong, Robinson was friendly and well-liked, though something of a loner. Teachers and classmates remember him as a skinny, rather clumsy boy given far more to indulging in cerebral pastimes like philosophy, poetry and art—he liked drawing caricatures—than in sports. Unlike his younger brother, Randall, captain of the basketball team, "he was kind of awkward and just didn't seem that interested," recalled James Carter, a playmate who lived on his block.

Though Max did find his way onto the basketball team at one point, his shortcomings on the court were flagrant and seemed, to friends, the source of great disappointment to his hard-driving father. Maxie Robinson was tough on anybody who made mistakes, they said, but he seemed especially tough on his older son. "He would publicly lambaste him for not being able to play," said classmate Ervin Watson. This, others noted, produced tension between the two—and, some friends believe, stirred up complex feelings of insecurity in Robinson that lingered for most of his life. Shepherd said she does not doubt that her father was openly perplexed by his son's lack of athletic aplomb or that he may at times have said so, since it was his way. But "he always talked about the many strengths Max had and appreciated those." The more profound disappointment, she said, was in young Max himself, who wanted desperately to do better but just couldn't. Even during his last days, she said, he was regretting how he had never learned to skip as a child. "We were at his bedside, saying, '*Skip?*' [But] those things stay with you. You never forget the failures. Max didn't."

Still, Robinson excelled in the classroom, particularly in science and math, and established himself, eclectically, as a student leader, a dramatist and a dynamic orator who entered contests and won. So versatile was he that in his senior year, in 1957, he was voted Boy Most Likely to Succeed. "He really had a gift for words," said classmate Jewell Moore Poe. "He was very much a thinker." And, others said, a challenger. "If he wanted to say something in class," remembered Watson, "you couldn't have stopped him from saying it. ... He just didn't back down if he thought he was right."

Upon graduation, Robinson went to Oberlin College as one of a handful of Armstrong students offered the opportunity to attend a predominantly white school. Watson recalled that Robinson made headlines in the black weeklies because of the scholarships he received, about $7,000 worth, due mainly to his talents in science. But after a year of average work at Oberlin, he left. One good high school friend, Air Force Col. Anthony Manning, said he believed Robinson had his sights on political science or medicine. But somewhere along the way Robinson apparently lost interest in both. Clarence Page, a *Chicago Tribune* editorial writer who is completing the autobiography Robinson started, balked at the possibility of racial problems: "It was just your basic dropout case. He just wasn't motivated to continue." But "this was something he deeply regretted most of his life."

Robinson entered the Air Force, but got a medical discharge for asthmatic bronchitis after about a year, then studied Russian at its language school at Indiana University. He then returned to Virginia and took courses at predominantly black Virginia Union University, where he met his first wife, Eleanor Booker.

Robinson "was trying to find himself," said his mother, Doris Griffin. So for a while he was a disc jockey at a rhythm-and-blues radio station in Petersburg, Virginia. He also maintained dog kennels and sold used cars. But Robinson had a family to support, and his frustration was growing over his inability to find the kind of job that suited his talents and his financial needs.

It was when he landed the job at the now-defunct Portsmouth station that he began thinking that television might be his calling. By the time he was fired for his appearance on camera, he was convinced.

He drifted to Washington, D.C., where he sold furniture before getting his first big break, in a trainee program at WTOP, now WUSA. "He looked just great," said James Silman, who was program director then. "He wanted to learn, and we were looking for somebody." Silman started him out as a "floor director" who erected sets, cued talents, cleaned the studios.

Before long, Silman said, he realized Robinson was capable of doing a lot more. He secretly gave him a test one day during a visit by John Hayes, president of Post-Newsweek stations, which owned WTOP.

The two were in a control room and Silman said he asked Robinson, over the intercom, to help with an audio check by reading a newspaper. When Robinson finished, Silman said, he and Hayes "looked at each other and said, 'Oh, my God.' Not only did he look good, but he had great camera techniques and this wonderful voice. We moved him immediately to the news department."

Robinson began paying his dues there on mundane fire and robbery stories. But soon, in 1966, a competing station, WRC, snatched him, making him the station's first black reporter. There he flourished, winning six awards, including an Emmy, for "The Other Washington," a series on life in the depressed black Anacostia district.

Robinson was on a roll, and even the fraying of his marriage—it finally ended in 1968—didn't impede his ambitions. He seemed no longer fulfilled as "just" a reporter at WRC, and began asking for an anchor job. He was turned down, and said years later that management felt the time wasn't "right." He was convinced that it was discrimination.

"At WRC I would walk down the hall, speak to people, and they would look right through me," he once said. And so he left in 1969, returning to the station that had given him his start.

Back at WTOP, he worked as a reporter, but made known once again his eagerness to be out front. This time his wish was granted, and Robinson was elevated to anchor the midday news—by then he'd been reporting for less than five years. Within two years, he was teamed up with Gordon Peterson to anchor the 6 P.M. and 11 P.M. newscasts, the most prestigious job at the station.

"Max had great presence on the air," said Post-Newsweek Vice President James Snyder, then the station's news director. "He was in command all the time. I didn't have to say, 'Here is this interesting guy and after we've trained him for ten years, he'll be okay.' Max had it from the beginning."

Peterson and Robinson turned out to be a magical pair, with just the right combination of warmth and authority to electrify a market that was decidedly black in its inner city but predominantly white in the suburbs. "Whites identified with Max as much as the blacks did," said Bob Strickland, a reporter at WTOP then, as now. "He was Max, not Black Max." Within three years the team had made it to the top of the ratings charts, and largely remained there throughout Robinson's tenure, another half-dozen years.

Those years at WTOP, by all accounts, were some of Robinson's best. He endeared himself to Washington, and it to him. He spoke at black churches and schools and fundraisers, rarely turning down a request to help, even when it meant forking over substantial contributions of his own to this cause, that group. "Max really did love black people," said Mitchell, "and he loved being adored by them." When a group of Hanafi Muslims took over three downtown Washington buildings in 1977, their leader called Robinson, who helped negotiate the release of hostages. He became a role model (he was a founding member of the National Association of Black Journalists) and to the end of his life was being approached, friends say, by people who reminded him of how he'd given them direction and inspiration during those years.

He entertained regally, too, and his became the parties not to miss, what with their interesting mix of blacks and whites, artists and politicians. Dressed at times in colorful African garb, Robinson would meander from group to group, drink in hand, putting on the kind of irresistible charm that, between his marriages, buoyed his already-solid reputation as a ladies' man. He was, simply, fun and had a sense of humor that friends argue could rival the best comedians.

His interests were as varied as the company he kept. He collected art—Romare Bearden, Cézanne, Jacob Lawrence, Richard Hunt—with such passion that in the end his collection, estimated to be worth more than $500,000, grew burdensome, he said, and he began selling it off. But he particularly liked reading books, especially books on black history and race relations. These topics he could talk about for hours nonstop, his friends say. And he would. The fervor, naturally, spilled over into the newsroom.

"It wasn't that he would pounce on any occasion to preach about race and racism," said Bruce Johnson, who came to WTOP as a rookie reporter and became close to Robinson, "but if you were open to that, Max was always available to talk about it."

And so while he could sometimes seem arrogant and not really into the grunt work of the journalist—always "strutting above the troops," as Johnson put it—Robinson could often be found holding court in his office, as at home, with young black reporters eager to get ahead. He became their advocate. "He was in and out the manager's office all the time with concerns about how young blacks were being treated in the newsroom," said WUSA's editorial director, Rich Adams, who was a reporter, then assistant news director during Robinson's tenure. "He was constantly butting heads with assignment editors over news coverage, too." Adams said that the preponderance of crime stories with black culprits irritated Robinson, and he complained that blacks were rarely interviewed on stories having nothing to do with race.

"I never felt any great joy at speaking out," he once told the *Washington Post*. "But I believe when there are fewer of us, we have to speak out. Malcolm [X] once said, 'When it hurts, don't suffer quietly.'"

Mitchell, a *Washington Post* reporter during those early years, recalled that Robinson was so intense that he occasionally convened "tribunals" at his house to query black reporters who he thought had violated some code of ethics in their portrayal of blacks. This was a throwback to his high school days, when Robinson played prosecutor in a student court dealing with minor rule infractions. Now, with black consciousness in full swing nationwide, Robinson was eager to use his talents to capitalize. "He was the self-appointed conscience and policeman for what he thought to be the ethical standards for black journalists," said Mitchell. "He just didn't think the journalist was this objective person in the bleachers." Though the meetings often ended up becoming cathartic "shrink sessions" for the handful of local black reporters trying to cope with the lonely grind at their jobs, some of them, said Mitchell, "didn't like being told whether what they were doing was or wasn't in the interest of blacks." But, as in his early years, "Max left no room for contradiction. If you were weak and mealy-mouthed, you just couldn't survive around him."

This intensity never waned. The higher his status, the greater his worldly trappings, his friends say, the bigger Robinson seemed to calculate his responsibility to "the cause," which in the '70s seemed particularly formidable, as there were so few blacks in the business. Robinson's new wife, Beverly Hamilton—they wed in 1973, some time after his annulled two-month marriage—was just as devoted to social change in her job as a social worker. The two, friends say, made a dynamic and inspirational pair in those days.

But Robinson was easily frustrated. "He felt he had the power to change things," said Adams, "and when he didn't see change right then, it bothered him deeply. He took everything so seriously." Indeed, said Adams, "He was the kind of guy who could read something about [racial] injustice in Mississippi and while it'd be something you and I would shake our heads at and say, 'What a shame,' Max, honestly, would brood for two days."

Only now, the brooding had another dimension with the death of Maxie Robinson. Depression would set in, and deep, friends say. Many times drinking would accompany the bouts and, on occasion, Robinson would find himself the talk of the town.

One night in 1973 after attending a restaurant opening, the anchorman and a few friends returned to his Washington apartment. Robinson had been drinking unusually heavily, said Bob Strickland, who was there that night, and before long he disappeared to his bedroom. "He just got into this depressed mood," Strickland said. When Robinson emerged, he was toting a pistol. He walked quickly onto his patio balcony, and before his guests could digest what they'd seen, he was firing at the ground.

"Everybody began yelling and screaming and saying, 'Max, what the hell!'" said Strickland. "I was saying, 'But you can't do this.' And he said, 'You're not thinking like those white people, are you?'"

According to Strickland, Robinson "just kept talking a lot about the racial situation generally, and about his father," who had died three weeks earlier. After emptying the pistol, Robinson began pounding it on a table in an effort to open and reload it. "He did this again and again," Strickland said. By the time the spree was over, Robinson had fired at least 20 rounds.

Some friends speculated that the incident grew, at least in part, out of anxiety over those early years during which Robinson believed he had not sufficiently satisfied his father, but also out of sheer love for the old man. He clearly idolized Maxie Robinson, and later erected an abstract stone sculpture on the patio of his house with a plaque in his father's honor. "I had a sense that there was an unfinished agenda, an unwritten chapter, in his relationship with his father," said Strickland. "But to the extent that can be blamed for his torment is open to question."

In any event, Robinson was arrested and fined $25 for illegal use of a firearm. He apologized, on-air, the next night. "Even a newsman gets out of joint once in a while," he said. "I am the same Max Robinson you have always known, except that today I'm a little bit wiser."

But problems continued and manifested themselves in unexplained absences from work. "I'm the one who'd get the call from Max's wife at 4:30 saying he wasn't coming in for the 6 P.M. news," said Adams.

Snyder said he realized Robinson drank a bit much at times, but in a business familiar with heavy drinking, "who's going to throw the first stone?" Although he missed newscasts more than was desirable and even showed up tipsy on occasion, Snyder went on, "it never got to the point where it was damaging to the operation."

Bruce Johnson recalled how he and Robinson went out between newscasts on Robinson's birthday and "got truly wasted." Returning to the studio, Robinson took his seat before the camera and, when the cue light came on, "he didn't miss a beat."

But it finally became apparent to some that Robinson was having to deal with a lot more than was evident to most. Snyder recalled the time the anchorman came to his house for dinner, and a young priest friend was visiting. "Max was very well known by then and the priest said, 'What is it that you do?'" Robinson told him, Snyder said, and the priest blurted somewhat jokingly, "Oh, you must be the token up there."

"Well it became frosty in there after that," said Snyder. "I mean, that was the end of the dinner party.

"The point," he concluded, "is that those things happened to Max."

There were other anxieties. Jim Vance, the star anchorman at WRC who confessed to a drug addiction several years ago and was rehabilitated before making a much-heralded comeback, said he hung out with Robinson into the wee hours many times during those days.

"One of the things that I think was eating at him, and eats at others of us, is a sense of impotence that almost increases proportionately with your level of apparent success," said Vance. "You start doing okay and you start doing a little bit better than okay, then you notice yourself being distanced from your brethren. You do all you can do—and Max certainly reached back—but the more you do, the more the dimensions of the despair become apparent and you get to the point that the anger is overwhelming."

At that point, Vance said, "You really need people around you who can see things in a different perspective, who can somehow make you know that it's not your responsibility to make everything right for everybody right at that minute, because then you start decimating yourself. Fatigue comes along with anger and frustration ... and it doesn't always release itself in constructive ways."

Robinson, his friends say, didn't always have people around who understood the frustration. "*He* was the king of the hill," said Mitchell. "I think a lot of blacks who were struggling themselves felt, What could we tell him?" And besides, said Vance, "You can't have a man who's breaking down barriers admit that he has a problem."

When the call came in 1978 to join ABC's "World News Tonight," Robinson, with some reluctance about moving from Washington to Chicago, took the job. (His last day on the air was proclaimed Max Robinson Day by the Washington city council.) It was fresh, at the least, he figured. A new challenge, a new arena. An opportunity to truly exercise power.

But the challenge at ABC turned out to be more multidimensional than he'd anticipated. In fact, by his own account, it was horrid.

For starters, the three-anchorman format was new, untested, and Robinson in some ways had the toughest assignment. Frank Reynolds, the consummate Washington reporter, remained in Washington; Peter Jennings, an established foreign correspondent, remained overseas, in London. It was Robinson who, shifted to Chicago, had to adjust to another part of the country, and beyond that, to cover breaking news stories, something he'd not done with any regularity for years, or shown any desire to do.

Much was riding on the success of the format, for this had been a stormy time for ABC News. It was routinely last in the ratings, and with the arrival of an off-beat Roone Arledge from the sports department, confusion seemed the order of the day.

Arledge, now group president of ABC News and Sports, has told the *Washington Post* that Robinson didn't seize the moment to try to make the situation work, but he also has conceded that there was a tendency among others to dismiss Robinson outright as incapable of carrying his weight as a reporter.

Not only was there pressure, then, to prove himself as a plane-grabbing reporter who could compete with those who'd spent their working lives doing just that, there was some bitterness, Robinson's friends say, that this was now even expected of him. "The bottom line is not that the anchor gets out there and gets his hands dirty, but that he looks good and sounds good," said Bob Reid, a producer for "Entertainment Tonight" who for more than 15 years has handled key network jobs. "That's what Max was accustomed to do and he was superb. Now, suddenly he was being judged by a different standard."

There were jealousies and resentment. "He was always being bad-mouthed," said one ABC insider in Washington. "The contempt was completely in-house, but it was something that filtered down to the lower levels and just took on a life of its own. It propagated until people here were talking about Max as if he were virtually a pariah. . . . It would have taken an extraordinarily strong person to survive that environment."

By his own admission, Robinson became paranoid, convinced that his Chicago colleagues were deliberately holding back information, not helping in ways they would have helped others of his stature. He began calling his friends—Reid, and *Fortune* magazine reporter Joel Dreyfuss among them—trying to lure them to Chicago to give him a hand.

"I got the sense that nobody had taken Max by the hand and said, 'This is the way we do this and this, and don't worry about that,'" said Reid. "Not coming up through the ranks can be very hostile, very alien—a maze and a morass, particularly when somebody is inventing the wheel."

Ray Nunn, his first producer, conceded that some of Robinson's frustrations "were not baseless." He said that Robinson had been led to believe that if he just lobbied hard for air time he could get it. But because of the mandates of news—that was a time of transition in administrations, and Washington was routinely the center of attention—"it could never be that way. He was given the wrong spear."

Inhibiting him the most, Nunn believed, [were] Robinson's own doubts about his talents. "He was a journalist with a sharp mind. But he never appreciated how good he was, how good he could become." In an interview with the *Washington Post* last May, Robinson acknowledged the problem: "I think one of my basic flaws has been a lack of esteem, not feeling great about myself. I never could do enough or be good enough. In fact, it probably was the essential problem I had throughout my career, throughout my life."

Yet, Milt Weiss, another of Robinson's producers, said Robinson "had an unusual ability to talk to all sorts of people. . . . He could get anybody to open up to him." And so he did have some successes: covering the nuclear reactor accident at Three Mile Island, floods in Indiana, unemployment in the steel mills, the problems of Dennis Kucinich, the flamboyant young mayor who was ousted after Cleveland went into default. Colleagues said Robinson seemed to do best when he could find an underdog.

But Chicago was not Washington, and Robinson did not have the cocoon of an adoring public to cushion the blows when they came. There were constant reports, mostly from columnist Gary Deeb, then writing in the *Sun-Times*, about Robinson's off-camera behavior and his on-the-job competence, or lack of it. He routinely was labeled "just a pretty face, a pretty voice."

Despite this load, Robinson forged ahead, still offering himself as mentor, man with the big heart. He could be found often in bars, buying drinks for everybody, mesmerizing the crowd with his stories and funny jokes. And, as in Washington, he still entertained, this time, though, at a fancy home on Lake Michigan, where guests could dock their boats, and later, at his nearby art studio loft.

"You couldn't *not* like Max. Everyone wanted a piece of him," said Monte Newman, who was to lure Robinson to a local Chicago station after he left ABC. Newman recalled being moved when Robinson showed up at an awards dinner with Malik, youngest of his four children. The two were dressed alike, in tuxedoes, and Robinson was noticeably proud, grinning from ear to ear. "How could you not think something special of this man?" asked Newman.

Yet at work colleagues noticed dramatic mood swings, weeks of apparently enjoying life and then days where Robinson was deeply depressed, bitter. Occasionally he'd show up dangerously late. "Max never let the show go to black," said Nunn, "but there were times when people were very, very worried." Friends report 3 A.M. calls from a Robinson in distress. Knowing about this, Strickland of WUSA said he'd call Robinson periodically from Washington to check up on him. At times, he said, Robinson reported doing fine. "He'd say, 'Oh, there're a couple of people nipping at my ankles . . . but that's okay. We know who the racists are.'" At other times, though, "you'd hear this sullen voice and when I'd ask how he was, he'd say, 'What do you mean by that?' And when I'd say I hear they're not treating you right, he'd say very snidely, 'Always the reporter, aren't you Bob?' He could be very abrasive . . . almost obnoxious, and you'd promise yourself you've washed your hands of him once and for all, but then you'd always come back . . . Max had his way of making you do that."

At first Robinson seethed and complained within the organization about his frustrations and rebelled in little ways. He refused to socialize with ABC's corporate advertisers, Mitchell said. "Max thought that was improper. He said he didn't sell advertisements. I'd say, 'Well, I'm counseling you to go, if only for an hour. It won't hurt.' And he'd say, 'Do you hear what you're saying?' You could never argue with Max's substance. But I knew it would only be a matter of time. This was a career out of control."

Robinson's anger soon was finding an airing in public places. On the speaking circuit in late 1980, he said in Los Angeles that Ronald Reagan's election was a sorrowful day for blacks. In other speeches, he complained about the industry generally and made it clear that his experiences at ABC were not all as sweet as they might have appeared. Lynn Small, marketing director of the Chicago Transit Authority, and other friends say they told Robinson to cool it. "You can nibble at the hand that feeds you," Small recalled telling him, "but don't bite it off." Robinson insisted on doing things his way, though. And in February, 1981, when he spoke at Smith College, he really lashed out. But this time the media picked up on the message and shared it with the larger public.

In the speech, Robinson complained about the skewed picture of the "orgy of patriotism" that was reported after Reagan's inauguration and the simultaneous release of the Iran hostages. He said the media were looking at the world through "cracked glasses" and complained that he and other blacks at ABC, as at other networks, had largely been left out of the inauguration and the hostage story.

He accused ABC of fostering its own subtle brand of racism, saying executives wanted him to speak out "like any old white boy" and not incorporate his history, culture or views—"and certainly not speak out of experience."

Robinson predicted there'd be criticism of the speech, but said that "only by talking about raciam . . . by taking a professional risk . . . will I take myself out of the mean, racist trap all black Americans find themselves in."

It was a risk indeed, and Arledge immediately called Robinson to New York for what turned into a three-hour meeting. Eight years later, outside the church at Robinson's memorial, Arledge recalled that Robinson had enlightened him at their meeting and in the period that followed. As a result of Robinson's input, Arledge said, as others have, he set in motion changes at ABC News that still affect blacks today. Now, for example, a black commentator appears occasionally on Sunday's "This Week with David Brinkley" show; Robinson had argued that blacks can be pundits, too—an idea some colleagues said was rebuffed initially.

But at the time, the repercussions of Robinson's public outbursts were great, and he issued a statement that attempted to defuse his charges about the company that paid his salary. Blacks still hailed him as a man with guts.

"We knew we could all have made that speech, and we knew corporate denial would come down on our heads like a sledgehammer," said Roger Wilkins, author, scholar and fellow with the Institute for Policy Studies, who once wrote for the *Washington Post* and *The New York Times*. "And so there was, at that moment in his career, the summation of the excruciating dilemma of most black journalists: to see and know more truth than the cultural and racial limitations of your society will let you tell."

Robinson tempered his public remarks after the Smith speech, but he brought back ill feelings when in July, 1983, he missed the funeral of his co-anchor Frank Reynolds. Producer Weiss said he and Robinson, who was to sit next to Nancy Reagan at the funeral, planned to fly to Washington together. But when Weiss arrived at Robinson's place the next morning, he said, no one answered after several knocks and doorbell rings, and he left alone. Robinson told him later, Weiss said, that he had not been able to sleep and took prescription sleeping pills that, in combination with liquor, made him pass out.

The episode was another Robinson embarrassment, and while ABC executives publicly played it down, it was widely believed to have been the last straw.

Within months, Jennings became the sole anchor and Robinson was moved to Washington to do the weeknight "News Briefs" between prime-time shows and anchor the Saturday evening newscasts. Robinson would later recall being teased as the highest paid per-minute TV person in history. He clearly didn't like it. It wouldn't last long.

Chicago station WMAQ soon appeared in hot pursuit. The bosses there wanted Robinson to co-anchor the weeknight news and were willing to pay him half-a-million dollars a year. It was a time of new beginnings: He'd recently ended the marriage to Beverly Hamilton. He left ABC and began at WMAQ in March, 1984. As at the network when he arrived, ratings at the station were pitiful, and Robinson was seen as the man who could best help turn them around. But, as at ABC, problems developed immediately.

The new anchor team lacked the chemistry that was so palpable between Robinson and Peterson in Washington. Nothing clicked. To boot, there were rivalries inside the newsroom, longtime station anchors "looking over their shoulders," as one insider put it, to make sure they were not being eased out of prestigious jobs by the former network star. The station continued to wallow in its turmoil. Robinson complained about feeling he was being undermined, of people tampering with his Teleprompter, of technicians deliberately leaving his microphone on so that viewers heard him chew out studio personnel. He told friends that things were so bad at WMAQ they were making ABC look like paradise. "There was no question he was unhappy there," said Monte Newman, then general manager.

And so, Robinson left one day in June, 1985, to attend an Emmy award ceremony in Cleveland. He never came back.

He told the *Washington Post* last year that he was treated by a doctor in Cleveland, then entered a medical rehabilitation program "to deal with the problems I was going through at that time."

After completing the program, in the summer of '86, Robinson tried to pick up the pieces. He did some public speaking and writing and took reporting assignments for "Essence," the TV feature show that grew out of the black women's magazine of that name. But the alcohol problem was still there, and his mother, Doris Griffin, encouraged him to seek help anew: "I had been on him a long time, you know, like mothers do. I didn't let it rest." In mid-'87 Robinson was treated at the Hazeldon Drug and Alcohol Rehabilitation Center in Minneapolis; he denied to the *Washington Post* that he had a drug problem.

He came out of Hazeldon determined to beat his alcohol problem, friends recalled. It was then that Robinson discovered he had AIDS. He told only a few close friends—even his mother didn't learn of it for a while.

Robinson remained in Chicago for the most part while he battled his illness, spending much of his time in his studio painting, which, friends said, gave him great spiritual pleasure. He even returned, as he always had, to his class reunion in Richmond. It was the thirtieth reunion this time, and they chose to honor him with a special award and make him the keynote speaker. No one had an inkling that Robinson was dying.

"Everybody knew that his struggle, being the first and all, had been so difficult," said Evelyn Graves, the president of Robinson's senior class alumni group.

"We just wanted to tell him we appreciated what he had done." It was the biggest reunion ever.

Several months later, in December, 1987, Robinson was admitted to St. Francis Hospital in Blue Island, Illinois, in critical condition. Robinson himself has recounted how he went "to hell and back" there, for the following February, he was released and for the better part of the year seemed to be making remarkable progress.

His hospitalization, meanwhile, had spurred an outpouring of support from scores of friends, including Oprah Winfrey, Sydney Poitier, Bill Cosby and Jesse Jackson. Others who were in regular contact say he seemed more peaceful than ever, meditative. Robinson himself noted this transformation when he was honored by Howard University's communication students at their Frederick Douglass awards dinner last November.

In the final analysis, he told them, money and material things "won't count. I can assure you—I used to have plenty of it ... Thought I was cute ... But I think I've grown that much. The love of friends and acquaintances, that's the most important thing."

Robinson had moved to Washington when his condition worsened. He wanted to be near his brother and sisters: Randall, who heads the lobbying group TransAfrica; Jean Yancy, public relations director for the Duke Ellington School of the Performing Arts, and Jewell Shepherd, the actress.

"He was never bitter," said Pat Fleming, a longtime friend who visited Robinson at Howard University Hospital. "He never said, 'Goddamn it, why me?'" In fact, she recalled, Robinson made the visits remarkably easy. "He was always ready to laugh, share a joke."

One Chicago friend said that, while still in Chicago, Robinson even talked openly about death. As soon as he got to heaven, "I'm going to sit down with [the late Chicago Mayor] Harold [Washington] and say, 'What the hell's going on?'" The friend said Robinson also described how he wanted to be buried. "He said his body should be wrapped in African cloth and put in the bottom of a pine box. He said, 'I want to be buried the way the West Africans were buried.'"

Robinson died December 20 at Howard University Hospital, but because of a Washington, D.C., law governing the burial of people with infectious diseases, his body was cremated.

Max Robinson, by his insistence on demonstrating integrity when it would have been far easier to shut up, "set a standard for us all," says Gil Noble, the host of WABC's "Like It Is."

For many, his career served, too, to point up the ugliest flaws in an industry where blacks, by and large, have made only marginal advances. "We work in settings where we've seen less competent white people supported, nurtured, apologized for, helped along and elevated," said Joel Dreyfuss. "Black people rarely get any of those positives."

Wallace Terry, author of the book "Bloods," and the first black correspondent for *Time* magazine, agreed. "When the media moguls look in your face," he said, "they do not see their son ... Max knew this."

Even in his dying days, Robinson spoke of that, and how, because of it, blacks should never think they've "arrived." "As visible as he was, for every person who said he was great, there was another who took the opportunity to put him in 'his place,'" said Reid. "I think this propelled him, too. ... There are certainly people who have obtained high positions and you barely know who they are. But Max was always trying to achieve the greater good for black people."

"He was always asking how we can maintain our integrity in an environment that's so contrived and superficial," said one ABC employee who worked with Robinson.

And at the Howard University program, where he made one of his last public appearances, he was still hounding this point.

Though thin, graying and using a cane—he hadn't been sure if he could "drag this body" to come, he told the students after receiving a long, standing ovation—Robinson gave thanks to those who had struggled before him. But he warned that things were still difficult.

"When you walk into the newsrooms of America and take your places, and at the first thing that goes wrong you say, 'Oh, my God'—that's the right one to call," he said, to some laughter. He quickly warned the students not to be surprised.

"This country," he went on, "remains very much a racist country. And there will be temptations to sell out."

But you must "try to keep your integrity," Robinson said finally, his voice quivering now, his eyes teary, "because you're going to find out in life that in the end, that's all you've got."

Diane Sawyer

"Star Power"

by Richard Zoglin

First there are the blond-haired good looks: striking but somehow wholesome, more high school prom queen than Hollywood glamour puss. Then there's the rich, honeyed voice: husky and authoritative, but free of the severe tone affected by some females in TV news. As a reader of the news, she is masterly: businesslike but warm, her eyes now wide with the drama of the day, now crinkling ever so slightly with concern. Diane Sawyer doesn't just deliver the news, she performs it.

But there's more than mere show-biz flair here. Sawyer is a fully credentialed reporter who covered Three Mile Island and the Iran hostage crisis. Later she demonstrated smarts and interviewing skills as co-anchor of the *CBS Morning News.* As a member of the formidable *60 Minutes* team since 1984, she has traveled from the garbage mounds of Cairo to the heart of the AIDS plague in Uganda, profiled the likes of Corazon Aquino and James Michener, and given then candidate George Bush perhaps his toughest TV grilling on the Iran-*contra* scandal. If she never seemed an indispensable cog in the powerful engine that is *60 Minutes,* she was no Tinkertoy either.

Have a conversation with Sawyer, and you cannot help coming away impressed. Intelligent, articulate, polished—and a bit calculated. (She calls a reporter at home to amend her earlier list of favorite reading: add Doctorow's *Billy Bathgate* and Mann's *Tonio Kröger* to a shelf that already features Flaubert, Henry James and John Fowles.) In earnest, carefully molded sentences, she strives to dispel the notion that she is strictly a TV creation. "I really love what you learn every day in the business," she says. "I love the breathtaking way we walk into people's lives and ask them anything we want and then leave. For a moment you have available to you the whole universe of a person's life—the pain and the suffering and the joy and the struggle. You can learn from it and take it with you and then come back the next day with somebody else. That's what I like to do."

Is it any wonder that Sawyer, at 43, is the hottest newswoman in television? The sort of star news executives battle over, make promises to, open their wallets for? Last February, after more than ten years at CBS, she was hired away by ABC for a reported $1.6 million a year. The primary lure: the chance to join Sam Donaldson as co-anchor of *Prime Time Live,* the new weekly show that will debut this Thursday at 10 P.M. EDT. In addition, ABC dangled occasional fill-in anchor duty on *World News Tonight* and *Nightline.* The prospect of losing Sawyer so rattled CBS's bigwigs that they virtually handed her a blank check in an effort to keep her; then, when she was irretrievably gone, they ran out and hired another high-priced star, NBC's Connie Chung, to fill the gap and save some face.

And yet the question nags: Is Sawyer really worth it? Indeed, are any of TV's high-profile news stars worth the money they are paid, the power bestowed upon them, the fuss made over them? At least a dozen network-news personalities currently earn more than a million dollars a year and vie for a few high-visibility showcases. Traditionally, these slots were limited to the morning and evening newscasts, but they are spreading into prime time as well. Along with Sawyer's program, this week will see the debut of another magazine show, NBC's *Yesterday, Today & Tomorrow.* Its hosts: Mary Alice Williams, a former CNN anchor hired by NBC to much fanfare in March; Chuck Scarborough, a popular local anchorman for New York City's WNBC-TV; and Maria Shriver, a Kennedy. CBS, meanwhile, is in the process of revamping its four-year-old magazine show *West 57th* around its newest star anchor, Chung.

In the commerce of TV news, these personalities probably earn their pay. Stars draw viewers, and that means higher ratings and higher ad revenue for the network. TV's top-rated magazine show, *60 Minutes,* earns an estimated $40 million a year for CBS; *20/20* brings in $15 million to $20 million annually for ABC. In a survey conducted for *Time* by Yankelovich Clancy Shulman, 52 percent of TV viewers polled said they consider the anchor "very important" in choosing which network newscast to watch, though only 41 percent feel that anchors deserve to be paid a million dollars.

The crucial question, however, is not whether news stars deserve the money but whether they deserve the stature. Although most are competent reporters, they have reached their positions largely because of qualities that have little to do with journalism: the way they look, the tone of their voices, their on-camera charm. Yet they have influence that betokens great wisdom and judgment. They are the people America listens to, relies on, trusts. The major events of the day are filtered through their eyes and ears. News becomes bigger news simply because they are present—in Paris for a presidential visit or Tiananmen Square for a nation's aborted experiment with democracy. The danger is that as stars become more and more important in the high-stakes world of TV journalism, they are overwhelming the news they purport to report.

Sawyer, more than any of her colleagues, embodies all the contradictions of TV news: that uneasy mix of journalism and show business, reporting and acting, substance and style. Her experience as a reporter, while not negligible, is on the slender side. Sawyer came to network news rather late, at 32, after spending nearly eight years as an aide to President (and then ex-President) Richard Nixon. As a correspondent, she won respect for her doggedness and intelligence, but she was helped by some shrewd career moves and smart packaging. At *60 Minutes,* for instance, she benefited from a corps of the best producers in TV news; still, according to insiders, she had difficulty with the format and was less productive than the show's other correspondents. "She's a monumental talent," says executive producer Don Hewitt. "But her coming to the broadcast didn't do that much for us. And her leaving has not even remotely crippled *60 Minutes.*" (She will be replaced this fall by Meredith Vieira and Steve Kroft, formerly of *West 57th.*)

Few TV newspeople, moreover, have moved in such glittery social circles. Sawyer has kept company with a raft of celebrities, from Warren Beatty to Henry Kissinger, and last year married director Mike Nichols. She was the subject of a glamorous (too glamorous for some of her colleagues) Annie Leibovitz photo spread in *Vanity Fair* magazine. At CBS she cultivated friendships with founder William Paley and president Laurence Tisch, both of whom have taken a personal interest in her career. Says a veteran CBS hand: "She's the best politician I've ever come across."

"Ambitious" is a word often used to describe Sawyer, but the fact is that others have had ambitions for her as well. In 1986, as her CBS contract neared renewal, Sawyer was avidly pursued by NBC. To keep her, CBS upped her salary to $1.2 million and promised to give her additional projects besides

60 Minutes: subbing for Dan Rather on the *CBS Evening News* and hosting a series of *Person to Person* specials, patterned after the old Edward R. Murrow interview series.

But the anchor stints were sparse (reportedly because Rather was jealous of her), and *Person to Person* never got off the ground, largely because of Hewitt's resistance to letting his *60 Minutes* star do outside work. That left an opening for ABC News president and chief starmaker Roone Arledge. In May 1988 he approached Sawyer with a proposal to co-anchor a new prime-time show he was developing. She declined, saying she did not want to leave *60 Minutes* in the lurch as it was gearing up for a new season. But when Arledge tried again in January, she was more receptive. A deal was consummated in two weeks. "I always thought Diane was very good," says Arledge, "but I never had anything right for her until I came up with this show. Look at the success that Barbara Walters has had: she is set apart from the rest of the industry. I think Diane will have that same kind of success."

Just what the new show will be was still in flux just days before airtime. Produced by Richard Kaplan, formerly of *Nightline,* the live weekly hour will be a mix of interviews, reports on breaking news stories and town meeting-like discussions. Sawyer describes it as a "lateral slice" of the week's news. Arledge compares its free-form structure to Olympics coverage: "The idea is that we will be all over the world where things are happening." What is most apparent is that *Prime Time Live* has been predicated on—and will succeed or fail because of—the chemistry between its two stars.

It's a match that might have been made in a Hollywood mogul's heaven: the loudest reporter on the White House lawn meets the classiest lady in TV news—"a sonata for harp and jackhammer," in Sawyer's words. The pair represent different roads to TV stardom as well. Donaldson, unlike most of his fellow TV news stars, gained fame because of his brash, sometimes abrasive reporting rather than his on-camera charm or polish. He and Sawyer plan to engage in unrehearsed, possibly disputatious colloquies about issues, but Donaldson insists that the clashes won't turn into routs. "One of my fears was that I would be perceived as the bully," he says. "But if we have a disagreement, Diane is not going to be intimidated. I will probably be the one getting the sympathy votes." "We have a natural adversarial relationship on a lot of issues," says Sawyer. "But it's not going to be 'Diane, you ignorant slut!'"

The star system, of course, is hardly a new phenomenon in TV news: Murrow, Walter Cronkite, and Huntley and Brinkley were certainly as popular as any of the current luminaries. But salaries and network bidding wars entered a new phase in 1976, when Arledge lured Walters away from NBC for one million dollars a year. The rise of superagents like Richard Leibner (who represents Sawyer, Rather, Shriver and Mike Wallace, among other network news stars) has brought about an escalation of salaries and an increase in the clout these personalities wield.

Today, as the networks fight to retain their dwindling audiences, prime-time news programming is becoming more desirable because it costs only about half as much to produce as entertainment fare. And to compete in the glitzy arena of *The Cosby Show* and *Dallas,* stars are a must. Other entertainment elements are creeping into these shows as well. On *Prime Time Live,* Sawyer and Donaldson will be joined by an unusual (for a news show) featured player: a live studio audience. Both *Yesterday, Today & Tomorrow* and the revamped *West 57th* will feature dramatized "re-creations" of events, a dubious enterprise that blurs the line between news and entertainment. (Even ABC's *World News Tonight* tried the technique two weeks ago, with mock-documentary footage ostensibly showing suspected spy Felix Bloch handing a briefcase to a Soviet agent. Anchor Peter Jennings last week apologized on the air that the footage had not been clearly labeled as a simulation.)

On the evening newscasts, too, stars are being hyped more than ever. Facing growing competition for the news viewer — from cable outlets like CNN, aggressive local stations and syndicated shows — the networks are trying to stress what makes them distinctive: namely, their anchors. That's why Rather, Jennings and Tom Brokaw can be seen jetting off to Eastern Europe or China whenever the President (or a Soviet leader) hops an airplane. Network executives gamely defend such trips on journalistic grounds, but they are primarily promotional gimmicks meant to showcase the network's resident Bigfoot. "We're almost defining news in such a way as to say something's not important unless an anchor is there," says Everette Dennis, executive director of the Gannett Center for Media Studies. "That's regrettable. Sometimes the specialists on a particular subject ought to be the ones dominating the coverage, not the anchors, who are by definition generalists."

News personalities, of course, bring special skills to their jobs that are not always appreciated. They must be able not only to report the news but to communicate it effectively. An appealing on-camera demeanor is no less important than a writer's prose style or a magazine's layout. "You have to be a special combination of person to be the focal point of a successful show," says NBC News president Michael Gartner, a former newspaper editor. "You have to be a good journalist, and you have to be able to deliver the message — which a print person doesn't have to do — in person, in somebody's house."

Yet an excessive focus on stars has its costs for the news division. For one thing, it diverts resources from bread-and-butter reporting. Salaries for top people keep going up even as the networks trim their news budgets to the bone. Says former CBS News president Ed Joyce: "You simply cannot pay a large stable of news stars these million-dollar salaries in the diminished economy that now exists in television without it coming from somewhere. My concern is that it is happening at the expense of the basic responsibility of network news organizations: to maintain bureaus overseas, to maintain bureaus domestically, and to cover the news coherently and responsibly."

What's more, these news stars — whom the networks must keep happy at all costs — are wielding more and more power behind the scenes. CBS's Rather, who is managing editor of the *CBS Evening News* as well as its anchor, is a force to reckon with at CBS News, with a major say in the assignment of reporters and even news executives. NBC's Brokaw too has been accused of becoming an "anchor monster," of engineering the departure of former News president Lawrence Grossman and of being reluctant to yield the spotlight to correspondents who might threaten him, such as Chris Wallace (who has left the network for ABC's *Prime Time Live*). In order to keep *Nightline*'s Ted Koppel happy, ABC gave him an unprecedented contract that allowed him to set up a production company and make news specials for both ABC and for independent distribution.

The anchors insist that their power has been overrated. "Careers did not go into decline at NBC because anyone argued with me," says Brokaw. "I protected Chris Wallace. I said it was a mistake to lose him." CBS News president David Burke has clipped Rather's wings a bit by shifting some of the anchorman's supporters out of key executive positions.

Then there is the problem of what to do when stars collide. Sawyer and Rather are a case in point. The CBS anchorman insists that he did not prevent Sawyer from anchoring the *CBS Evening News* and that he even told her she would be considered the front runner if the network decided he needed a co-anchor. Those close to Rather, however, are skeptical that he—or either of the other two network anchormen—would willingly agree to share his platform with a dynamic female like Sawyer.

Sawyer has proved that she can fend for herself in the corridors of power. Her determination to reach the top rung on the network ladder has been matched by her adeptness at making the right moves on the way up. That political savvy probably dates from her Louisville childhood. Her father was a Republican county executive active in state politics; her mother was a teacher. At 17, Diane won the America's Junior Miss competition. Her talent: reading an original poem about the Civil War and singing songs representing the North and South. A newspaper account at the time described Sawyer as a straight-A student who "wants to study foreign languages, for a possible career in diplomatic and foreign service. Her other interests include journalism."

Hearing that today, Sawyer laughs in surprise: "Really! I thought I wandered aimlessly into this profession." She went to Wellesley, majored in English and marched in one campus protest—against mandatory Bible class. ("I have to confess I was ambivalent about it, because I loved Bible class.") Meanwhile, she suffered through an identity crisis and an undernourished social life, which she traces to the Junior Miss "aberration." "I only dated four or five times in college," she says. "I went to my first mixer my first year, and I heard some guy say to his date, 'That can't be her. She's nothing special.' And I slinked out of the room and never went to a mixer again. I became very self-conscious."

After graduation she got a job as a weather girl at a TV station back in Louisville. Too nearsighted to see the western half of the map from the East Coast, she made jokes on the job. "I had no interest in the weather," she says, "and it showed nightly." Later she did reporting; her first assignment was to follow Supreme Court Justice William O. Douglas on a hike through Kentucky's Red River gorge. Toting the camera and recording equipment herself, she fell backward into the gorge while trying to get a shot. The Justice's comment: "Are you new at this, dear?"

"I felt that the journalist's perspective was home for me," Sawyer says, "but I really wanted to know something about making decisions, taking responsibility." That led her to Washington, where her father's connections helped her land a job in the White House press office. She started answering phones, was soon writing press releases and eventually became a chief assistant to Press Secretary Ron Ziegler. Her personal contact with President Nixon at the White House was limited: their only face-to-face encounter came when she accidentally barreled into him on the stairs leading to the Situation Room. The eager young press aide made a better impression with a piece she wrote for a magazine that expressed Nixon's feelings about his mother. The President called to compliment her; thereafter he dubbed her "the smart girl."

"She brought an intellectual spark to the press office and creativity that was invaluable," remembers Ziegler. Another colleague recalls, "She had a great deal of political sensitivity for someone her age. She was smart and cunning, very clever and resourceful. She was dogged in her approach to things: she covered all the bases." Loyalty was another of her hallmarks. One Washingtonian recalls sitting next to Sawyer in the cheap seats at a radio and TV correspondents' dinner in 1973. Satirist Mark Russell was taking swipes at Nixon's Watergate troubles, and the audience was laughing; even Ziegler seemed to roll with the punches. But Sawyer broke down in tears.

Dealing with the gathering Watergate storm, Sawyer recalls, was "bruising, nerve-deadening torment." Her response was to devour all the information she could about the scandal. "I read all the newspapers and all the testimony and all the lawyers' briefs," she says. "I became a kind of walking computer. Even the lawyers would call me occasionally became I seemed to have everything on file." Only after the famous "smoking gun" tape, released just days before Nixon's resignation, did Sawyer become convinced that the end was inevitable. She was one of the stalwarts who rode on the plane that carried Nixon to San Clemente after his farewell speech. What explains her loyalty? She ponders the question quietly for a few seconds. "When someone's life is shattered," she says, "there is only humanity."

To some friends, however, her loyalty went beyond reasonable bounds: Sawyer remained with Nixon for nearly four more years in San Clemente, helping Frank Gannon (whom she was dating) gather material for the President's autobiography. "I had the illusion of indispensability," she explains. Her job was to assemble all the on-the-record material about Watergate and the Final Days—an assignment that led to some tense moments with the former President. But she does not regret the experience (she and Nixon still correspond regularly): "I knew that being out there with him was going to be a seminar the likes of which one could never attend. I had a real sense of the Shakespearean, dark history that I was going to be a minor character in."

Her role in that Shakespearean drama caused something of an uproar at CBS, when, shortly after leaving Nixon in 1978, she was given a reporter's job by Washington bureau chief William Small. Several correspondents, including Rather, openly expressed opposition to her hiring. "Conversations would stop as I entered the room," she recalls.

Gradually, though, she earned her colleagues' respect. For several months she labored in relative obscurity, doing legwork on stories that rarely made it on the air ("They called me queen of the stakeouts"). Her big chance came after the Three Mile Island nuclear accident. She broadcast live reports from the reactor—borrowing a producer's tennis shoes so she could stand atop the microwave truck in the rain without slipping off—and got her first major exposure on the *CBS Evening News.* After a stint covering the 1980 presidential campaign, she was assigned to the State Department, where she impressed her bosses with her hard work and excellent sources. Says former CBS News president Richard Salant: "I think she was the best State Department reporter we ever had."

During the negotiations to free the Iran hostages, Sawyer's reports often wound up on the *CBS Morning News.* "I would sleep all night on two secretarial chairs so I could get up at 4 A.M., stalk the halls and see what I could get," she recalls. Her live exchanges with Charles Kuralt led to her being tapped as the show's co-anchor, and Sawyer made the leap from journeyman correspondent to network star.

As co-anchor with Kuralt and later Bill Kurtis, Sawyer helped boost the ratings for the No. 3-ranked morning show to their highest levels ever. Colleagues were impressed by her dedication. "She would show up at 2 o'clock in the morning and write her own copy," recalls a producer. "This was unheard of. There was no way you could not respect her." But soon she grew dissatisfied with the low priority the *Morning News* was given at the network and with the trivia she was sometimes forced to handle. "I thought this was not really what I should be doing," she says. "It was time to move on."

That's when Hewitt came calling with an offer for her to become *60 Minutes'* first female correspondent. Joining the old-boy network of Wallace, Morley Safer, Harry Reasoner and Ed Bradley was not easy, and reviews of her performance were mixed. Producers found her, as usual, to be a trouper—willing to go anywhere, endure any hardship for a story. "She has a lot of cold blood," says producer Anne de Boismilon. "You can never feel fear coming from her." Others, however, grew impatient with her for endlessly tinkering with stories. "She could drive a producer crazy fixing, then fixing again and again," says one source. "What she needed was a baby-sitter to tell her to get on with it."

Outside the office, Sawyer is praised as unfailingly gracious and generous. When relatives of co-workers are sick, she sends cards and fruit baskets; her thank-you notes are known for their eloquence. Her own life-style, meanwhile, is far from extravagant. In the New York City apartment she occupied while single, "She preferred no décor," says a close friend. "Basically, what she had was an awful little table in the living room with a couple of small couches and some dying plants." Admits Sawyer: "I'm hopeless. I'd just as soon send out for pizza and sit on pillows in front of the fire."

Her marriage to Nichols has changed some of that; they are planning to redecorate their brownstone on Manhattan's Upper East Side, and they have a house in Connecticut and a ranch in California. Sawyer is even getting involved in cooking. "She does it the way she does everything," says Nichols. "She cuts out 35 different versions of the recipe. We do it together. It is very detailed and sometimes complex." The pair met two years ago on a Concorde flight from London and went to lunch a couple of times to discuss doing a profile for *60 Minutes*. Nichols finally confessed that he didn't want to do the piece—but wanted to keep having lunch. "All of her is always available all the time," he gushes. "She uses more of her brain than almost anybody I know."

Sawyer's enthusiasms also run to tennis and movies, and Nichols has been introducing her to old films on the VCR (her most recent discovery: Renoir's *The Rules of the Game*). Nichols sat in on run-throughs of Sawyer's new ABC show and offered some suggestions about lighting and blocking. But, says Sawyer, "we're not very good consultants on each other's careers. We're very good, astute experts on each other and being happy." Notes a colleague: "She's like a kid, madly in love for the first time."

Sawyer resists dwelling on such personal matters: it pains her that her journalistic accomplishments are overshadowed by questions about her looks, marriage and glamorous life-style. "We're a Madison Avenue country," she sighs. "I'm not sure that we can make a distinction between newspeople and celebrities. And I think there is a distinction. The distinction lies in what you do every day—what you do to get stories and how far you will go and how much you will dig for them. All the rest of the attention that comes to you because you're on the air seems to me an irrelevance."

It is no irrelevance, however, to the executives who pay Sawyer and her fellow news stars million-dollar salaries and bet entire prime-time shows on them. Nor is it an irrelevance to the audience that tunes in, not to watch the *NBC Nightly News* or a new show called *Prime Time Live,* but to see Tom Brokaw or Diane Sawyer or Connie Chung. This is perhaps the ultimate irony of TV news in the celebrity age: reporters spend their careers trying to become stars, only to lament, once they make it, that they are treated as stars rather than reporters. The complaint may actually be sincere, but it almost doesn't matter. It's good for the image.

Bernard Shaw

"The Anchor Under Fire"
by Jeannie Kasindorf

"I went over to interview Saddam Hussein. I arrived in-country around the eleventh [of January]. They made it clear they couldn't schedule it for the

Jeannie Kasindorf is a staff member of New York *magazine.*

CNN principal anchor Bernard Shaw (photo courtesy George Bennett).

fifteenth, since that was deadline day, and I said, 'What date looks most likely?' They said the sixteenth or seventeenth." Bernard Shaw is explaining why he was in the Al-Rashid Hotel in Baghdad on the evening of January 16 and became one of the first reporters to tell the world that America had gone to war.

That moment was a long way from his childhood on the South Side of Chicago, where his father, a housepainter, and his mother, who cleaned other people's houses, would flood his own home with the newspapers that he learned to love. "My ritual on Sunday morning was to walk to a place called the Green Door bookstore near the University of Chicago, which was the closest place I could find a Sunday New York *Times*. Edward R. Murrow was my hero. I used to watch all the Murrow and Cronkite programs and watch *Meet the Press* religiously."

Shaw, 50, who speaks with the measured precision of a Cronkite or a Murrow, joined the Marines after graduating from high school and was stationed in Hawaii. While he was there, he read that Cronkite was on the islands. "I called his hotel room about 34 times and left messages to call Corporal Shaw. When he finally called me, he said, 'I can talk for a few minutes.' We talked for 45. He says I'm the most persistent guy he's ever met."

After leaving the Marines, he returned home and entered the University of Illinois. While he was still in college, he began working at WNUS, one of the country's first all-news radio stations. From there, he went to Westinghouse Broadcasting. He left the University of Illinois after three years when Westinghouse offered him a job in Washington. In 1969, when he was only 28 years old, he became Westinghouse's White House correspondent. In 1971, he left Westinghouse to become a CBS News correspondent, leaving there in 1977 to go to ABC News.

In 1979, there was a dustup at ABC News when Roone Arledge hired Carl Bernstein to be his Washington bureau chief. In the aftermath, George Watson, who had been running the bureau, left to help start CNN. Watson asked Shaw if he wanted to come on board as the new network's principal anchor. "I had been negotiating a new contract with ABC, but I was dissatisfied with the terms," Shaw says. "So I started talking to Ted Turner. The time period in which I was trying to decide, it seemed like agony to me. I'd only been married three years and our children were very small, and I couldn't selfishly take that gamble by myself; there were three other lives involved. It's no exaggeration; I walked around the dining room for two weeks, talking to myself, trying to decide. My wife, Linda, would wake up around one in the morning, come downstairs. So finally we just sat down at that dining-room table, and she said, 'Okay, you should take the job, because if you don't and CNN takes off, I won't be able to live with you.'"

When Shaw left for the Middle East on January 7, he and his wife didn't discuss the possible danger. "It was apparent to her," he says. "Keep in mind, she's gone through this before, when I was in Nicaragua and El Salvador. We just have a certain look that we exchange when I'm going off to someplace that's perilous." But once the Iraqis told Shaw that Saddam Hussein would not grant him an interview, he decided to leave. "I had a daughter and a wife and a son who wanted me back here," he says.

It is almost impossible to get Shaw to talk about his coup. "Anybody at CNN makes a mistake by gloating over our success," he says. "All of this is very temporal. This war is going to end. I don't think any journalist should get fixated on a success he or she has, because there are just too many talented people in this business."

Mary Alice Williams
"News Star Burns Brightly for NBC"
by Susan White

NEW YORK — Mary Alice Williams, the newest star at NBC News, sat stiffly at her desk, the straps of a heating pad dangling from the front of her suit jacket. For the first time in her life she was having back trouble, had been in pain for two weeks, had had X-rays, was being treated by a physical therapist. But still she was on the job, chin up, every hair in place, planning business trips to four cities that weekend.

"What am I going to say?" she said in her no-nonsense anchor voice. "That I'm sorry, my back hurts, so I can't do the news on the *Today* show? That I'm sorry, I know you planned for me to make this commencement address last September, but I hurt my back and now I can't do it?

"You can't do that to people. You've made a commitment, you've given your word. Right?"

In 1979 Williams made a commitment to Cable News Network, which had hired her away from WNBC, NBC's New York station. Although CNN has never billed any of its anchors as "stars," Williams came as close as anyone to earning the label. In 1982 she became a CNN vice president. And right from the beginning she had anchored CNN's *Newswatch* and *Primenews* programs.

But in March after much soul-searching, Williams left CNN to become an NBC star. As NBC news president Michael Gartner explained it, he heard she was available, called and offered her the job over the telephone. She gave him "yes" within 48 hours — in the same week, ironically, that one of NBC's biggest stars, Connie Chung, announced that she was moving to CBS.

Susan White works for the Knight-Ridder news service.

Gartner now predicts that "Mary Alice is going to be a bigger star" than Chung. In an interview last month he described Williams as "just wonderful ... an outstanding writer ... very pleasant to be around ... indefatigable."

"I loved CNN," Williams said slowly on the day we talked. "I love CNN now. I'm terribly proud of what those 2,000 men and women do over there. I stand in awe of what they do now, and of what we accomplished in a very short time. So it was very difficult to leave. And part of my heart stayed."

But NBC's offer was simply too good to pass up. Not only would she be an anchor for *Yesterday, Today and Tomorrow,* the prime-time news program NBC will unveil late this summer, but she would also have an opportunity to anchor every other NBC news program, even filling in for Tom Brokaw on *NBC Nightly News.*

"The new prime-time program ... is something that has never been done before," she explained. "It's a brand new idea. It's terribly innovative. And I figured, people don't often get a chance in a lifetime, and now I have had two."

Williams went to work immediately.

On her first day at NBC, Williams appeared on camera, as an anchor of the evening news breaks, and by the end of her first three weeks she had anchored every network news show. She earned Gartner's "indefatigable" compliment when he saw her on the *Sunrise* set at 6:15 one morning, doing the news wearing her heating pad.

Williams said that working for NBC is in many ways no different from working for CNN. She still writes most of her copy. She still sits in front of the cameras, reading words to an audience she cannot see.

But the size of the audience reached by the two news services is quite different.

"I am probably talking to more people in 30 seconds on NBC news than I was even with the global reach of CNN," she said. "On her third day at work, after anchoring *Nightly News,* she found out first hand how broad her new audience really was. When she stepped off the studio elevator onto the public first floor of Rockefeller Center, where NBC's studios are located, she saw a crowd of people waiting — for her.

"They followed me into the Fanny Farmer store where I went to buy Easter eggs," she said. "And I kept saying, 'Thank you very much, but I really have to get Easter candy for my family.' It was very strange."

Williams' family consists of her husband of nine months, CNN reporter Mark Haefeli; her mother, her three sisters and one brother; and her 12 nieces and nephews. Although she doesn't like to talk about her age ("I'm happy to be the age I am, but I don't see any point in belaboring it"), she is about 39.

"Family is still the most important foundation of my life," she said. "Even today. Everywhere.

"I had a father who was a psychiatrist, a brilliant, thoughtful man, who when I was first on television — I was just 18 — was there with me to guide me through the morass. Dad always made sure that I knew who I was. My mother and my sisters do that now."

Now, of course, Williams knows she is a star, or at least a star-in-the-making. Although her face isn't as familiar to NBC viewers as Brokaw's or

NBC journalist Mary Alice Williams (photo courtesy NBC).

Bryant Gumbel's, or the recently departed Chung's, it's a foregone fact that it soon will be. Even if *Yesterday, Today and Tomorrow* is a flop, Gartner seems committed to making Williams an integral part of his team. He sees in her the elusive quality that separates one attractive, intelligent woman from a crowd of attractive, intelligent women—and makes her a TV star.

"The fact is, if you are a real star," she said, "the news comes first."

Annotated Bibliography

Alter, Jonathan. "When CNN Hit Home: Was It 'the Night the Network Died'?" *Newsweek,* Jan. 28, 1991. How CNN News broadcast the first days of the war with Iraq.
Appelo, Tim. "Scoop! A Behind-the-Scenes Look at the Frontline Reporting That Made Television History." *Entertainment Weekly* magazine, Feb. 1, 1991. A diary of how CNN in Atlanta covered the first hours of the war with Iraq.
Arlen, Michael J. *The Viking Room War.* New York: Viking, 1969.
Auletta, Ken. *When the Good Times Stopped: Takeovers, Technology and the Decline of American Television.* New York: Random House, 1991.
Baker, Kathryn. "Rather Redux." *The American Way* magazine, vol. 22, no. 19, Oct. 1, 1989. The highs and lows of Dan Rather's career through mid-1989.
Barnouw, Erik. *The Golden Web: A History of Broadcasting in the United States,* vol. 2, 1933-1953. New York: Oxford University Press, 1968.
_____. *The Image Empire: A History of Broadcasting in the United States.* Vol. 3, From 1953. New York: Oxford University Press, 1970.
_____. *A Tower in Babel: A History of Broadcasting in the United States.* Vol. 1, To 1933. New York: Oxford University Press, 1966. Barnouw's three-volume history of broadcasting is often considered the definitive history of the industry in this country.
_____. *Tube of Plenty: The Evolution of American Television.* New York: Oxford University Press, 1975.
Bennetts, Leslie. "The Prime Time of Mary Alice Williams." *Vanity Fair* magazine, vol. 52, no. 9, Sept. 1989. A profile of Williams, formerly with CNN, now with NBC.
Bergreen, Laurence. *Look Now, Pay Later: The Rise of Network Broadcasting.* New York: Doubleday, 1980.
Biagi, Shirley. *Newstalk II: State of the Art Conversations with Today's Broadcast Journalists.* Belmont, Cal.: Wadsworth, 1987. Interviews with David Brinkley, Sam Donaldson, Charles Osgood and nine other television journalists.
Bilby, Kenneth. *The General: David Sarnoff and the Rise of the Communications Industry.* New York: Harper & Row, 1986.
Blair, Gwenda. *Almost Golden: Jessica Savitch and the Selling of Television News.* New York: Simon & Schuster, 1988.
Bliss, Edward, Jr., ed. *In Search of Light: The Broadcasts of Edward R. Murrow.* New York: Alfred Knopf, 1967. Murrow's scripts, in text form. Still useful to learn the art of writing for the ear.
_____. *Now the News: The Story of Broadcast Television.* New York: Columbia University Press, 1991.
Boyer, Peter J. "Taking on the World." *Vanity Fair* magazine, April 1991. Profile of Tom Johnson, CEO at CNN.

Brewin, Bob, and Shaw, Sidney. *Vietnam on Trial: Westmoreland vs. CBS.* New York: Atheneum, 1987. How and why General Westmoreland sued CBS.

Brown, Les. *Television: The Business Behind the Box.* New York: Harcourt, Brace Jovanovich, 1971. The financial aspects of the industry; now dated.

Campbell, Richard. *"60 Minutes" and the News: A Mythology for Middle America.* Champaign-Urbana: The University of Illinois Press, 1991.

Castlemen, Harry, and Podrazik, Walter J. *Four Decades of American Television.* New York: McGraw-Hill, 1982.

Chancellor, John, and Mears, Walter R. *The News Business.* New York: Harper & Row, 1983.

Comstock, George. *The Evolution of Television.* Newbury Park, Cal.: Sage, 1989.

———. *Sign Off: The Last Days of Television.* Cambridge, Mass.: The M.I.T. Press, 1982.

———. *Television in America.* Beverly Hills: Sage, 1980.

———. *The Tin Kazoo.* Cambridge, Mass.: The M.I.T. Press, 1975.

Dunkel, Tom. "Press's Mighty Pen Dulled." *Insight* magazine, Feb. 18, 1991. How television, especially CNN, beat the print press in coverage of the war with Iraq. This story accompanied the Glenn Emery article and the Jonas Bernstein article, "CNN at the Front Line of News," in *Insight* magazine.

Ellerbee, Linda. *"And So It Goes": Adventures in Television.* New York: G.P. Putnam, 1986. Ellerbee's chatty and wry media autobiography.

Emery, Glenn. "A Little Network Plays Giant Role in Gulf Coverage." *Insight* magazine, Feb. 18, 1991. CNN's coverage of the war with Iraq. A sidebar story to "CNN at the Front Line of News," reprinted in this book.

Epstein, Edward Jay. *News from Nowhere: Television and the News.* New York: Random House, 1973.

Esslin, Martin. *The Age of Television.* San Francisco: W.H. Freeman, 1982.

Frank, Reuven. *Out of Thin Air: The Inside Story of the Rise and Fall of TV Network News.* New York: Simon & Schuster, 1991.

Friendly, Fred. *Due to Circumstances Beyond Our Control....* New York: Random House, 1967. Friendly's behind-the-scenes autobiography.

Gans, Herbert. *Deciding What's News.* New York: Pantheon, 1979.

Gates, Gary Paul. *Air Time: The Inside Story of CBS News.* New York: Harper & Row, 1978.

Gelfman, Judith S. *Women in Television News.* New York: Columbia University Press, 1974.

Gitlin, Todd. *Inside Prime Time.* New York: Pantheon, 1983.

———. *Watching Television.* New York: Pantheon, 1986.

Givens, Ron. "Ted Koppel: 'Nightline' on the Front Lines." *Entertainment Weekly* magazine, Sept. 7, 1989. How "Nightline" scored a distinct scoop with Koppel's reportage from Iraq (before the war with Iraq).

Goldberg, Gerald J., and Goldberg, Robert. *Anchors: Brokaw, Jennings and Rather.* New York: Birch Lane (Carol Publishing Group), 1990. How Brokaw, Jennings, Rather and their news teams competed for the news in 1989. Highly recommended.

Graham, Fred. *Happy Talk: Confessions of a TV Journalist.* New York: W.W. Norton, 1990.

Green, Timothy. *The Universal Eye: The World of Television.* New York: Stein and Day, 1972.

Gunter, Barrie. *Poor Reception: Misunderstanding and Forgetting Broadcast News.* Hillsdale, N.J.: Lawrence Erlbaum Associates, 1987.

Hammer, Joshua. "Triumphant Ted." *Playboy,* vol. 37, no. 1, Jan. 1990. Profile of how Ted Turner launched TBS and CNN.
Harris, Mark. "Catching Up: Jennings and Koppel Reaffirm ABC's News Leadership." *Entertainment Weekly* magazine, Feb. 1, 1991. A sidebar article which accompanies the Tim Appelo article on CNN News, in the same issue.
Hewitt, Don. *Minute by Minute....* New York: Random House, 1985. Behind the scenes at CBS's "60 Minutes."
Hosley, David H., and Yamada, Gayle K. *Hard News: Women in Broadcast Journalism.* Westport, Conn.: Greenwood, 1987.
Iyengar, Shanto, and Kinder, Donald. *News That Matters.* The University of Chicago Press, 1987.
Katz, Jon. "The Air War at Home." *Rolling Stone* magazine, March 7, 1991. How the U.S. military gave the television networks only the shots the military wanted the networks—and the public—to see, during the war with Iraq.
_____. "Anchor Monster." *Rolling Stone,* Jan. 10, 1991. An analysis of the first ten years of Ted Koppel's "Nightline."
_____. "Collateral Damage to Network News." *Columbia Journalism Review,* March-April, 1991. Analysis of how network news must change to compete with CNN News in covering breaking stories.
Kaye, Elizabeth. "Peter Jennings Gets No Respect." *Esquire* magazine, vol. 112, no. 1, Sept. 1989. A profile of Jennings, from his early days to the present.
Kendrick, Alexander. *Prime Time: The Life of Edward R. Murrow.* Boston: Little, Brown, 1969. The first biography of Murrow.
Kenney, Charles. "Top of the News: Why Peter Jennings Is So Good." *Boston Globe Magazine,* Nov. 6, 1988.
Lemert, James B. "Content Duplication by the Networks in Competing Evening Broadcasts." *Journalism Quarterly,* 51, 1974.
Leonard, Bill. *In the Storm of the Eye: A Lifetime at CBS.* New York: G.P. Putnam's, 1987.
Lesher, Stephen. *Media Unbound: The Impact of Television Journalism on the Public.* Boston: Houghton Mifflin, 1982.
Lichty, Lawrence, and Topping, Malachi G. *American Broadcasting: A Source Book on the History of Radio and Television.* New York: Hastings House, 1975.
McCabe, Peter. *Bad News at Black Rock: The Sell-Out of CBS News.* New York: Arbor House, 1987.
MacDonald, J. Fred. *One Nation Under Television: The Rise and Decline of Network TV.* New York: Pantheon, 1990.
MacNeil, Robert. *People Machine: The Influence of Television on American Politics.* New York: Harper & Row, 1968.
_____. *The Right Place at the Right Time.* Boston: Little, Brown, 1982. The autobiography of Robert MacNeil, one half of PBS's "MacNeil-Lehrer Report."
Madsen, Axel. *60 Minutes: The Power & the Politics of America's Most Popular News Show.* New York: Dodd, Mead, 1984.
Massing, Michael. "Is the Most Popular Evening Newscast the Best?" *Columbia Journalism Review,* March-April, 1991. Why CBS and NBC have to play catch-up to ABC News.
Matusow, Barbara. *The Evening Stars: The Making of the Network News Anchor.* Boston: Houghton Mifflin, 1983. One of the first books about news anchors; now dated.

Mayer, Martin. *Making News.* New York: Doubleday, 1987.
Metz, Robert. *CBS: Reflections in a Blood-Shot Eye.* Chicago: Playboy, 1975.
Mickelson, Sig. *The Electronic Mirror: Politics in an Age of Television.* New York: Dodd, Mead, 1972.
––––––––. *From Whistle Stop to Sound Bite: Four Decades of Politics and Television.* New York: Praeger, 1989.
Midgley, Leslie. *How Many Words Do You Want? An Insider's Stories of Print and Television Journalism.* New York: Birch Lane (Carol Publishing Group), 1989. Memoir of the man who started in print journalism and became producer of "CBS Evening News with Walter Cronkite."
Murrow, Edward R. *This Is London.* New York: Schocken, 1989. Murrow's scripts from war-time England. A reprint edition of a classic, first published in 1941 and long out-of-print before this new edition.
Nash, Alana. *Golden Girl: The Story of Jessica Savitch.* New York: E.P. Dutton, 1988.
O'Connor, John E., ed. *American History, American Television: Interpreting the Video Past.* New York: Frederick Ungar, 1983.
Paisner, Daniel. *The Imperfect Mirror: Inside Stories of Television Newswomen.* New York: William Morrow, 1989.
Paley, William S. *As It Happened: A Memoir.* New York: Doubleday, 1979. As is the case with many autobiographies of the famous or infamous, this must be considered as self-serving. Lewis J. Paper's and Sally Bedell Smith's biographies of Paley are more impartial.
Paper, Lewis J. *Empire: William S. Paley and the Making of CBS.* New York: St. Martin's, 1987.
Persico, Joseph E. *Edward R. Murrow: An American Original.* New York: McGraw-Hill, 1988. Persico's and A. M. Sperber's biographies of Murrow are both exceptional.
Powers, Ron. *The Beast, the Eunuch, and the Glass-eyed Child: Television in the Eighties.* New York: Harcourt, Brace, Jovanovich, 1990.
––––––––. *The Newscasters.* New York: St. Martin's, 1978.
Quinn, Sally. *We're Going to Make You a Star.* New York: Simon & Schuster, 1975. Autobiography of a *Washington Post* writer who didn't become a star on network TV.
Rather, Dan, with Herskowitz, Mickey. *The Camera Never Blinks: Adventures of a TV Journalist.* New York: William Morrow, 1977. Rather's autobiography.
Reasoner, Harry. *Before the Colors Fade.* New York: Alfred Knopf, 1981. Reasoner's television memoirs.
Sanders, Marlene, and Rock, Marcia. *Waiting for Prime Time: The Women of Television News.* Urbana, Ill.: The University of Illinois Press, 1988.
Schoenbrun, David. *On and Off the Air: An Informal History of CBS News.* New York: E.P. Dutton, 1989.
Shayon, Robert Lewis, ed. *Walter Cronkite, Television and the News: The Eighth Art: Twenty-Three Views of Television Today.* New York: Holt, Rinehart & Winston, 1962.
Slater, Robert. *This ... Is CBS: A Chronicle of 60 Years.* Englewood Cliffs: Prentice-Hall, 1988.
Small, William. *To Kill a Messenger: Television News and the Real World.* New York: Hastings House, 1970.
Smith, R. Franklin. *Edward R. Murrow: The War Years.* Kalamazoo, Mich.: New Issues, 1978.

Smith, Sally Bedell. *In All His Glory: William S. Paley.* New York: Simon & Schuster, 1990. The newest unauthorized biography of the founder of CBS.
Sperber, Ann M. *Murrow: His Life and Times.* New York: Freundlich, 1986.
Trotta, Liz. *Fighting for Air: In the Trenches with Television News.* New York: Simon & Schuster, 1991.
Wallace, Mike, and Gates, Gary Paul. *Close Encounters.* New York: William Morrow, 1984. Wallace's memoirs of a life in broadcasting.
Westin, Av. *Newswatch: How TV Decides the News.* New York: Simon & Schuster, 1982.
Whitemore, Hank. *Ted Turner & CNN: How a Band of Mavericks Changed the Face of TV News.* Boston: Little, Brown, 1990. How Ted Turner gambled one hundred million dollars on CNN News. Highly recommended.
Yoakam, R. D., and Cremer, C. F. *ENG* (Electronic News Gathering): *Television News and the New Technology.* New York: Random House, 1985. A contemporary textbook for college and university students in broadcast news. How television news is taught in the electronic age.
Zoglin, Richard. "Life from the Middle East! CNN scores a reporting coup as TV dramatically captures the first major war in the era of instant worldwide communication." *Time,* Jan. 28, 1991. *Time's* version of the Jonathan Alter story in *Newsweek,* same week.

Index

Aaron, John 17
Abbas, Abul 110
Abbott and Costello 3
ABC (American Broadcasting Company) 1, 2, 3, 5, 12, 15, 20, 23, 24, 25, 29, 31, 32, 43, 48, 56, 91, 93, 95, 97, 99, 102, 108, 110, 113, 114, 118, 120, 123, 126, 134, 135, 136, 139, 142, 146, 157, 158, 159, 160, 161, 163, 164, 165, 166, 177, 185, 202, 205, 207, 208, 209, 210, 211, 214, 215, 216, 217, 218, 219, 221, 226, 230, 231, 233, 249, 259, 264, 271, 272, 273, 274-275, 276, 278, 279, 280, 281, 282, 285, 287
"ABC World News with Peter Jennings" 100, 102, 103, 104, 111, 116, 118
"The ABC's of Peter Jennings" 6, 209-221
"ABC's Person of the Week" 211
"ABC's Television Tiger: Sam the Man" 6, 197-202
"An Accident of Casting" 36-69
Accuracy in Media 150
Achille Lauro hijacking 110
Acme Newspictures 18
Acquino, Corazon 278
Adams, Rich 269, 270
"Adventure" 56
"The Advocates" 229
AFTRA 38, 40, 43
Agnew, Spiro 70, 72, 75, 192
Agronsky, Martin 12
AIDS 120, 178, 188, 212, 264, 275
Ailes, Roger 200, 251, 253, 254, 256
Alter, Jonathan 6, 186
Alton, Bill 142
The American Boy 86
American Film Institute 248n
American Heritage 207
American Home Products Company 67
Amusing Ourselves to Death 179
"The Anchor Under Fire" 7, 285-288
"Anchor Wars" 4, 6, 111-122
"Anchorman," origins of 113
Anchors: Brokaw, Jennings, Rather

and the Evening News 140, 250, 257-258
"Anchors: Who They Are; What They Do; the Problems They Face" 4, 7, 99-111
"And So It Goes," Adventures in Television 206, 208
"And So It Has Gone" 7, 205-209
Anderson, Jack 76
Anderson, Marian 14
Anderson, Terry 142, 144, 145, 146
"Animals, Animals, Animals" 164
Arbitron ratings 120
Arledge, Ann 162
Arledge, Joan 162
Arledge, Roone 2, 110, 114, 116, 118, 123, 146, 157-166, 198, 210, 272, 274, 280, 287
Arnett, Peter 148, 149, 150, 151, 152, 223, 224
Ash, Timothy 182
Aspin, Les 234
Associated Press 52, 76, 98, 142
"Association with PBS Is Still Good News for Roger Mudd" 7, 245-247
Astor, Brooke 162
Atkins, Norman 6, 209
Atlanta Journal 7, 245
Atwater, Lee 197, 253, 256
Austin American-Statesman 7, 122, 205, 248, 288
"Automation: Weal or Woe?" 14

Baker, Russell 48
Bakker, Jim 226
Bakker, Tammy 226
Baltimore Sun 7, 166, 235
Bani-Sadr, Abolhassan 234
Barrett, Nona 165
Batista, Fulgencio 23, 24
Battle Lines: A Study of Military/Media Relations in Wartime 151
Bazell, Robert 120
The Beatles 37, 196

Beatty, Morgan 5
Beatty, Ned 142
Beatty, Warren 279
Beckwith, Dave 256
Bernstein, Carl 287
Bernstein, Jonas 7, 47
Bernstein, Leonard 117
Berri, Nabih 110
Bettag, Tom 105, 250, 253, 254, 261
"The Beverly Hillbillies" 113
Big Story 151
Bigart, Homer 86
Billy Bathgate 278
Bistany, Joanna 161, 162
Blanchard and Davis 37
Blitzer, Wolf 224
Bloch, Felix 146, 281
Block, Kurt 124
Blonsky, Marshall 6, 225, 231
Bloods 277
Bloomingdale, Betsy 121
"Blurred Lines: TV Network News Is Making Re-creation a Form of Recreation" 7, 140-147
Boorstin, Daniel 212
Borovik, Artyom 232
Bosket, Willie 143
Botha, R. F. 226
Bradley, Ed 2, 7, 155, 166-169, 284
Braestrup, Peter 151, 152
Braver, Rita 123
Brinkley, Alan 51, 174
Brinkley, Alexis 170
Brinkley, Ann Fisher 51
Brinkley, David 3, 6, 7, 9, 11, 24, 25, 27, 33, 35, 36-39, 75, 113, 129, 155, 160, 165, 168-174, 197, 201, 213, 214
Brinkley, Joel 51, 174
Brinkley, John 174
Brinkley, Mary 171
Brinkley, Mary Nelson 171
Brinkley, Susan 174
Brinkley, William 171
Broadbent, Ed 217
"Broadcast News" 175, 177, 178, 181, 210
Brokaw, Meredith Auld 119-120, 175
Brokaw, Tom 2, 3, 4, 6, 91, 95, 96, 100, 103, 104, 105-106, 111-112, 114, 115, 117, 119-120, 121, 126, 155, 159, 174-181, 216, 217, 219, 220, 243, 246, 247, 249, 257, 262, 281, 282, 285, 289
Brooks, James 175, 177

Brown, Bob 185
Brown, Les 100
Brown, Pat 142
Bundy, Ted 210
Burke, Dan 158
Burke, David 102, 144, 145, 161, 162, 219, 282
Bush, George 91, 139, 148, 162, 180, 197, 200, 228, 229, 233, 250, 251, 252, 253, 254, 255, 256, 258, 259
"Bushwacked!" 7, 250-257
Business Week 95
"Business World" 165

C-Span 158
Cahill, Bill 255
"The Caine Mutiny" 262
"Camel News Caravan" 22, 38, 171
The Camera Never Blinks 115
Capital Cities/ABC 91, 100, 157, 158, 162, 163, 177, 210
Capital Cities Corp. 1, 135
"The Capital Gang" 185
Carroll, Earl 42
Carson, Johnny 37, 98, 165
Carter, James 266
Carter, Jimmy 195, 201, 233, 234; administration 194
Casey, William 259
Castro, Fidel 23-24, 190
CBC (Canadian Broadcasting Corporation) 118, 212, 243
CBS (Columbia Broadcasting System) 1, 3, 5, 6, 10, 11, 12, 15, 18, 19, 20, 22, 23-24, 25, 29, 31, 34, 37, 38, 42, 43, 47, 48, 51, 52, 60, 66, 67, 70, 71, 73, 74, 77, 79, 81, 82, 86, 87, 91, 93, 95, 96, 97, 98, 99, 100, 103, 104, 108, 110, 111, 117, 118, 120, 122, 123, 126, 129, 130, 134, 135, 136, 137, 138, 139, 141, 145, 155, 158, 159, 160, 161, 169, 174, 177, 192, 203, 204, 211, 214, 215, 217, 219, 229, 235, 238, 246, 252, 253, 254, 255, 260, 261, 279, 287, 288
"CBS Evening News" 180, 236, 250, 251, 252, 253, 258, 261, 262, 280, 281, 284
"CBS Evening News with Dan Rather" 100, 105, 114-115, 123, 133, 142, 143, 144
"CBS Evening News with Walter Cronkite" 58, 59, 77, 110, 116
"CBS Morning News" 278, 284
CBS Radio 171

CBS Records 135
"CBS Reports" 167, 168
"CBS Sunday Night News" 169
"CBS's Original News Anchor Signs Off" 7, 203-205
Ceausescu, N. 182
Center for Media and Public Affairs 148
Center for Strategic and International Studies 232
Center for Strategy, Technology and Policy 148
Center for Urban Education 64
Central Institute for the Deaf 137
Challenger explosion 104, 117, 211-212
Chambers, Robert 142
Chancellor, John 27, 28, 33, 45, 49, 67, 68, 119
Chandler, Cleveland 237
Chandler, Gloria 237
Chandler, Norman 237
Chandler, Toby 258
Channels magazine 100
Cheney State University 168
Chessman, Caryl 142
"The Chicago Conspiracy Trial" 141
Chicago Sun-Times 6, 56, 70, 273
Chicago Transit Authority 274
Chicago Tribune 16, 267
"Children's Express News Magazine" 139
The Christian Science Monitor 220
Christie, Agatha 209
Chung, Connie 19, 122, 123, 126, 127, 133, 141, 142, 145, 147, 182-183, 247, 249, 278, 285, 288, 289, 290
Churchill, Winston 11, 22, 27
CIA (Central Intelligence Agency) 148, 190, 259
Clark, Dick 213
Clark, Kenneth R. 7, 122
"Clinton and the Law" 14
CNN (Cable News Network) 2, 91, 95, 96, 99, 102, 121, 122, 126, 139, 146-153, 158, 159, 182, 183, 184, 185, 222-225, 245, 264, 278, 281, 287, 288, 289
Cohen, Richard 251, 252, 253
Colby, William 259, 276
Collingwood, Charles 16, 20
Colorado Springs Gazette Telegraph 7, 243
Colson, Charles 192
Columbia University 162
Compton, Ann 259
Connors, "Bull" 28

Corey, Mary 7, 155, 166
Cornish School of the Arts 42
Cosby, Bill 100, 119, 120
Cosby, Janet 168
"The Cosby Show" 145, 280
Cosell, Howard 163, 166
Cosgrove-Meurer Productions 142
Costello, Frank 12
Coughlin, Rep. Lawrence 148
Craft, Christine 123
Crier, Catherine 7, 181-185
Cronkite, Betsy 33, 35
Cronkite, Mary Kathleen 33
Cronkite, Nancy Elizabeth 33
Cronkite, Walter 1, 2, 3, 4, 6, 9, 12, 19, 25, 26-36, 38, 58, 59, 62-63, 67, 68, 70-90, 93, 96, 112, 113-114, 117, 119, 122, 143, 146, 155, 164, 174, 176, 177, 186-196, 204, 212, 214, 215, 221, 246, 247, 250, 257, 258, 259, 261, 262, 280, 287
Cronkite, Walter Leland, III 33
"Crossfire" 185
Crystal, Lester 56
Cuban missile crisis 148
"A Current Affair" 142, 146
Current Biography 170

Dach, Leslie 229, 230
The Daily Texan 7, 181, 222
Daley, Richard 191
"Dallas" 171, 280
Daly, John 12
Daniels, Faith 131
Dart, Justin 121
"David Brinkley's Journal" 171
Davis, Elmer 11, 43
Davis, Leslie 104, 108
Dean, John 197, 199
de Boismilon, Anne 284
Deeb, Gary 273
deMacias, Patricia Villarreal 7, 222
Dennis, Everette 281
The Des Moines Register 256
Desert Storm 150
Dewey, Thomas 13
Diamond, Edwin 6, 111
"Diane Sawyer; Star Power" 5, 277-285
Dillingham, Susan 153n
Dirksen, Everett 41, 47, 201
Dobi, Nancy 158
Doctorow, E. L. 278
Dole, Sen. Robert 252, 256

Index

Donahue, Phil 136, 220
Donaldson, Sam 2, 6, 122, 124, 126, 142, 155, 156, 159, 160, 165, 173, 197-202, 225, 259, 278, 280, 281
Dori, Mi 117
Dougherty, Richard 74
"Douglas Edwards with the News" 20, 203, 204
Downey, Morton, Jr. 95, 136, 220, 221
Downs, Bill 16
Downs, Hugh 160, 163, 185
Doyle, Robert 45
Dreyfuss, Joel 272, 276
DuBois, W. E. B. 226
Dukakis, Michael 200, 217, 226, 228, 229, 230, 231, 233
DuMont Network 21
Dunkel, Tom 153n
Dunsmore, Barrie 211

The Economist 43
"Ed Bradley's Two Muses: Work, Music" 7, 166-169
Editor and Publisher 36
Edward R. Murrow: An American Original 10
Edwards, Douglas 7, 21, 24, 61, 62, 112, 203-205
Edwards, May 203
Eisenhower, Dwight 11, 22
Ellerbee, Linda 7, 127-140, 205-209
Ellsberg, Daniel 79
Emery, Glenn 153n
Emmy awards 238, 239, 246, 275
"Entertainment Tonight" 116, 147, 272
Erlick, Ev 135
Erstein, Hap 7, 238, 239n
"Essence" 275
"Eyewitness to History" 34

"Face to Face with Connie Chung" 249
"Family Feud" 163
Farrakhan, Louis 159
FCC (Federal Communications Commission) 130
Feders, Sid 142
Fenster, Sol 144
"Fibber McGee and Molly" 37
Fitzgerald, Ella 117
Flanner, Janet 157
Flanner, Judy 6
Flaubert, Gustave 6

Fleming, Harold 29
Fleming, Pat 276
Forbes 207
Ford, Gerald 193
Foreign Affairs 66
"48 Hours" 145, 262
Fowles, John 278
Fox television 98, 109, 142
Frank, Reuven 19, 22, 24, 37, 54-55, 56, 60, 65, 67, 143, 146, 178
"Frank McGee Report" 68
Friedman, Kinky 206
Friedman, Paul 161, 219
Friedman, Steve 177
Friendly, Fred 13, 14, 17, 22-23, 34, 37, 56
"Frontline" 96
Fuller, Craig 254
Fulton, Tom 215

Gallup Poll 119, 259
Gannett Center for Media Studies 129, 281
Gannon, James P. 256
Gans, Hebert J. 64
Gardner, John W. 48
Garroway, Dave 20, 34
Gartner, Michael 124, 281, 288, 289, 290
Gazette Telegraph (Colorado Springs) 7, 243
Gemini space program 82
General Electric Corp. 1, 91, 93, 95, 100, 178
Gephardt, Richard 256
Gergen, David 161
Gifford, Frank 160, 161, 163
Gillespie, S. Hazard 44
Gingrich, Newt 201
Glass, Charles 212, 259
Goebbels, Joseph 149
Goldberg, Gerald Jay 140, 250, 257
Goldberg, Robert 140, 250, 257
Goldin, Marion 127-140
Golson, G. Barry 70
"Good Morning America" 102, 117, 138, 165, 249
Good News, Bad News 6, 111n
Goodman, Julian 68
Goodman, Kevin 7, 140
Gorbachev, Mikhail 117, 175, 180, 200, 256, 263
Gorbachev, Raisa 137
Gould, Cheryl 180

Gould, Jack 35, 62, 67
Grant, Cary 37
Graves, Evelyn 276
Graziano, Rocky 11
"The Great Billion Dollar Mail Case" 14
Greenfield, Jeff 95
Greenfield, Meg 202
Greensboro News & Record 7, 169
Greppi, Michelle 7, 245
Grey, Joel 83
Grossman, Lawrence K. 108, 119, 281
The Guardian Manchester 43
Gumbel, Bryant 249, 290

Haefeli, Mark 289
Haig, Alexander 256
Halberstam, David 179
Hanks, Tom 211
Harper's magazine 265
Harris, Richard 229
Hart, Gary 188, 230, 256
"Harvest of Shame" 112
Hayes, John 267
Hazelton Drug and Alcohol Rehab. Center 275
"The Health Show" 165
Heatter, Gabriel 11, 19
Hegert, Todd 7, 243
Helms, Jesse 258
Hemingway, Ernest 239
Herman, George 108
Hermanson, Hjalmar 61
Hersch, Seymour 79
Hewitt, Don 18, 20, 21, 25, 60, 97–98, 204, 211–212, 279, 280, 284
Hildebrand, Cynthia 144
Hill, William 54, 58–59
Hirohito, Emperor 238
Hitler, Adolf 15
Hoff, Charlie 151
Hoffa, Jimmy 12
Hoffman, Abbie 141, 143, 144
Hoffman, Anita 143–144
Hoffman, Jack 141–144
Hoffman, Wendell 24
Hold On, Mr. President 199–200, 202
Holliman, John 148, 149
Holloway, Diane 7, 248
Holmes, Larry 180
Home Testing Institute/TvQ, Inc. 37
Horne, Lena 167
Horowitz, Vladimir 110
Hottelet, Richard 12, 116

Houston Chronicle 260
Howe, Quincy 12
Hudson, Rock 188
Hume, Brit 160
Hume, Ellen 148
Humphrey, Hubert H. 37, 192
"Hunter" 145
Huntley, Chet 3, 6, 9, 11, 24, 25, 32, 36–69, 113, 170, 171, 176, 177, 280
Huntley, Ingrid Rolin 43
Huntley, Leanne 43
Huntley, Percy 42
Huntley, Sharon 43
Huntley, Tippy 43–44
"Huntley-Brinkley Report" 24, 27, 29, 34, 37, 38, 40, 49, 52, 58, 59, 68, 96, 114, 119, 170, 171, 176, 177, 280
Hurt, William 177
Hussein, Saddam 149, 150, 285, 287

"I Can Hear It Now" 13
I Never Played the Game 166
"I Was Trained to Ask Questions" 7, 257–263
"In Wake of 'Today,' Jane Pauley Learns America Loves Her" 7, 248–250
Insight magazine 147, 153n
Institute for Policy Studies 274
Institute of International Education 15
International Radio and Television Society 71, 214
Iran-Contra affair 252, 253, 256, 257, 259, 278
"The Iran Crisis: American Held Hostage" 165
Irvine, Reed 150
Isaacs, Harold 28
"Issues and Answers" 164
ITT (International Telephone and Telegraph Corp.) 53

Jackson, Jesse 230, 233, 264
Jacobson, David 142
James, Henry 278
Jarriel, Tom 185
Jenco, Lawrence 142, 145
Jennings, Kati Marton 111, 211, 216
Jennings, Peter 2, 3, 4, 91, 95, 96, 100, 102, 103–104, 109, 110, 111, 112, 113, 115, 116, 117, 118–119, 121, 123, 146, 155, 156, 160, 161, 163, 164, 174, 179,

180, 194, 209–221, 243, 257, 262, 271, 275, 281
Johns, Vernon 142
Johnson, Bruce 268, 270
Johnson, Lyndon Baines 27, 49, 81, 190, 191
Johnson, Maria C. 7, 155, 169
Johnson, Tom 7, 222–225
Johns, Alex S. 7, 99
Jones, James Earl 142
Joyce, Ed 130, 281

Kalb, Marvin 262
Kaltenborn, H. V. 11, 19, 171
Kaplan, James 6, 156, 174
Kaplan, Rich 159, 228, 229, 230, 280
Karr, Alphonse 123
Kasendorf, Jeannie 7, 285
Kast, Sheila 123
KCBS 203
Kefauver, Estes 11
Kelly, Leon 229
KELP 202
Kemp, Jack 256
Kendrick, Alexander 10
Kennedy, Ethel 162
Kennedy, John F. 25, 80, 148, 163, 166, 176, 190, 251, 260; assassination 25, 27, 29, 190, 260, 261
Kennedy, Robert F. 27, 48, 163, 166, 190
Kennedy, Ted 246, 251
Kennedy-Nixon debates 251, 256
Kenton, Stan 42
Khomeini, Ayatollah Ruhollah 118
KHOU 260
Khrushchev, Nikita 148, 170
Kiker, Douglas 52, 56, 64, 67, 68–69
King, Martin Luther, Jr. 80, 190
Kintner, Robert 23, 61, 98
KIRO 42
Kissinger, Henry 115, 232, 234, 279
Klein, Paul 68
KMBC 33
KNBC 119
Knight-Ridder 7
KNX 203
Konner, Joan 143
Koppel, Grace Anne 232
Koppel, Ted 2, 4, 19, 108, 122, 154, 159, 160, 161, 164, 165, 166, 196, 201, 225–235, 259, 282
Koslovsky, Vladimir 232
Koughan, Martin 251, 260

KPCB 42
Kravitz, Walter 53
KROD-TV 202
Kroft, Steve 279
KTSC 243
Kucinich, Dennis 273
Kuralt, Charles 10, 131, 155, 235–238, 239, 284
"Kuralt Finds Security on the Road Less Traveled" 7, 235–238
Kurtis, Bill 284
KXAN 249

"L.A. Law" 158, 198
Lack, Andrew 144, 145
Lane, Jane F. 6, 197
Langley, Jeanne Solomon 167
"Larry King Live!" 153
Lassie 37
Lawrence, Anthony 150
Lawrenson, Johanna 143, 144
"Laverne and Shirley" 114
Le Monde 118
LeCarré, John 245
Leech, Margaret 173
Legvold, Robert 232
Lehrer, Jim 7, 238–242, 243–245
Lehrer, Kate 240
Leibner, Richard 280
Leiser, Ernest 93
Lennon, John 196
LeSueur, Larry 16
"Let's Make a Deal" 142
Leventhal, Todd 151, 152
Levine, Irving R. 131
Levy, Alyssa 151
Levy, Mark 109
Lewis, Anthony 202
Lewis, Fulton, Jr. 11
Lichter, S. Robert 148, 151, 152, 153
Lieber, Paul 141, 144
Liebovitz, Annie 279
Life 12, 25, 248
"Like It Is" 276
Lippmann, Walter 13
"Little Network Plays Giant Role in Gulf Coverage" 153n
Lodge, Art 19
Loews Corp. 93, 178
Los Angeles Herald Examiner 7, 203
Los Angeles Times 3, 52, 96, 153, 222, 224, 262
Lowe, Rob 142

Index   303

Lower, Elmer W. 25, 214
Lucas, Diane 203, 204

M magazine 6, 197
McAndrew, William 23, 41, 56, 60
McCarthy, Eugene 74, 87, 88, 191-192
McCarthy, Joseph 11, 16, 23, 42, 112
McClennan, John 12
McGee, Frank 35
McGovern, George 74, 87, 191
McHargue, Kevin 7, 181
McLuhan, Marshall 66
McNamara, Robert 80
MacNeil, Robert 7, 164, 239, 242, 243-245
"MacNeil-Lehrer NewsHour" 96, 104, 122, 148, 149, 164, 238-239, 243, 244, 245, 247
"MacNeil Says 'NewsHour' an Ideal TV Anchor Job" 7, 243-245
MacRae, Gordon 213
Magid, Frank 95
The Main Source: Learning from Television News 109
Mankiewicz, Joe 136
Mann, Thomas 278
Manning, Anthony 267
Manning, Gordon 27
Maples, Marla 159
Marbella, Jean 7, 235
"March of *Time*" 14
Markle Foundation, John and Mary 109
Mead, George Hebert 116
Meese, Edwin, III 226
"Meet the Press" 287
Mercury space program 82
Meredith, Don 163
Meyer, Karl E. 64
Meyers, Joe 60
Michener, James 4, 278
Mickelson, Sig 34, 47
Milloy, Marilyn 7, 263
Millstein, Gilbert 56, 58
Minow, Newton 29
Mitchell, Andrea 124-126
Mitchell, Grayson 265, 268, 269, 271, 273
Monroe, Marilyn 163, 166
Monroe, William 3, 45
Morgan, Edward P. 12, 33
Morris, Joe Alex 224
"The Most Intimate Medium" 2, 3, 5, 26-36

Mother Jones magazine 67, 106, 121, 126
Moving On: Adventures in the Real World 206, 207,
Moyers, Bill 27, 182
Mubarak, Hosni 148
Mudd, Roger 7, 34, 48, 58, 63, 177, 245-247, 251, 261
Mulroney, Brian 217
Murdoch, Rupert 93, 98, 102, 109
Murphy, Thomas 157, 158
Murrow: His Life and Times 10
Murrow, Charles Casey 13
Murrow, Dewey 15
Murrow, Edward R. 2, 3, 9, 10-18, 22-23, 31, 37, 38, 42, 43, 56, 59, 62, 105, 112, 113, 247, 280, 287
Murrow, Ethel 15
Murrow, Janet 13, 15
Murrow, Lacy 15
Murrow, Roscoe 15
Murrow, William 3, 45
Museums and Arts Washington magazine 239n
My Lai incident 78-79, 193

NASA (National Aeronautics and Space Administration) 117, 163
NATO (North Atlantic Treaty Organization) 214
NBC (National Broadcasting Corporation) 1, 3, 5, 6, 11, 12, 15, 19, 20, 21, 23, 24, 25, 29, 31, 33, 35, 37, 41, 42, 43, 45, 51, 56-57, 60, 64, 66, 67, 68, 91, 93, 94, 95, 98, 99, 103, 106, 108, 117, 118, 120, 122, 124, 126, 129, 130, 131, 135, 145, 158, 159, 160, 161, 164, 165, 171, 176, 178, 205, 208, 217, 219, 237, 243, 246, 247, 249, 250, 278, 279, 281, 288, 289
NBC Entertainment Div. 142
National Association for Black Journalists 268
National Endowment for the Arts 248n
National Geographic 207
National Geographic Society 45
National Student Federation 15
NBC News 178
"NBC News Digest" 180
"NBC Nightly News" 4, 119, 142, 176, 177, 178, 180, 246, 249, 285, 289
"NBC Nightly News with Tom Brokaw" 100, 120-121, 127
NBC Radio 213

304   Index

Neiman Reports 64
"Network News Is: ☐ Dead; ☐ Dying; ☒ King of the Mountain" 3-4, 5, 93-99
The New Deal 50
New Jersey Institute of Technology 144
The New Republic 215
"New Star Burns Brightly for NBC" 7, 288-290
The New York Daily News 3, 52, 57, 96
The New York Herald Tribune 18, 52, 69, 86
New York magazine 7, 285
The New York Times 3, 7, 11, 35, 43, 48, 52, 55, 56, 57, 59, 64, 65, 66, 67, 77, 78, 95, 96, 115, 117, 121, 140, 151, 174, 202, 208, 212, 241, 261, 274, 287
New York Times Sunday Magazine 99, 225
New York University Dept. of Communication 179
The New Yorker 6, 36, 169
Newark Evening News 19
Newman, Edwin 3
Newman, Monte 273, 275
News Corp. 142
"The News Mission Study: Viewer Attitudes and Beliefs About Network and Local Newscasts 98
"Newsbeam" (CNN service) 151
Newsday 7, 263
"Newswatch" 288
Newsweek 6, 59, 95, 162
"Nickelodeon" 207
Nichols, Mike 279, 284-285
Nielsen Co. 102, 104
Nielsen ratings 30, 62, 68, 120, 127, 136, 145, 209-210, 262
"Nightline" 157, 159, 160, 164, 165, 214, 215, 225, 226, 228, 229, 230, 233, 234, 278, 280
"1986" 247
Nixon, Richard 70, 72, 88, 89, 137, 194-195, 251, 258, 261, 279, 282; administration 70, 72, 73, 74, 88-89, 114, 120, 137, 192
Noble, Gil 276
Norville, Deborah 249
Nuell, David 147
Nunn, Ray 272

Oberlin College 267
"Off Camera: Newswomen on Bosses, Bias and the Future of the News" 5, 6, 126-140
Ogonyok magazine 232
O'Heffernan, Patrick 148, 152
Olivier, Laurence 167
"On the Road" 236, 237
On the Road with Charles Kuralt 238
O'Neill, Tip 110
"Open Hearing" 15
Orenstein, Peggy 6, 126
Oswald, Lee Harvey 29, 190
"The Other Washington" 268
"Our World" 137, 138, 140, 205, 207, 208
"Outlook" 15
"Overnight" 137
Ozal, Turgut 148

Paar, Jack 20, 34
Page, Clarence 267
Paley, William S. 11, 13, 16, 20, 98, 204, 279
Pan Am Flight 103 210
Parade 155
Pauley, Jane 7, 119, 248-250
PBS (Public Broadcasting Service) 122, 139, 238, 239, 244, 247
Peabody awards 56, 238, 239, 244, 246
Pearl Harbor attack 11
Pentagon papers 79
People 178, 248
The People Machine 244
Perkins, Jack 67
Persico, Joseph E. 10
"Person of the Week" 117
"Person to Person" (Murrow) 10, 11, 12, 13, 17
"Person to Person" (Sawyer) 280
"Peter Jennings with the News" 29
Peterson, Gordon 268, 275
Petus, Mike 211
Pfeiffer, Michelle 248
Pierce, Fred 163
Pizzey, Allen 12, 237-238
Playboy 6, 9, 70, 186
"*Playboy* Interview: Walter Cronkite" 1, 2, 3, 6, 9, 70-90
Playwrights Preview Productions 242
Poe, Jewell Moore 267
Polk, George 211
Post-Newsweek Stations 267
Postman, Neil 179
Potomac Institute 29

Povich, Maury 142
Powell, Adam Clayton 49-50
Powell, Colin 150
Powers, Ron 6, 9, 70-71, 186
The Press and Journal 143
Presser, Jackie 117
"Press's Mighty Pen Dulled" 153n
"Prime News" 288
Prime Time: The Life of E. R. Murrow 10
"Prime Time Live" 142, 158, 159, 160, 165, 198, 249, 278, 280, 281, 282, 285
Pruden, Wes 202
Pulitzer Prize 242
Pyle, Ernie 239

Quayle, Dan 139, 152, 200-201
Quinones, John 118

Raduvolich, Milo 23
Rather, Dan 2, 3, 4, 26, 81, 91, 95, 96, 99, 100, 103, 104-105, 105-106, 108, 110-111, 112, 114, 115-116, 117, 119, 120, 121, 123, 155, 156, 159, 174, 177, 179, 180, 191, 194, 204, 210, 216, 217, 219, 220, 235, 238, 243, 246, 247, 250-263, 280, 281, 282
Rather, Irwin "Rags" 115, 119
Rather, Jean 260
RCA (Radio Corporation of America) 53, 100
Reagan, Nancy 119, 161
Reagan, Ronald 193, 194-195, 200, 221, 238, 251, 273, 274; administration 116, 117, 121, 126, 192-193, 251
"Real Life with Jane Pauley" 249, 250
Reasoner, Harry 35, 155, 164, 284
Reid, Bob 272, 277
Renick, Ralph 35
Renoir, Pierre 285
Reston, James 48
Reuters 243
Reveille in Washington 173
"The Revolution Will Be Televised: A Year in the Life of Catherine Crier" 7, 181-185
Reynolds, Burt 145
Reynolds, Frank 117, 164, 165, 216, 271, 274
Richards, Ann 207
Richmond News-Leader 246
Ridenhour, Ronald 78

Riland, Dr. Kenneth 44
Rivera, Geraldo 95, 136, 166, 220, 221
Robbins, Jerome 211
Robinson, Beverly Hamilton 269
Robinson, Doris 266, 267, 275
Robinson, John P. 109
Robinson, Malik 273
Robinson, Max 2, 7, 164, 212, 216, 263-277
Robinson, Maxie 266, 270
Robinson, Randall 266, 276
Rockefeller, Nelson 44
Rockwell, George Lincoln 46
Rockwell, Norman 121, 200
Rolling Stone 6, 111, 186, 209, 217
"*Rolling Stone* Interview: Walter Cronkite" 2, 4, 6, 186-196
"Rooneglow" 6, 157-166
Roosevelt, Franklin D. 11, 50, 174
Roper poll 63
Rosenberg, Howard 153, 253
Roth, Richard 150
RTNDA (Radio Television News Directors Association) 95
Rubenstein, Ann 123, 126, 127-140
The Rules of the Game 285
Russert, Timothy J. 108

Sadat, Anwar 193
Safer, Morley 31-32, 131, 284
Safire, William 202
Salant, Richard 47, 93, 95, 100, 143, 147, 192, 284
Salinger, Pierre 182, 232
Salisbury, Harrison 151
Sandburg, Carl 11
Sarnoff, Robert 61
The Saturday Evening Post 57
"Saturday Night at the Movies" 37, 52
"Saturday Night Live" 170, 211
"Saturday Night with Connie Chung" 141, 142, 143, 144, 145
Sauter, Van Gordon 100, 115-116
Savimbi, Jonas 226-227
Savitch, Jessica 207
Sawyer, Diane 2, 5, 19, 122, 123, 124, 126, 131, 142, 159, 160, 161, 183, 198, 219, 249, 262, 277-285
Say, Peggy 146
Scali, John 214
Scarborough, Chuck 142, 278
Scheffler, Phil 21
Schoenbrun, David 16

306   Index

Schorr, Daniel 200
Schultz, George 200
Schwartz, Herb 22
Schwartzkopf, Norman 150
Schwed, Mark 7, 203
"The Secret Life of Jim Lehrer" 7, 238–242
"See It Now" 10, 12, 13, 14, 15, 16, 17, 22–23
"The Selling of the Pentagon" 73
Sestasnovich, Stephen 232
Sevareid, Eric 11, 12, 16, 17, 20, 31, 35, 110
"Seven Lively Arts" 56
Shales, Tom 143, 180
Shamir, Yitzhak 173
Shaw, Bernard 2, 148, 149, 223, 224, 264
Shearer, Lloyd 155
Sheehan, Bill 163
Shepard, Jewell Robinson 265, 276
Sherr, Lynn 185
Shirer, William L. 16, 20
Shriver, Eunice 162
Shriver, Maria 127, 131, 142, 249, 278, 280
Sign Off: The Last Days of TV 6, 111n
Silman, James 267
Silverman, Fred 114
Simpson, Carole 125
"60 Minutes" 18, 97, 98, 104, 113, 114, 122, 126, 137, 142, 145, 159, 167, 169, 204, 211, 249, 259, 261, 278, 279, 280, 285
Small, Lynn 274
Small, William J. 6, 91, 171, 282
"Small World" 17
Smith, Desmond 6, 9, 18
Smith, Dorrance 160, 164
Smith, Howard K. 3, 12, 20, 27, 30, 32, 35, 48, 64, 75, 202
Smith, James 104, 108
Smith, Perry 152
Smithsonian 28
Snyder, James 268, 271
Snyder, Tom 119
Socolow, Sandy 21
Spencer, Susan 123
Sperber, A. M. 10
Stahl, Leslie 123, 197, 199, 200
Stanton, Frank 11, 25, 98, 204
Stanush, Michele 7, 205
"Star Power" 7, 277–285
State Department, U.S. 16

Steele, Shelby 265
Stengel, Richard 7, 250
Stevenson, Adlai 22
Strickland, Bob 268, 270, 273
Stringer, Ed 130
Stringer, Howard 141, 145, 255, 260
Stone, Gerald 142
Stone, Karen 165
"The Story of English" 245
Stossel, John 185
Sukle, Joe 143
Sullivan, Ed 37
Sullivan, Kathleen 131, 159, 165
"Sunday Morning" 237
Swaggart, Jimmy 105
Swayze, John Cameron 3, 11, 21, 22, 38, 51, 60, 61, 171
Swindall, Pat 245
Swing, Raymond Gram 17, 19, 42

Taber, Robert 24
Taft, Sen. Robert 22
Taylor, Charlotte 210
"Ted Koppel's Edge" 4, 6, 225–235
"Teddy" 246
Teeley, Peter 253
Television Critics Association 248n
Television Critics Circle, award 243
Terry, Wallace 277
Tet offensive 80, 81, 189
"This Is Korea—Christmas, 1952" 14
"This Is Murrow" 2, 10–18
"This Week with David Brinkley" 157, 164, 165, 170, 173, 201, 274
Thomas, Lowell 11, 12, 171
Three Mile Island 143
Time 2, 3, 7, 10, 57, 59, 63, 64, 95, 230, 250, 256, 257, 260, 277, 279
Times-Call 243n
Times, London 258
Times-Mirror 259
Times Mirror Center for the People and the Press 147, 149
The Tin Kazoo 6, 111n
Tinker, Tailor, Soldier, Spy 245
Tisch, Lawrence 133, 177–178, 260, 261, 262, 279; ownership of CBS 1, 91, 93, 100–101
To Kill a Messenger: Television News and the Real World 6
"The Today Show" 20, 34, 68, 99, 114, 119, 120, 138, 147, 164, 176, 177, 247, 249, 288

Index **307**

"Tom Brokaw: NBC's Air Apparent" 6, 174–181
"Tom Johnson: Q & A" 7, 222–225
"The Tonight Show" 188
Tonio Kröger 278
"A Touch of Wit: Journalist David Brinkley Has Seen It All and Reported It Well" 7, 169–174
Towson State University 167–168
"Tragic Fadeout" 7, 263–277
Tree, Marietta 162
Trese, Patrick 58
Trout, Robert 12, 20, 34, 63, 247
Trudeau, Garry 248
"True Stories" 145
Truman, Harry S 17, 22, 174
Tucker, Cynthia 149
Turkel, Studs 259
Turner, Ed 148
Turner, John 217
Turner, Ted 100–101, 102, 121, 185, 222, 223, 287
Turner Broadcasting Co. 93
Tutu, Desmond 226
"The Twentieth Century" 34
"20/20" 97, 113, 146, 157, 160, 162, 163, 166, 185, 249, 279
TV Guide 32, 49, 179, 248
"TV News Did Not Just Happen, It Had to Invent Itself" 3, 5, 18–25
Tyson, Mike 180

United Nations 42
United Press 171
United Press International 6, 19, 33, 51, 52, 76
United Press International writing style 58–59
"Unsolved Mysteries" 142, 146
USA Today 3, 96, 202
Utley, Garick 215

Valenti, Jack 48
Vance, Jim 271
Vance, Zebulon 171
Vanity Fair 132, 279
Vanocur, Sandor 67, 68, 165
Vieira, Meredith 127–140, 279
Vietnam war 31, 32, 49, 64–65, 77–78, 80, 189, 193
"Viva Max" 239
Vogue 6, 174

WABC 276
Wald, Richard 114, 161, 162, 165
WALK 43
WALK-FM 43
Wall, Irving 40
The Wall Street Journal 3, 7, 91, 96, 115, 121, 140, 148, 202
Wallace, Chris 198, 219, 281–282
Wallace, Mike 11, 21, 128, 280, 284
Walters, Barbara 126, 160, 163–164, 185, 198, 249, 280
"The War Turns in Cable TV's Favor" 153n
Warner, John 234
Warren Commission 190
Washington, Harold 276
Washington Goes to War 170
Washington Journalism Review 6, 93, 157, 210
The Washington Post 64, 115, 116, 143, 151
Washington State College 15
The Washington Times 7, 238, 239, 202, 238, 239n
Watergate 187, 192, 261, 282
Watson, Ervin 266
Watson, George 166, 287
Wayne, John 37, 200
WCBS 136, 169
Webster, Don 108
Webster, William 148
"Weekend" 207
Weiner, Irwin 161
Weiner, Robert 224
Weir, Benjamin 142
Weiss, Milt 272–273, 274
Welch, John F., Jr. 95
Welsch, Roger 236–237
Wentworth, Scott 142, 145
"West 57th St." 122, 127, 145, 235, 278, 279, 281
Westfeldt, Wallace 56
Westin, Av 118, 119, 162, 163
Westmoreland, William 80
Weston, Jim 14
WETA-TV 239
Wheatley, William O. 106, 180
"Wheel of Fortune" 120
White, E. B. 50
White, Susan 7
White, Vanna 120, 232–233, 234
Whitworth, William 6, 9, 36, 169

Index

Wick, Charles 135
Wicker, Tom 202
"Wide, Wide World" 11
Wilkins, Roger 274
Will, George 155, 160, 165, 173, 197, 201
Williams, Mary Alice 2, 7, 122, 123, 126, 127, 142, 183, 185, 278, 288–290
Wilmington Star-News 50, 171
Winchell, Walter 11
Winfrey, Oprah 136, 220, 276
Winters, Jonathan 239
WMAQ 275
WNBC 136, 278, 288
WNUS 287
Wolfe, Tom 209
"Women in Journalism Anchored by Lack of Substantial Change" 7, 122–126
Woodson, Carter G. 266
Woodstock 195
Wooten, Tim 123
World Journal Tribune 43
"World Monitor with John Hart" 21
"World News Roundup" 15, 120
"World News This Morning" 159, 161, 164
"World News Tonight" 146, 160, 209, 210, 216, 219–220, 271, 278, 281
WQED 207
WRC 44, 268, 271
WRNL 246
Wright, Robert C. 95
WRIV 43
WTOP 267, 268, 269
WTVJ 35
Wussler, Robert 93
Wyman, Thomas 110

Yancy, Jean Robinson 276
Yankelovich, Clancy Shulman 252, 279
"Yesterday, Today and Tomorrow" 122, 127, 142, 146, 278, 281, 289, 290
"You Are There" 146

Zahn, Paula 159
Zelman, Sam 3, 43, 45
Ziegler, Ron 283
Zoglin, Richard 7, 257, 277
Zousmer, Jesse 17

www.ingramcontent.com/pod-product-compliance
Lightning Source LLC
Chambersburg PA
CBHW032033150426
43194CB00006B/265